JOHN WAYNE GACY

JOHN WAYNE GACY

DEFENDING A MONSTER

SAM L. AMIRANTE

AND

DANNY BRODERICK

Skyhorse Publishing

Skyhorse Publishing books may be purchased in bulk at special discounts for sales promotion, corporate gifts, fund-raising, or educational purposes. Special editions can also be created to specifications. For details, contact the Special Sales Department, Skyhorse Publishing, 307 West 36th Street, 11th Floor, New York, NY 10018 or info@skyhorsepublishing.com.

Skyhorse® and Skyhorse Publishing® are registered trademarks of Skyhorse Publishing, Inc.®, a Delaware corporation.

www.skyhorsepublishing.com

10 9 8 7 6 5 4 3 2 1

Library of Congress Cataloging-in-Publication Data is available on file.
ISBN: 978-1-61608-248-2

Printed in the United States of America

For our kids:

Sammy, Jimmy,

Sofiabella,

and

Casey.

Jack and Patrick

Contents

Prologue

IN 1770, WHEN this country was in its birth throes, the most hated man in America was a man named Captain Thomas Preston. He was the commander of a small cadre of British soldiers who fired upon a gathering of disgruntled colonists, killing five. This event came to be known as the Boston Massacre. The five men who died as a result of this event are considered by most historians to be the first casualties of the Revolutionary War.

As is always the case, there were two sides to the story as to why this tragedy occurred. The colonists, led primarily by Sam Adams, one of the most outspoken writers and revolutionaries of the day, claimed that the British fired upon a peaceful crowd and killed five patriots without just cause. The British soldiers claimed that they had fired upon an angry mob in self-defense.

There are two reasons that will cause good men to abandon their long-standing, dearly held morals, values, and principles and revert to more primitive, barbaric practices to resolve conflict. That is when their hearts are filled with anger or when their hearts are filled with fear.

Because the colonists were angry over taxes imposed by the British without representation, along with other perceived injustices, and because they were fearful of the sheer might of the British Crown, in general, and of the soldiers that were now being billeted in their town to quell potential uprisings, in particular, their hearts were filled with both.

They wanted revenge against the British captain and the British soldiers under his command. Evidence be damned, facts be damned, they wanted revenge that was swift and sure. They wanted the heads of the captain and his men on a spit.

One man came forth and said loud and clear, "I stand for the law."

The man that took the soldiers' case when no other man would stand in their defense was John Adams.

John Adams, one of our nation's true founding fathers, a signer of the Declaration of Independence, our first vice president, our second president of the United States, a man of principle. (He was also Sam Adam's cousin and friend.)

His response was said to be this: "Counsel is the last thing an accused person should lack in a free country." He agreed to defend these men in spite of what it might do to his reputation, to his law practice, or to his future plans. He took the case because he believed that free men had certain rights. These were among the heartfelt principles on which he built his life.

Those principles are woven into the fabric of our Constitution. Those principles represent *our* principles as Americans. Every person accused of a crime shall have the right to a speedy and public trial by an impartial jury of his peers. Every person so accused shall have the right to face his accuser in a court of law. Every person so accused shall have the right to counsel.

Many men have fought and died to preserve those principles, those rights.

So keep that in mind when you hear someone say that this crime is too gruesome, or this person is too dangerous, or this issue is too complicated to allow those principles to stand.

(This includes the frightened flock that today seeks to exclude terrorists from those principles.)

Keep in mind that the very men that John Adams defended were uniformed members of an army of a foreign power that would soon become an enemy. Still, they had their day in court. There is no just cause or justification to usurp the Constitution.

Remember the words of Judge Louis Garippo when he said through tears of pride, "What we do for the John Gacys, we'll do for everyone."

I will serve, protect, and defend the Constitution of the United States against all enemies, foreign and domestic.

That is the oath we ask our president to take, together with every other person in public service. Every member of our military takes that oath. Every lawyer takes that oath. Every American citizen lives by that oath.

It does not say, "I will serve, protect, and defend the popularity polls, or the will of the people, or the frightened masses." It does not say, "I will serve, protect, and defend the Constitution, *unless* . . ." There are no conditions or qualifications.

When harried and nervous people jump in front of microphones and scream and rail that we should suddenly do something in direct contravention to that upon which we have based our very system of justice; when they tell you that we should abandon that which men have fought and died for and which has worked so well since the beginning of this beautiful experiment that we call America in favor of that which we have always criticized about lesser countries . . .

Kindly . . . invite them to pound sand.

In all criminal prosecutions, the accused shall enjoy the right to a speedy and public trial, by an impartial jury of the State and district wherein the crime shall have been committed, which district shall have been previously ascertained by law, and to be informed of the nature and cause of the accusation; to be confronted with the witnesses against him; to have compulsory process for obtaining witnesses in his favor, and to have the Assistance of Counsel for his defence.

—The Sixth Amendment to the Constitution of the United States of America

1

"SAM, COULD YOU** do me a favor?"

A telephone call, seven short words, a simple-enough request. That's how it all began.

I knew the guy on the other end of the line. Everyone on the Northwest Side did. He was a political wannabe, one of those guys that was always around, talking about all the big shots he knew, hoping that the importance of others would rub off on him, a nice-enough guy—maybe a little pushy, a bit of a blowhard, telling tall tales, but still, a nice-enough guy. He was a precinct captain for the Norwood Park Township Regular Democratic Organization, and so was I. He was actually one of the best precinct captains they ever had, better than me, some might tell you. He really brought in the votes for that tiny organization.

I had met him at one function or another. He always bought a full table at all the fund-raisers, ten tickets, which translated into a sizable contribution to the party; and then he'd fill the ten seats with kids that looked like they really didn't wear business suits very often, unsophisticated . . . that would be a kind way to put it. They were usually his employees, young kids that worked for his contracting business.

Plus, he was on the Norwood Park Township Street Lighting District as a trustee, the secretary-treasurer, and I did some volunteer work on the side for the district. I was their lawyer. So I knew him.

"What's the problem, John?"

"You know all of the coppers over in Des Plaines, don't you, Sam?"

"Sure, John, I know most of them. We all used to work on different sides of the same building. I have worked on cases with most of them. Why?"

"Well, the Des Plaines police are following me around wherever I go. I have no idea why, but they're starting to cause problems for my business. It's really beginning to annoy me, Sam. It's getting nuts. Could you ask around and try to find out what the fuck they want, what they think I did, why the hell they are harassing me like this?"

He seemed genuinely upset—livid, one might say.

"What do you mean following you around wherever you go? How do you know?" Maybe he was just paranoid, imagining things, I thought.

There was a disgusted chuckle at the other end of the line. "If I am at a restaurant having breakfast in a booth, they are in the booth next to me. If I stop at a gas station to get gas, they are waiting across the street for me to finish. Wherever I go, they follow. No matter how fast I drive or how slow I drive, they are always right behind me. They sit outside of my house all night long until I leave in the morning. Then we all leave together. My neighbors are starting to complain."

Hmm, maybe this wasn't just paranoia.

I sat there wondering why in the world the Des Plaines police would have any interest whatsoever, but especially such an intense interest, in this rather-overblown, self-important hanger-on.

"How long has this been going on, John?"

"A few days, I think."

"And you have no idea why they are interested in you?"

"One of them said something about a missing teenager. I don't know. I sure as hell don't know anything about any missing kid."

"Let me see what I can find out. I will look into it."

"I'll owe you one, Sam. I really appreciate this."

"Call me tomorrow."

"Thanks, Sam."

I hung up the phone and thought for a second about how John Gacy had once been to my house in his capacity as a contractor. My wife and I were planning an addition to our home to accommodate our expanding family. Our second son, Jimmy, had been born, and we wanted to add a new room, a nursery. That's what my wife, Mary, called it, anyway. I called it a bedroom.

We did not end up hiring him, but we seriously considered it. So, like I said, I knew him. I thought I knew him pretty well. What I didn't know, however, what he didn't mention during our short telephone conversation, was this:

On Monday, December 11, 1978, just three short days previous, John Wayne Gacy had an appointment at Nisson Pharmacy, a busy drug and sundries store located at 1920 E. Touhy Avenue in Des Plaines, Illinois. He had done some remodeling work at that establishment in the past, and when brothers Phil and Larry Torf, the owners of the store, decided to add some shelving and make some other changes, Phil called John.

Mr. Gacy arrived in his brand-new black four-door 1979 Oldsmobile 98 promptly at 5:30 p.m., as agreed, and parked in front of the store just off Touhy. There was snow and slush left over from a typical Chicagoland December snowfall, which would melt some during the day and freeze up solid during the night. John negotiated the puddles left over from the day's thaw and thought about offering to return with his snowplow to clear the parking area completely, thereby alleviating the puddle problem—he did plowing as a side business—but once inside the store, he was distracted by other things and never made the offer.

He shivered as he unzipped his black leather bomber jacket, stamped his feet on the matting just inside the door, and shook off the damp chill from the outdoors. He immediately saw Phil Torf coming from the rear of the store to meet him, and he lumbered his rather-cumbersome two-hundred-plus-pound five-foot-nine-inch frame down the aisle, big fleshy hand extended in greeting. As he passed the cash register, he smiled at the young cashier, Kim Byers, bundled up in an ill-fitting oversized light blue nylon down parka because she was exposed to the arctic blasts from the open doors every time a customer came in or went out. He made a mental note to attempt to sell the Torf brothers on a revolving door system to replace the simple double doors that presently existed and were the only thing blocking out the crisp December air. *They are heating the outdoors and exposing their poor little cashier to the elements in the process*, he thought. *She might catch her death from a cold or flu.*

He wasn't sure if he remembered Kim from his last extended visit to the store when he did the previous remodeling job. Back then, he was an employee of P.E. Systems, a firm that specialized in remodeling and design for the pharmacy industry. He had learned a lot from his time spent with that company, and now he was returning as the proud owner and proprietor of PDM Contractors (Painting, Decorating, and Maintenance), the company he had founded after he left P.E. Systems.

John and Phil shot the shit for quite a while before the contractor got down to business, taking measurements and figuring out a quote. During his time at the store, he was introduced, or in some cases reintroduced, to many of the employees; most of them were young kids working part-time after highschool to make some extra spending money, save for college, or save for a car.

One such part-timer was Rob Piest, a fifteen-year-old sophomore and budding star gymnast at Maine West High School in

Des Plaines. Rob fell into the save-for-a-car category, and he was becoming increasingly frustrated at the seemingly insurmountable task of saving enough money to purchase a reliable car on his $2.85/hour wage at the pharmacy. He had looked at a Jeep and was getting close to his goal; he had $900, but it seemed to him to be taking forever. He wanted to make more money. He was fuming a bit because his employers had rebuffed his previous requests for a raise.

Rob had not been introduced to John Gacy; he was much too busy working, but he thought he had overheard the contractor talking to Linda Mertes, a longtime employee at the pharmacy, about his policy to pay his young workers $5 per hour to start. He couldn't believe that a highschool kid working part-time could make that much money. Linda later confirmed this fact to Rob, and he was intrigued, to say the least. Imagine making nearly twice as much money each and every hour! Rob was fast approaching his sixteenth birthday, and he, like every other teen his age, wanted to be ready when that magical age arrived—sixteen years old, the age when he would finally get his driver's license.

At 7:15 p.m., when Mr. Gacy finished his business at the pharmacy and left the store in his shiny new car, Rob was slightly disappointed. He hadn't had the opportunity to approach the man with an offer to work for him. He had, however, noticed that while the contractor was taking measurements and "walking off" the store, writing up his proposal and speaking with Mr. Torf, the guy seemed to be looking at Rob, watching him work. This happened more than once during the time the man was in the store. Rob was sure that the fat guy with the fancy new black luxury cruiser was impressed with his hardworking style, his attention to the task at hand, the overall way he worked so hard at his job. Maybe if he approached him later, called him on the phone or something, Mr. Gacy would give him a job that paid $5 per hour. If that happened, Rob would be driving his own brand-new Jeep before he knew it.

Meanwhile, John Gacy was speeding south on Interstate 294 on his way home from what he was sure was yet another successful bid for a new remodeling job. He had become adept at schmoozing the potential customer. He had long ago realized that he wasn't just selling the job, the work itself—he was selling himself. There were hundreds of guys that could do that job as well as he could, although he did pride himself in his attention to detail. He considered himself a perfectionist; lots of contractors did good work, but they didn't have his stories, his jokes, and his knack for befriending the customer. The $1,600 proposal that he had left with Phil Torf was money in the bank as far as he was concerned.

As John negotiated the ramp that led to the Kennedy Expressway and moved to the right lane where he would exit south at Cumberland Avenue, he looked at the seat next to him, then all around the interior of the car. "Fuck," he muttered to himself. "I left my damn appointment book at Torf's place." John was close to his home at 8213 W. Summerdale. It was just east of Cumberland, so he decided to continue home to check his answering machine before he made the trek back to Des Plaines. He also figured he might as well take his black Chevy pickup with the snowplow attached on his return. Maybe he would pick up some further business while he was there. Perhaps it would not be a totally wasted trip.

When Gacy checked his answering machine, he was reminded that he was late for another appointment that he had made with Richard Raphael, a business associate who lived in Glenview, Illinois. John knew he had to hurry but he figured Des Plaines was on the way to Glenview. It would all work out.

Had he not forgotten his address book, he would not have gone back to the pharmacy that evening. He would have driven straight to Glenview.

That evening, when John Wayne Gacy pulled up in front of Nisson Pharmacy for the second time, it was just past 8:00 p.m. He had made record time traveling back because he rarely paid any attention to speed limits. He thought of himself as someone far above those poor little souls that had to bother themselves with such mundane rules. He was much too important a figure to have to worry about speeding tickets. He would simply have them "fixed." He knew all the right people in all the right places.

As his pickup truck squeaked to a stop in front of the drugstore with its second set of headlights blazing above the snowplow, he noticed the kid that he had seen stocking shelves earlier carrying some trash out to the Dumpster in the alley. He watched as a young girl threw a snowball at him and ran away to join her friends, giggling and laughing. She was obviously someone he knew from school or from the neighborhood. The kid was wearing the same blue nylon parka that he had seen on the cashier earlier that evening. It was Rob Piest.

"You are a hard worker," Gacy said through the side window of his truck.

Rob looked up, squinting into the bright lights over the plow. John switched them off, allowing Rob to see who was talking to him.

"Oh, hi, Mr. Gacy." He pointed to the pickup truck. "Different ride."

"How did you know my name?"

"Linda told me. She said something about you looking for help . . . or something."

"I could use a hard worker like you. I bet I pay better than your boss, Phil, does too. You interested?"

"Yeah . . . yes, I am, sir, but I gotta get back inside right now. I can't let Mr. Torf see me talking to you about a job. You know what I mean. Plus, I'm on the clock."

"Loyalty, I like that. It's one of the qualities I like most. If I hang around till you get off, could we talk then?"

"Sure, but my mom is coming to pick me up at nine o'clock."

"I'll hang around. I have some more measurements that I have to take anyway," Gacy lied. "Then we can talk. It won't take long to exchange information. Right? Would that be OK?"

"That would be great, Mr. Gacy." Rob ran into the store. He was giddy. He could already see himself driving his brand-new Jeep.

John watched Rob enter the store and throw his jacket on some boxes near the cash register. Then he sauntered into the store as if nothing had happened, where he immediately saw Phil holding his appointment book.

"Did you forget something?" Phil asked, smiling, taunting him.

About five minutes before nine o'clock, John, while he futzed around pretending to remeasure the shelves in the store, saw a woman, who was obviously Rob's mother, enter the pharmacy. She spoke to some of the other kids and to her son and then meandered toward the greeting card section to wait for her son to finish up. John went outside to his truck. He surreptitiously eyed Rob and nodded toward the door as he left, all in keeping with their plan to meet without alerting Phil Torf.

Minutes later, Rob grabbed his coat, mumbled something to his mother about what he was planning, and ran out the door.

Rob Piest was never seen alive again.

"WHAT'S YOUR NAME? What do your friends call you?" Gacy asked this as soon as he saw Rob bound enthusiastically out of the pharmacy. John had the engine running, and the cab of the truck was beginning to warm up.

"Rob . . . Rob Piest."

"Hop in, Rob."

"Ah . . . , Mr. Gacy, my mom is inside the store. She is here to pick me up."

"Don't worry, Rob, I'll take you home. She will understand. Won't she?"

"But, sir, it's her birthday. My family is waiting at home for me so we can cut the cake and sing 'Happy Birthday' . . . all of that. I really have to be quick about this."

Everyone who ever knew John Gacy knew one thing about him—he was a master manipulator. He could sell ice cubes to Eskimos. He had the Polish version of the gift of gab. John had already decided that this young man was coming home with him. He was not taking "no" for an answer.

"You love your mother," he asked the question in the form of a statement, a foregone conclusion.

"Well, yeah, of course I do," Rob promptly answered.

"Imagine coming home with the news that you have landed a new job that pays $5 per hour to start, a job with perks and a future. She would be happy for you, wouldn't she? That would make her happy, wouldn't it?"

"Sure, it would."

"And what better present could you give to your mom on her birthday than to make her happy? Isn't that the purpose of a present?"

"I guess so . . ."

"I have been watching you work, Rob. You have a great work ethic. I am also impressed by your devotion to your mom. Hell, I love my mom too. All true men should love their mothers. But I need for you to fill out some forms if you are going to work for me, and those forms are in my office at my house, which is about twenty minutes from here. I can have you back in about forty or forty-five minutes, an hour, tops. Only, in an hour from now, when you walk into the house, you will be able to tell that wonderful mother of yours that you have a new, well-paying job, that you have doubled your salary. What do you say? I have an appointment myself that I must get to after I drop you. You do want the job, don't you?"

"Are you saying I have the job, Mr. Gacy?" Rob was bubbling over with excitement. Five dollars per hour! He could easily make

$100 per week. He would have enough for his Jeep well before his birthday in March. This was a dream come true.

"You will when we finish filling out those forms. We have to comply with all of the legal stuff, after all, right? No employer can afford to play fast and loose with the goddamn IRS."

Rob glanced back at the door of the pharmacy, thought for a second about how happy his mom would be when he told her about his new job; then he put his hand on the passenger-side door handle of the truck, opened the door, and jumped up into the pickup. He looked at his new boss.

Mr. Gacy had a big toothy grin peaking out from below the bushy mustache that he wore, creasing the flabby jowls hanging off his beard-stubbled face. "Welcome aboard," he said through his ear-to-ear smile. He was pleased with himself. And then they drove off.

"I have a good feeling about this. I think this just might work out well for both of us," John said as he drove at breakneck speed.

"Don't you worry about getting a ticket, Mr. Gacy?"

"First, call me John, or Colonel. I'm an official Tennessee colonel. All my guys call me Colonel or John. Mr. Gacy was my father. Second, you will come to know that you are about to start working for a very important guy. I know people. I know some of the most important people in this city. I'm a personal friend of Mayor Bilandic's. Plus, I'm connected. Syndicate connected. You will learn a lot working with me, kid. Wait and see."

Judging by the way Mr. Gacy drove, Rob tended to believe what he was being told. Nobody would drive like this unless he was pretty sure he was not going to get in trouble for it.

"Plus, you will find that working for PDM is fun. We work hard, don't get me wrong. But when work is done, we play hard too. You do like to party, don't you?"

"Sure . . . I guess."

"Do you have a girlfriend?"

"I date. I guess. I go out with girls that are a few years older than me, usually." Rob blushed, but he was also a little proud. "I do all right." They both laughed. It was unnecessary to say more.

"Well, I'm very liberal minded when it comes to all that. The guys that work for me often use my house as a place to party. I have a well-stocked party house—no parents allowed." Again, the big toothy grin.

"Well, I'm looking forward to it. I really need the money. I want to buy this car that I have my eye on. It's a Jeep, actually. So I will work really hard, Mr. Gacy, err . . . ah, John. I promise. You won't regret this."

"You seemed hungry, eager to work, to do a good job. At least that is what I saw back at the pharmacy. You never even took a break. Everybody else seemed to be using my visit as a chance to slack off, but you just kept working. I like that."

"Well, I need money right now. I would do almost anything for money."

This statement elicited a new, kind of creepy, version of the same smile. Gacy chuckled low. "That's what I like to hear. You're going to do fine, just fine."

When the truck careened into Gacy's driveway at his Summerdale address, splashing and sliding, Rob was glad to be in one piece. It had been quite a ride. However, John was right. They had arrived in just over twenty minutes. John pulled the truck past the circular drive in front of the house and along the side. The house was completely set off from the neighbor's house by a huge hedgerow along the side of the driveway. It had to be at least eight feet high and was a bit of an eyesore. *I guess this guy really likes his privacy*, Rob thought. He also saw the brand-new Olds 98 parked in front. The car had spotlights on both sides of the windshield and a CB antenna sticking into the air. The passenger-side spotlight was red. This supported some of the stories that John had told to Rob on the drive there. He must really be an important guy. His car was like a cop car, or even a mayor's car. It looked important.

Gacy ushered Rob into his house through the back door, which opened into a large recreation room, obviously an addition to the original structure. The room had a large black recliner opposite the TV, a pool table, a well-stocked bar with barstools in front next to a refrigerator, and then a corridor that led to the rest of the house. A little yapping dog was making a bit of a racket and jumping up and down, so John let him out into the backyard.

"Check it out. Make yourself at home," Gacy said as he pointed the way to the rest of the house." He took off his black leather jacket and dropped his car keys on a table. "You will probably be spending a lot of time here."

In the front of the house, a newly constructed temporary wall divided the original living room. The smaller living room left by this division was full of plants and pictures of clowns, very little furniture. As Rob looked around, he saw more clown portraits and clown knickknacks. John's office was also in the front of the house, as well as a couple of bedrooms. Rob didn't venture that way but returned to the rec room.

"What's with all the clowns?" Rob asked casually.

"I'm a clown."

Rob laughed.

"No, really, no joke. I am a registered clown. I'm Pogo. I entertain kids in hospitals and seniors at old folks' homes. I do tricks for the kids, tell jokes for the old fogies. I march in parades. It's a hobby. I'll show you some of my tricks. Hey, you want a beer or something?" John was bending down, head into the refrigerator. "I'm having one," he said over his shoulder.

"Thank you, Mr. Gacy . . . ah . . . John. I'm not saying I would never have one, but I have to think about my mom's birthday, remember?"

"Oh, lighten up, Rob, this is your interview. Don't disappoint your future boss during your first job interview. That's not a good idea, is it? We can be at your parents' house in twenty minutes. Sit down. Have one beer. Let's talk." John was now standing in front of the refrigerator, holding two beers, still sporting that same creepy smile.

Rob was torn. On the one hand, he could picture his very close-knit family at home. By now, almost a half hour after he should have been pulling into the driveway in his mother's car, they were all beginning to wonder where the heck he was—his mother worried, his father starting to get a little pissed, his brother and his sister perplexed, the birthday cake waiting. He had never done anything like this in the past.

On the other hand, here was this unusual man offering him the job of his dreams, a pathway to the car of his dreams. He sure as hell had never had an adult offer him a beer before. That he thought was a little strange. But what could it hurt? If having a beer with his future boss would solidify the job offer—close the deal, so to speak—why not? If spending fifteen or twenty minutes with this dufuss would get him this job, he felt he had to do it. His parents would not be mad at him once he explained that he had secured a great new $5-an-hour job. He had been to highschool parties before. It was not the first time he had accepted a beer from someone. He took the beer from John Wayne Gacy's fat, stubby fingers. Tragically, it would be his last.

He took a sip and sat down on one of the barstools. He watched John sit in his recliner. Then he asked, "So you have some papers for me to fill out?"

John looked annoyed. "You are really all business, aren't you? You have to learn how to relax, Rob." John rose out of his recliner and stomped off toward his office in the front of the house, shaking his head. "I'll get the papers," he said, sounding exasperated, "but I want to get to know you a little bit before we make this final. I don't hire just anybody. My guys have to be a *good fit* for the way we work. I told you, we work hard. But we also play hard and . . ." His voice trailed off as he got farther into the front part of the house. Rob could not hear the rest of what John was saying, but he had heard enough. He had no intention of blowing his chances to get this job. He tried to relax. He tried to ignore the alarm bells that were already starting to clang in his head.

In his office, Gacy was smiling. He knew he had just set the hook. Any further attempts by this fish to get off the line would be futile.

When Gacy returned from his office, he was holding some items of paperwork that looked like official IRS forms and a job application, but he was also carrying something else that made the hairs on the back of Rob's neck stand. He was holding a set of handcuffs.

"OK, we are going to fill these out," Gacy said, raising the papers above his head, shaking them. "But first I have to show you something cool. Watch this." John put the papers down on the bar. He twirled the handcuffs around on his index finger. He began to make moves like a showman. He was doing his clown act. He was smiling, not threatening. He overacted his big, sweeping moves like a magician. He began humming some kind of stupid show tune. He showed Rob the handcuffs. Abruptly, he yanked them taut, demonstrating that they were quite real, quite strong. Then he slapped them on his own wrists, first one then the other. Again, he showed them to Rob. Again, he yanked them taut. They clinked. Clearly, John was in handcuffs. He yanked them taut again, harder. He turned around, facing away from Rob; and in seconds, he turned back. When he did, he was twirling the handcuffs on his index finger.

Two things happened. The fear that had first gripped Rob when he saw the handcuffs drained away completely. He was fully disarmed. Plus, he was actually astonished. This was a real, professional, well-executed trick.

"How did you do that?" Rob asked, completely befuddled.

"That's nothing," John said. "Watch this." He handed Rob the handcuffs. "You put them on me. Only this time"—John turned around, placing his hands behind his back—"you cuff my hands behind my back."

Rob was actually intrigued. He was totally taken in. He slapped the cuffs on his new boss's wrists. Then he inspected them, checking them for trick latches. There were none.

"OK, are you satisfied that I am clearly handcuffed, unable to escape?"

Gacy had a flair for the dramatic. Rob could hear the drumroll.

Gacy turned around, facing Rob. Then in seconds, he was standing there twirling the handcuffs on his index finger once again, with a big gawking smile on his face.

"What the fuck!" Rob exclaimed. "How the heck did you do that?"

"I'll show you. It's easy. Give me your right hand."

Rob didn't think. He simply slid off the barstool and raised his right hand and held it out in front of him.

Gacy took his right hand, slapped a cuff on it, spun Rob around, and handcuffed his left hand into the handcuffs behind his back.

The two of them had walked into that house less than fifteen minutes before this moment, and suddenly Robert Jerome Piest, age fifteen, was standing face-to-face with John Wayne Gacy, age thirty-six, with his hands locked in handcuffs behind his back, unable to free himself.

"OK, John, what's the trick?" Rob was smiling, innocent, waiting to learn the trick that his boss was going to show him.

"The trick," John Wayne Gacy sneered, "is not being dumb and stupid." He was holding a shiny tiny silver key. "Everyone knows that the only sure way to free yourself from locked handcuffs is to have the key. Do you have the key, Rob? Or are you dumb and stupid?"

Rob looked at John. He couldn't believe it. It was as if he was looking at a different person. Gone was the goofy, creepy, familiar ear-to-ear smile. It had been replaced by a grave, stern, dead stare. But it wasn't just that minor change that had caused the transformation, everybody stops smiling from time to time. It wasn't that. Gacy's eyes had gone lifeless. They had lost life's twinkle. There seemed to be nothing behind them. No personality. No person. Rob thought he detected a brief flutter in the eyelid. The transformation struck a level of fear into Rob's heart that wasn't fear. It was terror.

Rob felt his mouth dry up and his heart start to pump. A single tear welled up and streaked his cheek. The moment lasted a lifetime.

Then like in a terrible B horror film, the telephone shrieked. Gacy looked toward the front of the house. When he looked back at Rob, he was John again, just like that.

"I'll let the machine get it." John was so offhanded as he said this Rob couldn't believe his ears. It was as though nothing had happened. Rob actually began to question whether anything *had* happened. Maybe it was all in his head, this silly fear. Gacy walked a few steps toward the corridor that led to the front of the house, leaving Rob standing there in handcuffs. He raised a finger and listened. He was listening to the answering machine. Rob couldn't make out what was being said or who was talking.

"That was your boss, your other boss, Phil Torf. Your parents must have called him. We have to get you home. They must be looking for you already." John Gacy was holding that small silver key between his fingertips. "Let's get those cuffs off of you."

Rob thought he was losing his mind. Had he simply imagined the whole terrifying interaction that had just occurred between them? Did he just scare himself half to death, or was there something unearthly sinister about this guy? As John was about to remove the handcuffs from Rob's wrists, Rob recognized that John was talking and that he had not heard a word. He was too busy reliving his terror, questioning it.

"So the trick is to learn how to palm the key so perfectly that no one ever even suspects you have it." Rob heard the tail end of Gacy's lecture. John was showing him how to hide the key between his fingers in such a way that he could still show his audience both of his palms. It was a pretty good trick. It had sure as hell fooled him. But what about those feelings, that fear—was it real?

Again, the phone rang.

Gacy again walked to the corridor so he could hear the answering machine. Rob stood there, still in handcuffs.

"Is your father's name Harold?" John asked when he returned to the rec room.

"Yes, that's my dad. What did he say?"

"The machine answered. I just heard him on the tape. He knows you're here, though. So you don't have to be in such a rush. He didn't sound pissed."

"Well, he wouldn't sound pissed when he's talking to you . . . or leaving a message. But that doesn't mean they are not worried or angry that I am missing my mom's birthday." Rob was concerned. "We should probably start heading towards home."

"Before we do, before I remove those cuffs, I want to ask you a question. You told me that you would do almost anything for money, right?"

"Yeah, John, I'm a hard worker, a very hard worker. I'll do anything you ask. You cannot work me too hard."

"Yeah, yeah, we already talked about that. I know that you are a hard worker. But I was thinking about something else. Remember that I told you about how I was very liberal minded about sex? Well, I am. Now, don't get me wrong, I'm no fruit picker. I ain't a fag or anything like that, but a long time ago, this guy and I were out trying to pick up girls, and he said something interesting to me. He said that I had maybe a fifty-fifty shot at getting laid that night—or of even picking up a broad at all, for that matter—but he had a one hundred percent chance. I thought he was full of shit, of course.

But he said it was true because if he struck out trying to pick up a girl, he just went out and picked up a guy. He said that it feels just as good to get a blow job from a guy as it does to get one from a girl. All you do is close your eyes."

As Gacy rambled on with his story, which Rob found repulsive, Rob felt the fear growing inside him again. *When something seems too good to be true, it usually is*, he thought. *This guy was some kind of weirdo.* Rob realized he was in some stranger's house—an old, weird man's house, locked in handcuffs. He began to feel that he was going to cry. He didn't want to. He wanted to be strong. He felt that he had to hold it together.

Gacy was continuing his story. "So I tried it. I let him do it to me, and believe it or not, he was right. A blowjob is a blowjob. No shit. Now, I say it again, I am no fruit picker. I ain't gay. You can't be gay if you are thinking about girls when you are doing it, right?"

To Rob, it felt as though the walls of the room were closing in on him. He had no deep-set prejudice against gay people. That was not the problem. If Gacy had said that he was gay and came on to him, he could have sidestepped that without an uncomfortable incident. He had done it before. Most people had. But he was in handcuffs! This was different! He tried not to insult his captor.

"John, that type of activity is just not in me," he offered meekly. "It's just not me."

Gacy looked at him. At first he looked surprised, as though he had not expected that reaction, as though he just assumed Rob would go along. Then it looked like he was getting angry.

"I have a lot of money. I could help you get that Jeep," he said.

"No," was all Rob could muster.

"Suppose I just fucking rape you, you little fucking liar," Gacy growled. "You said that you would do anything for money. You led me on! You lied to me!"

Gacy moved toward Rob, reaching out at Rob's pants, at his fly. He grabbed Rob by the waistband of his jeans and pulled him closer. Rob was unable to resist. He yanked at the handcuffs. They would not give. Gacy unzipped Rob's zipper. He reached inside and touched him, grabbed at him. John tugged down on Rob's jeans. Rob could feel his buttocks and thighs being exposed. No matter how hard he struggled, the handcuffs made it impossible to fight off this crazed man twice his size. Rob was now past terror. Was this a nightmare, or was it real? Why couldn't he just wake up?

At this point, Rob started to break down. He began to sob uncontrollably. "Stop this! Please don't do this!" he screamed.

He looked at Gacy, whose face immediately began to soften. Then to Rob's amazement, he began to apologize profusely, over and over again. *What the fuck is this*, Rob thought, *a goddamn roller-coaster ride? One minute this fucking nut is scaring the shit out of me, and the next minute he's Mr. Nice Guy.* His heart was returning to its normal beating.

John removed the handcuffs, and as Rob rubbed his wrists a bit to restore his blood flow, he said, "I hope you understand, Mr. Gacy." He didn't want to set him off again. He chose his words carefully. "I would do it if I could, but I can't. I am just not that way."

"Don't say anything. It was a dumb idea," John said. "Dumb and stupid. I'm really sorry if I made you feel uncomfortable or scared. I ain't no fag, Rob. You have to believe me. I am no kind of fruit picker."

"You had me going there."

"Forget about it. Let's never talk about it again, OK? You still want the job, right?"

"Yeah, yes, I do. I really need the money." At this point, Rob would say anything that he thought John wanted to hear. Wild horses could not have dragged him back to that house, but he had to say something.

"OK, then, we start from scratch. This never happened, right? And it will never happen again, OK?"

"OK, John, but I really have to get home. Is that all right?"

Suddenly, John was all for the idea. He began moving around as though he was getting ready to leave, mumbling, making sure he had everything, patting his pockets. Rob was somewhat relieved, but still frightened. It had been an interesting first meeting, to say the least. That was the understatement of all time.

"Make sure you bring those papers. We can fill them out in the car," John said offhandedly, pointing at the bar.

Rob grabbed the papers from the bar as he watched John Gacy walk around his house, preparing to leave. He thought it ironic that after all that had occurred, the papers were an afterthought. That was ostensibly the main reason they had gone to John's house in the first place. Unbeknownst to Rob, he was about to learn another reason that he was there—the real reason.

Rob had his hand on the doorknob. "I thought you were going to kill me, John. I thought you were some kind of crazy person." Rob looked back at John Wayne Gacy, who was standing behind him

"One second, I'll show you one quick trick for the road. Put down your coat for a second. You'll love this." Gacy had a length of rope in his hand and the handle of a hammer without a hammerhead on it. He was tying knots into the rope, very meticulously. He had done this before. He was practiced. He slid the handle of the hammer between the knots. "Now, watch this," he said.

Gacy slid the rope over Rob's head. It was loose, not threatening.

"Why are you putting it over my head?" Rob asked, nervously laughing.

"Just watch," Gacy whispered.

Those were Rob Piest's last words.

In a split second, Gacy had twisted the hammer handle twice, instantly tightening the rope around Rob's neck. To struggle was a mistake, because that made the rope tighter. To panic was fatal. Unfortunately, Rob panicked. The hammer handle was lodged tightly, permanently against Rob's back. Gacy no longer had to hold on to it. The rope would not unwind; it would not loosen. Rob's eyes bulged as he gasped for air and clawed at the rope. He was free to scramble and struggle as Gacy passively watched, thumbs in his waistband. The more he struggled, the tighter the rope got.

Gacy whispered again, "Dumb and stupid." He shook his head as though he was looking at the proverbial two-year-old caught with his hand in the cookie jar. "Dumb and stupid."

Rob fell to the floor. He thrashed, he struggled, he fought valiantly, but, as stated, Gacy had done this before. He was practiced.

The last thing Rob Piest heard out of the velvet blackness of approaching death was Gacy's telephone ringing.

John Wayne Gacy left Robert Jerome Piest lying on the floor gagging, surrendering, sucking in his final breaths of oxygen as he went to answer his telephone. "You think you can fool me, you fucking little lying homo," Gacy spat out as he lumbered off.

It was just past ten. Rob and John had been in John's house a little over a half hour.

On the phone, Richard Raphael was angry. John never showed for their meeting. Gacy made several disjointed excuses. His uncle was sick. His uncle might die. He might have to go to the hospital. He was too tired. He forgot. They would meet at John's house tomorrow at 7:00 a.m. "Don't be late." Gacy was completely unaffected by the night's tragic, morbid occurrence. Richard Raphael noticed nothing whatsoever wrong or different about Gacy's voice when they spoke. Same old John.

Gacy closed Rob's eyes and manipulated his face in an effort to soften the grotesquely contorted frozen facial features of the strangled boy and stuffed a wad or two of paper into Rob's mouth because he didn't want him to leak fluids all over the place. He lifted the limp corpse of Rob Piest, carried it down the hall, and placed it onto his own bed in his bedroom.

Again the telephone rang.

"Now what?" Gacy mumbled. He answered the phone while Rob Piest's body lay quiet.

On the line was Gacy's aunt Leone Scow, his mother's sister. "Uncle Harold has taken a turn for the worse," she said. "They don't think he will make it through the night."

Gacy looked at his silent houseguest. "I have a few things to attend to, but I will be at the hospital as soon as I can get there, within the hour."

"Hurry, John," Aunt Leone said through stifled tears. "It's time."

It seemed that John Gacy was surrounded by death, a death merchant that drew death toward him. Now he had to go and perhaps watch some other poor schmuck gasp his last breath, unless he kicked it before John arrived. "Fuck, this is bullshit," he grumbled as he lumbered grudgingly down the hall back toward the rec room.

He surveyed the room. There were two half-empty bottles of beer, one on the small table next to his chair and one on the bar; some IRS forms and an application for employment, which had floated to the floor when Rob involuntarily released his grasp on them; and a light blue parka draped over a barstool. Otherwise, the room was in its normal meticulously kept condition. Gacy was a fastidious housekeeper, a "Felix," a place for everything and everything in its place. He emptied the beer bottles into the kitchen sink and pitched the empties into the garbage. He groaned as he bent down to pick up the papers off the floor and groused silently about how he was getting older. *I can't even touch my toes anymore*, he thought. He put the papers back in his office, in the filing cabinet where they belonged, passing Rob's corpse on the bed in his room as he wandered about as if it wasn't even there. He picked up the parka and checked the pockets. He pulled a piece of paper from the right one. It was a receipt from Nisson Pharmacy for photograph development. "I guess the kid won't be picking up those pictures," Gacy was muttering to himself.

He wasn't crazy about the fact that he had to go out into the cold winter night to Northwest Hospital to tend to his aunt Leone and his uncle Harold and any gathering relatives, but he had become the go-to guy in the family, the strong shoulder. He had no choice in the matter. The women needed him. He absentmindedly dropped the photograph receipt into the garbage can in the kitchen and put the blue parka by the back door. He would dispose of that later, when he went out. How incongruous a sight—here was this frumpy, middle-aged community leader wandering back and forth from room to room in his stocking feet, shirt untucked from bending over, scratching his belly from time to time, doing light housework, straightening up his little home, and all the while, the dead body of a young boy was getting cold on his own bed.

Gacy let the dog in, went to his bedroom, and stripped Rob's clothes off of him, folded them, and stacked them into a neat pile. The underwear had been soiled, so he put them in a separate plastic bag. He picked up the pile and added it to the parka waiting by the back door for ultimate disposal. He got into the shower and scrubbed off the evening's events and watched them circle the drain, shaved, and dressed in slacks and a shirt suitable for the impending hospital visit.

The telephone rang again. It was just past 10:30 p.m. The voice of one of his valued employees, David Cram, came over the line, saying something about Christmas trees. Gacy explained that he was going out and would call him tomorrow. His uncle was dying. On his way out the door, he picked up the neat stack of Rob's clothes. He looked at the blue parka. *Why would I throw this away? It's a nice coat. Someone I know might want it, maybe Dave or Mike.* He brought the coat into the utility room of his house and left it there. En route to the hospital, John dropped the rest of Rob's clothes into a Salvation Army donation box in a strip mall not far from the house. He tossed the plastic bag into a nearby trash can. Then he continued on to Northwest Hospital.

Rob Piest's naked young body remained where John had placed it, in the stark, cold bedroom of a madman.

2

JOHN **G**ACY **WOKE** the next morning at 6:00 a.m. He had a busy morning ahead. The naked deceased form that was once Robert Piest was lying on the bed next to him. Gacy lay there, momentarily thinking about his situation.

He had arrived at Northwest Hospital at around 11:00 p.m. the previous evening, but when he entered his uncle Harold's room, it was empty. Nobody was there, not even Uncle Harold. He had passed away during the hour that John had spent tidying up and rushing to the hospital. His corpse had been transferred to the morgue, and Aunt Leone and any other visitors had left the hospital. Now they were mourners, not visitors.

John decided to drive over to Aunt Leone's house at 7304 W. Cullom Street, but when he arrived there, it was clear that no one was home. The house was dark, doors locked tight. John looked down the block to 7300 W. Cullom, the home of Aunt Leone's brother. There the lights were blazing, including the Christmas lights. *Everybody must be over there*, John thought, so he parked and went to the door.

John spent the requisite time consoling his aunt Leone and her daughter, Joyce Konakowski. He offered appropriate condolences to all, patted hands, hugged relatives, had a beer with them; but at about 11:50 p.m., he begged off, saying that he had an early morning. He promised that he would call his mother and his sister in Arkansas first thing after he woke and break the sad news.

Now, with less than six hours of sleep, he was going to be hard-pressed to accomplish all the things that he had to do. Plus, he had the meeting scheduled in an hour at his house with Richard Raphael, the business associate and friend that he had blown off the night before. "That fucker will be right on time too, the punctual prick," he said out loud to no one. He looked at the corpse lying next to him and thought, *You can't be here when we start the meeting. That would be a distraction.* But what to do? There wasn't a lot of time.

John was naked, but for dingy white underwear. No time to waste, though; so he stood up, stretched, shook off sleep, and reached for his bedmate's arm and pulled the body close to the edge of the bed. He bent down and got under as much of Rob's corpse as he could. He lifted with his legs, shifted and adjusted until he could hoist the 150-pound body over his shoulder, fireman-style.

It had been eight hours since life had coursed through Rob Piest, and rigor mortis was nearly complete. The sounds of snapping and cracking that emanated from the stiffened body, together with the gurgling of transferring fluids and the release of air from the lungs would have made the average pro linebacker pass right out. Gacy simply considered this whole matter one big necessary pain in the ass, like he considered most physical chores. Grunting and sputtering like a sumo wrestler, he trudged to the hall where the trapdoor to the attic was. He balanced his load, then reached for the tiny rope loop on the trapdoor. The door was enhanced by a spring mechanism, and it opened easily. A telescoping ladder unfolded and came to rest on the floor in front of him.

Gacy was strong, but he was flabby and noticing his age. Beads of perspiration exploded off his face and neck and dripped to the carpet. He took each step of the ladder as though he was working with free weights, but soon he had Rob's remains stored just to the right of the trapdoor in the attic. "That is good enough," he groaned, letting out a huge breath and wiping sweat from his brow with his forearm. He raised the ladder and the trapdoor, and it closed. Nothing looked out of place. John dragged his sweaty, naked fleshy and overweight white body back down the hall toward the bathroom, picking his underwear out of his butt crack and bitching and moaning about what a pain in the ass *that* was. "Why the fuck did I make a stupid appointment at seven fucking o'clock in the motherfucking morning at my own goddamn house? Jeez!"

John remembered that it was his duty to call his mother and tell her about the death of Uncle Harold. He had volunteered to be the one to notify her the night before. He was worried, however, about how long his mother would keep him on the goddamn telephone. He had shit to do. He decided that she would just have to understand that he had business to attend to and would have to cut the phone call short.

When Richard Raphael arrived at John Gacy's house with another business associate and friend, Gordon Nebel, at 7:00 a.m. sharp, Gacy had shit, showered and shaved, let the dog out, called his mom, made coffee, and put out a coffee cake. He greeted them with his standard-issue ear-to-ear smile. There was absolutely no hint that anything was amiss. The fact that John had failed to make the appointment the night before was quickly forgotten, especially when his guests heard about poor Uncle Harold.

The Chicago Bears had lost Coach Jack Pardee to the Washington Redskins at the end of the 1977 season, and the new coach, Neil Armstrong, was leading the team to a dismal, losing season in 1978. This became the topic of discussion between the men for the first part of the meeting. "Fuckin' Bears," they all agreed. The one bright spot: the Bears had beaten the hated Green Bay Packers, 14–0, on Sunday and were looking forward to a grudge match against Pardee's Redskins next weekend.

Soon the conversation turned to business; however, just as the men began to get to the crux of the intended issues for discussion, a shopping center job, the phone rang. John considered letting the answering machine get it but thought better of that. He went ahead and answered the telephone while Raphael and Nebel continued to discuss the job. As it turned out, the phone call would prove to be somewhat important, at least to John.

"Mr. Gacy, my name is Officer Adams from the Des Plaines Police Department. We are investigating the disappearance of a teenage boy that worked at Nisson Pharmacy. We understand that you were at the pharmacy last night, and we are wondering if you could help us out."

The blood drained from Gacy's face, and his heart jumped into his mouth; but outwardly he appeared quite calm. "How can I help you?" John asked tentatively. "What could I possibly do?"

"Well, the parents of the boy are very concerned, as you might imagine. They are here at the station with me right now, and we were wondering if you could shed any light on this matter. The boy's name is Robert Piest. There is some indication that he was going to ask you for a job. Did he do that, Mr. Gacy? Did you meet or talk to him last night?"

"I met several kids at the pharmacy. Most of them were girls. I saw boys working there. Was this kid tall or short? I did not talk to any of the boys, or, at least, not to get their names. I talked to Linda with the brown hair and glasses. I might have asked one boy if there was any more shelving in the back. I don't know . . . does that help?"

"Did any young man ask you for a job, or did you offer a job to any of the young men?"

"Absolutely not . . . no, I did not. No job offer."

"Did you see or talk to any of the employees outside of the pharmacy . . . after you left the pharmacy?"

"There was a kid taking out trash."

"Did you speak to him?

"No, why would I? No, of course I didn't. I just got into my truck and left."

"Did you see anything at all that seemed unusual, sir?"

"I'll be honest with you, Officer—I just got into my truck and left. I wasn't paying a lot of attention to the pharmacy at that time. I was finished there."

"I see. Well, let me give you a number to call in case you think of something that might help us. Would that be OK? Do you have a pen, sir?"

"Yeah, sure . . ." John scratched out a number on a piece of paper and hung up the phone.

John Gacy downplayed the hell out of the importance of the call when his business associates asked him what it was all about. "It was nothing. Some kid is missing, and he worked at a place where I was bidding a job last night. They wondered if I saw anything. No big deal. Cops . . . what the fuck do they know?" The men were back to business without much hesitation.

When the meeting broke up later that day and John was once again alone in his house, he busied himself with paperwork and mundane chores. Of course, he knew that he had a pressing task ahead of him, but it was broad daylight, not the best time of day to dispose of a body. He called Nisson Pharmacy at approximately 5:00 p.m. Larry Torf answered, and John asked if Phil was around. Phil and John were closer friends than John and Larry were, and John thought he might be able to pry information about the police investigation out of Phil without making him suspicious. To John's dismay, Phil was not in. Therefore, John spoke to Larry about the job, asking if the glass company had communicated with him, if delivery had been set up—perfunctory nonsense to justify the call.

John had made plans to take his aunt Leone and her daughter, Joyce, out to dinner, and he believed that his best course of action was to go about his normal business. To that end, he was in front of Leone's house at 6:00 p.m., as planned. He had no idea whether or not unknown forces were gathering against him, but he figured that he might as well not worry about things that had not yet happened. There would be plenty of time to worry about such things once they happened—if they happened. He was a bit concerned about the call from Officer Adams; however, what could he do about it? He decided to put it out of his mind. After all, what did cops know? He took Leone and Joyce to the Sizzler Restaurant on Harlem Avenue near the Harlem Irving Plaza and had a nice dinner where he further consoled his loved ones and reminisced about good old Uncle Harold.

When John returned home, he called his employee and friend Michael Rossi. They had previously spoken about going out to procure a Christmas tree for Gacy's house. Rossi said he would come over around 9:00 p.m. or a little after that.

WHAT JOHN GACY did not know was that forces were, in fact, conspiring against him, so to speak; and, perhaps, he should have been worried—very worried.

When Rob Piest did not return home the previous evening, his parents sprang into action. They did not wait. They did not dally. They knew their son. His two siblings knew their brother. Rob would not have just disappeared without a word. He was not a troubled kid. He was not a runaway. He was a good, responsible, conscientious young man who had a great relationship with a loving, caring, attentive family. After calling all of Rob's closest friends and acquaintances, calling Nisson Pharmacy and speaking with Phil Torf and obtaining John Gacy's home number, after personally calling John Gacy's house and talking to an answering machine, Harold Piest, together with his wife, Elizabeth, and their children, Ken and Kerry, decided it was time to go to the police. The family did not want to admit it, but they all knew something was very wrong.

Missing person reports had always been considered routine by police departments all across the country. In many cases, it was stated policy to wait twenty-four hours before even beginning the concerted process that went into a lengthy and expensive search. This was not because the police departments, and their collective members, did not care deeply about each missing person reported. It was because so often, frankly, in most cases, the reported missing person would turn up in short order with some lame and embarrassing excuse concerning where they were, or, particularly in the case of teenagers, the missing person had voluntarily, purposefully left home, the typical runaway. Therefore, it was often a tall hurdle for the family of a missing person to impress upon a specific desk sergeant or watch commander that their "missing" person was somehow different from all of the other "missing" persons.

This was not a problem for the members of the Piest family, however. When the four remaining members of the Harold Piest family walked into the Des Plaines Police Department sometime just before 11:00 p.m., united in their purpose and solidified in their resolve, they were a force of nature. They first spoke to the watch officer, George Konieczny.

Although Officer Konieczny explained that at that hour all he could do was take down the information regarding Rob's disappearance and move it through the system—and he advised the Piest family that they should go home and wait for a call from the detective in charge of the case—he was inspired by the obvious concern that was evident on the part of the family. He finished his report at 11:50 p.m. and added a personal note to the report, which emphasized the concern and believability of the family with whom he had met. He had his watch commander sign off on the report and immediately transmitted the pertinent information contained therein to the radio room. The statistical information contained in the City of Des Plaines Police Department case report #78-35203 concerning Robert Jerome Piest, male, Caucasian, age fifteen, slender to medium build, brown hair, brown eyes, tan Levi's jeans, white T-shirt, brown suede shoes, light blue nylon parka, last seen in the area of 1920 Touhy Avenue, Des Plaines, was sent out to every Illinois jurisdiction over LEADS (Law Enforcement Agencies Data System) within two hours.

The Piest family left the police station and drove the short distance to the family home. They were beside themselves with worry. They had no intention of waiting for word from some unnamed, yet-to-be–assigned-to-the-case detective. They immediately split up into a makeshift search party using the two family German shepherds to assist them. Harold, Ken, and Kerry spent the entire night searching every dark corner of the city of Des Plaines and the immediate surrounding area while Elizabeth stared at the silent telephone, waiting for it to ring, and wept. If Rob was hurt and in some bushes or in a forest preserve somewhere, they were going to find him. They could not sit idly by while the wheels of the government bureaucracy slowly churned.

At 8:30 a.m., the exhausted, sleep-deprived troop trudged back into the Des Plaines Police Department. They asked the officer at the front desk if they could see the youth officer assigned to the case. At least they could put a name and a face to the person that would be helping them find Rob.

They were led past bustling uniformed officers attending to this and that, the organized chaos of the inner offices of a busy police department. Finally, they were shown into a conference room where Officer Ronald Adams joined them, holding a copy of Officer Konieczny's report. Officer Adams perused the report and eyed the personal Post-it note attached. He looked at the determined family in front of him, and he too was immediately convinced that this was no typical runaway case. He had been in the youth division for six years and had handled many claims of "missing" teens. Experience told him that this claim was real. He suspected foul play but did not tell the family that. He asked the Piests to remain in the conference room while he went to his office and began making telephone calls.

When Officer Adams retuned to the conference room about a half hour later, he did not have good news.

"I spoke to Phil Torf. He has not seen or heard from Rob. I asked him about Mr. Gacy. He confirms that Mr. Gacy was at the store twice last night, once to discuss a remodeling job and again because he forgot his appointment book. He does confirm that Mr. Gacy had mentioned that he too hired highschool boys to work for his contracting business. This was in the context of a conversation concerning Mr. Torf's many young highschool–aged employees. Mr. Torf never saw Rob talking to Mr. Gacy. He said that after you called him last night, he called Mr. Gacy but spoke only to the answering machine. Mr. Gacy has not yet returned the call."

Officer Adams was looking at an array of disappointed and dejected faces.

"I also talked to Mr. Gacy . . ."

These words elicited an immediate response.

"You talked to him?" was the chorus from the momentarily hopeful family.

"Yes, I talked to him. He confirms that he was at the pharmacy last night but insists that he did not meet Rob or speak to him. He says he did not offer anyone a job."

After all faces fell, Officer Adams went on to explain that at Phil Torf's suggestion, he had also talked to Kim Byers, another young employee at the pharmacy. She specifically stated that at around 9:00 p.m., Rob had told her that "that contractor guy wants to talk to me" just before he ran out the door. However, she had not actually seen Rob talking to Mr. Gacy either inside or outside the pharmacy.

Then Officer Adams launched into an all-too-practiced soliloquy about the necessity for the family to allow the police to do their job. It was a bad idea and quite improper for family members to intrude into an ongoing missing person investigation, and at times, it could be dangerous. It was best if the family went home and waited for developments. They would be the first persons contacted, of course, as soon as there was any update in the search.

The family thanked the officer and left the station, dejected and broken, their hopes for a quick resolution to their nightmare dashed.

Officer Adams later discussed the matter with his lieutenant, Joseph Kozenczak. He was not in any way giving up on the case. Lieutenant Kozenczak, after having read Konieczny's report with the personal note attached and having discussed the facts with Adams, was easily convinced that the matter was urgent. He gave the go-ahead to pursue the matter posthaste with an emphasis on their suspect and the last person reported to have seen Rob Piest, one John Wayne Gacy; and he assigned another officer, James Pickell, to help out. At 3:00 p.m., a fourth member of the force joined the team working on the case. A young detective, Mike Olsen, came in early to help the others. He and Adams used a copy of the Maine West Highschool student directory, which had been given to them by the Piest family, to contact all of Rob's friends from school.

The other officers used police channels and shoe leather to check to see if Mr. Gacy had a criminal record of any kind and for any other pertinent information about the case.

By the evening of December 12, the Des Plaines police knew the following about case #78-35203 and the suspect, John Wayne Gacy:

The black 1979 Oldsmobile that John Gacy drove, bearing license plate number PDM 42, was registered to PDM Contractors Corporation, as was the Chevrolet pickup with the snowplow attached.

Not a single friend or relative of Robert Jerome Piest had seen or heard from him since nine o'clock the previous evening.

Not a single friend or relative of Robert Jerome Piest considered him a likely candidate to run away from home. He had no recent troubles, no problems at school, no fights with girlfriends, friends, or family. He was a good student, an athlete, a hard worker, and a responsible young adult.

Linda Mertes confirmed that she had spoken to Robert Jerome Piest about the fact that John Wayne Gacy said that he hired his new employees at a starting pay of $5 per hour. She had specifically, although jokingly, mentioned that Rob should get a job with Gacy.

Kim Byers confirmed that Robert Jerome Piest had told her that he was going to talk to some contractor about a job just before he left Nisson Pharmacy at approximately nine o'clock the previous evening.

Elizabeth Piest confirmed that Robert Jerome Piest had told her that he was going to talk to a contractor about a new job just before he left Nisson Pharmacy at approximately nine o'clock the previous evening.

John Wayne Gacy had been arrested and convicted for the crime of sodomy in Waterloo, Iowa, and had been sentenced to ten years in the Iowa Men's Reformatory at Anamosa on May 20, 1968. He had been granted early release and had been paroled to Chicago, Illinois, on June 19, 1970.

John Wayne Gacy had been arrested and charged with aggravated battery and reckless conduct on June 22, 1972, in Northbrook, Illinois. This case had been dismissed.

John Wayne Gacy had been arrested and charged with battery on July 15, 1978, in Chicago, Illinois, Sixteenth District, and said charge was pending and unresolved.

Needless to say, John Wayne Gacy became the primary suspect in the disappearance of Robert Jerome Piest. There was evidence of both deviant and violent behavior in his past. As far as anyone knew, Gacy was the last person to see Rob. It was time to pay this guy a visit. It was time for Mr. Gacy to go on the record.

After a twelve-hour day, Officer Adams had family matters to attend to at home; however, he was replaced by Detective David

Sommerschield, who was brought up to speed by the other officers. Somebody said it. No one remembers who, but it got said; and unfortunately, all agreed:

"We have to get this motherfucker. This son of a bitch is either holding . . . or, more likely, has done something much worse to Rob Piest, no fucking question about it."

Sometime around 9:00 p.m., exactly twenty-four hours since the last time anyone had seen Rob Piest, the four police officers piled into two unmarked squads—Kozenczak and Pickell in one, Olsen and Sommerschield in the other—and screeched out of the dark garage of the Des Plaines police headquarters, headed for the home of John Wayne Gacy. They had no clue what to expect when they arrived.

Rob Piest's body remained resting silently in the attic above the hallway in Gacy's house.

Michael Rossi had worked for PDM Contractors for about two years and, along with David Cram, had become a trusted and essential member of John Gacy's contracting business and one of Gacy's best friends, in spite of the nearly twenty years that separated their ages. Rossi had learned enough about the business to run jobs on his own, thereby freeing Gacy to take in more work. He had begun his employment as a green sixteen-year-old kid but had matured into an integral cog in the success of PDM Contractors.

As one of the perks of his job, Rossi was also allowed to use the company van, with the name of the company painted on the doors, as one of his personal vehicles. Rossi also drove a white 1971 Plymouth Satellite, which he had purchased from John. It was in the PDM van, however, with tunes cranked up and cigarette smoke billowing from the slightly open driver's window, that Rossi arrived at Gacy's house at about 9:20 p.m. as planned.

When he bounced into the circular drive in front of the house and the headlights of the van swept across the front yard, he noticed two men standing at the front door of the house. One of the men had his hands cupped on the sides of his face and was looking in the small diamond-shaped window in the otherwise-solid front-entrance door. He also saw two matching unmarked Ford sedans parked in front on the narrow city street lined on both sides with parked cars. The two cars stood out.

Rossi, like everybody else on the planet, had often thought that if the police wanted some of their vehicles to be unmarked, to be "undercover," they might want to throw a set of hubcaps on them or allow the manufacturer to put a piece of chrome here or there on the damn things. The two vehicles parked in front of Gacy's house might just as well have had "police vehicle" painted in neon on the side doors. Rossi swallowed hard and wondered why two plainclothes policemen were standing on his boss's front stoop. Not for any particular reason—he wasn't doing anything wrong, not just then anyway—but Rossi just didn't like cops.

A lone old-fashioned decorative streetlight burning on the front lawn of the house cast long shadows across the small yard as Rossi opened the creaking door of the van, exited the vehicle with a jump, crunched through the snow that blanketed the cold ground, and approached the two men. Christmas lights blazed on houses and in yards up and down the block. Gacy had yet to decorate. His house was noticeably dark.

"If you are looking for John, he won't hear you. He is probably watching TV in the back room." Puffs of condensing breath accompanied his words like tiny clouds due to the crisp, wet December air.

"Are you friends with Mr. Gacy?" Lieutenant Kozenczak asked.

"Who's asking?"

"My name is Lieutenant Kozenczak. This is Officer Pickell from the Des Plaines Police." Kozenczak showed a badge.

"I work with John, and we're friends."

"What is your name, sir?"

"Michael Rossi."

Just then, Detective Sommerschield appeared. He and Olsen had been checking out the rear of the house. The detective signaled that Gacy was in the rear of the house. He had seen him through a window in the back.

"Mr. Rossi, I am going to ask you to wait here with these officers." Kozenczak pointed to Olsen and Sommerschield. "Keep him here," he said to them. "Jim, come with me."

"Is John in trouble?" Rossi asked.

"We just want to ask him some questions."

"Do you guys have a warrant?" Rossi sounded a bit like a brat, like he had watched way too many cop shows. This brought light chuckles from the officers. Then he was ignored.

What Mr. Rossi didn't know or didn't understand when he asked the question was this: The police can walk up to any person's door anytime they want to, without a warrant, without probable cause, without an apparent reason of any kind, just like a Jehovah's Witness or a door-to-door roof repair salesman can. They simply knock on the door and proceed to ask questions as they investigate a case, and they can ask for the citizen's cooperation in their investigation. Often they are doing this to exclude or eliminate a person from their investigation. Sometimes they are hoping that a suspect will in some way slip up or give himself or herself away. However, when the police do act without a warrant, when they are at the early stages of their investigation, the cooperation by the citizen is voluntary. Therefore, the citizen can refuse to cooperate.

When the two officers identified themselves, Mr. Gacy flashed his patented ear-to-ear smile and invited them in.

"How can I help you guys?" Gacy asked without concern. "I heard you at the front door, but I had to take a piss. What's up?"

Thus began the first of what would later prove to be many, many face-to-face conversations between officers of the Des Plaines Police Department and John Wayne Gacy. This particular conversation at times got slightly contentious. Mr. Gacy continued to state with conviction that he had no idea who Rob Piest was, that he had not offered anyone a job, had not spoken to any employee of Nisson Pharmacy about a job, that he had been in the pharmacy on business and when that business was completed, he left, alone. He admitted that he might have asked a male employee if there was more shelving in the back room of the store, but he did not know the name of the employee, nor did he talk to him or anyone else outside the store. He was sorry that he could not be of more help, but that was all he knew. When he arrived home after he left the pharmacy, he was informed by telephone that his uncle was near death; later, his uncle died. That was what his attention was directed to for the remainder of the previous evening, and that was his primary concern at that moment.

Kozenczak and Pickell were not so easily convinced. They had statements from at least two persons indicating that the man sitting in front of them so comfortably in his big black recliner was the last person to talk with their missing kid. They also now knew Gacy's criminal record. The conversation went around and around until Kozenczak began to suggest that Mr. Gacy accompany them back to the station to make a formal written statement. At this point, Gacy became emphatic.

"I have a goddamn funeral to plan, grieving relatives to attend to. I am waiting for a long-distance call from my mother in Arkansas at this very moment. Arrangements have to be made. I can't leave."

"Call her now," Kozenczak prompted. "Call her right now, we'll wait."

Gacy, completely exasperated, feigned a call to his mother, knowing that she would not answer. "I have to wait for her call," he said. "I'll come down to give a statement later tonight if it means that much to you."

"When can we expect you at the station, Mr. Gacy?" Kozenczak was not letting up.

"I don't know . . . maybe in about an hour or so."

"We will be waiting, sir. We need a statement from you. We have a job to do, Mr. Gacy."

"Look, you guys can check out everything that I have told you. I was at Northwest Hospital last night, and then I was with my aunt who just lost her husband and her daughter who just lost her goddamn father. Don't you guys have any respect for the dead?"

As Officers Kozenczak and Pickell grudgingly left the house, they had absolutely no way of knowing that at times during their short visit to the home of John Wayne Gacy, as they walked around the house, they were standing just two and a half short feet below the body of the very boy that they sought and just two and a half short feet above the most gruesome makeshift graveyard that has ever been recorded in the annals of crime.

———————

WHEN ONLY ONE unmarked squad car slowly pulled away and splashed through melting snow and ice on the unplowed, ice-rutted city street and one repositioned itself and parked on an intersecting side street, headlights off, Michael Rossi went to the back door and confronted his friend. "What the fuck is all this shit about, John? One of those fucking cop cars is still sitting out there." Rossi had been slightly grilled about John by the two other detectives while they all waited out front on the circular driveway. "What do these son-of-a-bitching cops want? Did you do something?"

"Hell, no. They are just looking for some fucking kid, probably a runaway. I don't know shit about it. They can't find the fuckin' kid, and they were asking for my help. Fuckin' cops. What do they know?"

"Well, they were asking me a lot of weird-ass questions, John."

"They're cops. What the fuck do you expect? Wannabe suburban cops. Don't pay them any attention. I'm gonna make some calls about this. They are going to hear about this from their superiors . . . motherfuckers."

Rossi looked at his boss. He wasn't sure what to think. Being friends with John Wayne Gacy was never all that easy. He told so many stories; it was always hard to tell the truth from the bullshit. If you believed everything he said, you would have to be an asshole. How could any one person be all of the things that he said he was? One day he was a special auxiliary cop on some secret assignment, the next day a mob guy with ties to the highest levels of "the Family." It would be impossible. Rossi had learned to take his tall tales with a grain of salt. Rossi decided that he wasn't going to worry about it at that moment, though. At least for now, it seemed that the commotion was over.

"Well, are we going to look for a tree?" Rossi asked, trying to put the events of the evening behind him.

"It's too late now, but I'm gonna get the ornaments down from the attic. We'll go tomorrow." Then Gacy smiled. "Let's fuck with them."

"What do you mean? Fuck with who?"

"You said one of their stupid unmarked squads is still parked out there. Let's fuck with them."

Minutes later, as Officers Olsen and Sommerschield looked on, Rossi walked out to his van, got in, fired up the engine, and slowly pulled up along the side of the house, out of their view. Then he slowly backed up again and stopped. The two officers could not see what was happening on the other side of the van. Suddenly, both vehicles, the van and Gacy's big black Oldsmobile, took off out of the circular drive and tore off heading east down Summerdale, spitting snow and ice and fishtailing as they went. It all happened so fast that the two police officers had no time to follow, and by the time they did shoot down Summerdale in pursuit, both the van and the Oldsmobile had disappeared into traffic on Cumberland Avenue and were gone.

Gacy aimlessly drove through neighborhoods without apparent purpose, and when he was sure that he was not being followed, he returned home and got started. He had promised to be at the Des Plaines Police Department in about an hour. There was no question that he was going to be late . . . but how late? That would determine if the sons of bitches would be back sniffing around, being cops, making nuisances out of themselves. John was committed to go and give them their damn written statement, but he had some things to do first.

Once he was alone again, Gacy went out to his garage and picked up an old rolled-up orange rug that he had not thrown away, even though it had not been used for months and was worn and soiled beyond its usefulness. He lugged it into the house and unrolled it out on the floor underneath the attic trapdoor in the hall. He pulled down the trapdoor and climbed the telescoping stairs. He yanked and pulled at the inert object that had once been Rob Piest and positioned the body at the top of the stairs so that he could simply let it slide down by guiding it along on the rails of the ladder. He certainly had no intention of lifting the fucking thing down. That had really been a pain in the ass when he was putting the kid up there. He certainly didn't look that heavy. He was a wiry little kid, for chrissakes. *I guess muscle really does weigh more than fat,* he thought as he guided the body down to the floor and onto the rug, grunting and groaning, spitting and perspiring as he did it, while his little dog looked on with head cocked, quite perplexed.

Gacy left the body while he let the dog out into the backyard. He went to his car and popped the trunk. He returned, rolled the body of Rob Piest in the old rug, picked it up with one final colossal grunt, and waddled out to the trunk of his car.

Once the body was safely in the trunk, Gacy relaxed. He let the dog back in and locked up the house. He drove out of his driveway, constantly checking his rearview mirror for sedans without chrome. There were none. He headed south on Interstate 294 to where it connected with Interstate 55 and drove south on 55 toward Joliet.

The huge suspension bridge that spans the muddy brown Des Plaines River, where it intersects and churns 150 feet below Interstate 55 is bleak, unlit, and foreboding at night, especially when the traffic is light. It looms out of the darkness and suddenly fills the windshield when approached at high speed. The area surrounding the bridge is mostly forested and pitch-black. The only lights in view are a mile away and just to the east, where a huge Exxon oil refinery—with thousands of small twinkling lights on the various, odd-shaped structures and pipelines—glistens like a miniature Emerald City in the distance.

As Gacy approached the bridge, he began to slow well below the minimum speed limit of forty-five on the interstate. A Peterbilt semi, hauling cross-country, grew in his rearview mirror, then thundered by with a windstorm in its wake, shaking the big Oldsmobile like a toy. He was just about to stop on the bridge when he heard a warning of a "smokey" in the vicinity of the bridge over the CB. He immediately hit the gas and sped up. He exited at Arsenal Road a short distance ahead and maneuvered the long dark cloverleaf, crossed over I-55, and returned to the highway in the northbound lanes heading back toward the bridge. He searched ahead. Where was this trooper? Gacy then proceeded past the bridge again to the exit for Bluff Road. He again did a turnaround by crossing over the interstate. While on the Bluff Road bridge, he stopped. He looked both ways, north and south, and saw only the distant taillights of a truck getting smaller as he watched. There was no trooper, no "smokey," as far as the eye could see in any direction. It was only then that Gacy realized that the "smokey" in question . . . was him. His car had the spotlights and antenna. His car looked like an unmarked cop car! He had designed it that way.

It was approaching midnight, and it was cold. December was taking hold in a big way, especially out there in the fuckin' sticks. Cops were waiting for him in the Des Plaines police station. He was late. If he didn't hurry, they would probably be back at his door, pestering him. Gacy was annoyed. He was sick of this whole exercise. It was becoming a bother. What a pain in the ass. What was he so worried about? He had done this before. He got into his car and floored it. He screeched around the cloverleaf and entered the southbound lanes again. He shot over the bridge at a dangerous speed and screamed back down to the Arsenal Road exit. He repeated his turnaround maneuver; only this time, he accomplished it in half the time. He wanted to be headed north. He wanted to be headed home.

Gacy screeched to a stop on the big suspension bridge at approximately the midway point. He popped the trunk and got out, grumbling and bitching like this whole matter was an enormous imposition on his time. He wrestled the contents out of his trunk and, with a gross, guttural yell that echoed through the night, flung it over his shoulder. He again waddled under the weight, and when he reached the railing, puffing and gasping, he hoisted his load up onto the top rail.

John Wayne Gacy released the body of Robert Jerome Piest into the blackness below. The only sound was the howling of the December wind through the massive iron girders of the bridge. Then seconds later . . . a distant splash.

ON HIS WAY back to the city, Gacy rarely let the speedometer dip below 90 mph. The drive back was normally at least an hour without traffic, and he was trying to improve on that time. He wanted this business with the damned Des Plaines police to be over. He would give his goddamned statement and be done with it. He was very late, but Gacy intended to get to the police department come hell or high water.

Interstate 294, also called the Tri-State Tollway, is actually a bypass. It allows truckers and travelers that are passing through Chicago to avoid using I-94, the actual interstate route, which slices right through the heart of downtown Chicago. The Tri-State skirts around the city to the west through dozens of densely populated suburbs. The area is much too populated to have the common style of rest stops along the roadway, so the State of Illinois has constructed oasis-style rest stops, which are built over the tollway like a bridge but with restaurants and gas stations and public restrooms. As Gacy screamed under the Hinsdale Oasis, pedal to the metal, a truck was exiting the oasis and entering the highway, but had not picked up full speed. Gacy had to change lanes, normally a simple maneuver; however, black ice had formed on the pavement due the midday thaw and the nighttime hard freeze. The big Oldsmobile began to fishtail. Gacy overcompensated. Suddenly, he was in a free skid. The car hit a snowbank, and it exploded all around him. The car continued to slide fully off the road and landed completely askew in snow, ice, and mud, ten feet from the highway.

"What the fuck else is going to happen tonight?" Gacy screamed at the windshield. "What!"

He wasn't hurt; he was pissed—totally pissed. Here he was, trying to do the right thing, following through on this asshole cop's requirement that he show up and tell him the same fucking thing that he had already told him. And now this. What next?

He took a deep breath, got out of the car, and surveyed his predicament. As he walked around the car, with each step he took, his shoes poked through the thin layer of ice atop the snow and plunged into the sloppy mud underneath. What a fucking mess. He was stuck, no question about it—good and stuck.

Gacy went into the trunk and hoisted his spare tire out and put it on the ground in front of the rear drive wheel. He was trying to use this little Chicagoland trick to get traction, but it was futile. The clock was ticking, and his opportunity to get to Des Plaines was slipping away when at about 2:00 a.m., a tollway employee, Dennis Johnson, noticed the disabled vehicle. He pulled up and asked Gacy if he needed a tow truck. At first, Gacy resisted this. It cost big bucks, and he thought he could get the car out eventually. But upon reflection, he finally agreed, and a tow truck was called. It came twenty minutes later, and the car was winched free from the mud, ice, and snow.

A report of the incident was filed with the Illinois Tollway Authority. It stated that at 2:30 a.m. on December 13, 1978, a 1979 Oldsmobile 98, bearing Illinois plate number PDM 42, was tended to and freed from a spinout at mile marker 29 in the northbound lanes of Interstate 294.

At 3:20 a.m., Gacy presented himself, caked in mud and totally disheveled, at the front desk of the Des Plaines police headquarters and asked for Lieutenant Kozenczak. He was told that the lieutenant had waited as long as he thought was reasonable but then had to leave. Mr. Gacy would have to return in the morning.

3

So THERE'S NO question about it. It's true. Mr. John Wayne Gacy left out a few pieces of pertinent information when he called me the first time. What I didn't know about my new client vastly outweighed what I did know about him. However, and I haven't mentioned this yet, John Gacy was my first client. He was, actually, my one and only client. Plus, I was intrigued by the puzzle he presented. Needless to say, I took his call quite seriously.

Don't get me wrong: he wasn't the *very* first client that I had ever had in my life. It's not like I had never seen the inside of a courtroom before. I had. It's not like I had never represented a person in court before. I had. In fact, I had been living in courtrooms for the past five years. That's what you do when you work for the Office of the Public Defender of the County of Cook, State of Illinois. You live in courtrooms. You live there, you eat there, and often enough, you sleep there.

Doesn't that title sound impressive, the Office of the Public Defender? Then you have the really impressive part, the County of Cook, State of Illinois part. Sounds pretty important, huh? What the office is, in reality, is a conglomeration of disparate, harried individuals, most of them very new to the profession, scurrying here and running there like chickens with their heads cut off, overworked and underpaid, many of whom are asking themselves daily, "Whose friggin' idea was this?" Men and women of all stripes that had finally come to the conclusion that perhaps they should have listened to that parent, that mom or that dad, who told them time and time again to become a doctor or a stockbroker, maybe a banker, anything but a lawyer. Son (or princess), they would say, the jokes they tell about lawyers are true. Don't you know that? People don't make those things up. They are true stories. Sharks? Professional courtesy? You have heard the shark jokes, right? That is exactly what lawyers are— they are sharks. Is that what you want? To be a shark? But of course, we didn't listen. No one seems to listen to their parents at that age.

And me, I was their boss. Sam L. Amirante, supervisor, Third District Office, the boss of the entire disparate and harried troop. I had already done my years of harried scurrying, and I had been promoted. So I was their boss, at least I was until the day that I submitted my resignation.

I had, in fact, submitted that resignation only a few days before I received the fateful call from Mr. Gacy. I had finally decided it was time to strike out on my own, to hang up the proverbial shingle, to become a private criminal defense attorney. I had done my intern-ship. I had worked in the mill that was the PD's office. I had been trying cases for five years—lots of misdemeanors, lots of felonies, a couple of murders—and it was time.

So I leased an office in a building in Park Ridge with several other lawyers, friends of mine. I moved in a few sticks of sec-ondhand office furniture that I picked up, including my first desk, which, if you have ever had a first desk, then you know . . . is a great feeling. I tacked up my diploma, license, and other lawyerly documents and mementos on my freshly painted wall. I put my wife and kid's pictures on the credenza, and presto, I was a criminal defense attorney for hire.

When John Gacy called me, I was in jeans and a sweatshirt. I didn't have any clients to see because I didn't have any clients.

So why get dressed up? I was so new at being a private criminal defense attorney I still had a check or two coming from the PD's office for vacation that I had never taken. Therefore, when I say that Mr. John Wayne Gacy was my first real client, that would be true.

Mr. Gacy called the right guy, though. I say that without blushing because I was absolutely dedicated to my job, passionate, immersed. In spite of the fact that my dad was one of those parents that wanted me to be a doctor, and that some people look down their noses at lawyers, until they need one, that is. Then everybody loves their lawyer. In spite of the fact that being a lawyer is a 24-7 job that sometimes precludes what most people would call a normal life. I loved being a lawyer, still do. It suits me.

I'm not sure why Gacy called me. There was a lot of wild speculation by others about that. Did I chase the case? Did I steal it from the PD's office? Who was this young upstart, and why was he representing this guy? Why was he in front of all those cameras?

Well, during my time at the public defender's office, I had met a lot of people. By coincidence, the Des Plaines police headquarters was in the same building as the Third District Office of the Public Defender, and I'm a likable, amiable sort, I guess. So I kinda knew everyone, and everyone kinda knew me.

That could explain why Gacy chose me to represent him. I was connected. I had clout. People might think that, I suppose. However, I choose to assume that it was because of my stellar reputation as an up-and-coming young trial attorney, together with my rugged, movie star good looks and my winning, ebullient personality. Actually, I'm just over five feet tall and come from a long line of short, stocky proud Italian men with gruff voices and easy smiles. If I shave too early in the morning, by five or six o'clock in the evening, I tend to look a little like Nixon did when he debated Kennedy. I've actually been mistaken for the defendant once or twice in the courtroom after a long day, so I don't know why he picked me. I guess I'll never know; he never told me, unless, of course, it was because he knew that I was an authentic true believer, one of the last of the breed, and proud to be.

I was also very active in Cook County politics, so I got to know many of the local politicians through political channels. Gacy was always impressed with that. I knew nearly all of the prosecutors. I had tried cases against most of them; the others I had met at political fund-raisers or bar association meetings. In spite of the huge size of Cook County and the greater Chicagoland area, the legal community is comparatively small and quite tight-knit. Everybody's reputation precedes them. I had a good reputation, if I do say so myself. Gacy knew that. Maybe that was it. Suffice it to say, he called me. I was now his lawyer.

In keeping with my promise to my new client, I started making some calls. At this point, I was doing him a favor just like he had asked. I had not been officially retained. But I was understandably curious as to why this guy, this pudgy, unassuming, glad-handing, small-time politician was being followed around twenty-four hours a day by the Des Plaines police. This was an unusual amount of attention to pay to anyone, except the most serious of suspects. The more I checked into it with clerks and others, the more curious I became. Nobody, but nobody, was talking. If they knew anything, they were not saying. There was, however, a bit of a buzz about the case. Even the local press had become marginally interested in the missing teen from the northwest suburbs, Rob Piest.

I finally called assistant state's attorney Terry Sullivan. Terry was the supervisor of the Office of the State's Attorney in the Third District. Essentially, he was my counterpart; he was the chief prosecutor in that district, I was the chief public defender. We had worked on several cases together and had become friends.

Terry's a great guy, a big tall lanky guy with a head of thick, wavy reddish blonde hair, a great smile, very disarming, lots of Irish charm. However, if you made the mistake of underestimating Terry in a courtroom, he would crush you like a bug. I had seen him do it. It was fun to watch some hotshot defense attorney who thought his shit didn't stink get his hat handed to him by Terry. He was a tough prosecutor and a good lawyer.

After making a few preliminary calls, I heard that Sullivan was becoming involved with the *Gacy* case and was conversant with the facts. I figured he could help me.

At first, we exchanged small talk. He asked me how I liked private practice so far, general chitchat. He immediately clammed up, however, the moment he knew that I was calling about the Gacy matter.

"Your guy is dirty, Sam. We are on him for this, and he is going down." Terry was not kidding around.

"Terry, this guy is involved in democratic politics—he's a damn precinct captain in Norwood Park, for chrissakes. He is a successful businessman. Everybody knows this guy. You are making him out to be some sort of hide-in-the-shadows kind of pedophile creep."

"That's exactly what I am making him out to be, Sam. He's a bad guy, a real bad guy. I can't tell you much, but I can tell you that." Sullivan was adamant.

"Look, if it turns out that you guys are right, it will all come out. But in the meantime, you guys are ruining his reputation. You are ruining his business. And all of this is based upon mere suspicion, because he happened to be in the wrong place at the wrong time. All we are asking is that you back off on the surveillance a bit, at least until you know more."

"We know plenty now, Sam."

"But you can't tell me what it is, right?" I was quite sure that Terry was using an old prosecution trick: Pretend that you know more than you do, and perhaps your opponent will let his guard down and give up information by accident.

"That's right. You know how this shit works, Sam. I can't jeopardize my investigation. It's nothing personal."

We volleyed back and forth without any kind of progress. Now I was truly curious and determined to figure out what was going on.

"You do realize that you are probably forcing me to file a lawsuit against Des Plaines and all of the coppers involved. This is harassment, Terry, plain and simple. We will get a TRO. I cannot speak for my client without discussing it with him first. But I can tell you that I will be recommending it. I have no choice, Terry. You are leaving me no choice."

"You do what you have to, Sam."

Terry Sullivan knew that I would not make such a claim unless I meant it. Still, he was not talking. We were running out of things to say to each other. I had determined one thing for sure. Something serious was brewing concerning my new client, Mr. Gacy.

"Keep me in the loop as much as you can, OK, Terry? I'll send you a courtesy copy of the lawsuit if and when we file it. "

"You know I will, Sam."

Herb Volberding was the mayor of Des Plaines. I knew him through my work with the Democratic Party in the northwest suburbs. He took my call. When I was done talking with the mayor, one thing was clear: Gacy needed a lawyer. For whatever reason, there were forces that were targeting him for the disappearance of this teenager, and they were quite unmoved by arguments to the contrary.

When I spoke to him by phone, Mr. Gacy was very upset. He told me that his house had been searched, that he had been kept in the Des Plaines police station for a period of time, very much against his will, and that the police had seized two of his vehicles. Funny, Sullivan must have forgotten to mention all of that. I told Mr. Gacy to come into my new office at 222 S. Prospect in Park Ridge.

When he walked into my office on Friday, December 15, 1978, at 11:30 a.m., Gacy was no longer just the political wannabe that told his tall tales and hung around the fringes of the Democratic Party in Cook County; he wasn't just the semisuccessful contractor and founder of PDM Contractors; he wasn't just the precinct captain that had brought in more votes for the Democratic Party organization of Norwood Park Township than any other precinct captain; he wasn't just the registered clown, Pogo, that marched in parades and made little sick children laugh; and he wasn't just the primary suspect in the disappearance of a local teenager, one Rob Piest, who, for the record, I still believed was a victim of circumstances. Now he was something very different. Now he was only one thing to me: Now he was my client, my first.

GACY APPEARED IN my office with that ear-to-ear smile of his as if he didn't have a care in the world. He was upset and indignant that he had been subjected to what he considered mistreatment by the Des Plaines police, but he seemed unconcerned about the potential consequences of these activities, what all this might ultimately mean to him, not unlike what one might expect from an innocent man.

We quickly caught up regarding mutual acquaintances and routine jibber-jabber concerning local politics and politicians. This part of the conversation, the small-talk part, was over very quickly because we both knew why he was there. I got the impression that he knew this matter was serious, even though he was trying his best not to act like it.

"So, John, I don't know of a more pleasant way to put this. I am not going to try to sugarcoat what I am about to tell you. It is clear, after having talked to several people regarding your concerns about being followed, that you are, without a doubt, a target . . . let me rephrase that—you are *the* target of an investigation being conducted by the Des Plaines police regarding the disappearance of a local teenager, Rob Piest. Now, why don't we start by you telling me why they might think that you have something to do with this?"

"This is bullshit, Sam."

"I know, John. I know it is bullshit. But there has to be a reason why these coppers, and at least one very persistent, very capable assistant state's attorney, have locked on to you the way they have, and I need to know what that is. Why don't you just start at the beginning and tell me exactly what happened?"

Gacy muttered and grumbled something about how he was an important man and this was a travesty, an outrage. He wasn't talking to me. He wasn't talking to anyone. He was simply bitching out loud. He couldn't sit still, he was so angry. Finally, he began . . .

"Well, on Monday, last Monday, I had an appointment at Nisson Pharmacy to bid a job . . ."

Gacy calmed down as he continued to tell his story. We stayed in my office for six hours. I happened to have the time available. I also felt that under the circumstances, it was important to learn everything there was to know about Mr. John Wayne Gacy.

4

PROCUREMENT OF A search warrant is not a simple matter. The Constitution of the United States requires that a showing of probable cause must come first. This is not always easy. The citizens of the United States do not take kindly to persons coming onto their property without a good reason. They sure as hell do not want police officers looking through their underwear drawers or the secret compartments and hiding places in their homes, reading their mail, and invading their space, unless they have a pretty goddamn good reason.

A search warrant allows the police to do just that, by the way. They may search anywhere that the delineated items in the warrant might be found. So if the police officers are looking for something small, which could be hidden in any small place within the home, a warrant allows them to literally look anywhere they damn well please during the search. Therefore, a showing of probable cause can be quite a high bar. Even the most state-minded of judges takes this requirement seriously. For this reason, the drafting of a complaint for warrant has become a bit of an art form.

For example, if the police are looking for a stolen car, and they have reason, or probable cause, to suspect that the said car is in a particular garage attached to a particular house, they couldn't very well justify the search of the house, or certainly not the drawers in that house, if they are looking for a car. However, if the keys to the car or the registration documentation are included in the items delineated as targets of the search, they can search anywhere that a set of keys or a set of documents might be hidden. Which, of course, means that they can turn the whole damn house upside down. Then, if they happen to stumble across a pound of marijuana or a bag of illegal pills while carrying out a legal search for the keys, well, so be it. Therefore, the officers investigating a crime and the prosecuting attorneys assigned to a case take great care in the preparation of a complaint for search warrant.

When Lieutenant Kozenczak approached Terry Sullivan with a request that a warrant granting permission to search John Gacy's home be issued, of course, Terry agreed. Kozenczak did not have a good feeling upon leaving Gacy's house, and he was not shy in sharing his thoughts on the matter. By now, all the police officers working on the case and the assistant state's attorney were on the same page. They all believed that Gacy was involved with the disappearance of Rob Piest and that either he was holding Rob against his will or, and this was the nagging fear that concerned each and every investigator working the case, he had done something much worse to him.

Assistant state's attorney Terry Sullivan had assigned most of his day-to-day responsibilities to members of his very competent staff and had literally moved into the offices of the Des Plaines Police Department, lock, stock, and coffeepot, in order to devote his full attention to the Piest/Gacy matter; and he brought with him one of his lead investigators, Greg Bedoe, of the Cook County sheriff's police. Bedoe was immediately accepted to the team of Des Plaines police officers that were assigned to the case. Sullivan told Kozenczak to draft up a complaint for search warrant and submit it to him for approval. Kozenczak had to admit that he had never had occasion to draft one before. That is when Bedoe was dispatched by Sullivan to help out.

As the days progressed, a cohesive team began to emerge out of the rather random group of investigating officers, many of whom had never worked together before, never even met. Of course, there were the standard clashes of egos and interdepartmental squabbles. These were tough cops from different divisions and different departments. That is to be expected. Standard pecking orders were being disrupted. Who outranked whom was sometimes in question. However, there seemed to be a higher purpose at stake that transcended the normal boundaries between individuals, the different divisions of the department, and between those various divisions and the outside help that was occasionally required. A unity of purpose began to overshadow all other elements.

The City also had a group of young undercover investigators, known as the Delta Unit, that drove old beater cars, allowed their hair to grow out, wore mustaches and grungy facial hair and jeans and ratty T-shirts, all in an effort to infiltrate the drug scene in that suburb, what the kids called "narcs." This unit, made up of three officers—Ron Robinson, Bob Schultz, and Dave Hachmeister, together with their sergeant, Wally Lang—volunteered and was ultimately assigned to the twenty-four-hour surveillance of Mr. Gacy and his associates. Mike Albrecht, who had previous dealings with Mr. Gacy and had been involved with the investigation from the beginning, soon joined them in their efforts.

The help of Delta Unit was enlisted following the first visit to Gacy's house by Kozenczak, Pickell, Olsen, and Sommerschield. Those men left that house with the nagging belief that something was wrong there. Something was very wrong.

Therefore, a team was forming, a dedicated team with a single purpose—get Gacy.

When Bedoe and Kozenczak put their heads together to draft the complaint for search warrant, they paid particular attention to the evidence that existed at the time. They called on the others for help. They wanted to include everything they had on this guy.

They wanted to have the leeway to search every square inch of that house.

They had a report about Gacy's arrest in Waterloo, Iowa, but they did not have the specifics. They wanted to know more. Let's face it . . . sodomy? They had to know more. This was a case about a missing kid. What they, together with the other members of the team, unearthed was not good news . . .

Sodomy has always been a catchall charge. It could denote any number of lewd offenses—things that lawmakers just didn't want people to do, plain and simple.

In Gacy's case, however, it was quite specific.

It seems that upon moving to Waterloo, Iowa, Gacy joined the local chapter of the Jaycees. He thought of himself as civic minded and had been a member of the Jaycees in every town that he had ever lived. He met a man named Donald Voorhees, a state senator and local businessman. Mr. Voorhees had a fifteen-year-old son, Donald Jr. Gacy heard that Donald the younger was known around town to be homosexual. Gacy approached this youngster and offered to pay him for sex. An unusual relationship grew between the boy and Mr. Gacy, which resulted in threats of blackmail and potential violence. Ultimately, it ended with charges being filed against Gacy—ten counts ranging from sodomy to unlawful restraint and extortion. In spite of a presentence investigation and report that recommended probation, Judge Peter Van Metre in Black Hawk County, Iowa, sentenced Mr. Gacy to the maximum sentence of ten years at the Iowa State Penitentiary in Fort Madison—a sentence that was converted to ten years at the Iowa Reformatory for Men in Anamosa, which he didn't fully serve because, as started prior, he was paroled to Chicago in June 1970.

That was enough for Kozenczak and Bedoe. Gacy had an unsavory history with young boys. He had been to prison for committing sodomy on a young boy! Their missing person was a young boy! They scribbled up a complaint for search warrant and brought it to Sullivan. They took great care to make the delineated search items vague and generic so that they could search with abandon. They now knew, at least for their purposes, that they had the right guy. Gacy was a predator, a creep that had targeted victims just like the Piest boy in the past. He fit a profile. He was the guy.

5

GACY SAT ACROSS from me, well back in his chair, ankle on a knee, casually recounting the events of the past few days as if he thought all of this was a huge inconvenience, an imposition on his busy day. He certainly didn't come off as a person with a guilty conscience. I had interviewed hundreds of individuals that were suspects of a crime during my years at the PD's office, maybe thousands when you think about it, several a day for five years. Often, the guilty ones lean forward on the desk with a sense of urgency, practically begging you to believe them. Their eyes often dart around as though someone is about to break in and grab them.

Gacy, on the other hand, had relaxed. He and I could have just as easily been discussing last weekend's football game or the state of the economy, rather than what was, in point of fact, the closing of a net around him from which he would never be freed. There was something, though—something that gnawed at me. The guy just couldn't seem to get through a sentence without mentioning how this was all related in some way to how he knew that big-shot politician or another rich and famous guy. It seemed such a non sequitur, as if he really did not understand the gravity of the situation. He was detached, disconnected. There he sat, implicated in the disappearance of a human being, under suspicion for perhaps kidnapping, abduction, or worse; and he was nonchalantly going on and on about his political connections. He wondered aloud more than once why Chief Alfano, the chief of police in Des Plaines, had let this go on as long as it had. He knew the chief well, according to him. They had met at some function or at one of the many fund-raisers he attended. Eventually, the chief would surely put a stop to all this nonsense. It was as if he thought he was insulated from all potential harm because he had once shaken the hand of the chief of police of the City of Des Plaines, Illinois. He mustn't have read the papers too closely. In the state of Illinois, governors routinely wind up doing time.

He recounted with great specificity the entire tale regarding his two visits to Nisson Pharmacy and his visit to Northwest Hospital to attend to his dying uncle Harold. He gave me the addresses and the life histories of his aunt Leone, her daughter, and her brother, told me how he went to comfort them on Monday night, all of it very plausible and very much verifiable. He mentioned Phil Torf and his brother, Larry. He told me about Linda with the dark hair and glasses at the pharmacy and the short kid that he had asked about shelving in the back. He even told me that he had failed to meet with his business associate, Richard Raphael, and that he agreed to meet him and Gordon Nebel, whom he called Uncle Gordon, at 7:00 a.m. the following day. He left out the events that took place between 9:30 and 10:00 p.m. He also told me that he left the pharmacy alone.

Gacy mentioned that he thought that the interest the police had in him might be related to drugs. He said that he did have a conversation with Phil Torf about the fact that Phil claimed to have grown some good pot on the roof of a building that he owned at Devon Street and California Avenue in the city. He was worried that some of Torf's employees had heard this discussion. However, he had spoken to the coppers on the phone, and they had been to his house twice now, and this had never come up.

"Speaking of the cops having been to your house," I chimed in, "why don't you tell me about that?"

"Which time?" Gacy asked blandly, as if the police go to every-one's house.

"Both. Start with the first time," I said.

"OK, I was sitting in my rec room watching TV when I hear a knock on the front door. I was expecting one of my guys, one of my foremen, Mike Rossi, and he would not normally go to the front door, but I still thought it must be him, so I didn't answer the door. I knew he would eventually figure it out to come to the back. I had to take a piss, so I did. When I finished, there was a knock on the back door. I did wonder what the fuck was up, cuz Rossi would normally just let himself in. I answered the door, and it was two cops. One says his name is Kozenczak. I let them in. No big deal. They say they are looking for some kid. I told them everything that I just told you. That's not good enough for them . . . so we argue a little bit, nothing to get upset about. They say they want me to come to the station to give a statement. I told them I was waiting for a call from my mom in Arkansas. It's a long-distance call, I say. She's gonna call collect. Her fucking brother-in-law just died, her sister's fuckin' husband . . . and I can't go."

"Did they say that they were going to arrest you?" I asked.

"Hell, no. They were just being cops, trying to intimidate me. Fuck them. I woulda called Bob Martwick or Chief Alfano before I would have left with those two assholes. They didn't know who they were talking to. I know people. It was OK, though. They were just doing their job. I told them that I would come down to the station later, and that seemed to satisfy them. So they left. Then a few min-utes later, Rossi walks in. I didn't know it, but they had Mike cooling his heels out front the whole time with two other coppers—"

"They sent four cops to your house, four detectives?" I inter-rupted, a bit incredulously.

"Yeah . . . why?"

"Well, that would be a little unusual, John—not that it means anything, necessarily, but it's a little bit unusual to send out four police officers, especially four ranking police officers, to take a simple statement from a potential witness." I was taking notes, wondering. This was a bit strange.

"Yeah, well, that was the first night they put a car outside the house. The fucking thing stood out like a sore thumb. They had a car parked just down the block. Rossi and I saw it."

"I see . . . did they stay there all night?"

"No, they left after a while."

"Did you go in to the station to give a statement?"

"Yes . . . but . . . well, Rossi had some pot with him, and after all the commotion, we decided to get high. Plus, I had a few drinks and a Valium or two. So I didn't make it into the station until about 3:30 a.m. or so. By that time, no one was around to take the damn statement. So they told me to come back in the morning. Hell, I thought cops worked all night."

"That was smart," I said sarcastically. "Did you go in the next day?"

"Yeah, I woke up early, made some calls for work and some regarding the funeral arrangements. I went to get a haircut, but there was a line, two people were in front of me. I don't like to wait around, so I went over to Democratic headquarters to use the phone over there. I called the Des Plaines police and got connected to Kozenczak. I asked him if he still wanted me to come in. He said that he did. Why, I don't know. But I went right over. I got there about eleven thirty or so. I thought this was all a total waste of time. What else could I tell them? I had already told them everything I knew."

"They like to get you on the record. They like to get a statement in writing."

"I guess . . . Anyway, they put me in a conference room with a cop named Jim, the same one that was with Kozenczak the night before at the house. I told them everything that I have told you, the whole story, step-by-step. Now, it was getting late. I had been there for over two fucking hours! I was starting to get pissed. I had a meeting at the funeral home. I had jobs going on that had to be checked. I had shit to do. They let me use the phone. I guess they thought that was enough. But sometimes they would all leave, and I was locked inside this room . . . locked in!"

"Did you feel like you were under arrest?"

"Fuckin' A. Wouldn't you?"

"Did you ask to leave? Did you tell them that you had pressing matters to attend to?"

"Sam, after a while I was screaming at these guys. I'm not some kind of pussy. I'm not a fruit picker. I know my fuckin' rights. At one point, an assistant state's attorney, Terry Sullivan, came into the room and grabbed me by the arm. He said something about how they were not done taking my statement and that it wouldn't be much longer, that I should be patient. Patient? Patient! It was going on three goddamn hours!"

"OK, OK, what happened next?"

"I called Leroy Stevens. He's a lawyer that has represented me on my corporate matters, a few other things too. Nothing big."

"Then what?"

"Leroy called Sullivan and told him to let me leave."

"I take it that this didn't work?" I knew that a call from a lawyer would not have rattled Terry in any way. As I said, he was a tough prosecutor.

"Right . . ." This time, it was Gacy that dripped sarcasm. Then he went on. "They had me locked in a room, no fuckin' bathroom in there, I might add, for so goddamn long that I finally laid down on the floor. I was going to take a fuckin' nap. Then a couple hours later, Stevens gets there. By then, they had me in another room, where they were telling me to sign my statement and a waiver of my rights."

"Did you sign those documents?"

"I told them to get Stevens in there."

"That was smart. What happened next?"

"Well, there was a bit of an argument about that, but, finally, Stevens told me to go ahead and sign the fuckin' thing and—"

"He did what?" I interrupted. This surprised me. I tried not to let on. It was not my practice to second-guess other lawyers. I wasn't there. I wasn't in that room.

"First he asked me if I knew anything about this whole matter . . . anything at all about this missing kid, other than what I had already told them. I said no. Then he told me to sign the fuckin' thing so that we could be on our way. Why? You wouldn't have advised that?"

"I have no idea what I would have done. I wasn't there. But normally, I would not recommend that a client give a voluntary statement or sign a waiver. I like to let the police and the prosecutors do their jobs themselves. Why do it for them? They are professionals, right? They don't need our help."

"What difference does it really make?"

"Look, John, everybody has heard about the scheming, low-life criminal defense attorney, using trickery and loopholes to get their dirty, rotten bad-guy clients off, scot-free, thereby unleashing them into our society again to prey on the defenseless. All of the TV cop shows and *Dirty Harry*-style movies put forth that message. And unfortunately, many people believe it. Now, don't get me wrong, I love those movies, and nobody wants the bad guys in those movies caught and punished more than I do. I root for those cops and those prosecuting attorneys. But I live in the real world, and in that real world, it's not so cut-and-dried. What nobody hears about is that, sometimes, the prosecution does the same goddamn thing. Don't forget, prosecutors are lawyers, and lawyers like to win. They have plenty of tricks and loopholes in their own repertoire. And one of those tricks is to get some poor unsuspecting innocent sap to give a written statement in the very early stages of the investigation, often under a great deal of duress and pressure; have them sign their name to it; and stick it in a file. Then a year and a half later, during the trial, if that poor sap, now the defendant, changes one word of their story as written in that statement, they wave it in their face and call them a liar, right in front of a jury. My job is to make sure that does not happen to the people I represent. So normally, I advise against giving any kind of statement. However, there are exceptions to every rule. Plus, and one cannot diminish this fact, not every lawyer represents his client in exactly the same way. Who's to say who is right or wrong in their approach? One thing is sure in this case, however—you already signed the fucking statement. So the point is moot, isn't it?"

"Yeah, I guess so . . ." At this point, Gacy sat up and put his hands on the other side of my desk. He seemed to fidget a bit, ever so slightly. He was starting to lean forward out of his chair.

"What else happened while you were in there?" I asked.

"Well, they had taken all of my personal possessions, my wallet, my keys—everything that I had in my pockets. When they gave everything back to me, they did not give me my keys. That's when they told me and Stevens that they were searching my house, that they had a search warrant to do so."

"Did they show you or Mr. Stevens the warrant?"

"No . . . and then the motherfuckers told me that they were going to hold my car—confiscate my fucking car! I asked them how the fuck I was supposed to get home, and they all just looked at Stevens. Then, when I get home, I find out that they grabbed my pickup too. This shit is getting out of hand, don't you think, Sam? What are my options here? Do I have any?"

"They are following up on what they believe to be leads regarding their case. However, the mere fact that they have not arrested you tells me that they have nothing solid. It may be time for us to sue them, to go on the offensive. This is harassment, plain and simple, unless you are not telling me something. Have you left anything out, John?"

"I have told you everything that I can recall, Sam, everything."

I looked at my knew client for a very long minute and then said, "OK, John, let's try to figure out what is making these guys so sure that you have something to do with this kid's disappearance. I want to know everything about you, not just what happened in the last three or four days. I need prior arrests, prior employment, prior marriages, family life—everything."

Over the next several hours, he went on and on about his life. I learned a lot about my new client.

John Wayne Gacy was born to the union of John Stanley Gacy and Marion Elaine Skow/Robinson on Saint Patrick's Day, March 17, 1942, at Edgewater Hospital in Chicago, Illinois. His parents remained married until the death of John Stanley on Christmas Day, December 25, 1969. He grew up under the thumb of a domineering father of Polish heritage, a hardworking, hard-drinking man with a Jekyll-and-Hyde personality, who was the dispenser of harsh corporal discipline, sometimes for no known reason, and whom John Jr. spent his entire life trying to please without success.

John was a sickly, flabby, uncoordinated kid who was unable to perform at sports, unable to bond with the kids his age, and unable to shake his own nagging, overwhelming belief that he was an outsider and a misfit. This low self-image was routinely and continuously reinforced by that domineering, uncompromising dad, a man who would routinely refer to his son a dumb and stupid sissy, a fag, a fruit picker, or worse.

He was a middle child; his sisters, Joanne Gacy Casper eighteen months his senior, and Karen Gacy Kuzma eighteen months his junior, were a countervailing force to their father's scorn and seemingly continuous berating of their brother. Together with their mother, John's only true source of comfort at home were the female members of his family. It seemed that John could never do anything well enough to satisfy his overbearing father.

John was a hard worker; he began working at various odd jobs at the age of fourteen. He always was considered the go-getter of the group on any job that he ever had.

When he was eighteen years old, he "ran away from home." I found it unusual for a grown man to tell me that he ran away from home, considering he was eighteen at the time and of legal age to do as he pleased. I saw this as an insight into his personality, although I didn't necessarily know what it meant.

It seems that John had saved enough money to buy a car, and he intended to buy a used car on his own. His father convinced him to accept a loan from him to buy a better car. In doing so, John's father maintained a level of control over his son. When John did something that John Sr. didn't like, John Sr. would ban John from using "his" car, the car on which a debt still remained in favor of John Sr.

One night, his father was exercising the power that he had over his son, and John decided to leave rather than obey. John drove to Las Vegas, Nevada. He arrived there with $36 in his pocket. He did not like the heat, however, and was already homesick when he had a blackout episode. He passed out in his car on a side street and was taken to Southern Nevada County Hospital as a result. The bill for the ambulance ride was, coincidentally, $36. Gacy went into the ambulance service office to explain why he could not pay the bill, and instead of encountering a dispute, he walked out of the office with a job. John worked for the ambulance company until they found out that he was only eighteen years old, too young to drive an ambulance. That did not deter John. He had met a man, Bud Bishop, at the Palm Mortuary while working at the ambulance company, and he was hired there. In spite of the fact that he was employed and making it in Las Vegas, supporting himself, he missed his mom, his sisters, and even his dad. After three months, he left Las Vegas and headed home. He was back living under his father's roof.

As he spoke, I began to realize that he was telling me about a life lived without a connection to anything or anybody. He was recounting a life that he lived without knowledge of how to do so. Like a pinball, he just bounced from setting to setting.

After he returned home, he began his adult career.

His first real job was at the Nunn Bush Shoe Company. He claimed that he tripled the sales of the store in which he first worked. He was promoted to manager and traveled for that company in 1963.

He moved to Springfield, Illinois, in 1964, where he met and married his first wife, Marlynn, in September of that year.

He joined the Junior Chamber of Commerce (Jaycees) in Springfield and rose quickly through the ranks. He ran membership drives, organized parades, basically volunteered for everything. He was chosen Outstanding First-Year Member in his Springfield local, and he was chosen third among all members honored as Most Outstanding First-Year Member of the Jaycees in the entire state of Illinois. It was a happy time for him.

His local Jaycees chapter also honored him as Man of the Year in 1965.

He ran the largest Christmas Parade in Central Illinois that year.

He was riding high, proving to his father once and for all that he was not the failure that his dad had always predicted he would be. Plus, he loved the limelight, the pats on the back, the attaboys. He couldn't get enough of that stuff.

His father-in-law owned three franchise locations of the Kentucky Fried Chicken food chain in Waterloo, Iowa. The newlyweds decided to move to Waterloo in 1966, and John was trained as a manager there.

Again he joined the Jaycees; again he soared through the ranks of its membership.

John was living the life of a successful young married man on his way up.

He told me that life was not all perfect in Iowa, however. He said that he did not like working for his father-in-law, and he was experiencing sexual confusion. He and his wife practiced wife swapping during this time, but even that did not satiate him. He knew one thing, though—he hated homosexuals, and he was no fruit picker.

Then, in spite of what he had just said about homosexuals, he proceeded to explain that while his wife was in the hospital giving birth to their firstborn, their son Michael John, he had his first sexual experience with a man.

The man, Adam Johnson, was an employee at one of the Roberts' brothers' stores, the Nunn Bush franchise where John worked in Springfield. The two decided to celebrate the blessed event, the birth of his son, by going out scouting for chicks—a questionable decision, to begin with. But that aside, after several drinks, Adam suggested that Gacy's approach to getting laid was all wrong. He said that Gacy had, at best, a fifty-fifty chance of finding a girl and getting laid. But he, Adam, had a 100 percent chance of having sex that night. Gacy certainly did not believe him, and, of course, he asked how that was possible. Adam said that if he struck out finding a woman to have sex with, he simply found himself a man. He punctuated this theory with a statement that a blowjob is a blowjob, doesn't matter who it comes from, man or woman.

Later that evening, to hear John tell it, he found himself magically transported to Adam's bedroom, where Adam was putting into practice that very theory of his. John says he has no memory of how he got there—he said something about going for coffee, but it turned into more drinks—but he does admit that he accepted the act of oral sex being offered by Mr. Johnson, adding, "That didn't make me a fag, that didn't make me a goddamn fruit picker. I was only bisexual."

John went on to explain that his second sexual encounter with a man was in 1966 in Waterloo, with Rick, a young employee of the Kentucky Fried Chicken stores that John managed. Of course, he reiterated his abiding hatred for homosexuals after telling me all about Rick.

My client was clearly confused sexually, I thought.

Then he told me about a series of events that helped greatly to explain why the Des Plaines police, Terry Sullivan, the mayor, Herb Volberding, and others were so convinced that Mr. Gacy was involved in the disappearance of Robert Piest.

My client explained that he had done time for the crime of sodomy in the state of Iowa.

At first, Mr. Gacy described the crime as "sodomy of film." I believe that John was so accustomed to marginalizing this matter over the years to others that he thought he could do the same with me. This was a mistake for two reasons: One, I was a lawyer; and I knew that no such charge exists, in Iowa or anywhere else—at least I'd never heard of such a charge. And two, Mr. Gacy had brought with him a stack of papers. Most of those papers were evidence of his many accolades and awards. However, among those accolades and awards were some of the charging documents and presentence reports that were generated by the State of Iowa regarding that very charge. A perfunctory review of these documents made it clear to me that the charge was simply sodomy, together with a plethora of ancillary charges.

I asked him what "sodomy of film" meant. He seemed to realize that I wasn't buying that description of the charge, so he launched into his story.

One of the reasons that he was so very successful at attracting new members to the Waterloo chapter of the Jaycees, he explained, was that he made it fun to be a member. He made it a lot of fun.

The parties that he arranged in support of his membership drives included the showing of heterosexual stag films, the presen-

tation of live girly shows, and, in many instances, the use of prostitutes to convince prospective members that it would be a great idea
to join the Jaycees.

This worked, by the way. It worked quite well. After one of
these parties, twenty-five new members tripped over themselves
to join up in a single night. John had caused the membership of
his small chapter to swell to levels never before seen in its history.
He was toasted and proclaimed a genius by his peers. Everybody
loved John. Apparently, he was not the only man in Waterloo that
liked to kiss his wife good-bye as he left for a Jaycees meeting that
could have doubled as a Nevada bordello. Once again, John was
Man of the Year.

He was planning to run for president of the whole group, and
he had the support among most of the membership. He enlisted
the help of a local politician and fellow Jaycees member—Donald
Voorhees, a businessman and an elected Iowa State senator—to run
his campaign. "He wanted to be on the side of a winner, the winning team," John proclaimed.

That is when John's super-duper nonstop train to happy town
derailed.

Mr. Voorhees had a son, Donald Jr. There was a rumor that the
son was a known homosexual and that he was amenable to having
sex with men for money. Gacy could not resist. He approached
this fifteen-year-old boy and, as he tells it, offered to pay him for
sex. The two haggled over the price but eventually agreed on the
payment of $5 for oral sex. Gacy reports that he could not reach a
climax as a result of this encounter and said that Donald Jr. owed him
one, to which the young man agreed. A relationship grew between
the two, and they had oral sex on at least two other occasions,
according to John. John became a friend to the father and a friend
to the son, unbeknownst to either. At some point, young Donald
needed money. He wanted to buy an amplifier, and he went to
Gacy to borrow money. When Gacy insisted on sex, the young man

threatened to expose their relationship to his father and others. The situation exploded into a scandal—ownership of certain stag films, which were in the possession of the senator, was attributed to John. This resulted in accusations being exchanged between both parties, ultimately resulting in John being charged with several felony counts. John Gacy was sentenced to the maximum sentence of ten years in prison. A presentence report classified him as an "antisocial personality," but he was still recommended for probation.

Gacy lost his wife, his children, his good standing in the community—he lost everything. Most importantly, while he languished in jail, he lost the man he could never please. His father died on Christmas Day 1969, and in keeping with his prediction, he would always remember his son as a dumb and stupid faggot and a failure.

We then discussed Gacy's plan to turn his life around after he was paroled. He had started a new business, which was quite successful, and he had reentered society. Once again he was becoming a respected civic and community leader, a precinct captain, the leader of the Polish Constitution Day Parade in Chicago. Hell, he had just recently been rubbing elbows with the president's wife, Rosalynn Carter, for chrissakes. She was the guest of the city for the parade. They had been pictured together.

John presented himself as a guy with a past who was just trying to put it all behind him and make a new life . . . and now this. Based on what I knew at that time, I had to believe him. What a sincere face he put on. Poor John.

Before he left my office nearly six hours after he had arrived, John Wayne Gacy wrote me a check in the amount of $3,000. I had been officially retained.

6
___

A S TEDIOUS AS it is to investigate and then draft the documents necessary for a warrant, that is also how much fun it can be to finally
execute one, at least sometimes. Come on, imagine being able to
invade someone's home, break the doors down if you have to, and
snoop to your heart's content. For some . . . that's heaven.

After having the warrant signed by Judge Marvin Peters at 3:10
p.m., December 13, 1978, a team was dispatched to the Gacy residence armed, with keys to the doors and imbued with a sense of
purpose. They were like a pack of dogs on the hunt, sniffing here,
poking there, in drawers and under cabinets, searching for something that would tie this creep to their missing boy. Some of the
younger guys actually hoped to find Rob Piest tied up and hungry,
hoping against hope that he would be found. The more seasoned
among them knew better. There was seldom any good news that
resulted from situations such as this. They were usually just fact-
finding, evidence-gathering missions.

David Cram was at the Gacy house, quite coincidentally, when
the search team arrived. He was there in a work capacity, to pick
up items that he needed for the job that he was on that day. He
was shown a warrant and a badge by one of the officers, and he

explained his presence there. He then beat feet as fast as he could, glad that the officers did not detain him for any reason.

They all knew that the owner of the house would not bother them. Gacy was being allowed to spin his endless stories, tell his tallest tales, and in general go on and on about just how important of a guy he actually was. Eventually, even Gacy got sick of this routine, although he did so long after the poor officers had tired of his spiel.

Finally, Gacy started barking about going to appointments that he had. He had to meet with a funeral director. He had business to attend to. At that point, the officers at the station simply put him in a room, gave him a can of pop, and locked the door. He wasn't under arrest. He wasn't in a cell. He was in limbo—a kind of land that time forgot while the team did their job at his house.

Most of the officers who took part in the search of the house noticed a slight odor that was unidentifiable. It was faint, but it was there. It became somewhat stronger when the thermostat turned on the fan for the heating system. Gacy also had a little dog that yapped incessantly during the search, but such were the trials of the job. At least it wasn't a big one. That could have caused a problem.

When the search was over, the following report was filed, and the items recovered were categorized and logged into evidence:

JOHN WAYNE GACY

	TE/TIME THIS REPORT
	15 Dec 78 1245 Hours

ORIGINAL OFFENSE	3 OFFENSE CHANGED TO
Missing Person	

	5 ADDRESS
Pest, Robert J.	2722 Craig Drive, Des Plaines

NARRATIVE:

1st Search. Items recovered.

The following is a list of items recovered by Reporting Officer on a search warrant served on the 13th of December 78 at 8213 West Summerdale in Norwood Park Township, the residence of John W. Gacy, tx 457-1614.

Located in the bedroom on the northwest side of the residence on top of a dresser which was against the south wall next to the closet were 2 adult paperback books. Taken from the first drawer in that dresser from a plastic bag was 1 switchblade knife. Also taken from a cigar box, which had the name Swisher Naturals, a name of cigar, located in the second drawer of that dresser was a clear plastic bag containing a crushed green plant like material. Also cigarette papers were taken. Taken from the second drawer was also 2 paperback books about "gay people." Found in the middle of the top of three cabinets in this dresser was a temporary Illinois driver's license to a Michael B. Baker. It had a D.L. Number of B260-5425-8212 and the number on the license was 0784008. This was located in a Folgers Coffee Can. Taken from the top shelf of the closet in the northwest bedroom located on the left side of the top of the closet were 8 brown envelopes containing adult books. Taken from the second drawer of that same dresser on the south side of the northwest bedroom from a shoe box were 2 pictures that appeared to be of the same male subject. Taken from a dresser located along the east wall of the bedroom on the northwest of the residence, second drawer, were 7 colored adult films. This was on the left hand side of the dresser. Taken from the right hand side of this dresser in the first drawer was 1 Marlboro cigarette box containing crushed green plant like material. Taken from a jewelry box located on top of this dresser underneath a tv was a Maine West High School ring for the year 1975 with the initials J.A.S. inscribed. Taken from the bottom of this jewelry box was an Illinois Driver's License to a James G. O'Toole, D.L. Number of 0340-4475-4295. Taken from the middle compartment of the three compartments of the dresser in the northwest bedroom along the south wall located in a box was 1 brown plastic bottle containing 7 unidentified pills, blue in color, 1 red and blue capsule, suspected Tuinal, 10 yellow pills, suspected Valium, and 3 blue pills, suspected Valium. Located in the second drawer of this same dresser was 1 clear plastic bottle containing 3 blue pills of suspected Valium and 4 capsules of Amyl Nitrate. Also from the second drawer was obtained 1 glass clear cigar tube with 4 green pills, suspected Tapase. Also taken from the same dresser, top drawer left side, was 1 dark brown bottle of suspected Atropine Sulfate, Prescription #8080-453477, made by Lilly, and had Number 15 on it. Also taken from the second drawer in this dresser was a clear plastic baggie containing possible starter pistol blanks. Located in the bedroom of the southwest corner of the residence in a dresser on the north side of the room, situated between the closet and the doorway, was 1 pair of handcuffs and keys located in the top drawer left side. In the same drawer on the right side was 1 box for an Edge Mark Pistols, Mod. 1969, Cal. MM6, made in Italy. On the very top of the dresser is another small compartment located when this drawer was taken out in the left hand corner in the rear was a white plastic bottle containing 21 pink pills of suspected Preludin. Located in this bedroom behind the bedroom door was a two by four, approximately 30 inches in length with two holes drilled in each end. Taken from the bathroom in a top drawer located to the left of the sink and along the wall was a 1 cc hypodermic syringe. Also in this drawer was a Swedish Erotica Film Book with adult pictures. Also located was 1 red address book. In a cabinet above the toilet was 2 adult books, paperback. Located in the office

6 CASE STATUS	☐ CLEARED/ARREST ☐ CLEARED EXCEPTIONAL	☐ UNFOUNDED ☐ INACTIVE FILE	X ☒ FURTHER ACTION REQUIRED	7 DATE/TIME REPORT COMPLETED 15 Dec 78 1320 Hours
8 PROPERTY EVIDENCE RECOVERED YES ☐ NO ☐		9 LEADS MSG REQUESTED YES ☐ NO ☒		☐ CONTINUED ON C.I.D. CONTINUATION REPORT ☒X
11 REPORTING OFFICER-PRINT Det. J. Kautz	STAR 217	12 REPORTING OFFICER SIGNATURE		

R.D. # 78-35203

C.I.D. CONTINUATION REPORT / DES PLAINES POLICE   PAGE ___2___

area of the residence in a desk which is just to the south of the front window in the top right side drawer was 1 Brevettata 1949 Caliber 6mm starter pistol. Located in the garbage in the kitchen were 7 Polaroid colored pictures of what appears to be drug stores. Also was located 1 plastic tag with the name Charo Raphael, Pres., Raphco Incorporated, 831 East Lake Avenue in Glenview, Illinois 60025. Located in an utility room in the garbage was an adult paperback book. This is the end of the items which were recovered and inventoried in the search of the residence.

R.D. # 78-35203

C.I.D. CONTINUATION REPORT ☐

REPORTING OFFICER SIGNATURE

Also found but not listed on the original report was a receipt for photographs, which had been dropped off for development at Nisson Pharmacy. This item was recovered from the garbage bag in the kitchen of the Gacy home. A supplemental report was filed regarding that item.

The implications attendant to the items found in Gacy's house during the search go without saying. The suspect was either gay or bisexual, had drugs, drug paraphernalia, and what were potentially items of torture, weapons, and potential weapons; the consensus was quite simple to reach. What more proof did a good cop need? This guy was going down. Everyone agreed.

As for Mr. Gacy, he had been released without being charged from the Des Plaines police station. Upon his arrival home, he was greeted by the aftermath of the search of his residence. He was shaken by the experience. His normally tidy home was in complete disarray. Before he had a chance to assess the mess, or even really check it out to see what the police had taken from the home, he received a welcome call from his trusted employee and friend David Cram. Gacy was particularly happy to hear from David because he had no desire to stay in the house. He was worried that he was being watched, and he was uncomfortable with the mess. He also wanted help with the cleanup. Although his car and his snowplow truck had been confiscated, one of the PDM vans was available, and he used that to go pick up David Cram that night. Cram was still shaking in his boots from his chance meeting with the Des Plaines police earlier that day when they came to Mr. Gacy's home to execute the search warrant. Gacy grilled him about that.

Mr. Cram later gave a statement to Officers James Pickell and Ronald Adams regarding the activities of the evening following the search of Gacy's home and other matters.

After spending some time at the Golden Bear Restaurant on Forest Preserve Drive near Harlem Avenue where he and Gacy feasted on cheeseburgers and coffee, and David listened to Gacy grouse on about the fucking cops, they returned to Gacy's house. Cram tells the police officers what happened next and about a variety of other things:

Officer: "Did he walk through the house?"
Cram: "Yes he did."
Officer: "Where did he go?"
Cram: "Crawl space."
Officer: "Down under the house?"
Cram: "Yes."
Officer: "Did you see him go down there?"
Cram: "Yes I did."
Officer: "When he went down there, what did he do while he was down there?"
Cram: "Okay, he seen the mud on the floor. Complained about that. Went into the crawl space with a flashlight and the lights were on also. Went down in there, walked about, didn't even take a full step. He just went around in a complete circle and came back out."
Officer: "Did he walk around at all down there?"
Cram: "No, he went down into the crawl space, crouched down, 'cause there's not much clearance to stand up under there. He went around in a complete circle. All he did was check it out and then came back up into the house."
Officer: "Did he go anywhere else in the house?"
Cram: "Attic, bedrooms, bathroom, laundry room, kitchen, back room, every space in the house."
Officer: "And did he indicate that he found anything else to be missing?"

Cram: "Just what I said, and he'd have to stumble over it. You know, if there's anything else."

Officer: "Okay, what time did you leave John's house?"

Cram: "Oh, about I'd say 1:30, quarter to two. 1:30 quarter to two somewhere in there."

Officer: "Would that be in the morning, or . . ."

Cram: "Ah, yeah that would be morning, early."

Officer: "On which date?"

Cram: "Ah, Wednesday."

Officer: "So, are we talking about the early morning hours? Would that be Wednesday or Thursday?"

Cram: "The early morning would be on Thursday. Thursday morning."

Officer: "Did he ask you anything about while you were in his house and the police officers were there?"

Cram: "Yes he did. He said what were they looking for. What did they take? And also they had a few bags. There were probably other bags, because they were like mailing envelopes of some sort, brown, and he said those were the books. He said were there about five of them and I said; 'yeah,' and he goes what have they done with the books and I said they might have taken them with."

Officer: "Did he say what kind of books they were?"

Cram: "He said dirty books."

Officer: "Dirty books?"

Cram: "Like that would be Playboy, all the way down the line, who knows?"

Officer: "Okay, do you recall what time you left John's house?"

Cram: "Approximately quarter to two."

Officer: "Okay, where did you go?"

Cram: "We took a ride past the police station to see if his truck was, his car was left in the lot."

Officer: "Did he tell you what his intention was?"

Cram: "Yeah, if they were there, that he wanted to pick them up, the truck up, because he needed transportation on the jobs. If the car was there, he was going to take that, so that either a truck or a van would be supplied for the men to haul materials, and so on and so forth."

Officer: "Do you recall what time you got to Des Plaines?"

Cram: "I wasn't paying attention to the watch, but I arrived home at around 2:30. Give or take a few, 10–15 minutes anyway, and it had to be between the time I left John's house and the time I arrived home; and I live in Chicago and it's approximately a 20 minute drive."

Officer: "And you said you left John's house at what time?"

Cram: It was approximately a quarter to two."

Officer: "Okay, you said earlier, I believe, that you left about 2:30, or am I mistaken?"

Cram: "No, I arrived home at two thirty or so."

Officer: "Did you have any more conversation with John after you got home?

Cram: "After he dropped me off, the next time I talked to him was on the phone the next morning."

Officer: "That would have been Thursday morning?"

Cram: "Yes, Thursday morning."

Officer: "What time did you have a conversation with him?"

Cram: "Must have been around 10 o'clock, 9 o'clock, somewhere in there. I talked to him on a job site. He was at a job site. He carried a radio beeper with him and I had him return the call, requesting another job."

Officer: "Okay, where were you working on Thursday morning?"

Cram: "Democratic Precinct Headquarters, which is on Montrose."

Officer: "Do you recall what time you finished working at the Democratic Police Headquarters? Or, the Democratic Precinct Headquarters?

Cram: "Yeah, about 5:25. I called in on his radio, or his telephone answering service. Left a message. Time out 4:35 and went back in the office. Knocked over paint. Had to clean that up, so it was about 5:25 when I left, so I called a cab from there. I arrived at his house at 6 o'clock, 'cause I stopped off at the Hunger Dog on Cumberland for a hot dog or Italian Beef and I arrived at the house at approximately 6 o'clock. From there I met with the Lieutenant and other police officers."

Officer: "And what date was that?"

Cram: That was on Thursday."

Officer: "Did you work for John on Thursday?"

Cram: "Yes I did. Wednesday is when the investigation was right?"

Officer: "Wednesday is when the police officers were at his house."

Cram: "That's when it was, Wednesday, not Thursday, it was Wednesday when I worked for him. Thursday I worked for the Fox Valley Shopping Center with Rich and Raphael."

Officer: Did you have any conversation with Mr. Gacy at that time?"

Cram: "Once in the morning when he picked me up so I could drop him off at his house. He originally wanted to get a rent car with him and go pick up his vehicles at the police station, and he said he couldn't get his vehicles back, so he'd have to do it himself. That Richard would meet me out at Fox Valley Shopping Center."

Officer: "And what happened, how did you get out there?"

Cram: "I took the van."

Officer: "And how did you get the van?"

Cram: "From John Gacy."

Officer: "And how did you get to his house?"

Cram: "John Gacy picked me up at my house."

Officer: "Do you recall what time you finished working at Fox Valley?"

Cram: "Yeah, 11 o'clock at night."

Office: "And what night was that?"

Cram: "Thursday."

Officer: "Did you have any conversation with Mr. Gacy after that?"

Cram: "No I didn't."

Officer: "Did you take the truck home?"

Cram: "Yeah, from Fox Valley Shopping Center at 11 o'clock I rolled into his house to pick up a wheelbarrow and unload headboards. I picked up the wheelbarrow and proceeded home."

Officer: "Did you work Friday morning?"

Cram: "Yes I did. 7:30 in the morning I picked up Michael Rossi at his house. Following him. Met Michael Rossi at his house, followed him, he drove his own vehicle. Followed him to North Avenue job. He parked his car at the North Avenue job, which is at North Avenue and Pulaski. Both of us drove over to a lumberyard, Southernland Lumber, which is about 4 or 5 blocks from the North Avenue job. Picked up materials on the job, went back to the job with those materials. I picked up extra material that was on the job site. That I dropped off at John's garage for storage. Stopped off before going back before going back to the North Avenue job for the second load. Stopped off and got gasoline, delivered the material from Century Tile and what material was in his garage I delivered that also. Brought it back to the North Avenue job. Made one more stop at

Southernland Lumber to pick up something. From there I left the city to go to Fox Valley Shopping Center."

Officer: "Did you have any conversation with Mr. Gacy when you met with him?"

Cram: "I ran into him. He pulled up in the driveway on the first trip out to his house before I stopped and got gas and I was loading up materials from his house."

Officer: "And did he say anything?"

Cram: "Well, he just asked me you know, has the police got in contact with you and stuff like that."

Officer: "Did he discuss anything at all about the police being at his home or related to his activities?"

Cram: "No, he said that he spent the night at his sister's house."

Officer: "Where is that?"

Cram: "Approximately in Carpentersville. Somewhere around Carpentersville."

Officer: "Can I ask you about your personal feelings about Mr. Gacy?"

Cram: "Well, it's hard to explain him. Sometimes he's the nicest guy in the world and sometimes he's evasive."

Officer: "Has he ever indicated to you that he was arrested?"

Cram: "Yeah, he said he was arrested a sodomy. I believe the word is. It's something to do with dirty films and stuff like that. Yeah, dirty films I believe it was. And prostitution. I think it was prostitution."

Officer: "Did he say where the arrest took place?"

Cram: "I believe it was Ohio or Oregon. Or one of the southern states down south."

Officer: "Have you ever known Mr. Gacy to have an argument with anybody?"

Cram: "Oh, I argue with him all the time."

Officer: "I'm talking about physically. Did he ever fight with a person?"

Cram: "Oh, yeah, he and Michael Rossi were at Ma's Bar in Cicero, Little Joe, and they were out bar hopping. Michael, his friend and John. John was driving his own vehicle. Now, this is just the story between the two of them, okay? Now one has one story and one has another. They both coincide pretty well, but I wasn't there so I can't say. But, the story that I got was from Michael. John wanted to shoot pool and he felt like he was being teamed up on. They were exchanging words, goofing around like guys do and John took it personal and said "Hell with ya," and walked out of the bar. He walked out into the street. John's version, he walked out into the street, drove around the block once, came back in. He double parked out in front of the bar, which was across the street from Ma's bar, was going to walk back in supposedly to give Mike a ride back to his car, 'cause his car was parked on the north side. Michael was mad because he's stranded in Cicero, Illinois, and they also previously exchanged words earlier that day, had an argument. John pushed Michael earlier that day at a restaurant and they went outside and had a discussion and came back in, you know, buddy, buddy. Well anyway, Michael had a few drinks and walked across the street. Met John halfway in the middle of the street. Knocked away two guys; one knocked his mother and went at John, where he proceeded to fight with John. John didn't strike no blows. He tried to hold Michael back. Michael swung at him and John said the other guy, Michael's friend, hit him three times. And with that John went to the hospital for a couple of days."

Officer: "Do you know the name of Michael's friends?"

Cram: "No I don't."

Officer: "Do you know what hospital John went to?"

Cram: "That I don't know neither, but it should be on the police report."

Officer: "Well, what police department was called?"

Cram: "Cicero Police. And the court was being held at First Avenue and Highway 65, right there at that court building. And they gave Michael a year's probation."

Officer: "Mr. Gacy signed a complaint against Michael?"

Cram: "Signed a complaint against Michael, and was going to have Ma charged with Dram Shop Act for serving, you know, for having that on and so forth, but after Michael . . . This went on for about two months, I guess, Michael didn't work for him. Just before his court date, John called Michael up asked him if he would like his job back. John's reason for this is no matter whether there is personal conflict or not. There should be no reason why I should penalize myself because of the job, because of my job, 'cause Mike knows the system; Mike knows the carpentry. So, Michael accepted a position with John at $10 an hour. His salary and so on and so forth would be recorded at his job."

Officer: "Do you know anything about the investigation that we are working on? Do you know what it's about?"

Cram: "Ah, yeah, I from what I think it's about some guy from Les-on Drugs or something like that, isn't it?"

Officer: "Okay, now, is there any reason for you to think that perhaps Mr. Gacy could be involved in this?"

Cram: "Well, like I say, John is a funny person, you know, I mean in my past history from associating with people that don't put nothing past nobody."

Officer: "Is there in your knowledge anything about Mr. Gacy that would cause you to believe that something similar to this might have happened before?"

Cram: "Well he is a bit of a bragger, so on and so forth and he lives in a fantasy world, I believe. Now how much is fact and how much is fiction that's left up to the individual to decide. But, he claims that he does work for syndicate and so on and so forth, you know. But, that's neither here nor there. I don't have actual proof of the individuals, you know, actual proof that I could come right out and stake my life on it."

Officer: "Has he ever told you that he has been involved in something like this before?"

Cram: "Ah, yeah, he said he was, you know."

Officer: "What does he say?"

Cram: "Well, he said he, well let's see if I can get this right. He said he set people up before and he's just a few things, just basically like that."

Officer: "Did John have any statement to make to you about whether or not he was involved in this?"

Cram: "Ah, yeah, he said I did not have nothing to do, I swear to you that I had nothing to do with this one, with this guy."

Officer: "Did he lead you to believe that perhaps he was involved with somebody else?"

Cram: "Ah, yeah, you could come to that assumption."

Officer: "Can you talk about that a little more?"

Cram: "Well, just by the way, I don't know. I imagine an innocent man would conduct, I mean he would get a little pissed off at the whole matter, rather than be shaken by it. Okay, I realize that it is a serious charge and everything, but why would he be upset as far as nervous and drawn out and, you know, go spend the night at his sister's house and be afraid of his own shadow more or less. Like I said, it's personal opinion."

Officer: "Have you ever found anything suspicious around his home or property?"

Cram: "Well, okay, he's had a couple of wallets in the garage, you know, with identification in it. The identification was a driver's license, library card, military I.D. from maybe the Army Reserve or something like that. That was a little while back, school I.D., college I.D. I believe it was from DeVry Tech, DeVry Tech, DeVry Tech. I believe that's where it was from, DeVry Tech School I.D."

Officer: "Do you recall any names on this identification?"

Cram: "I can't think of the names, no."

Officer: "Now, how many wallets did you find?"

Cram: "About three."

Officer: "Where were they?"

Cram: "They were in the cabinet, garage and the storage. Where he keeps his, ah, nails and keeps his office supplies and just little junk, more or less."

Officer: "How long ago did you see these wallets?"

Cram: "About six months after I was working with him."

Officer: "Did you mention finding these wallets to Mr. Gacy?"

Cram: "Yeah, I asked him if I could use the I.D. He said I was underage, so on and so forth, and, ah, to go out with my older partners to do drinking. He said, no, you don't want those."

Officer: "Did he say why?"

Cram: "He said 'cause they were some people that were deceased."

Officer: "Would you repeat that?"

Cram: "Deceased. No longer living."

OK, David Cram . . . not a brain surgeon, and so on and so forth, ya know. But, David provides significant insight into the personality of John Gacy. Who was this guy? What was he like? What did his friends say about him? If it were not for Mr. Cram, a sizable piece of that puzzle would be missing.

7

WHEN THE DELTA Unit first began their twenty-four-hour surveillance of Mr. Gacy, he would lose them pretty much at will. The team was trying to remain inconspicuous. This didn't work well at all. They would be parked in some inconspicuous place, hidden down the street from his house, and Gacy would hurry out of the front door; jump into his car and tear off, fishtailing on the wet ice as he went; and disappear into traffic on Cumberland Avenue, before the guys could get their car out of park.

The members of the team decided that they couldn't care less if Gacy spotted them or if he knew that he was being followed. Their job was to keep Gacy in sight, not to play private detective. This not only solved the problem, it gave rise to one of the most unusual surveillance scenarios in the history of modern police work. Before long, Gacy was having drinks with the members of his surveillance team . . . while they were surveilling him.

Friday, December 15, was one of the days that Gacy had completely eluded the surveillance team. Gacy could have been on the moon for all they knew. They had actually alerted the authorities at O'Hare Field in an effort to thwart any attempt by Gacy to leave the country. The team was determined to make this time the last time that they allowed this to happen. They had been embarrassed once too often. They each took an unmarked squad car and set out to find Mr. Gacy. At about one o'clock that afternoon, Wally Lang recognized Gacy's rental car parked outside of my office while my client was inside speaking with me during those six long hours and he, Lang, immediately alerted the others. They all converged on 222 S. Prospect.

The city of Park Ridge is approximately five miles due north of Gacy's neighborhood in unincorporated Cook County. At 5:30 p.m., when John left my office, the guys from Delta Unit were out in full force. Three cars were waiting for him to leave—one with Wally Lang inside, one with Bob Schultz, and one driven by Ron Robinson. Gacy and I agreed that I would follow him to, or, in the event that we got separated, meet him at Uncle Gordon's, the home of Gordon Nebel, one of Gacy's closest friends and business associates.

We were about to get separated.

Mr. Nebel lived on Lawrence Avenue in the suburb of Norridge, very close to Gacy's house and not far from where I lived with my wife and kids. Therefore, it would stand to reason that Mr. Gacy would travel south on Cumberland Avenue to get to Uncle Gordon's. It was the easiest and most direct route.

I was about to discover that my new client was sometimes a bit unpredictable and that he had absolutely no aversion to "fucking with the cops." When Gacy saw that three unmarked squads were glued to his rear bumper, he slammed on his brakes in the middle of Friday-evening rush-hour traffic and, with tires screeching, pulled a U-turn and tore off northbound, bouncing over a curb in the process and waving the middle-finger salute at his tails as he roared by them in the other direction.

Not to be outdone, Ron Robinson immediately cranked his steering wheel hard to the left, thereby blocking the considerable amount of traffic approaching in the northbound lanes of Cumberland Avenue and pissing off a slew of unsuspecting homebound commuters. Tires screeched, horns blared, tempers flared. No more Mr. Nice Guy on the part of Robinson or the other Deltas. This maneuver allowed Lang and Schultz to clumsily turn around and tear off northbound in pursuit of Gacy. Robinson quickly followed and now the whole caravan was northbound, speeding crazily in the wrong direction.

Welcome to the private practice of criminal law, Sam.

GACY DRAGGED HIS ragtag tail around the northwest suburbs of Chicago for a while, driving as though he was begging to get pulled over. The Deltas simply hugged his rear, clearly making the statement that Gacy was under surveillance and that, if there was any doubt left, it was in no way any kind of a secret anymore. There had previously been such standoffs between Gacy and his tails, but this was a line in the sand being drawn by the Delta Unit. No longer would Gacy be able to shoot off on errant frolics of his own. Wherever he went, they would also be. It actually became a game that both sides played with relish.

I took my sweet time. I wasn't going to be lulled into some kind of road race with this crew. When I arrived at the home of Gordon Nebel, I saw at least two unmarked squads, and I was pretty sure that a woman who was hanging around was also watching Gacy. (I was wrong about that one.) Gacy was inside Nebel's apartment. I walked up to Shultz, who was sitting in his car smoking a cigarette.

"Hi," I said. "I'm Sam, Sam Amirante."

"I know who you are, Sam. You left the PD's office, eh?"

"Yeah, and I am going to be representing Mr. Gacy. He knows that he is being followed."

This elicited a long chuckle from Schultz. "Yeah, I would say that he does," he said through intermittent laughter.

I had to chuckle too.

I handed him one of my freshly printed business cards and asked that I be called if any kind of an arrest was made. He said he would see to it.

JOHN WAYNE GACY

WHEN I ARRIVED home that night, I took stock. I had my first client, and he seemed to be a doozy. He certainly had his problems, but, as it turned out, I had problems of my own. My oldest son, Sammy, was sick, not just a-case-of-the-sniffles sick—he was go-to-the-hospital sick. He had a high fever, and he was lethargic; and as new parents, my wife and I were beside ourselves with worry. I thought that the PD's office was a pressure cooker. I was learning that private practice had its very own brand of stress. You cannot call in sick when you alone are the entire staff.

My wife, Mary, and I took our Sammy to the nearby Resurrection Hospital and we took our newborn, Jimmy, to my mother's. Thank God for her. Thus began a parent's worst nightmare—the waiting. We set up a schedule whereby my wife would spend each day sitting with our son and I would spend the nights. I would catch a nap in a chair next to my son when I could.

As I sat in an uncomfortable hospital chair during the wee hours of the morning on that first night of what would prove to be many long nights to come next to my infant son, I thought about the craziness of the day. I had nagging questions: How could my client be guilty of this? He was a well-liked, gregarious ham of a guy who certainly didn't hide in the shadows. He was a successful businessman. He had won awards and accolades from his peers everywhere he lived, everywhere he went.

He was no angel, that was true. He sure as hell couldn't drive worth a shit. He was a menace behind the wheel. Plus, he did have a past. Sodomy, for chrissakes. That nagged at me. However, Gacy's past could just as easily be the explanation for why the police and the prosecutors had made this honest mistake.

If I were investigating this case, I would be drawn in the direction of this suspect, no question. He was there at the drugstore, and he had done time for this creepy fucking crime—I would be all over him. But when would he have had time to be involved in some kind of elaborate abduction of this teenager? He was at Northwest

Hospital with his relatives. If John was involved, where was this kid? The cops had been over his entire house with a fine-tooth comb, hadn't they? They followed him wherever he went. They knew his every move.

When all was said and done, it didn't matter, really. A defense attorney doesn't have that luxury. If we waited for that client that was pure as the driven snow, we would be very lonely people. Police officers do make mistakes, but they don't make that many mistakes. Ninety-five percent of the people that walk into a lawyer's office did exactly that with which they are charged. That's no secret. There are no Perry Masons; lawyers sometimes represent guilty people. When your uncle Charlie got that DUI last year, he was actually drunk as a skunk when he got it. When your sweet angel, Suzie—the apple of your eye, your one and only daughter, the one that looks just like your dear departed mother—was charged with possession of marijuana the other day, she was high as a fucking kite when it happened. Sorry. People make mistakes.

People can do terrible things without being terrible people.

My job is not to judge. My job is to make the State prove their case beyond a reasonable doubt. That is our system, the absolute greatest system on earth, a system that is the envy of the civilized world. Let other countries lop off the fingers of suspected thieves without a fair trial. Let other countries stone alleged adulteresses to death in the street. Let other countries make their defendants prove their own innocence against the overwhelming power and presence of the State. I'll stick with this country. And I would gladly die in defense of that system of justice. Hundreds of thousands of good men have. I was a marine, and once a marine, always a marine. I had taken that oath. We, as a nation, don't do everything right. Our history is fraught with blunders. But we got that part right, the part about innocent until proven guilty—on that we were right as rain, right as right can be. Sometimes people don't fully understand that. That's OK. I understand it, and that was all that mattered then.

I loved my father. He was my hero, simple as that. He didn't have an Ivy League education or a big fancy job in one of the towers of industry. He just worked hard every day, loved his wife, took care of his kid, put one foot in front of the other day after day. But maybe my old man did make one tiny mistake. He didn't make many, but maybe he did make just this one. He wanted me to be a doctor because he didn't like lawyers, but maybe it wasn't so bad to be a lawyer. I didn't think so anyway. I was proud. I was an intricate cog in that very system that I would defend with my life. And . . . I had my very first client.

I looked at my own son and thought of the Piest family. What were those poor parents going through right now? My son was ill, but he was right there beside me, and he was receiving the constant care that he needed. What would it be like to not know where he was, not know whether he was alive or dead? I couldn't fathom it. The thought of it made me shudder.

I had almost dozed off when Mary walked in with a nurse.

"How's he doing?" she whispered.

"At least he is sleeping," I said. I smiled at the nurse.

"Did you get any sleep?" My wife was concerned. She was looking in my eyes. I could see it.

"Some," I lied.

"Well, you can go. Try to lay down before you go to the office."

"I will," I lied again.

I kissed my son. I kissed my wife, and I left the hospital, ready to do battle. The sun was just peaking over the blue water of Lake Michigan nine miles to the east. It was dawn on the first full day of my representation of Mr. John Wayne Gacy. I was walking alone through the parking lot to my car, and I realized just how alone in the world I really was. If it was true that Gacy had done what they thought he did, then he was not going to have anyone on his side. I would be criticized for defending him. But I would be his one and only voice. I was just one guy. I felt the endless sprawl of the great city of Chicago all around me. I was a dot. I felt the miles of corn and the quaint little towns out there in the vast state of Illinois. I was a speck. I knew that the world would find it hard to appreciate my position. Perhaps many would not understand. That was OK with me, though. I knew my job. I had a job to do, and I knew what it was.

If the People of the State of Illinois thought that my client was guilty of these horrible charges, these accusations, then they were just going to have to damned well prove it.

8

I REMEMBER SAYING IT when we were walking out of my office. I did say it. I had no way of knowing, however, that he was going to take me quite so literally. I said it, though, so I'm to blame. I said, "John, call me anytime."

From that day forward, I talked to John Gacy more than I talked to my wife.

I needed to find out everything that I could about the investigation of my client. I talked to John about Leroy Stevens. Stevens had represented Mr. Gacy's corporation, PDM Contractors. He had also worked with John on some relatively minor scrapes that John had gotten himself into.

I determined that Mr. Stevens was on a weekend hunting trip, and I would have to wait until Monday to speak to him.

I talked to everyone I could think of that might have information about the case. One thing that became clear as a result of this preliminary investigation: Elements of the press were becoming interested in the story. One of the suburban papers, the *Daily Herald*, was running stories about Rob Piest as a missing person. They had also gotten wind of the Gacy angle. Although the *Herald* was a strong publication, it had regional editions that were specific to certain segments of Chicagoland, referring to the greater Chicago metropolitan area. Many of the stories were quite local in nature. Not every story that was reported in the south suburbs was reported in the north suburbs. Therefore, the story had not yet spread to all of their editions.

However, I also determined that a reporter from Chicago's ABC affiliate, Channel 7 News, Sylvia Cesneros, had been speaking with Terry Sullivan about the case. Chicago is the third largest television market in the United States. If the press grabs hold of a story and slants it a certain way, the public believes it. If Channel 7 reported the story and named John Wayne Gacy as the primary suspect in a case concerning a missing teenager in the Chicago suburbs, it could then be reported nationally. If that happened, my client's thriving construction business would be history, and it would not matter one whit if he did it or not. Perception has a funny way of becoming fact in our society.

I began to research the law regarding temporary restraining orders and police harassment. If a story concerning the harassment of a citizen by the police was reported instead of one about a missing teen, that could save my client's business.

The Des Plaines police, however, together with the entire prosecutorial arm of the State of Illinois, had other ideas.

The items found as a result of the execution of the first search warrant of Mr. Gacy's home were bearing fruit, as were other items of information that the investigation had unearthed. The investigation of one Robert Jerome Piest, a missing teen from Des Plaines, Illinois, was about to take on a life of its own; and the participants in that investigation would never be the same again.

A young man named Jeffrey D. Rignall had reported an incident that allegedly occurred on Chicago's Near North Side. Mr. Rignall was a resident of the state of Florida, but he claimed that he was visiting a friend here in Chicago. He said that he was walking alone at approximately 1:30 a.m. on March 22, 1978, when he was picked up by a man in a black Oldsmobile with spotlights on it. He and the driver drove around the side streets in the Lincoln Park neighborhood and shared a joint.

According to Mr. Rignall, when the marijuana was gone, the driver suddenly covered Rignall's mouth and nose with a rag that was soaked with a substance that caused him to pass out. When he awoke at 4:30 a.m., he was lying behind a statue in Lincoln Park with burns and bruises to his face and pain and bleeding from his rectum. He felt that he had been raped, although he had no recollection of the experience.

Rignall actually went so far as to take matters into his own hands. He rented a car and cruised the area where the incident took place. He finally saw the car that he was sure he had gotten into that night. It was a black 1979 Oldsmobile with spotlights on its doors, bearing the license plate number PDM 42.

John Wayne Gacy was arrested for battery four months later on July 15, 1978. The case was still pending in court.

During the first search of the Gacy house, the team recovered a Main West Highschool class ring with the initials JAS engraved on it. By coincidence, Main West Highschool was where Rob Piest was a student, and that intrigued the hell out of the boys in Des Plaines. Was there a connection between the Piest boy and the owner of that ring? John Wayne Gacy had no children living with him in the house, nor had he ever had a child or relative that attended Main West Highschool. Where the hell did the ring come from?

Through diligent detective work (actually, it was a process of elimination—which students had the initials JAS and where were they) it was discovered that the ring belonged to a student named John Szyc.

A quick investigation into the whereabouts of Mr. Szyc determined that John Szyc was last seen on January 20, 1977; he was another missing person.

Now there were two missing young men connected to Gacy and one that claimed that Mr. Gacy had raped him. What had started out as a simple missing person case was expanding into something much more sinister.

Then Michael Rossi called the Des Plaines Police Department. He had been interviewed as part of the investigation, and it seems that he decided to cooperate more fully. Maybe he talked to a lawyer, or maybe he talked to his wife—who knows? However, he had information that made your skin crawl.

Gregory Godzik, seventeen years old when he disappeared, was last seen December 12, 1976. Young Mr. Godzik once worked for John Gacy.

Finally, and perhaps the most frightening of all, James Mazzara who once worked for Mr. Gacy, was found floating facedown in the Des Plaines River approximately seventy miles southwest of the city of Chicago.

When the investigators talked to Mr. Gacy's former wife, Carol, she told them that a person that previously worked for John, a person whom she always liked, might be someone with information for them. The young man's name was John Butkovitch. Only problem—nobody had seen him in quite some time. When asked, Gacy had said that Butkovitch had left town.

The eerie, frightening, nagging, undeniable truth was this: If you were a young man and you had a connection to John Wayne Gacy, chances were that you might turn up missing in short order. The investigation had turned from a search for an individual, a single missing person, to a full-on murder investigation centered on several cold-case files from all over Cook County. However, the team remained tight-lipped about what they knew because they did not want to tip off Gacy before they had the necessary evidence to arrest him. They also did not want me to go running into court and get a restraining order that could cripple the investigation. They did not want this story to explode in the press or in some other way get back to Gacy, because they didn't want him to flee the jurisdiction. But the names Piest, Rignall, Szyc, Godzik, Butkovitch, and especially Mazzara began to haunt the dreams of each and every member of the investigation team.

9

WHEN THE POLICE investigate a crime or pick over a crime scene, they never know which tiny piece of evidence will be the piece that finally tips the scales, that cinches it once and for all for the prosecution and convicts the defendant. So they bag everything. They try to leave no stone unturned, no speck or hair or fiber uncollected. Such was the case with the execution of the search warrant on Gacy's home.

The circumstantial evidence against John Wayne Gacy was mounting. Gacy had a past that involved untoward advances on a young boy. Missing employees and others with complaints connected to Mr. Gacy were turning up like bad pennies. Claims that Mr. Gacy had committed violence against others, sometimes with a sexual intent, had come to light. This information was quite sufficient for the team investigating him. They knew that they had the right guy. Unfortunately, no item of evidence that had been discovered so far that tied Mr. Gacy to Rob Piest. And after all, at present, this was a missing person investigation. The team was supposed to be finding out what happened to Rob.

During the search of Gacy's home, Lieutenant Kozenczak noticed a small piece of paper sticking out of the kitchen garbage bag. It was orange in color and had a serrated or perforated edge where it had been torn from the other side of a form. It was a receipt for photo development. When you drop off film to have it developed, you get a receipt. It was that kind of receipt, and it had a number on it, 36119, along with the name and address of Nisson Pharmacy stamped on it. Naturally, this begged the question: Did Gacy have his pictures developed at Nisson Pharmacy, a store that was nearly ten miles from his house?

That was an interesting question, because it seemed unlikely that anyone would travel that far just to have pictures developed. There were places to have pictures developed on nearly every corner, weren't there? Maybe Gacy simply wanted to do business with a potential customer of his. One hand washes the other and all that. But if not, if that receipt was not Gacy's, then whose was it? It had certainly been recently discarded. It was lying on top of all of the other trash.

Other questions plagued the nights of every person involved with this case.

Many, many questions, very little time. When Terry Sullivan heard me say that I was considering, or, more precisely, that I was recommending a petition for a TRO, he knew that he had a very specific time configuration. A TRO would seriously gum up the works for his investigation. Not only would he and his men lose the ability to follow Mr. Gacy wherever he went, it would, in some sense, shift the burden to the State to show that they were not harassing Gacy. Complaints for search warrants might come under a bit more scrutiny. The filing of any document or petition in court is by definition a public record, as are the hearings that flow from the filings. Once I filed documents in court, the press could discover all this information and report on his every move. Witnesses could be put on notice that they didn't necessarily have to talk to his investigators. Those witnesses might run out and get their own pain-in-the-ass attorneys. Nothing worse than a bunch of goddamn defense lawyers milling about, looking over your shoulder. Terry turned the intensity of the investigation up to eleven.

Members of the investigation team were running themselves ragged. Long hours and total dedication to what had become a cause, a mind-set among the team; this was the norm. Wives and children temporarily lost Dad. Where was Dad? He was working. When would he be home? When the case he was working on was finally over!

For the officers that had no families at home, the investigation became pretty much 24-7. They slept when they could. They would get a good night's sleep when this creep was behind bars.

Investigators headed out in every direction to chase leads.

Officer Adams went with an Officer Kautz to speak to the parents of John Szyc. They spoke to Mrs. Richard Szyc, his mom. She told them her son was last seen January 20, 1977, almost two years prior. She explained that she and her husband had searched for their son to no avail. They had gone to his apartment and found that it was undisturbed, that no foul play was evident; but it was also clear to them that their son had no plans to leave town. The apartment had all of his things in it. There were even tax forms, which were half completed, laid out on a table. John was in the middle of filing his taxes for the year 1976. That was certainly not indicative of a person planning to leave town.

The Szycs paid the rent for the month of February on their son's apartment and left things as they were for their son, believing that he would return.

However, they were told by the Chicago police officers that were assigned to the case that John had been seen since January at various places. These "spottings" are common in missing person cases. This erroneous information that had turned up during the Chicago police investigation did two things: It gave the Szycs hope. They believed that John was somewhere and would someday be in touch. It also caused the investigation of John Szyc's disappearance to be dropped to a very low priority. Why would the police keep looking for a person that was alive but obviously did not want to be found?

The Szycs waited through the month of February, but when no word came from their son, they moved his things back to their house to store. The Chicago police later contacted them and told them that their son had sold his car. There was some indication that the seller needed money to leave town. The police believed that the car was later used during the commission of a robbery; however, their son was not a suspect. The police believed that John had simply moved away. They did not close the file, but it was certainly placed on the back burner.

The appearance of Officers Adams and Kautz gave Mrs. Szyc new hope. These were the first members of any police department that had shown any interest at all in their son's case, and she wanted to be as helpful as possible to the officers with this apparent new interest. She gave the officers all of her son's personal papers, which included the documentation on John Szyc's car. Before he disappeared, John Szyc drove a 1971 white Plymouth Satellite.

When Adams and Kautz returned to Des Plaines, someone noticed that another person involved in their investigation drove a white 1971 Plymouth Satellite: Michael Rossi had the very same car. A quick check of the registration on Mr. Szyc's car and Mr. Rossi's car revealed some very interesting information. The VINs (vehicle identification number) on the two autos were the same but for one number. Szyc's car had VIN RH23G1G239297. Rossi's car had VIN# RH23G1G739297. Everyone in the room looked at each other with astonishment. Rossi was driving John Szyc's car!

Of course, this would have to be confirmed with the records in Springfield (the state capital), but that was for court; that was for the lawyers and judges and juries. Everyone in that room knew that it was the same car. Whether the different VINs were the result of a change that was a mistake or it was done on purpose, it didn't matter. No two VINs could be that close and both belong to a white 1971 Plymouth Satellite and both be involved in the same investigation. Same car, same investigation—the odds were infinitesimal. There was no question in the officers' minds. Rossi was driving John Szyc's car. Then someone said it: "Hey, didn't Rossi say that he had bought that car from his boss, John Gacy?"

After the expenditure of $5,000 on a private investigator, the parents of Gregory Godzik were no closer to finding out the whereabouts of their son, who had been reported missing December 12, 1976, to the Chicago police two years ago, almost to the day that Rob Piest was last seen.

Gregory was last seen by his girlfriend at approximately 1:30 a.m. on that date. He left her saying he was thinking about going to a party in Niles, Illinois. His car was found in Niles, but no Gregory. Unfortunately, just like in the Szyc case and so many other missing person cases, there had been reported sightings of Mr. Godzik following the date of his disappearance. This convinced the Chicago police that Mr. Godzik was a runaway and not a missing person. A file still existed, but it had not been touched in nearly two years.

Prior to his disappearance, Gregory Godzik worked for a contracting firm, PDM Contractors. The Chicago police had interviewed the owner of the firm, one John W. Gacy, and were told that not only did Mr. Gacy not know where Gregory had gone, he had sent a few days' pay that was owed to Gregory to his parents. Although Gregory Godzik had worked for Mr. Gacy for only a short time, he was a good worker, and Mr. Gacy was also concerned about his well-being and his whereabouts.

As clear as clear could be, that was how sure the members of the investigation team were that John Wayne Gacy had something to do with the death or disappearance of these many missing boys. There was absolutely no doubt in any mind in the Des Plaines police headquarters. None. Yet, nothing that they had on him was concrete. Nothing that they had discovered tied Gacy to any of one of these boys in any way that was not circumstantial. They had to keep searching, and they had to do it fast. They were all quite sure that I would walk in at any moment with a TRO, and that would be the end of it all. The clock was ticking.

10

AS FAR AS I knew, I was representing a man that was simply in the wrong place at the wrong time—a man with a past, granted, but a man who was trying to put that part of his life behind him, a man who was a likely suspect due to that past record, but someone that was being mistakenly, albeit reasonably, targeted by a police force that was looking for answers.

He had done what he had done back in Waterloo, but he was taking all appropriate steps to turn his life around, and now this incredible snag had arisen. From my perspective, I was representing a successful, hardworking businessman, a tireless political soldier and precinct captain, a volunteer that did the hard, behind-the-scenes work on behalf of ethnic causes, giant elaborate parades, his local Democratic Party, and little sick kids. He was a clown, for crying out loud. How bad of a guy could he be? OK, he did have a funny way about him. He was a bit of a braggart and a blowhard, but that didn't make him a kidnapper or a stalker or whatever the Des Plaines coppers and Sullivan thought he was.

My job did not rely, however, on what I thought about John Gacy or what Terry Sullivan or Herb Volberding or any of the guys over in Des Plaines thought about him. My job was to defend his interests, and that was what I intended to do. After my son's illness, it was my only focus.

I began by cracking books. Lawyers turn to the law at times like these, and this was where you could find me—with my nose buried in law books concerning the issues of police harassment, temporary restraining orders, illegal search and seizure, and like topics. I split my time between the hospital and the law library. I had absolutely no clue as to what I had actually signed up for. It was the calm before the storm. Christmas was fast approaching, and I had two little kids. Little did I know what was about to happen to my life and the lives of everyone around me. As snow floated softly to the ground outside my lonely office window in quaint, affluent little Park Ridge, Illinois, where lights burned late into the night, a storm was brewing—events were unfolding that would focus the attention of all of Chicago, all of Illinois, all of the nation, and eventually all of the world on that sleepy, quiet town and the surrounding northwest suburban area of our fair metropolis.

As I worked the case, Gacy was in constant contact. He was calling both at my office and at my home. I guess he felt I should know every little thing that happened. He said he was making friends with the team of police officers that were assigned on his tail. At first, I thought he was kidding. He wasn't. He and the members of the surveillance team were now having drinks regularly. They had been out to dinner on a couple of occasions. Gacy had them over to his house. Usually, Gacy paid the bill; however, on at least one occasion, the officers sprung for dinner and quite often picked up the tab for the many, many rounds at the many, many bars that Gacy frequented. Gacy was a night owl, and he dragged the members of the Delta Unit from bar to bar until the wee hours of the morning. It didn't matter what ridiculous time of the night or early morning it was, Gacy knew of a bar that was open. He would enter each watering hole like a conquering hero, working the crowd like an old-school politician, introducing the members of the Delta Unit as his bodyguards. More often than not, Gacy and his "bodyguards" would arrive at Gacy's home after a night out on the town just before sunrise on the following morning.

I was also still finalizing the decor and tenor of my new office. Of course, I wanted my first office to be perfect. I brought in pictures and knickknacks from home, together with boxes of law books that I had collected over the years. I was just settling into my office. It was becoming my home away from home.

I was spending as much time as possible at the hospital where my son, although showing signs of improvement, was still not out of the woods. He was running a high fever, and it was evident that he was going to have a protracted stay at the Resurrection Hospital. I was getting very little sleep during this time, because I was spending most nights with my son. Occasionally, because he knew he could find me there, Gacy would stop at the hospital to check in rather than call. He actually seemed concerned about my son's well-being and on one occasion brought a little stuffed animal and gave it to Sammy.

When Leroy Stevens returned from his hunting trip on Monday, John Gacy went to see him at his Jefferson Park office. I spoke to him by phone, and it became evident to both Mr. Gacy and me that Stevens was not interested in becoming immersed in what was shaping up to be a complicated and time-consuming criminal defense case. He had represented Gacy primarily on corporate matters, and he was content to have things remain that way.

However, it was decided that he would file the civil case for harassment, including the matter of a petition for a temporary restraining order against the Des Plaines Police Department. Although I had already tendered my resignation from the public defender's office, I was still owed back pay for vacation time that I had not taken. We determined that we did not want any question to arise as to my status, which might serve as a defense to the lawsuit. I had a complaint drafted and a petition for TRO, and Stevens agreed to file it as the attorney of record.

On Tuesday, December 19, Gacy went to Steven's office, and the two of them left together and went to the Jefferson Park Chicago Transit Authority station with the intention of taking the train downtown to the Chicago Loop. In Chicago, the CTA operates an elaborate electric train system as well as the bus routes throughout the city. Much of the train system is on tracks that are elevated, and therefore, the entire system is affectionately referred to as the "L."

Before they left, Leroy Stevens bought lunch for everyone at Gale Street Inn, one of Chicago's most famous rib joints; then after lunch, Gacy dutifully informed the present members of the Delta Unit—Robinson and Schultz—of their destination and gave them time to park their car in a legal spot, considering that they would all be downtown for quite a while. The relationship that existed between Gacy and his police tail was an unusual one, to say the least. Believe it or not, the entire motley crew—including Gacy, Stevens, Robinson, and Schultz—rode together on the train to the Daley Center, which was the city's main civic center filled with courtrooms, and most of the main offices of the city and the county, named in memory of the great Chicago mayor Richard J. Daley. Any important office that wasn't in that building was across the street at city hall.

Stevens stayed on the train when they reached the stop for the Daley Center, claiming that he had Christmas shopping to do while Gacy and crew disembarked and went into the Daley Center, where Gacy had permits to apply for and other business to transact. In reality, Stevens took the train a couple of extra stops to the Jackson St. Station. That is where one would exit if one has a case to file in the federal district court. Stevens had such a case to file. The case: *John W. Gacy v. the City of Des Plaines et al.* The case included among its pleadings a request for a temporary restraining order against the police force of said city. It was filed and scheduled for emergency hearing on the following Friday, December 22, 1978.

The following day, I forwarded a copy of the file stamped Complaint at Law, the petition for TRO, together with the information and notice regarding court dates to all opposing parties as required by law, and I made sure that Terry Sullivan received a copy, as promised.

When Gacy told me the story about how he, Robinson, Schultz, Stevens, and Stevens's secretary all had a pleasant lunch, including drinks, at the Gale Street Inn—all of it paid for by Stevens—and then rode the train downtown together, I had to laugh. This was such an unusual occurrence that I would have been surprised to hear that it had ever happened during any serious investigation of a suspect in all of history. This was a testament to the unusually gregarious nature of this man whom I represented. I could see how he had been given all the various awards and accolades that he had. He was truly a Man of the Year type of guy.

He would speak to the clerks and cashiers behind counters and at desks like they were old friends. He shook the hands of middle-level politicians with smiles and jokes all around. During his visit, a man who seemed to be a good friend approached Gacy, and handshakes and backslapping were exchanged. Robinson and Schultz could not help but be impressed. The friend was Illinois attorney general Bill Scott. Gacy was clearly in his element among politicians and public servants. Frankly, that was because he was one of them. Gacy was a "pitch in and help out" kind of guy, and everybody knew that about him.

The more I looked into this matter, the more this became evident. I couldn't help but be further convinced that the targeting of my client had to be a mistake. After all, John Gacy could have simply disappeared at any time. If he was as guilty of these charges as the members of the prosecution seemed to think he was, wouldn't he have just run away, disappeared forever? Wouldn't anybody? He certainly had ample opportunity to do so. Instead of running away, Gacy was facilitating the surveillance. He would tell the Deltas where he was going in advance, just in case they somehow got separated. He bought drinks, bought dinner, and invited them into his home. He just did not act like a guilty person. His overall demeanor was that of someone without a care in the world.

There is a song, which won the old-time blues and jazz singer Dinah Washington a Grammy in 1959. It's a great song. Everybody's heard it. It's called "What a Diff'rence a Day Makes." No song could have been more apropos for me than that one on that Wednesday night. "Twenty-four little hours," the song goes on. If someone had a crystal ball and they told me what was going to happen to me in twenty-four hours, I wouldn't have believed them.

11

AT THE DES Plaines police station, there was serious concern about the fact that a court date for a hearing on a TRO had been set and was looming, staring the investigation straight in the face. The team needed a break in this case before Friday, or it was likely that the investigation of this man, Gacy, would be greatly hampered, if not completely shut down.

In spite of extensive circumstantial evidence linking their prime suspect to the disappearance not only of Rob Piest but also of other young boys that had each been in some way connected to Gacy, they still had nothing concrete, nothing that they could point to linking Mr. Gacy to any of those missing boys. As it stood, there were a few kids that had a vague connection to Mr. Gacy in years previous who may or may not be missing. Each of the missing teens could in fact simply have run away from home.

One thing that was definitely true: No judge would allow the members of a police force to doggedly pursue a suspect in the manner in which they were pursuing Gacy on such flimsy evidence. The placement of a team of investigators on the tail of a citizen of the United States—the constant following of that person in a way that was beginning to affect his business activities and his reputation in the community—was the very definition of police harassment. This would not be allowed absent clear and convincing evidence that this level of surveillance was absolutely warranted. They needed evidence to warrant the continuation of such activities—hard, conclusive evidence. And what evidence had the investigation actually produced?

Other than an indication that Rob Piest was "going to ask that contactor guy for a job," or words to that effect, had anyone seen Rob Piest talking to John Gacy? Had anyone seen them together? Was there any evidence whatsoever that Gacy had ever met or spoken to Rob Piest, let alone left the pharmacy with him on the night of December 11? Clearly, there was not. No actual evidence unearthed to date tied John Gacy to Rob Piest in any way.

The 1971 Plymouth Satellite that now belonged to Mike Rossi had been legally transferred through the Secretary of State's office from John Szyc to joint ownership between a John Grey and Michael Rossi. On a later date, the transfer from joint ownership to sole ownership in the name of Michael Rossi had been completed, presumably upon full payment for the vehicle, a very common transfer. Not only was the transfer a legal and seemingly proper one, it also had the obvious discrepancy of different VINs. The single digit that separated the two numbers may just as well have been the Grand Canyon. At present, there was no concrete proof that it was even the same vehicle.

Sullivan and the members of his team knew exactly what had happened. It was clear to them. John Wayne Gacy had killed John Szyc, stolen his car, and fudged a legal transfer by transposing a single digit of the VIN. He also used the name "John Grey" rather than "John Gacy" in making the transfer to cover his tracks. Who could question any of that?

But wait a second, hadn't there been sightings of John Szyc reported on dates following the date that he had first been reported missing? Weren't there reports in the Chicago Police Department file that indicated that John Szyc had sold his car because he needed money to leave town? Wasn't it true that the automobile in question, the 1971 Plymouth Satellite bearing the same VIN as the one owned by John Szyc, had been reported as having been involved in a robbery after the date that Mr. Szyc was reported missing?

When a transfer of title is made at the office of the Secretary of State, the documents are routinely filled out in pen and ink, sometimes even smudgy pencil. Isn't it possible that the handwritten, perhaps scribbled, name "John Gacy" could have been mistaken by an overworked and underpaid clerk in the Secretary of State's office to read "John Grey?" Maybe the *a* and the *c* looked like an *r* and an *e* and "Gacy" became "Grey" in the eyes of that poor harried clerk. It's a simple-enough mistake, isn't it? Couldn't that also explain the transposition of a single digit on the VIN as well? In fact, isn't that a more likely explanation of these discrepancies? Do we as a people automatically assume foul play every time a mistake is made on a form at the Department of Motor Vehicles? One would certainly hope not.

And what of Gregory Godzik? What about Charles Mazzara? Well, what about them? Gregory Godzik clearly had once worked for Mr. Gacy. But what did that have to do with the price of tea in China? The parents of Mr. Godzik believed their son was missing . . . maybe worse. So what? Take a stroll down Hollywood Boulevard, take a walk down Duval Street in Key West, check out the Haight-Ashbury district in San Francisco, go to any strip in any town where teenage runaways gather; and you will see the faces of hundreds of young men and women with whom parents have had no contact. The parents of each and every one of those kids have probably reported them missing and they pine for their child's return. Such is the heart-wrenching nature of the problem of runaway teens. The mere fact that Gregory Godzik's parents did not know where Gregory was and Gregory had once worked for John Gacy meant exactly nothing in the general scheme of things. It was not proof of anything at all.

And what of the tragic story of Charles Mazzara? It was true that Charles once worked for John Wayne Gacy. It was also true that, sadly, Charles had been found dead of an apparent drowning in the Des Plaines River some seventy miles from the city of Chicago. Now the sixty-four-thousand-dollar question: What did those two facts have to do with each other? The answer is obvious. Absent actual, concrete proof to the contrary, absolutely nothing. Gacy ran a construction company, a non-union shop. Construction is a seasonal profession. Employees come and employees go. That is the nature of the business. That is the nature of the trades. Pick any construction company and track the lives of every person that worked there over a period of years, and you will find that some of those former employees are now deceased. Unfortunate as it may be, some of those deaths will have been tragic—all young deaths are tragic, aren't they? The fact that a former employee of John Gacy was now dead, however tragic, meant absolutely nothing in a courtroom. In a courtroom there has to be proof.

Lastly, there was the frightening story told by Jeffrey Rignall, which actually resulted in charges being filed against Mr. Gacy. That's some cold, hard evidence, right? Let's see, Jeffrey, an admitted homosexual, had voluntarily hopped into an automobile with a total stranger, in an area of town frequented by male prostitutes; and then as a result of this folly, he experiences a horrific, traumatic experience, most of which he tells the police that he doesn't remember. He takes matters into his own hands, rents a car, and scours the neighborhood for a car that he thinks he remembers from that night. Weeks later, he finds such a car and reports the plate number to the police. Months later, a man is arrested for battery. Jeffrey, now a Florida resident, cannot always be in court to testify against the perpetrator due to the distance. The case was on the verge of dismissal for want of prosecution.

There are a lot of things that make being a police officer or a prosecutor a tough job. Occasionally, you get shot at. Occasionally, you might have to shoot someone else. Tough things, those, no doubt. But how tough would it be to absolutely know in your soul that some prick is a danger to others, a danger to kids, is probably out there murdering people, and not be able to prove it? Not an enviable position to be in, huh?

As Terry Sullivan reviewed his present situation, he knew that if no new evidence were to come to light, but quick, I was likely to win my motion, and the intense, hands-on investigation of Mr. John Wayne Gacy would be over. Search warrants would be much harder to get approved, surveillance would be curtailed or ended, the investigation could be seriously stalled, and Mr. Gacy would then be free to either take steps to cover his tracks or, worse, skedaddle from Chicago for all time.

Then late Tuesday night, the break that the prosecution needed materialized.

Kim Byers was a swimmer. She was on the swim team at Maine North Highschool, and on Tuesday night, December 19, she was participating in a big swim meet. Following the meet, a couple members of the investigation team finally caught up with her. She was a busy girl, a very busy girl.

A full-time student, an employee at Nisson Pharmacy, and a member of the swim team, she was a typical teen, always running from place to place. This was the first night that there was time to talk with the policemen regarding Rob since that first night. They had some more questions for her.

It seemed that on the night of December 11, Kim Byers was working the cash register when John Wayne Gacy walked in for his appointment with Phil and Larry Torf. The police had asked her many questions before regarding the disappearance of Rob Piest, but tonight they were concentrating on just one single piece of evidence, a receipt for photographs. They showed it to Kim.

Yes, that was hers, she admitted. That night, that Monday night, she had turned in some film for developing. She filled out the form with her name and address and ripped off the receipt. She was wearing Rob's coat that evening while she worked the cash register because it was freezing cold up front by the doors. They did not have revolving doors, just a set of double doors; and therefore, she would get a huge blast of frigid air every time a customer came in or went out. Rob let her wear his blue nylon parka. He was so nice.

She had put the receipt in the pocket of Rob's coat. She remembered this for certain. Why? Because she was an employee, she really didn't need it. When the film came back from developing, she could simply search for her own pictures herself, a little perk of being an employee. She didn't need the receipt like a customer would. But she had put the receipt in Rob's pocket on purpose. She thought Rob was cute. She wanted him to find it. It would give them a reason to talk, you see. It would give them a reason to talk . . . maybe about the pictures. She remembered putting that receipt in the pocket of Rob's coat because she did it on purpose. It was a conscious decision. She wanted Rob to find it.

There was only one way that Kim Byers's receipt for photographs had wound up in John Wayne Gacy's kitchen garbage bag. Rob Piest was in that house. Rob Piest had been in John Wayne Gacy's house! At last! An actual connection—this was a piece of physical evidence, this was the long-sought-after link between young Rob Piest and Mr. Gacy. It was as good as a fingerprint.

12

FIVE DAYS BEFORE Christmas Day 1978, five days following the day that John Wayne Gacy first officially retained me as his lawyer, two days before the scheduled date for the hearing on our pending petition for a temporary restraining order, December 20, Wednesday, was an interesting day in my life, a very interesting day.

I was at the hospital almost all night and had barely had a wink of sleep. That morning, I had a court date for a damned speeding ticket—my own damned speeding ticket—downtown at 321 N. LaSalle Street, Chicago's traffic court.

I headed down to the city to do what Abraham Lincoln had warned against—to represent myself in court. I believe the age-old adage about how a man that represents himself has a fool for a client has been attributed to him. Whoever said it, I was about to do it.

The calls from Mr. Gacy started first thing in the morning and continued throughout the day. Every time I called my office to check for messages, there was a new message. Finally, I could avoid it no longer. I called John Gacy.

Don't get me wrong, I was happy to be representing him, my one and only client; but he had been calling me five to ten times a day, each and every day. I had a very sick son, a law practice to get up and running, other clients to attract, my own stupid traffic ticket to deal with, a wife that was justifiably concerned about her infant son, a mother that was watching our other son, plus, there was never anything new that Gacy had to say. He was starting to sound a little like a broken record. Nevertheless, I called him from my office.

"John, how are you today?" As I spoke, I was staring at a picture of Rob Piest that was in yesterday's *Daily Herald*, which someone had left on my desk. The story was front page above the fold.

"I have to come in to see you . . . today. I want to talk to both you and Stevens." Gacy sounded urgent. I wondered what new bit of sage advice he had to offer or what new pressing question he had to ask.

"John, unless there is something new that you have to tell us, I don't see the necessity of you coming in here today. You know how sick Sammy is. You know that I need to be at the hospital. You were here at the office last Friday for six hours. We talked about everything at that time. I do not believe that there have been dramatic changes since that day that warrant another meeting. It's Christmas, John. Are you done with your shopping? Don't you have Christmas shopping to do? I know I do."

"Give me a break, Sam. These cops are breathing down my goddamn neck. This is not a normal Christmas for me. I have to see you guys. It can be late this evening. That way, you guys can do whatever you have to do first. But it has to be tonight."

Welcome to the private practice of law. Your time is truly not your own.

"OK, John," I said with some obvious signs of exasperation—exasperation that Gacy completely ignored, I might add. "Come in tonight at ten thirty. I'll call Stevens and ask him to be here."

I called Stevens, and he agreed, after much consternation, to meet me at my office at 10:30 p.m.

THE APPOINTED TIME of 10:30 p.m. came and went. No Gacy. Stevens and I stared at each other, fuming. I'm Italian. I'm passionate. I believe that I was fuming on a level that far exceeded Mr. Stevens's. I had just about had it with our mutual client.

I showed Stevens the article in the *Daily Herald*. It read:

> Son missing, parents 'fearing worst'
>
> The second son of a close-knit family, Robert Piest was not about to miss his mother's birthday December 11. He just wasn't that kind of kid.
>
> "He was very considerate of our feelings," his mother, Elizabeth, said. So when he failed to return to work where his mother was waiting to pick him up that day, his family started to worry. Later that evening, they called Des Plaines police.
>
> That was a week ago. Robert Piest still hasn't come home. His parents are prepared for the worst. Des Plaines police think the youth is dead.
>
> "Right now we are fearing the worst," said his father, Harold. "And that way anything else we find out is only a plus."
>
> Monday night, Elizabeth, Harold, and their daughter, Kerry, 21, sat talking of "Rob," as they called him, in the comfortably furnished living room of the Piests' home, 2722 Craig Drive.
>
> The time that has passed since her son's disappearance appeared to show in Mrs. Piest's face. A thin woman with dark hair and brown eyes, she smoked several cigarettes within a half hour. The room was softly lit, much of the light coming from a Christmas tree covered with tinsel.
>
> Circular mirrors underneath the base of the tree reflected light out toward the room. There were no presents under the tree.
>
> Harold, middle-aged and middle height, with thick, short brown hair combed well back, reclined in a plush couch. He didn't seem comfortable.

They described their son as a good boy, the kid who was on the school's gymnastics team, had his share of girlfriends, loved to play pinball, and liked studying electronics.

Harold, who is an accounting manager for an area packaging firm, said, "We are all very close . . . we know each other's feelings." Harold has been involved in scouting all his life, and was very proud that his son was about to earn the coveted rank of Eagle Scout.

The last member of the family to see Robert was his mother. She went to pick him up from work that night, at Nisson's Pharmacy, 1920 Touhy Avenue, where Rob worked part-time.

Mrs. Piest said she arrived at the drugstore at 9:00 p.m. to pick up her son. She met him inside.

"Then he was going outside to talk to a guy. He said it would be only a few minutes. I didn't pay much attention to it and didn't know if he was going to talk to him outside the store, or inside . . . I just said, 'I'll wait for you and browse around.'"

Mrs. Piest said she knew that Rob was to talk to the man about a summer job, but little more than that. She said she didn't know who the man was.

Minutes later she checked outside to find Rob, but he was gone.

Harold called the police at 11:00 p.m. The family knew something was wrong from the beginning.

Mrs. Piest said that the usual routine on work nights was for her to pick up her son at school, usher him to work and then home.

"We'd pick him up at 5:45, take him home for a bite to eat, then take him to work. Sometimes I bring him some hot food in the car. We didn't like him walking around at night."

The family isn't quite sure of the next step, but it wants to maintain the public's interest in the case.

Son missing, parents 'fearing worst'

by BILL GRAHAM

THE DAILY HERALD

Arlington Heights   PADDOCK PUBLICATIONS

52nd Year—126   Tuesday, December 19, 1978   40 Pages — 15 Cents

Oil price increase jolts West

ABU DHABI, United Arab Emirates (AP) — The decision by OPEC oil ministers meeting here to raise prices 14.5 percent jolted the Western financial world Monday, driving down the dollar and the Dow Jones stock averages and darkening the U.S. economic picture for 1979.

Related story on Page 3

(Continued on Page 3)

WHEN NORTH POINT State Bank was closed by state officials Saturday, some depositors wanted to withdraw their money, but most just wanted to ask questions and be reassured. Secretary Loraine Furmanski said an assumed 200 calls in a 90-minute period early Monday.

Lawsuits forced closing of bank

by RON SONNETTI

Money safe, depositors assured

by NANCY CUTLER

(Continued on Page 4)

Designing to begin for commuter parking garages

THE DAILY HERALD   Tuesday, December 12, 1978   Section 1

Businesses bracing for oil cost hikes

by JOHN N. FRANK
and NANCY GOTTLER

Consumers will get a lesson in oil economics next year as costs for everything from food to flying rise and the likelihood of a recession increases.

The immediate impact of OPEC's 14.5 percent oil increase will be felt in the gasoline pumps, but almost every industry will be affected.

"The ripple effect throughout the economy is widespread. You're going to see it spread through the whole economy, gradually," says Theodore Tung of the Continental Bank, Chicago.

THE INDUSTRIES most likely to face higher costs first will be plastics and petrochemical manufacturers.

"We will pass it along, definitely, but the impact will be less than the percentage increase on a barrel of oil," said Ed Collins of the Society of Plastics Industries, a New York-based trade organization.

The plastics industry uses 1.5 percent of the total crude oil consumed in the United States, Collins said.

Air carriers could face higher ticket prices next year because of high jet fuel prices, United Airlines, the nation's largest air carrier, estimates it will pay an additional $93 million for fuel based on its first full consumption. Trans World Airlines estimates added fuel costs will increase its operating expenses 16 percent.

SHOPPERS WILL see supermarket prices climb because of hampers' reliance on petroleum-powered farm machinery.

"Energy uses are a big part of our costs," says Peter Blewitt of the American Farm Bureau Federation. "Transportation costs are likely to be felt almost immediately in the marketplace. When a farmer's gas costs go up, he is likely to pass that on to the supermarket."

And after the food leaves the farms there will be even more costs added because shippers and processors use petroleum to get food to consumers.

"It affects all industries in the sense that the consumer will be paying a little bit more for gas, a little bit more for heating oil; and that takes a little bit more from discretionary income," said Norbert Neil, vice president, Home Trust and Savings, Chicago.

LESS DISCRETIONARY income, money not needed for necessities such as food and housing, means less spending for cars, retail goods and leisure time activities.

"This adds to the forces generating a slowdown in the economy," Neil says. "It makes a recession probably won't be hurt anyone."

ly more likely."

"People will go to one less restaurant, one less movie, buy one less suit of clothes," said Arnold E. Safer, an economist at Irving Trust Co., New York. "It's going to be damaging."

Safer and other analysts say the damage to the economy could lead to a recession, even though OPEC tried to diffuse the shock by spreading the increase over most of the year.

"THE ECONOMY WAS in pretty bad shape anyhow. This probably makes it worse," said Michael Evans, president of Chase Manhattan Bank's Chase Econometrics division. Evans, whose predictions of a 1979 recession have been more dire than most, said the fact the increase was spread out "moves the recession from the first half of the year to the second."

He said the oil companies have stockpiled crude for the last couple of months in anticipation of an OPEC increase and won't begin buying large amounts of crude again until the second half of next year, when the increase will be larger than it would be if they began large-scale purchases in the early part of the year. So consumer shock cities will be greater in the second half of the year.

Chuck Rolls, owner of Arlington Best Cab Co., a fleet of 12 cabs, said he will have to ask Arlington Heights officials for a rate increase next year.

"WE PAY FOR gasoline just like everyone else," he said. "A couple of cents increase I can live with, but ultimately, we will have to go back to the village and ask for a price hike. I don't know if it will affect our business, but we probably won't have a choice."

Michael Bingham, co-owner of Suburbanyer Bus Service, which has a contract with Elk Grove Township Dist. 59, said the price hike will be passed on to the taxpayers.

"We have a contract with the school district that says the gasoline price goes beyond a certain amount, the difference will be paid by the school district," he said. "So it will affect the taxpayers."

Richard Foss, owner of Executive Chauffeuring in Wheeling, expects a boost in business. Higher gas prices close the gap between the cost of driving to the airport and the cost of taking a limousine, he said.

"When gas prices go up, it leads to drive customers to us because rather than use their own car, they'd rather go with us if we keep our rates reasonable," he said. "Business probably won't be hurt anyone."

ABOUT 200 persons of Chinese descent, some carrying signs that read "Who lifted your uncles in Korea in the '50s — the Red Chinese," demonstrated peacefully in the Daley Center Monday in Chicago. They protested President Carter's plan to recognize mainland China as the official government of the Chinese people. Other signs read, "Long live Free China" and "After Taiwan, which ally will be next?" No one was arrested.

Israel peace talk stand hardens

Egypt Monday recalled its military delegation to the stalled Washington peace talks, Israel hardened its rejection of new Egyptian proposals carried by Sec. of State Cyrus Vance as his second Middle East shuttle.

Israeli Prime Minister Menachem Begin told political supporters, "We must be ready not to accept Egyptian suggestions which run endanger the welfare of our nation, even if they are favored by the United States."

While Knesset news secretary Jody Powell said President Carter is "concerned and disappointed" that an treaty is in sight, but does not believe he can have a solution.

"PEACE will have to be made between Israel and her Arab neighbors," Powell said. "We are more

than willing to be of assistance in the process. There's no way the United States can impose peace."

In Cairo, government officials said the three-man Egyptian military team in Washington, headed by Maj. Gen. Taha ElMagdoub, had been ordered to return home. Begin announced a similar decision Sunday.

Begin told a meeting of his government coalition there was a "vise in position" and "the United States" to recall his Israeli positions.

"Not just now, say the American position is corrosive," Begin said. "There are articles in important newspapers which say there is no reason to blame Israel as if it caused the postponement of the signing of the peace treaty."

"THE TRUTH is the opposite. We were ready to sign the peace treaty without official interpretations, without expressing from the Camp David accords and the responsibility for not signing the treaty, so far as we know, falls on Egypt."

Begin emphasized that Israel has "closed no doors" and remains ready to sign a peace treaty with Egypt "provided it will not be devoid of all meaning."

Jordan's King Hussein Monday held the British Broadcasting Corp. he remains unwilling to accept any settlement with Israel that does not include return of all Arab territories occupied in 1967, including Arab East Jerusalem.

He said he continues to reject any

separate deal between Israel and Egyptian President Anwar Sadat.

ISRAEL's firm rejection of the latest peace proposals by Begin and Foreign Minister Moshe Dayan coincided with a demonstration from Cairo.

Egypt's own President Anwar Sadat accused Israel was "perpetuating" and "obstructing a peace treaty." He relied on the Jerusalem government to change its position and make agreement possible.

Dayan, and Israel will not assume peace talks until Sadat drops five new demands relayed by Vance. Begin said Israel's peace proposals were "fair" and would not include return of all Arab territories occupied in 1967, including Arab East Jerusalem.

United Press International

Woodfield 76 to begin in spring

by JOHN HUDSON

A developer of Schaumburg's massive Woodfield 76 commercial and residential complex still breakground early next year with construction of a theatre office building.

"It's just a small step," said Howard Kanfner of Bennett & Kanfnweiler Associates, Chicago. "But it's a first step and that's when the hardest to accomplish."

Although plans and zoning for the project were approved nearly four years ago, construction was delayed by financial "uncertainties" and the "general sloppiness of the nation's economy," said Kanfner.

GROUNDBREAKING FOR THE office building and a parking lot should begin in the spring, said Schaumburg

Planning Director Steve Bovett.

The building will be at the east end of a 297-acre parcel on Golf Road north of the Woodfield Shopping Center.

Bovett said the project's first phase also will include the construction of two more 16-story office buildings, but he did not know when work might begin. The three buildings and shared parking lot will occupy 23 acres east of Union Oil Co. of California's headquarters.

Ultimately, Woodfield 76 is to include approximately 1,200 residential condominiums, a 1,000-room hotel, stores, restaurants and its own transportation system, possibly a monorail. Kanfner said the construction may take as long as 20 years.

None of Bennett & Kanfnweiler's as-

sociates would identify tenants for the office building nor disclose the price of the construction project.

THE ESTIMATED COST of the entire project was $200 million in 1976. Kanfner would say only, "I can say just from looking at the rising cost of everything else that it is going to go up."

Tishman-Midwest Inc. of Chicago will construct the office buildings for the 16-acre parcel said John Quin, project director. He said Bennett & Kanfnweiler are "choosing at the bit" to disclose more details but have agreed to "wait until early January to participate in a broad release of information."

The village agreed in 1968 to build a theater and museum on the Woodfield

76 property and has collected nearly $1 million in cash and land from other developers for the "cultural center."

Dist. 214 building program OKd

The High School Dist. 214 Board of Education Monday night approved a building and remodeling program that is more than $1 million more costly than it was when adopted last summer.

BOARD MEMBERS briefly discussed whether they should spend money to remodel and build additions for the district's eight high schools when they have been worrying about declining enrollments bringing future school closings.

"We still do have a responsibility to educate the students that are with us," said board member Marilyn Quinn. The district cannot eliminate

programs now because of what has to have many bring, she said.

"I'm 100 percent in favor of extending the budget by this 10 percent and proceeding," said board member Eugene Hoerl. He said the board should not again begin playing apart the plan to use what could be cut. "We did trim for approximately the last four years."

HE SAID the district has been criticized for putting away more than an million in savings. That money will pay for the improvements. "If we back off on any of these projects that we sent back in July we'd go ahead

with, we need to sort to any and all criticism."

Architects' cost estimates for the improvements total $7 million, 17 percent more than the original budget. Construction will start in the spring.

Quinn, Hoerl, board members Robert Buchheister and Al Potterton and Pres. John Guttrie voted to direct architects to proceed with the plan unless the ray new budget.

Board member Harris Best objected, saying he does not oppose the plans but thought the district could save money by having maintenance workers do some of the remodeling.

'Good boy' is missing, parents expect worst

(Continued from Page 1)

Roberta Piesel

live on every night was for her to pick up her son at school, labor him to work and then home.

"He'd pick him up at 6:45, take him home for a bite to eat, then take him to work. Sometimes I bring him some hot food in the car. We didn't like him walking around at night."

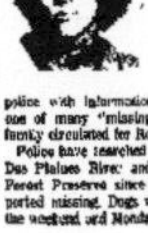

THE FAMILY isn't quite sure of the exact step, but it wants to maintain his public's interest in the case.

"There might have been someone at the drugstore that night who saw something; maybe something that they thought was unimportant, but something that would help us in the search. If they read about what happened, they might call us," Mrs. Piesel said.

She said that two parents phoned

police with information after seeing one of many "missing" posters the family circulated for Bob.

Police have searched sections of the Des Plaines River and Cook County Forest Preserves since Piesel was reported missing. Dogs were used over the weekend and Monday.

Patty Hearst's parents split because of pressure

SAN FRANCISCO (AP) — Patricia Hearst's parents have separated after 40 years of marriage because of the pressure brought on by their daughter's kidnapping, trial and jailing, a source close to the family said Monday.

Randolph Hearst, president of the San Francisco Examiner, and his wife Catherine, began living apart last summer, said the source who asked not to be named.

Hearst has purchased a home at Paso Robles, inland from the San Francisco Castle at San Simeon

on the California coast. Mrs. Hearst is living at the family home in Hillsborough on the San Francisco Peninsula, according to the source.

Patricia Hearst was kidnapped by the self-styled Symbionese Liberation Army Feb. 4, 1974. She currently is serving a seven-year prison term for joining her SLA abductors in a bank robbery 19 weeks after the kidnapping.

She will be eligible for parole within months of her sentence and could have served 21 months of her sentence.

Jones' son confesses to murders

GEORGETOWN, Guyana (UPI) — Stephan Jones, the 19-year-old son of Peoples Temple prophet Jim Jones, Monday made a surprise confession that he murdered a cult official and her three children in the bizarre Nov. 18 orgy of death.

Young Jones was immediately arrested after his admission at a magistrate's hearing for another cult member charged with the slayings of Temple official Sharon Amos and her children at the cult's Georgetown headquarters.

Stephan, who earlier had declared, "I hate my father," and blamed his father for the mass suicides and murders of more than 900 Temple followers at the Jonestown commune, was called for a hearing for Charles Edward Beikman.

"I killed those people and I'm trying to throw it off on the accused," Jones told the court exactly who made it after the shocking deaths of Rep. Leo Ryan, three newsmen and a defecting cultist triggered the mass deaths at Jonestown.

Beikman looked startled at the unexpected confession, but said nothing.

Jones was taken into police custody. Prosecutors said they were continuing filing final murder charges against him and Beikman.

Prosecuting Attorney Carling Weisman indicated if the charge of murders unfounded if the confession stands. At the hearing, the present inquiry would have to be halted and new proceedings started.

Earlier Monday, Magistrate Ian and Christian refused to allow the state to introduce into evidence a

statement from Beikman that amounted to a confession, ruling it inadmissible.

AFTER LISTENING to two hours of legal arguments by Weisman and defense attorney Rex McKee, Clothian said he did not believe the statement was made voluntarily.

Jones was called to testify about the statement and made his startling confession near the witness box. After a brief afternoon recess, the hearing was adjourned until today.

"There might have been someone at the drugstore that night who saw something, maybe something that they thought was unimportant, but something that would help in the search. If they read about what happened, they might call in," Mrs. Piest said.

She said that two persons phoned police with information after seeing one of many "missing" posters the family circulated for Rob.

Police have searched sections of the Des Plaines River and Cook County Forest Preserve since Piest was reported missing. Dogs were used over the weekend and Monday.

Stevens looked at me and shook his head. We shared a long unspoken moment. Who knew what to think?

The phone rang. It was Gacy.

"I'm running a little late," he said. "I'll be right there. I'm on my way."

I rolled my eyes and told Stevens the news. We both shared stories about our client in his absence while we waited.

At about eleven thirty, Gacy finally arrived. He looked trashed, disheveled, frightened.

He asked if I had anything to drink around here. He already looked like shit, eyes bloodshot and bleary, face haggard and drawn. He seemed to be coming apart. He obviously knew something I didn't. I wasn't so sure that I should contribute to his condition, but I was pissed that he had dragged me out, days before Christmas, away from my sick son. Plus, he arrived late; now it was damn near the middle of the goddamn night, so . . . what the fuck. It was Christmastime, and an investigator in the Third District had given me a bottle of VO in honor of the season. It was out in my car. I looked at him and finally said, "Sure, John, why not. Wait here. I'll go get it."

On the way back into my office from my car, I noticed the two poor saps saddled with the thankless, mind-numbing job of tailing

Gacy and reporting his every move. The temperature had plummeted. It could not have been much more than zero, maybe less. The ground crunched underfoot, and you could see your breath. Everything glistened. I stopped by their beat-up excuse for an unmarked squad and leaned into the driver's-side window.

"It looks like we might be here for a while. You guys are welcome to sit in the reception area if you want." I pointed at my office. "At least it's warm."

They both lit up. All I saw were chattering teeth. They looked at each other and shrugged as if to say, "Why not?"

"OK, Sam . . . thanks. I think we'll take you up on that," Mike Albrecht said. I knew Mike from around the station in Des Plaines. At least I knew who he was.

We all hotfooted it into my office together, shivering and crunching the snow.

"You guys can stay out here in the waiting area. Do you want anything?" I raised the bottle and my eyebrows. They both declined. "OK, make yourselves at home."

I locked the glass door that separated the reception area from the rest of the office.

Back in my office, Gacy and Stevens had both turned to stone. They didn't seem to be doing much chatting. Stevens was also pissed off that Gacy had dragged us out on such a night. I got the feeling that he was quite ready to wash his hands of this whole matter—of Gacy, of me, of everything. I think he was glad that I was coming into the case.

The only glasses that I had on hand were the plastic inserts to those silly brown cup holders for coffee that snapped together. We didn't bother with the holder part. I poured a splash into Gacy's cup, maybe an ounce, and he looked at me and smiled a crooked, strange smile. He waved his other hand in a way that meant he wanted me to keep filling. I filled his cup to the brim. He inhaled it. He waved his hand once more and mumbled, "Again." He guzzled the second cupful as fast as the first. Then he set the cup down on the table. He looked at me.

"OK, John, you've had your drink. You said you had something to tell us. You said it was important. Let's make this ridiculous trip out into the frigid night worthwhile," I said, annoyed, impatient.

He started talking, rambling really, but it was all the same drivel; he was repeating his same old tune. I looked at Stevens and shook my head.

"John!" I bellowed. "We don't have the time or the patience for this shit! What the fuck are we all doing here tonight? You said you had something new to tell me! Something important!"

I grabbed the copy of the *Daily Herald* off my desk and slammed it down on the table in front of him. I pointed to the picture of Rob Piest on page 3. I nearly put my finger through the table as I did it.

"Do you see this kid? Do you see him? This is a good kid! This is a good kid with good parents! He's missing!" I was screaming, pacing now. I left the paper on the table in front of him. "You called me for a reason, John. You said you had something to say to me, that you needed to talk. Now, what the fuck did you want to say? And don't give us any more of your tired, worn-out shit!"

Gacy looked at me through tired, bloodshot eyes. I could see him surrender. His demons were winning. He looked down at the paper in front of him, shoulders slumped, beaten. He was ready. He picked up the paper and pointed to the picture of Rob Piest.

"This boy," he said, gently tapping the picture with his fingertip. "This boy is dead. He's dead. This isn't the boy from the drugstore . . . but this boy is dead. He is in a river."

Time switched to slow motion. I looked at Stevens and then back at the pathetic, broken lump of a man in front of me. I guess I had some suspicions; if I was honest, they were there, nagging questions put there by Sullivan and others, the mayor. They were all so sure. But until that moment, I wanted to believe my client. I wanted him to tell me that he had driven Rob to the Greyhound station or that Rob was staying with Rossi or Cram and that Gacy had given him a job and that Rob wanted to leave home. Something. Something else.

The gravity of his statement was beginning to register. I looked at Stevens again, puzzled, then back at Gacy. I was shaking my head. Something wasn't right. "What the fuck are you talking about, John? That is Robby Piest, the Piest kid, the kid from the drugstore, the kid that everybody has been looking for. That's him."

Gacy looked at me. His sagging, dead, watery eyes pierced me.

"So . . . many," he softly murmured, barely a whisper. He dropped his head again, slowly shaking it from side to side. He looked back up again with a surprising, newfound sureness. He looked at Stevens . . . then back at me. I was caught in a dead stare.

"I have been the judge . . . jury . . . and executioner of many, many people. Now, I am going to be my own judge, jury, and executioner."

I looked at Stevens. He was white, like chalk, mouth agape, eyes bulging. As the words sank in, my heart started to pump harder and harder. The words . . . "many, many people" . . . those words . . . What on earth was this guy telling me? Then it hit me. That's what wasn't right. I knew something wasn't right. That was it. This guy . . . this guy sitting right in front of me . . . my client . . . this guy had killed so many people, so many kids, that he was confusing Rob Piest with one of the others . . . one of the many, many others.

My heart felt as though it was trying to pump motor oil instead of blood. I slowly sat down in my chair. "What are you trying to say, John? What exactly are you telling us?"

John started talking. He talked for hours. We just sat with our mouths open and listened.

"You guys have to let me do this my way," he began.

"I have to do this my way! I will be my own judge, jury, and executioner. OK, Sam, OK?" His words were slurred, and his eyes were vacant, bleary, dripping.

"What are you trying to say, John?" I whispered.

"I killed people," he mumbles. "Fucking male prostitutes. Greedy fuckin' liars! I never forced sex on anyone in my fucking life. Never! Never forced it. It was for money . . . most of the time. Money. It was always these greedy fuckin' hustlers . . . and then they would change their tune . . . say they wanted more, more, more money. Fuckin' liars. Mostly kids. Some men . . . maybe thirtyish. I don't know. I don't know them all!"

"Maybe thirty people?" I asked in disbelief. I can't imagine what my face looked like. I know my body was having a field day. It never ceases to amaze me how physical the reaction to some words can be. Like when someone suffers a great loss, there is a physiological response. People sometimes pass out. They cannot catch their breath. They hyperventilate. That was happening to me on a smaller scale. I wasn't sure what to think, what to do.

"No! Thirty years old . . . but yeah, yeah . . . maybe thirty of 'em. Maybe thirty. I'd say at least thirty."

That took my breath away.

"I buried them. I buried them all. Well, no, that's not right. I ran out of room, so some are in the river. The Des Plaines fucking River. The river.

"Want to know the first time I killed? I'll tell you about it. But, you gotta let me do this my way . . . my way . . . my fucking way.

"You can do that . . . right, Sam? Right . . . Leroy? Right? I'm gonna take care of this whole thing. I'll take care of it. I know what I have to do. I ain't coming back from this. This ain't no jail sentence. This is the ball game, the whole fuckin' ball game, ya know? OK, want to know about it? Want to? Want to?

"Hey, I want you guys to know something . . . I ain't no fag. I hate fuckin' fags. Nobody hates fags more than I do. Nobody. Got that? Got it? I told you that before, Sam. You already know that. You know that little piece of information . . . but I am liberal minded when it comes to sex. Liberal. So I could be considered bisexual. I could.

"Anyway . . . what happened was this. It was January 2 . . . maybe the third . . . but I think the second. Cuz, cuz . . . I took Carol out for New Year's. We stayed out late. Went to Bruno's and stayed there till at least three in the morning. Then we went home to my house. We were not married then. We were dating and . . . and . . . and . . . for some reason, my mom wasn't there. I was living at the Summerdale house, and my mom lived with me. But . . . but . . . she must have been staying at her sister's. Yeah, yeah . . . cuz she would not drive with anyone that was drinking—she didn't drive herself—but she didn't want to ride in a car with a drunk person. So she must have been staying with Leone or something like that. She wasn't there, though."

The rambling nature of his narrative was hard to follow. He jumped from subject to subject. However, we could not stop listening.

"We had sex that night . . . till dawn, me and Carol. In fact, she got pregnant from that night. She got pregnant, but then she had a miscarriage from that night. So then I took her home. I took her home at, like, at seven in the morning."

"What year are we talking about, John? How long ago was this?" I interjected.

"Oh . . . sorry . . . this was 1972, or maybe '74, no . . . the very first days of 1972. I remember cuz somebody died. Somebody died in my family. I can't remember who . . . but it had to have been on my father's side. It had to have been a relative of my dad because the funeral home was DeBrecht on Western Avenue. DeBrecht was for my dad's family. My dad's side uses that funeral home. I believe I left Carol at seven in the morning . . . this is Saturday morning, so . . . Friday was New Year's Eve, right? That's right, I think. So,

I go to the funeral . . . I mean the wake, and you always go back to someone's house for dinner. I had to have done that. I would say that I did do that. I don't remember everything, but I am sure that I was drinking at someone's house, some relative's house; they were all playing cards and drinking. Everybody always drinks a lot in that crowd, and they play cards for money, lots of money. After a while, the arguments start. This is a routine . . . it happens every time. I don't like to argue, so I say I'm gonna go. And I go. I leave my relative's house, and I decide to take a drive.

"It was twelve or one in the morning when I left. I was wandering around, driving around, and I went downtown. I was right in the Loop, right downtown. I was driving on Clark Street, and I parked on Clark down by the Greyhound bus station. I was down by the Greyhound bus station, and I run into this guy. And I'm trying to fill this in, trying to remember. It was a long time ago, and I was drinking that night; but in my head I can remember talking to this guy. I don't know his name. I never did, never asked.

"I guess I just said hi to him . . . started talking to him. I don't know the conversation verbatim. It's a little foggy . . . the memory. But I remember that he was saying he had time to kill . . . he said he had time to kill. He said he had missed a bus and he was stuck in town . . . or maybe he was laid over, but he had to kill time until noon . . . that would be noon the next afternoon . . . so . . . like . . . ten or eleven hours; and he was just fuckin' around, nothin' to do till then."

"What did he look like?" I asked, for no apparent reason. I couldn't believe what I was hearing. This guy was telling us about his first murder, the first of many. I was, I hate to admit, enthralled. It was like having a book read to you or watching a movie. It didn't seem real.

"I think about nineteen or twenty years old, blond headed. He had, I think, Levi's on, and uh, some sort of uh, uh . . . lumberjack . . . jacket-type thing and uh, uh, uh, large belt buckle on his pants.

His jacket or shirt was blue and white checks or green and white . . . I can't recall. Blond hair, short haircut, blue eyes, and like a flannel shirt . . . It's all kinda foggy, but I remember . . . I remember.

"He said he had time to kill. I said something about how I was just screwing around, just screwing around. And said, if you want a ride . . . you can ride with me, you can just ride around with me. And he said that would be cool.

"So, we were just riding around, rode down State Street. There were Christmas decorations. The State Street lights . . . all beautiful and shit. Just riding . . . and . . . I started the conversation. I said to him . . . I asked if he liked sex or something . . . if he had ever gotten blown or that . . . like, had a blowjob. And, I talked about sex stuff. I asked if he had ever gotten blown by a guy. He didn't seem to think there was anything wrong with that.

"He said he was hungry . . . hungry. We went to my house. We went out the Kennedy Expressway towards my house. And we went to my house. I said I'd make him some food. I made him some sausage. We had some drinks. We sat around eating and having a couple of drinks. This was sometime around . . . I'd say two in the morning."

"We went into the back bedroom. This was the one with the green carpeting, the one in the rear, not the present one, not the master bedroom with the red carpeting. This was the one with the green carpet and the twin beds. That was my room at that time. Plus, if my mom ever came home, then we would just hop in different beds . . . you know . . . we went back there, and we got into oral sex . . . or whatever. You know . . . ah . . . we blew each other, gave each other blowjobs."

I had to ask, don't know why, but I had to ask. "John, this was voluntary on both of your parts? He wanted to do this?"

"Fuck yeah! Fuck yes! He wasn't any less into it than I was. He had done it before . . . plenty. You can tell. I can tell. Besides, you really can't force someone to suck your dick, can you? Not really.

Maybe with a gun or something, but even then . . . think about it . . . they might . . . they could bite your fuckin' dick off, right? Clean off! In one quick bite! Like a fuckin' hot dog. Would you risk that? Who would risk that? You'd have to want a blowjob pretty fuckin' bad to risk that. I never forced anyone to have sex with me. Why would you? Why? What fun is that? Ya know? Who wants that shit? No fun. No fun.

"So anyway, then we fall asleep. Went to sleep. He was in one bed by then and me in the other. Then I wake up, and he has a knife. He's coming at me with a knife!"

"Wait a minute. He was coming at you . . . with a knife?" This didn't sound like a murder to me. I looked at Stevens. He didn't look like he thought it was a murder either. "What happened next?" I added.

"He tried to stab me. He fuckin' was trying to stab me!"

"Where did he get the knife?" I asked.

"From the kitchen. It was the knife I was cutting the sausage with—my knife, my kitchen knife. It was lying on the counter in the kitchen. He was just wearing his jeans, but no shirt, no socks, nothin' else, just pants. And he was coming at me. He was right on top of me. You know . . . arm raised in the air, knife clutched in his hand . . . he was trying to stab me. So, I grabbed at him, grabbed his wrist and wrestled him, pushed him off me. I startled him, surprised him, you know. He didn't think I was going to wake up. I was lucky I did cuz I'd be dead otherwise. He was some kind of hustler. Probably done that hundreds of times before, you know, go with a guy in a strange town, go have sex with him, wait for him to fall asleep . . . kill him. Whatever, I don't know. We didn't fight or anything. We had sex and fell asleep. So, this was some kind of thing of his. There was no reason for it. He was some kind of sleazy, greedy hustler. I wrestled him out of that room.

"I flew out of bed and knocked him off his feet. We fought and wrestled out of the room and all the way into the front bedroom, and uh . . . uh . . . then . . . uh, I think that's when I, uh . . . that's when I got stabbed, cuz that's what made me mad, cuz that's when I got the knife . . . took the knife from him and stabbed the fucker in his chest four or five times. I was bleeding on him, and he was bleeding, and I was worried that he was going to bleed all over my rug. That really made me mad. The son of a bitch was going to get blood all over my rug! But then I realized we had wrestled into the room with the wood floors, so it wasn't so bad. I could clean that."

John pushed his sleeve up and showed us a nasty scar on his arm.

"See this . . . you see that fucking scar? That's where he stabbed me or cut me . . . or whatever. That's what made me mad . . . the fuckin' guy was going to kill me. But, then he started . . . you know, after I got on top of him . . . I had my knees in his chest, and I was struggling to get the knife from him . . . that's when he started saying that he was sorry, that he really wasn't going to hurt me. That he didn't mean it. He didn't mean it . . . didn't fucking mean it . . . I was bleeding all over the guy from my arm. He said something like he didn't mean it or something. Stupid fuck! Dumb and stupid. I just kept stabbin' him till he stopped fighting. Then all you could hear was the, like, the gurgling of blood in his lungs or something, I don't know. There was gurgling, a gurgling sound.

"So, now I'm scared shitless, right? I didn't know what the hell to do. The first thing I went and did is I went into the bathroom, I think with the knife . . . yeah . . . cuz I washed the knife off and was washing my arm off, or was washing my arm and washing the knife, and I went and put the knife in the kitchen. Then I went back by him . . . uh . . . uh . . . I went back by where he was. I didn't know what to do with him so . . ."

"What about calling the police, John? That is when you would have wanted to call the police, don't you think?" I was dumb-founded at what I was hearing.

"I don't know, Sam, I was scared. You know . . . I was scared cuz I had been in trouble before . . . you know . . . in prison before.

I thought I couldn't call the police because of that . . . that whole thing. I don't know. I don't know. I didn't know what to do. Then I see that we are right in front of the closet, where the trap . . . the trapdoor to the basement . . . the crawl space is . . . and I just opened the trapdoor and shoved him . . . I just threw him down there."

"John! You acted in self-defense! Why the hell didn't you just call the goddamn cops?" I couldn't believe this.

"Sam, I don't know, I don't fuckin' know. I was fresh out of prison. I was scared out of my mind. I just threw him down in the crawl space, and then I started, you know, uh, uh, I started collecting all of his stuff, picking up all of his clothes and stuff. That was . . . his clothes were still in the bedroom . . . on the floor in the bedroom and on the dresser, and his coat was in the living room—it was still in the living room. Now, I gotta pick up Carol later that day and take her to the wake. Sunday . . . she was going to go with me . . . you know . . . on the second day . . . the last day of the wake, and then the funeral is on Monday. I can't have this fuckin' guy in the middle of all this. I want him gone. I just don't want to think about all that . . . you know? I can't think about it. So, I clean up all his stuff . . . and he was gone. He was in the crawl space . . . but he was gone, right? I'll worry about that later. I'll worry about that later, ya know? So, I leave him down there, and I straighten up and get rid of his clothes. I found a locker key in his pants pocket . . . like from the Greyhound station. That was in his pocket. Plus, my arm is cut to shit. I didn't know what to do. I really didn't know what to do.

"So, then I do pick up Carol, and she sees this cut on my arm and tells me I might need stitches, and she wants to know how it happened . . . fuck . . . what a mess. So, I tell her . . . I told everyone I was cutting carpet, and, uh . . . uh . . . uh, I slashed it with one of those razor things, those razor knives . . . and that I cut it that way. We go to the wake, and then . . . after . . . we go to the hospital. We went to . . . the wake was on Western Avenue at DeBrecht, I said that . . . I told you that. So, we just drove down Western to St.

Elizabeth's Hospital. We went down to the hospital and got the cut looked at. They put a butterfly stitch or a bandage. Then we went back to the wake. Also, my sister—my sister Joanne—said I should go to the hospital, and she's a nurse . . . she's a nurse, so, uh . . . uh . . . uh, her and Carol were both saying that I should go to the hospital, so we did, and then we came back to the wake.

"Then after the wake, we went out with my sister. We were out for dinner or something like that with my sister, and I . . . kinda like . . . well, I wasn't thinking about that fucker in the crawl space. He was out of my mind . . . like . . . so we just went out to dinner with Carol and my sister Joanne."

"You didn't have any guilt, no remorse?" Obviously, this was not a normal person. I remember that as my assessment at the time. This guy needed help. He was not all there.

"No. I just . . . it just was completely blocked out. Did . . . did . . . didn't think nothin' of it—not at all. There was nothing. That was the same with the others too. I didn't feel nothin'. Most of these assholes were hustlers, like that first guy. They killed themselves anyway. Most of them killed themselves. I'll tell you. But after I got home from dinner with my sister and Carol, I . . . I . . . I was just, tired, you know. So, I went to bed, and in the morning I went down in that crawl and buried the guy, ya know, buried him down there. It wasn't easy either . . . no way . . . cuz . . . cuz . . . cuz it's really short down there. Like it's about two and a half feet to the bottom of the floor joists . . . those big joists that run the length of the house. You have to chop with a spade and kind of dig with your hands, or what not. But I did it. I got it done. The ground was loose down there, and there was an odor because of the wet clay. There were four houses in that area, on our block, that had to have sump pumps due to the moisture. There was always an odor down there since we moved in. Four houses in a low spot on that block . . . we were one of the four. We never could completely get rid of that odor.

"I remember that stupid belt buckle, that big belt buckle. He was buried with his pants on and that big belt buckle. I never asked him his name, and if he ever said it, I never got it. I never knew it. Just a greedy, stupid hustler. I put him beyond the uh . . . uh, he was beyond the second supporting post . . . uh . . . uh . . . going east. I can show you. I can show you guys. I'll show you everything. I know exactly where they all are. We can go over there."

That was the last thing in the world that I wanted to do. I looked at Stevens. The look on his face was telling. I changed the subject. "So, John, I guess you are saying that Rob Piest is also dead. You said that, right?" We were all looking at one another. Gacy was not in good shape.

"You mean the kid in that picture. Yeah, yeah . . . he is. He is dead. He is in the river."

After he said that, he went somewhere else in his mind.

"Carol moved in a month later . . . in February of 1972. She brought her fuckin' mother with her, the bitch. I didn't like her—not Carol . . . I liked Carol. I hated her fuckin' mother, though. Plus, Carol had two kids . . . two little girls. We got married in July of that year, and my mom moved out because she didn't think there should be two women running the house. Carol's mother was supposed to move out in August, after her divorce. In fact, my mother wanted her to move in with her . . . my mom wanted Carol's mother and her to move in together. But that never happened. That bitch stayed with us for a year. Well, in June . . . June 1973 . . . I had a stroke or somethin'. . . . I almost died. Dr. Levy came out to the house . . . he was my doctor—he was my doctor all my life—and he was so pissed off because it was four in the morning and I was having this attack, or what not, and Carol's mother never even got up out of bed. She just laid in the bed, the bitch. And that's why I had the goddamn attack in the first place. Carol and I were arguing about her still being in the house. She had to go after that, and I had to kick her out. She had to be evicted . . . kicked out."

"But you were talking about that kid in the picture . . . the boy in that picture. He wanted a job. He wanted to work for me. He wanted to buy a Jeep. I really don't know what happened there. That wasn't like me. Normally, I would be out cruisin' . . . you know, looking for someone to have sex with . . . late at night. I don't know. That kid wanted a job. He said that he would do anything for money. He was all hopped up on buying this car . . . a Jeep or some shit. I thought he was hustling me. We went back to my house. It didn't go well at all. He wasn't a hustler . . . he was just a kid. He was just a kid. I really don't know what happened there.

"After that first guy, the guy that I just told you about, the Greyhound guy, I got married—you know, pretty soon after that, I got married to Carol. She moved in and then we got married. I wasn't with any guys after that for a long time, a long time, ya know. I had a wife and two little girls and a fuckin' mother-in-law. It was like Grand fucking Central Station around there. I was working my ass off trying to build up the business and stuff—you know, trying to get jobs and doin' jobs, working all over the city. Plus, I was volunteering for everything with the party, the Democratic Party in my neighborhood, and I started having my parties. Like, I would have these "yard parties." But they were bigger than that. They were huge parties that politicians and everyone would come to. We would have hundreds of people, sometimes like four hundred people—four hundred people. And I had my self-made family . . . . I called it self-made family. I had two beautiful little daughters, Tammy and April. They were Carol's kids, you know, but I loved them too. They were like my kids too. In 1974, we had the Luau party, a party with a Luau theme, grass skirts, and shit like that—Hawaiian, ya know. People dressed up Hawaiian.

"In 1975, we had the Western barbecue party, and it was a big one. Hundreds of people came. But by then, Carol and I were fighting all the time. It was becoming clear that we would probably not stay together. Other good stuff was happening, though. The business was good, and my political connections were better. I got on the county board. But I also got divorced. I had been having sex with guys for a pretty long time, and I had learned that it was pretty easy to pick up young boys in the city . . . like in Boystown area by Diversey and Broadway, also in Bughouse Square and in Uptown. These areas were good. Uptown had poor kids that needed money real bad, and Bughouse Square was full of hustlers that were there to sell their shit . . . sell themselves. Now, that didn't make me no fag, though. I still had sex with Carol . . . sometimes . . . not that often . . . but we did till we started fightin' all the time. I hated her mom . . . plus, I was never home. I worked ten, twelve, maybe fifteen hours, and then I would go downtown a lot . . . cruising around in the middle of the night. I drank a lot and smoked pot. Sometimes, I would bring those kids back to my garage. My garage was my private place. Carol rarely went out there. After she was gone, I could bring people home as much as I wanted to.

"Also, Carol was going off to stay with friends a lot, and once she went down to stay with my mom in Arkansas, after Ma broke her hip. So, she wasn't there a lot . . . even before we got divorced. That's when this thing happened . . . this thing I have to tell you.

"I had this kid working for me, John Butkovitch. Carol knew him. Little John, she called him. Cuz . . . you know, I was Big John . . . he was Little John. He was at the house all the time, all the time . . . playin' with the kids, you know, over for dinner. Carol liked him. He was with me for about a year or so when we got into an argument over money. Money . . . ya know . . . the root of all fuckin' evil. He said I owed him money. He said I owed him back pay, but I . . . I . . . I didn't. I . . . I . . . I showed the kid where he owed me money. He owed me money. I didn't owe him money. He had this apartment that his dad got for him, and he bought a rug and some stuff on my account, on the PDM account, so he could get a contractor discount and shit, you know. He was fixin' up his place, and he got carpeting. Now, he was paying me back just fine. The bill started at around $600, and he had paid it down to $300. So, I was fine with all this. No problem, as far as I was concerned. But John got it into his head that I owed him a couple a hundred bucks or somethin', and this was bullshit, I tell you—pure bullshit. But he comes over talkin' shit, brought a couple of buddies with him, yellin' and screaming about how I better pay him, or there is going to be trouble. Like I'm gonna get my ass kicked. I just got everyone high. We smoked some pot . . . drank some beers. We calmed the whole thing down. No big deal, you know . . . Next thing I know, he's lying on my floor . . . dead.

"I was cruising—you know, driving around, just driving around. This is the same day . . . only at night . . . the middle of the night. John, Little John, had left my house with those guys, all his buddies. They all left, and they were all drunk and high when they left, and everything was fine. I thought. That's what I thought. Then I see him in Uptown, while I'm drivin' around. He shows up. He's like in the street, in the middle of the fuckin' street, waving at me and yelling that he wants to talk to me. We are not through yet about this money thing. He's in the middle of Sheridan Road, and he is ranting about money. So, I tell him to get in . . . inside the car . . . he's blockin' traffic. We go back to my house to drink . . . you know . . . drink some more. Carol's not home, so . . . what the fuck, right? Now, we start drinking, and he's hammered, he's real drunk, and I'm feeling no pain at all. I'm drunk too, I guess, you know. And the damn argument starts up again, you know, all over again. So, then, we start fighting, arguing back and forth. I got a heart condition, plus, he's a kid, a lot younger than me. So, I trick him into a pair of handcuffs that I use for my clown act. I'm a clown, you know, a registered clown. I do parties. You knew that, I think, Leroy. Did you know that, Sam? Did I tell you that?"

I just shook my head. I didn't want to interrupt, frankly. Continue the story, I was thinking.

"So, he's in these cuffs. I tricked him. But now he is very pissed off cuz I'm not taking the cuffs off of him. I don't want to take them off until he sobers up, stops screaming at me about this fucking money, you know, stops his goddamn yelling. I don't want him hittin' me or some kinda shit like that. I don't need any kind of shit like that. Now, this is where it gets a little foggy. I'm not exactly sure how this all happened, but I must have strangled him—you know, with this rope."

My client was obviously a bit drunk as he sat there. I had just watched him guzzle about sixteen ounces of straight whiskey right in front of me, two eight-ounce cupfuls. Plus, he was drinking previously that night. But this wasn't just a drunk man on a rant. We were listening to a killer, a true killer. I could never describe properly how offhandedly he said those words. "I must have strangled him—you know, with this rope." It was as if he was telling us that he had brushed his teeth that morning, mentioning some kind of inconsequential part of the overall point that he was making. Stevens and I could not believe what we were hearing. We just kept looking at one another, awestruck.

"Yeah, he was laying on the floor when I woke up. He was blue in the face, ya know, like they say, and he had a rope around his neck and the handcuffs—he still had the handcuffs on. I don't remember everything, but I think I tricked him, you know, cuz that is what I did with a lot of the others. I would use a rope, the rope trick, and I used it kinda like a tourniquet around their necks. That's how I would do it. That's what I did with that kid you were pointing to, that kid in the paper. What's his name? Robby . . . or somethin' like that. I did the rope trick on him. He was crying, scared. I didn't really mean to scare him. I thought he was something very different. I thought he was a hustler like the others. But, really, he was just a kid. The kid had his hand on the door to leave. He even said that he was so scared that he thought I was going to kill him. I knew I couldn't let him leave. I knew I couldn't . . . That would not have been good. That would not have worked out. He was too scared . . . too fuckin' scared. I thought he lied to me, but maybe he didn't. Maybe he wasn't lying. Maybe he just wanted a job, ya know?

"These other kids weren't like him, that's for fucking sure. They were hustlers, greedy little liars and hustlers. One was a bigger liar than the next. I used to go down to the park, Washington Park. They called it Bughouse Square, and these kids would offer blow-jobs for money. Sex for money, and then they would try to hike up the price after they had already told me a certain price. They would try to hike it up, you know, raise the price up. Extortion, plain and simple. Or, this was something else, I would take these guys back to my house, and they would see that I was a successful businessman in a nice neighborhood, and they would figure out that I couldn't let everyone know that I was bisexual or shit like that. They could see that I wouldn't want my neighbors to know about these guys. They could see that. And then they would start to threaten to tell the neighbors. Right then, they would say they were going to go right out and tell the neighbors everything. They should have kept their fucking mouths shut. They didn't know who they were dealing with. So, they would get the rope trick. I wasn't afraid of the neighbors. Lots of them knew me. They knew what I did. They have eyes. They can see my house from theirs. I just hate fucking liars, greedy lying homos. Fuckin' fagots!

"I had to get rid of this guy, though. I had to get rid of Little John. Then Carol, before I could do that, Carol came home. I had wrapped him in a tarp and put him in the garage . . . in the garage, ya know. Then Carol came home, so I couldn't bury that one in the crawl space. So, I have to figure somethin' else out. So I buried him out in the garage. There was already a place that I was gonna use for drainage out there. So, yeah, he is out there.

"There . . . well . . . after I got divorced. There are a lot under the house . . . like out under the bedrooms, down there. I can show you. I'll show you."

"We did some diggin' down there. Rossi did a lot. He was down there for eight hours one day. He was down diggin' trenches all day. I said they were for tiles. I told him tiles . . . you know . . . for the smell. We always got that musty smell when it rained. So, Rossi dug up the trenches for that.

"There was this kid with a weird spelling of his name. He spelled it S-z-y-c, but you said it *Sink* . . . like a sink, you know, in the kitchen. We were partying, drinking, smoking pot, taking pills, ya know. And everyone was runnin' around half-naked. See, this guy was a female impersonator and a dancer. I don't know . . . I don't know. It's all in a fog, you know? It's not that I don't want to remember . . . I try . . . but I can't remember it all. We did a lot of drinking . . . see . . . a lot of drinkin' and a lot of drugs. But we were partying, and I went to bed, and when I woke up, that kid was lying on the floor in the other room, ya know . . . the one with the red carpet. He was on the floor. He was naked on the floor, ya know. And Rossi had dug those trenches in the crawl, so he went down there. I threw him down there.

"Rossi was in the living room . . . sleeping on the couch. He wanted that kid's car, so we went down . . . the car was parked on Clark Street, so we just drove down there and got it. We just drove there in the morning and looked for the white Plymouth Satellite with the banged-up fender. It was parked on Clark across from the Newbury Theatre, right there on Clark Street, right down there. And Rossi drove it, and I drove my car and brought it back to my house. Now, I said I wanted $300 for that car. Rossi said he didn't have it, but we worked that out, and that became Rossi's car. He drove that car. There was a bunch of stuff in the trunk. There were license plates and women's clothing, weights, a television, and jewelry and stuff . . . lots of stuff. So, we cleaned that all out . . . all of that shit . . . and Rossi drove that car. So, that guy is down in the crawl space. He is down there. I threw him down there and put him in one of those trenches and covered him up. I only dug like five of those holes down there. I had those kids dig the rest. They dug them for me. There was trenches dug down there for the drainage . . . for the drainage.

"So, there are lots of guys down there. They are all in that basement . . . that crawl space down there under the house, ya know. Maybe twenty or thirty. Some are in that crawl, but a few are in the river. I put some in the river . . . five . . . ya know . . . it was five of them that I took out to the river. There were five of them . . . and that kid that you were asking about is one of those five. He was the last one. We can go there. I'll show you. That kid was not supposed to happen, ya know? But when it did . . . I had to go out to the bridge.

"Yeah, when I took him out there, I heard that a smokey was around, so I had to drive back and forth. You know, go down to the next cloverleaf and turn around. Then I figured out that it was me . . . ya know . . . it was my car. Oh, and there was a barge too. I didn't want to drop the fucker on that."

Gacy was starting to slur his words even more than he did at the beginning of this diatribe. His whole demeanor was beginning to wilt. It was clear to me that the massive amounts of alcohol that he had ingested both in front of us and before he arrived were beginning to beat the shit out of him. He was not going to last much longer. How right I turned out to be.

"There was this little fucker from Franklin Park—Joe or something . . . I forget. My memory is for shit . . . total shit. I cannot hardly remember anything . . . nothing. Sometimes I wake up in the morning and find strangled kids in my house, dead strangled kids, and I have no idea how they got there . . . no fuckin' idea what happened. I remember heading down to the park . . . Washington . . . you know . . . Bughouse Square . . . I told you that. I said that already. I remember goin' there, but I don't remember coming home, no idea . . . ya know . . . how I would get my ass home or what happened while I was out. But I have to get the bodies out of there. They don't belong there . . . ya know . . . ya know . . .

They don't belong there, do they? Sometimes, I get little flashes of memory, though. Like watchin' a movie that isn't a good copy. It keeps coming in and out, ya know. It is in bits and pieces . . . bits and pieces . . . little bits and pieces of life."

His rambling was getting scatological, and his tongue was getting thicker as he continued on. I was watching a man becoming unglued, sluggish. His chin was getting closer to his chest, his eyelids heavy, his head bouncing with every word as happens only with a drunk. The booze was catching up with him in a big way. I wanted him to clarify his rambling monologue. Mainly, I suppose, because I couldn't believe it all. I'm sure part of me didn't want to believe it. I looked at him dead in the eye. "John," I said, "are you telling us that you killed . . . you killed thirty people . . . thirty kids? That is what you are saying, right? You killed all these kids and buried them under your house?"

"Well . . . not all of them . . . not all are in the crawl space . . . ya know . . . ah . . . some are in the river . . . you know . . . you know . . . ah . . . in the river . . . like I said.

"I'll take care of it, though. I'll be my own judge, jury, and executioner. I'll be my own . . . I'll handle this myself. I'll take care of this . . . I'll take care of this. I have to handle this my own way."

I could feel my own heart beating, sense my own breathing. I looked at Stevens. We were both in a clinical state of shock. He looked back, eyes wide, head slowly moving from side to side. He could have been the bad actor in a worse movie watching the mummy approaching.

Finally, the booze won. Gacy's chin hit his chest. He was sound asleep.

13

THE LAWYER IN me immediately kicked in. I began to think solely in my client's best interest.

"He needs immediate psychiatric help," I said. We had to find him a shrink—right now. I looked at my watch. It was 3:30 a.m. *Fat chance*, I thought.

"It's three thirty in the morning, Sam." Stevens was looking at me like I was as crazy as Gacy.

"We gotta try . . . hospitals are open all night. I know, I used to work in one, a long time ago. This guy is going to kill himself. You heard him, Leroy. He plans to off himself—'I'll be my own judge, jury, and executioner.' He's going to commit suicide. What else could that mean? Right? He is a danger to himself and others. He can be committed. That's the standard."

Gacy wasn't going anywhere. He was comatose, snoring and snorting, in a state of complete slumber—let's be honest, he was passed out—sitting upright but slouched into his chair in such a way as to keep him from falling.

We both got on phones. It seemed a little crazy, but what else were we going to do? If he were having a heart attack, he would need a medical doctor. He was having what I would describe as a complete breakdown; he needed a head doctor. We had to at least try. We had to try something.

While Gacy snored, while Albrecht and his partner, Dave Hachmeister, killed time just thirty feet away on the other side of a piece of plate glass, we feverishly called hospital after hospital, begging to speak with anyone in the psych department, getting rebuffed time after time. Phone books were open on the conference table, cigarette smoke hung in the air, sleeves were rolled up, and the coffeepot was working overtime. We used whatever clout we could pretend we had, throwing our law degrees around as if they meant something to the poor receptionists who were unlucky enough to have taken the call. Finally, believe it or not, we found a psychiatrist at a hospital on the North Side of Chicago—Louis A. Weiss Memorial Hospital—who said that he would meet with us at 9:00 a.m. He seemed to understand the urgency.

Stevens and I decided to take turns going home to shower and shave, thereby leaving one of us to monitor our client. Neither one of us knew what Gacy would do when he came to. But we had a plan. All we could do was attempt to implement it.

Stevens was first to leave.

I sat alone with John Gacy, who sounded a little like a walrus in heat.

I pulled a few books on commitment of persons into a locked facility off of a shelf. I couldn't concentrate on the written word, however, no matter how hard I tried. I thought over and over again about that with which I was going to be faced, about what I had been told. It was a heavy burden. I was trying to play the tape out to its logical end. What was this going to be like? Clearly, my life was about to change. I was defense counsel for a serial killer.

John stirred. He snorted and rubbed drool from the corner of his mouth.

Then it happened. John suddenly sat up—stiff as a board, perfect posture. He opened his eyes and stared out into nothing. The look in his eyes was unlike any that I had ever seen. He was awake, it seemed, but not exactly.

"John?" I stood in front of him, looked at his eyes. They were vacant, no personality behind them, no person. It was if he didn't see me although I was standing right in front of him. I waved my hand in front of his face.

"John! You OK?" I wasn't yelling, but I was speaking at much higher decibels than normal conversation. He ignored me, totally. He started to stand . . . and I'll be damned to hell if he didn't put his arms out in front of him like a terrible movie's attempt to indicate sleepwalking. It was almost funny. It would have been funny if this guy hadn't just admitted to killing twenty or thirty people. He was standing now, like Frankenstein, arms extended, stiff as a board, everything, his whole body, rigid. His eyes were rolling around in his head. His eyelids were fluttering rapidly.

"John!" This time I yelled. I was waving both arms, palms facing out, in front of his face. Nothing, no response. I had a baseball bat that was a memento from Comiskey Park, my beloved White Sox. I picked it up and gently put it up to his chest. It looked like he was leaning on it, being led by it. He started walking forward. This had to have been a sight. Gacy was maybe five feet nine. I am five feet two if I stand up straight. He was walking forward, and I was walking backward, bat extended. We looked like Quasimodo and Phoebus.

"John! Can you hear me? John!"

I led him to the couch in my office and herded him gently down onto it. He lay down like a five-year-old, curled up, and went right back to sleep, as though nothing had happened. I was surprised he didn't put his thumb in his mouth. The only time I had seen anything like it before was with little kids that wander in a half-sleep state at the direction of their parents into a bed. This whole damn night was becoming surreal, absolutely fucking surreal!

"Well, at least we won't have a problem getting this guy safely behind locked doors in a nice psych ward," I mumbled to myself. I decided that Gacy was safe where he was and that I would check on the Delta boys out front in my lobby. I brought a pot of coffee with me. I figured they deserved it. They had been following this nutcase for days. They probably had a few stories.

"How are you guys doing out here?" I asked. "Want some coffee? He's sound asleep and will likely be that way for a while."

When Stevens returned, it was my chance to get a shower and a change of clothes. I told Stevens that I would be back as soon as possible. I told him about the "Frankenstein" incident and showed him where the bat was.

When I got home, I said to my wife, Mary, "This case is going to be big—really big. You remember the Richard Speck case? Well, this case is going to make that case look like a misdemeanor. I cannot tell you much cuz of the privilege, but get ready. This is going to be a big case, and it is about to break wide open. The shit is about to hit the fan."

That actually turned out to be an enormous understatement.

When I returned to the office, Gacy was still passed out, and the boys from Des Plaines were still sitting in the outer lobby of my office. Actually, Albrecht was lying down on the floor trying to catch a nap. It didn't seem to be working because he greeted me with a smile as I came through the doors.

Stevens said that all was well. Gacy hadn't moved.

We sat there planning how we were going to take our client immediately to Weiss Memorial Hospital, where he would be evaluated and a decision would be made to admit him. That would give us time to breathe, and then on Friday we would have our hearing. It was a good plan. We were proud. We had somehow succeeded on behalf of our client and had made these arrangements, as unlikely as that seemed, at 3:30 a.m. This was all going to work out.

The one variable that we had not planned on was the head-strong Mr. Gacy.

When Gacy awoke, he was Lazarus rising from the dead. It took a while for him to get his bearings. He looked around at his strange surroundings, bewildered, like a lost child.

"Shit," he groaned, "I slept here . . . all night? What time is it?"

"It's a little after seven, John. We have got a big morning ahead. We found a place that will take you. We have to take you to a hospital. You have an appointment at 9:00 a.m."

It's funny. I had this naive belief that Gacy was simply going to accept my advice, that he was going to appreciate all the trouble that Stevens and I had gone through on his behalf. That was a mistake.

"What the fuck are you guys talking about? Hospital? I got shit to do today. What in the fuck are you guys talking about?" Gacy looked honestly perplexed, confused.

"John, you told us some heavy shit last night. Don't you remember?"

"Remember what, Sam? What the fuck is with you two guys this morning?" John wasn't kidding. He had no clue as to what we meant, what we were talking about.

"Look, John, there are two coppers waiting patiently for you out in our lobby. You came here last night with this urgent, overwhelming need to talk. Are you saying that you don't remember anything about what you told us last night?"

Stevens and I just looked at one another, incredulous. I thought last night was surreal. This was beyond surreal, beyond description. We were sitting in a room with a man that had confessed to the murder of twenty, maybe thirty, people. He had told us that his basement or crawl space or whatever you call it was a fucking graveyard, a gruesome graveyard filled with young bodies. And now . . . he didn't remember? I could not believe my own ears. I finally knew what people meant when they said that. I honestly could not believe my own ears.

That's when I realized just how fucked in the head this guy, my client, actually was. I don't care how drunk or high a person is—for chrissakes, you cannot possibly forget that you confessed to murder . . . can you? That's not possible, is it? I must have looked like some kind of cartoon character, the picture of confusion. I put a hand on each of his shoulders and looked him straight in the eye.

"John," I said slowly, deliberately, "you told us everything. You told us about the crawl space."

Gacy, again the confused child, kept looking back and forth, first at Stevens, then at me, then back again for a very long minute. Then he said, "Oh . . . ah . . . I . . . I . . . I told . . . I told you guys about that, huh? I told you about that?"

"Yeah, John, you told us everything. You told us about the crawl space, about the river. You talked for hours, John. You told us everything."

He just shook his head slowly from side to side while he took it all in. He was a study in befuddlement. Then his face took on a complete change. He became determined or something. It wasn't readable.

"Well, I can't think about this right now. I've got things to do today. I've got shit to take care of, you know—work to do, shit to do."

With that, John Wayne Gacy stood up, looked around for his coat, picked it up, and started heading for the door. I grabbed his arm.

"You need help, John, you need lots of help. We made an appointment for you. You have an appointment with a psychiatrist this morning. You should keep that appointment. We will . . . Stevens and I will drive you."

He looked at me. All he said was, "I can't, Sam. I gotta do this my way. I gotta go. I gotta go."

He turned and walked out of the office with the two members of his tail scrambling to their feet and rushing out behind him.

14

A T THE DES Plaines police headquarters, Terry Sullivan and members of the investigation team were feverishly putting together a complaint for a new search warrant. A review of the newly existing evidence was bolstering hopes of procuring said warrant and allowing for a further search of Gacy's home. On this Thursday morning, four days before Christmas and just one day before the hearing on the petition for a TRO, the mood was much better than in days past, because everyone believed that a warrant was imminent.

Now, they had the photo receipt.

They also had something else.

It seems that during one of the times that Gacy invited members of the surveillance team into his home for dinner and drinks, Officer Robert Schultz, a member of the Deltas, smelled something—an odor that he believed he recognized. This revelation came to Officer Schultz—and to him alone, in spite of the fact that dozens of members of the search team had crawled all over that house during the first search on December 13, including into the crawl space, and never mentioned anything specific about an odor. In spite of the fact that Lieutenant Kozenczak and Officer Pickell were in the house on the night following Rob Piest's disappearance and never mentioned anything specific about an odor. In spite of the fact that Gacy's house was essentially an open office for his company, where employees were in and out of the home all the time, basically on a daily basis, and no specific odor was ever mentioned. In spite of the fact that Mr. Gacy had yearly parties to which literally hundreds of people came and during which his house was open to one and all, and nobody ever seemed to complain specifically about an odor. In spite of all of that, Officer Schultz was now willing to swear, under penalty of perjury, that he smelled the odor of putrefied human bodies in that house.

This was a gamble on the part of the prosecution because an odor, a bad odor, can be caused by so many different things. It is next to impossible to distinguish between the odor of a dead human body and the odor of the carcass of an animal—a rat, a raccoon, a bat, the list goes on. If every house that had an unusual odor emanating from it was subject to search, almost any house could be searched. That could be the reason that there is a multibillion-dollar industry in products that claim to rid houses of all the various odors that they all seem to have.

Nonetheless, the members of the investigation team wanted into that house; and they wanted into that house before Friday, before the hearing on the TRO, and they were willing to do whatever it took to accomplish that goal. Therefore, they literally drove the complaint for search warrant over to the home of Judge Marvin J. Peters on Thursday night and had him sign the search warrant at 7:15 p.m. The gamble paid off, by the way. The complaint for search warrant read as follows:

SAM L. AMIRANTE AND DANNY BRODERICK

COMPLAINT FOR SEARCH WARRANT

Joseph Kozenzak, officer of the Des Plaines Police Dept. complainant
now appears before the undersigned judge of the Circuit Court of Cook County and
requests the issuance of a search warrant to search (the person of _____
John W. Gacy M/W 5'-9" 195 Lbs. Brown hair Blue eyes
_____ and

8213 W. Summerdale, Norridge, Ill. Located in Cook County
(Premises, City and State)
and seize the following instruments, articles and things: the body of Robert Piest and/or
remains thereof

which have been used in the commission of, or which constitute evidence of the
offense of _____MURDER

Complainant says that he has probable cause to believe, based upon the
following facts, that the above listed things to be seized are now located upon the
(person and) premises set forth above:

I, Detective Lt. Joseph Kozenzak of the Des Plaines Police Dept., have been investi-

gating the disappearance of Robert J. Piest, M/W 15 DOB: 16 Mar 63 5'-8" tall brown

hair with a slim build. During the course of my investigation evidence was gathered

through a search warrant indicating that the missing boy, Piest, was in the residence

belonging to John W. Gacy located at 8213 W. Summerdale, Norridge, Ill. within

48 hours after he was reported missing from Nisson Drugs at 1920 Touhy Ave. in Des

Plaines. The search warrant referred to above was the search warrant execuited on

13 Dec 78 at 8213 W. Summerdale Ave. Norridge, Ill. signed Judge Marvin J. Peters.

Recovered during that search was a customer reciept #36119 from a film developing

envelope with the name and address of Nisson's Pharmany stamped on it in ink. Further

_____
Complainant

Subscribed and sworn to before me on _____ 12-21 _____ 1978

_____
Judge

153

JOHN WAYNE GACY

investigation revealed that this receipt had last been in the possession of
Robert Piest, prior to the time he had disappeared.
        immediately

On December 21, 1978 I had occasion to speak to Officer Robert Schultz, Star #215
of the Des Plaines police department. Officer Schultz has been a Des Plaines police
officer for the past eight and one-half years. He told me that on Tuesday,
December 19, 1978 at 7:30 p.m., he was at the John Gacy residence at 8213 W. Summerdale, Norridge, Ill. on surveillance assignment. At that time, John Gacy approached
Officer Schultz's police vehicle and asked him if he would like to enter his residence. Officer Schultz responded in the affirmative and entered the Gacy residence
via the kitchen entrance with Mr. Gacy. Once inside Officer Schultz immediately
detected an odor similar to that of a putrified human body. Officer Schultz further
indicated that during his tenure as a Des Plaines police officer, he has smelled
the odor of at least forty (40) putrified human bodies, and that the odor he detected
in the Gacy residence smelled similar to the odor of putrified bodies he has smelled
in the past.

Attached hereto and incorporated by reference is the search warrant referred to in
paragraph one, i.e., the search warrant bearing the State's Attorney's Office number
78-1-003792, which was issued on December 13, 1978.

For the above-mentioned reasons, I pray that the court find probable cause and permit
this search warrant to issue.

Lt. Joseph Kozenczak
COMPLAINANT

SUBSCRIBED AND SWORN TO BEFORE ME ON ___12-21___, 19_78_

154

investigation revealed that this receipt had last been immediately in the possession of Robert Piest prior to the time he had disappeared.

On December 21, 1978 I had occasion to speak to Officer Robert Schultz, Star #215 of the Des Plaines police department. Officer Schultz has been a Des Plaines police officer for the past eight and one-half years. He told me that on Tuesday, December 19, 1978 at 7:30 p.m., he was at the John Gacy residence at 8213 W. Summerdale, Norridge, Ill. on surveillance assignment. At that time, John Gacy approached Officer Schultz's police vehicle and asked him if he would like to enter his residence. Officer Schultz responded in the affirmative and entered the Gacy residence via the kitchen entrance with Mr. Gacy. Once inside Officer Schultz immediately detected an odor similar to that of a putrified human body. Officer Schultz further indicated that during his tenure as a Des Plaines police officer, he has smelled the odor of at least forty (40) putrified human bodies, and that the odor he detected in the Gacy residence smelled similar to the odor of putrified bodies he has smelled in the past.

Attached hereto and incorporated by reference is the search warrant referred to in paragraph one, i.e., the search warrant bearing the State's Attorney's Office number 78-1-003792, which was issued on December 13, 1978.

For the above-mentioned reasons, I pray that the court find probable cause and permit this search warrant to issue.

Lt. Joseph Kozenczak
COMPLAINANT

12-21   19 78

SUBSCRIBED AND SWORN TO BEFORE ME ON _____

There was a reason for the urgency in obtaining the search warrant of Mr. Gacy's home other than the impending hearing on Friday morning—a good reason. John Wayne Gacy had been arrested.

———————————

JOHN GACY LEFT my office early on Thursday morning, very much against my advice and the advice of Leroy Stevens. He hurried out past Albrecht and Hachmeister and tore off southbound on Prospect Avenue, with an unmarked squad in tow and others on the way. Everyone involved in the case seemed to sense that this day would be different from the past several days, different from any other day of the investigation. Radios were squawking, and plans were being thrown together concerning this particular day.

Gacy drove in his inimitable style, speeding through populated areas and school zones like they weren't there, all at a time when the town of Park Ridge was waking up, moving about, people rushing to work, school buses picking up small children.

John's first stop was the Shell gas station, where he had his business account. The owner, John Lucas, was a friend and business associate. It was clear from a distance that John was not himself. He was walking around stoop shouldered and hollow, obviously in some sort of funk. Something was wrong. Albrecht and Hachmeister didn't know what happened during the night in my office, but they were sure it was something significant.

"It's over," Gacy said to Lucas. "Those guys are going to kill me." He said this while pointing to the boys from Des Plaines.

"What the fuck are you talking about, John? You don't look so good, ya know? What's wrong with you?"

"My life is over, man . . . my life is over. Listen, don't take no more charges on my account . . . unless it's me, ya hear me? No more charges."

Gacy started popping pills as soon as he left the office, Valiums, and they were starting to kick in. It wasn't enough that he was hungover as hell, that he had been drinking all night long, and that he hadn't fully slept it off. Now he was gulping down pharmaceuticals like candy. He walked up to Lucas's employee, the kid that was pumping his gas, Lance Jacobson. Gacy stuffed a plastic baggy full of joints into Jacobson's pocket—in plain sight of the Deltas.

"Take these. I don't need them. Take them, Lance."

Jacobson tried to give the baggy back to Gacy more than once, but he wouldn't take it. He, Jacobson, didn't feel like getting busted by one of the obvious cops that went everywhere Gacy went; so he gave the baggy to his boss, hoping his boss would know what to do with it. Lucas, treating the baggy like a hot potato, then gave the baggy to Officer Hachmeister of the Delta Unit. He was shaking his head and repeating, "There's something wrong with Gacy. There is something wrong with Gacy . . ." Dave Hachmeister put the pot in his pocket as he watched Gacy hugging everyone he could and saying very final "good-byes." It looked like Gacy was going on a very long trip and he was saying bon voyage.

Albrecht and Hachmeister were angry with Gacy for blowing through school zones at 60 mph.

"I'm gonna bust you on just the principle of it, John! Now you slow the fuck down in areas with kids and pedestrians," Hachmeister was screaming.

Gacy was hurt. "You guys have to stop yelling at me. This is the end, and you know it." Gacy, stooped and deflated, mumbled another rather fatalistic statement. "This is my last day. This is it . . . you guys know that."

Albrecht was convinced that Gacy was telling them that he intended to commit suicide. That would not do. This guy was going to face the music, no easy way out for him. Albrecht was going to see to that. He walked over to his car and got on the radio. Other members of the investigation team were on their way. That made him feel a little better. He had no intention of letting the past eight days of his life be a wasted effort.

Gacy's next stop was his house on Summerdale. He didn't stay long. Then he drove to his friend Ron Rohde's house. There, more farewells took place, complete with tears, hugs, and pats on the back. The members of the surveillance team were watching Gacy completely self-destruct. In some ways, it was sad. This glad-handing, gregarious pol (Chicago for *politician*) of a guy had been reduced to a sniffling, sad excuse for a man, trudging about in a Valium-induced haze, acting out fond adieus like the world was coming to an end. This all simply reinforced the idea on the part of several of the Deltas that Gacy was planning something drastic. He looked like a man on a mission whose time was short.

Gacy's driving was becoming erratic. He left the Rohde home and traveled to David Cram's apartment, where Mike Rossi was in the process of quitting his employ with Gacy. On his way there, Gacy could have been arrested for the way he was driving, which was nothing new, of course; however, it was markedly worse than usual. There was some true concern that he would commit suicide by bridge abutment.

Rossi was unloading equipment and tools in some sort of futile effort to cut his ties with John. This was a joke. Rossi had quit many times in the past. It never lasted. It didn't this time either. Before long, Rossi was in Cram's house with John. They all seemed to be planning whatever destination Gacy had in mind. The Deltas could see Gacy in tears, animated, acting like a person in great grief.

The next stop for this pathetic, sad train with Gacy leading the way was Di Leo's Restaurant on the Northwest Side, Gacy's home turf. There he met Leroy Stevens. Once again, Gacy showed signs of a man that was living his last hours on earth. He hugged everyone that he knew, often with tears flowing. He said it again and again, "It's over for me." "They're gonna kill me." "This is it for me." He did not seem to be in his right mind. He was not himself. This was clear to Albrecht, Hachmeister, and the others. After all, these were guys that had been with him every minute of every day for the past week and a half. They had eaten with him, drunk with him, partied with him. They could see him coming undone. More and more, the Deltas were convinced that Gacy intended to take his own life.

When Gacy left the restaurant, his car was rocketing north on Milwaukee Avenue, like he was a man possessed; only now, Rossi was doing the driving for him.

"If he is going where I think he is, we may have a problem." It was Albrecht's voice coming over the radio speakers. "His father is buried in that cemetery, Maryhill Cemetery. It is straight ahead on Milwaukee, at about Dempster Avenue. He always said he wanted to be buried there. Maybe he is going there to die, ya know? Why else would he be traveling on Milwaukee, of all roads? Anyway, that sounds like him, the morbid son of a bitch."

The radios crackled with the concern of officers that had put their all, their everything into an investigation that was now threatening to end without closure, without Gacy having been brought to justice. If he killed himself, they might never find Rob Piest or see any kind of conclusion to the other leads that they had unearthed regarding a number of other missing young boys.

After hearing the concerns of his men, with the frantic efforts to finish and present the complaint for search warrant ongoing back at the station, Lieutenant Kozenczak finally gave the order to attempt to arrest Gacy if they saw an opportunity. Any reason would do at this point.

However, they needed an actual reason. Sure, any reason would do, but what would that reason be? What did they actually have on him? They could stop him and give him a ticket for his driving, that was sure. But wait, he wasn't even doing the driving. They could give Rossi a ticket. Of course, that would not do. They needed a solid arrest to be able to hold Gacy while the search warrant was executed.

These guys were so used to watching Gacy break laws for which they could not arrest him because of the larger nature of their investigation, they were getting rusty.

It was Albrecht that suddenly remembered the pot that had exchanged hands at the gas station.

———————————

TERRY SULLIVAN STOOD in the makeshift investigation's command room at the Des Plaines police headquarters, listening to the squelch of many radios and the metallic, anticipation-filled voices of the members of the surveillance team, all of whom had arrived on scene for an event that was the culmination of a great deal of hard work, long hours, and a lot of patience. All four Deltas—Albrecht, Hachmeister, Robinson, and Schultz—together with their boss, Wally Lang, were in hot pursuit of the car driven by Rossi and carrying John Gacy at breakneck speeds through suburban traffic on north Milwaukee Avenue.

Terry had a decision to make. The complaint for search warrant was a few short hours from being completed. He had spoken to Judge Marvin Peters, the judge that had signed the first warrant, in an effort to smooth the process of getting this new search warrant signed. Terry had actually gone through the draft language of the complaint to ensure that the judge had no problem with it and that a finding of probable cause would be forthcoming. It was further decided that, if necessary, the complaint could be brought to the judge's home that evening and he would sign it there. Once signed, the members of the search team would be free to search Gacy's home, including his crawl space.

Sullivan was convinced that such a search would turn up evidence sufficient to charge Gacy with murder or, at a bare minimum, kidnapping. The warrant was drawn up on the basis of murder, however. And everyone involved with the investigation, including Terry Sullivan, just knew that this was going to be the basis of Gacy's eventual arrest. That was the unfortunate truth of the matter. No one believed that Rob Piest was still alive.

Sullivan was hearing the excited voices of his men stepping all over one another, speaking at once, and claiming that they were convinced that Gacy was going to off himself before an arrest could be effectuated, and maybe take Mike Rossi with him. He also had the hearing on my petition for TRO up in court the following morning, which could throw a monkey wrench into this whole damn thing—jeopardize the authorization of the warrant and put the investigation back to square one.

Should he give the order to arrest Gacy or wait until the search warrant was executed and new evidence would undoubtedly be discovered?

When he heard that Gacy had transferred marijuana to young Lance Jacobson and that the said transfer had actually been witnessed by a couple of Deltas, that was quite enough. Delivery of marijuana is a felony even if no money changes hands. One need not sell marijuana to commit the crime; they need only to deliver it. An arrest on felony charges would allow the police to hold Gacy for a significant period of time while the final steps to procuring the warrant were being taken.

"Take him down," Sullivan told Kozenczak.

———————————

THE SCENE WAS like the filming of a movie. On a rare crisp, cloudless sunlit Thursday in December, four days before Christmas 1978, John Wayne Gacy breathed his last breath of free air. At about 12:15 p.m., near the intersection of Milwaukee Avenue and Oakton Street in the village of Niles, Illinois, it played itself out much like what one that has watched any of the thousands of police dramas produced by Hollywood might imagine. Three unmarked squads carrying five plainclothes policemen—each of whom were men that had given their lives over the past eight long days and nights to the surveillance, pursuit, and apprehension of this particular man—swooped in, surrounding the car in which John rode shotgun and corralling it to the curb with screeching tires, dipping bumpers and appropriate flourish, and, with sidearms drawn, approached the passenger side of the vehicle.

"Get out of the car, John," Officer Ron Robinson calmly commanded, with his pistol inches from Gacy's ear. "You are under arrest."

John was bent over the trunk of his rental car on the busy suburban corner, handcuffed and placed into the back of a police car, in keeping with police procedure and in a way befitting one of fiction's best melodramas. Gawkers stopped their busy last-minute Christmas shopping to take in the scene and point.

They were only a few blocks from Maryhill Cemetery.

"Why are you guys doing this?" the confused and broken suspect wondered allowed. "What have I done? I thought we were friends . . ."

This time Mr. Gacy didn't have a key to the cuffs held between his fingertips in the palm of his hand. This time it was Gacy that was . . . dumb and stupid.

A ragtag procession of unmarked squad cars and Gacy's rental car driven by Rossi snaked its way back to Des Plaines police headquarters through the upscale northwest suburban area of Chicagoland. This was just the very beginning of a saga that would grow exponentially and would soon be splashed across headlines and TV screens worldwide.

I didn't know it then, but I was about to have my fifteen minutes. I was about to become famous.

AFTER GACY LEFT my office early that morning and it was clear that he was not going to follow my advice and allow me to get him the psychological help he desperately needed, Stevens and I just shrugged and shook our heads. What could we do? We both said something about how we would see each other tomorrow for the hearing in federal court and went our separate ways.

For me, I couldn't remember a time that I felt as tired as I did at that moment. I hadn't had more than an hour's sleep in days, what with Sammy in the hospital and this certifiable nutcase that I now represented. I had pulled countless all-nighters in college and law school during midterms or finals. I had felt pressure before, coupled with a lack of sleep. I had negotiated the gauntlet that was law school. I had studied for the two-day nightmare that was the bar examination. I had been involved in many trials, many of them serious and high profile during my years at the public defender's office. But nothing compared to this—nothing. I was running on pure adrenaline, and only pure adrenaline. My body needed rest. *Welcome to the private practice of law, Sam.*

Alone in my office, I put together the files that I thought I might need before I left to go somewhere—I had no idea where—as the weight of the night's incredible scenario began to descend like a mountain on my shoulders. Did my memory serve me? Had my client really confessed to the murder, the serial killings of many, many . . . was this a fucking dream or what? I had to get some sleep. Then I would be able to sort all this shit out. I had to at least take a nap. My head was spinning.

I stopped by my parents' house, where my ma was watching Jimmy, my younger boy. There wasn't much I could say to her. I just thanked her for helping out with Jimmy and said that I had to lie down for a little bit. I fell onto the couch in the living room and was dead to the world in seconds, still wearing my suit and tie.

In what seemed like two minutes later, but was actually a couple of hours, my mother was standing over me.

"Sam! Wake up, Sam. They called from the office. They need you. Your client was arrested. You know that client you have . . . Geezy, Casey . . . what's his name?"

I looked at my own mother as though I didn't know her. "Whaaat?" I tried to focus.

"Your client was arrested, Sam."

"For what?" I asked, still struggling to come to.

"For pot, she said, the girl at the office. I don't know what she means. You have to call her."

"Pot? Pot? What the fu—"

15

"WHAT NOW? WHY are you guys holding him?" I bellowed as I stormed into the Des Plaines police headquarters forty minutes after my mother woke me. "You guys are asking for problems, you know that, don't you? The hearing on our TRO is tomorrow." I walked up to Terry Sullivan. "Terry, why the hell are you holding him?"

"Possession and delivery of marijuana, Sam—a felony, I might add," Terry said. "We also found some pills on him in an unmarked bottle. We think they're Valium. They have to be tested. We probably won't charge him with that, unless we have to."

I reached into my pocket and pulled out my money clip. "OK, OK, what's his bond? We'll post it."

"Not so fast, Sam," Terry said. "We are running his prints, processing him. You know the drill here. We can hold him until his prints clear. Then he has to go in front of a judge. This is a legitimate felony charge."

"This is harassment, Terry, harassment, plain and simple. He has a right to post bond, and you know it. A pot charge? Come on, man, really? Let's get him in front of a judge and have a bond set."

"All in due time, Sam. We are possessing him as fast as we can, but we are having a small problem with our fax machine. We have to fax his prints to Springfield, you know that. They are looking into it."

By now everyone in the room knew that the marijuana charge was preliminary, a pretext. Everyone knew that there was a greater reason for this circus. It seemed like every police officer on the entire force was in the room—certainly, all the principals involved in the investigation were there, buzzing around, busying themselves with one thing or another; but actually, they were there to be part of the final process of taking Gacy down. Of course, I still had to do my job. I wanted to speak to my client.

"Well, give me a room. I want to talk to him," I said.

Soon I was pacing back and forth in front of a shell of John Gacy in a locked interrogation room without windows, drab industrial-color cinder block walls, with a couple of government-issue chairs and a government-issue table where Gacy sat slumped and sullen.

"Keep your fucking mouth shut, John. They told you that you could remain silent, right? That is exactly what you do, remain silent."

"Sam, it's over, it's over . . . my life is over. I just want to get this shit over with, you know, get it all over with, clear the air." John's eyes were dripping, bloodshot, and sunken due to lack of sleep. He had a two-day growth of beard and looked like a hobo. He was in the same clothes that he had slept in last night, and he was in a drug- and alcohol-induced haze, his head rotating on his neck like it was not connected to his body.

"You don't have any idea what you want. You are in no shape to be making decisions of any kind, let alone decisions that are going to affect the rest of your life. You just keep your mouth shut. You had an appointment with a shrink this morning. That's where you should be right now, not here. You need help, John. Now, just take my advice, and keep your mouth shut. You are not required to say a word, so don't! Got it?"

Gacy then said something that threw me. I was about to find out just how crazy my client really was. "I want to get out of here. Do you want me to fake a heart attack? I can do that. I can."

"John, what the hell are you talking about? No! That's the simple answer. What's wrong with you? You cannot fake a heart attack. We have to get you into a facility, a hospital. You need help, John. You are not yourself. You are not making any sense."

"I have to do this my way, Sam. I know . . . I know th-th-th-that you are just trying to help me, that . . . that you are on my side. I know that. But you have to believe me. I have to do this my own way."

I shook my head slowly. I was concerned that if given the chance, he would try to commit suicide. He still had his belt and street clothes. If a person were determined to do it, there was always a way to do yourself in. I didn't want him to be left alone. I sat in the other chair in the room and watched my client put his head down in his arms. I stared at him for a very long couple of minutes.

"John, just keep your mouth closed," I said. "I will try to get—"

I was going to tell him that I intended to get him some help. I never got the chance. John raised his head. His face was an odd mix of ashen gray and vein-popping purple. His eyes were vacant and fixed. It was as if I wasn't in the room. His eyelids began to flutter much like they had on the previous night in my office, and his eyes rolled back in his head. All I could see was white where his eyes were supposed to be. Believe me, that is a frightening sight. His body began to shudder and shake as he flipped out of his chair and onto the floor. He lay there shaking, flopping around like a fish on a pier. I thought, *Twenty minutes ago he was talking about faking a heart attack, now he's fucking having one?* I jumped up and ran to the locked door and began pounding on it.

"Hey! Gacy's having some kind of seizure," I yelled. "He's on the ground. Hey, open the door. Someone call an ambulance."

Immediately, an officer came to the door. "You OK in there, Sam?" I don't think he knew exactly what to do.

"Call 911! Call an ambulance right now!"

The door flew open, and cops swarmed to the door, gawking. There was yelling beyond that, people screaming to call the paramedics. Gacy kept flopping around on the floor. White bubbly drool was running out of the corner of his mouth, and his color had gone off the charts. It looked as though his head might just pop like a thermostat cartoon.

I loosened his collar and tried to make him comfortable. Police officers gathered around shouting various forms of advice, all of which I ignored.

Paramedics burst through the door with a stretcher. They bent down over him and immediately assessed that it was time to go to the hospital. They put an oxygen mask over his mouth and nose and lifted him onto a gurney. Suddenly, my client was being whisked off to Holy Family Hospital with sirens blaring.

I suppose it wasn't really a surprise to anybody—not to me or to any of the investigation team—when we later learned that Gacy was not really having a heart attack. Upon arrival at the hospital, and after a short examination by hospital staff, it was clear that nothing physical was wrong with him, at least not anything life-threatening.

When I heard the news, it affected me differently than most, though. Most of the police officers believed that Gacy was just a bullshit artist—that was no surprise to anyone. Half of what he said was either bullshit or an exaggerated version of the truth, a Gacy version of things. And I suppose that I was somewhat on that bandwagon. I had described him as a blowhard and a braggart to others before. However, this time my perspective changed. I saw his face. I saw his eyes roll back into his head. I saw the color of his skin, the involuntary nature of his seizure. I was in that room with him. So I now knew something I didn't know before. My client was not normal; something was very wrong with him that ran much deeper. More than anyone else, I should have been able to dismiss Gacy's feigned illness as a stunt, a ploy for sympathy, something very typically Gacy. Hell, he had announced to me his intention to fake a heart attack. But that was no fake heart attack in the way that others might expect. He was not simply pretending. Gacy had experienced a physiological event, a physical response to what he perceived as a threat. He was not just "acting." The paramedics, trained professionals, determined there to be an emergency. Gacy was in actual physical distress.

Suddenly, I knew that his entire medical history—with all its documented seizures, strokes, and maladies—was likely one long psychological manifestation of a man unlike any other man, a man miswired at the factory, so to speak, a good old-fashioned crazy person, a person that had a lifelong record of known, documented illnesses and hospital admissions. But in spite of the very impressive nature of the charts and notes regarding his health, in spite of the many diagnoses of his condition over his lifetime, I knew that many or most of those problems had originated in this man's head. It wasn't his body that was weak or broken, as the charts and the medical history might indicate; it was his brain that wasn't working right. His problem was in his mind. His brain was profoundly broken.

That was the only explanation that I could come up with to account for the things that I had seen and heard over the past twelve hours. During the previous night, I had seen the same reaction in his eyes that I had seen today. That fluttering of the eyelids, that change in personality—I had seen it twice now, and although I am not a doctor, I know what I saw. This was not something as simple as a guy who faked illnesses or medical emergencies. This was something far more significant.

Once Gacy was out of my presence, he began to start telling parts of his story to just about anyone that would listen. Frankly, his decision to do so pretty much sealed his fate. He began confessing to many of the members of the Delta Unit, guys that he considered his friends, explaining that he had told Stevens and me everything.

To their credit, the officers involved in questioning were careful to continually remind John of his right to remain silent so that his statements would be admissible in evidence one day. It was at this point that Gacy began telling others about Jack Hanley, John's idea of an alter ego, another personality within him. Although Gacy had never mentioned this name to me or to Stevens in all of our long and exhausting conversations, the name "Jack Hanley" would prove to figure heavily in the Gacy story in the days and weeks and months to come. For now, Gacy was on what lawyers like to call a frolic of his own.

"My lawyers work for me," he would say. "They cannot tell me what to do, who to talk to, or what I can talk about."

In Gacy's mind, Gacy knew best. Unfortunately, nothing could have been farther from the truth.

16

CHUCK GORDON WAS nineteen years old and on his first date with a pretty young girl named Ronda, whom he had met the week before at a nearby bar. They sat on her grandmother's front porch exchanging stories, shivering against the cold, getting to know each other a little bit better before they finally had to say good night. He was fidgeting, contemplating that very first good-night kiss when the night sky to the west of the little Norwood Park bungalow where her grandmother lived was suddenly lit up. "It looked like they had moved Wrigley Field a few miles to the west and they were playing a night game in December," he would later say. "I couldn't believe how bright it was."

Chuck's memory of that Thursday night, just four days before Christmas, was just one of the hundreds of memories recounted by persons that happened to be in the vicinity of 8213 W. Summerdale on the evening of December 21, 1978, the night that the search warrant on John Wayne Gacy's home was executed. Chuck was from suburban Elmhurst, and it was by sheer chance that he was in that neighborhood on that fateful night.

I left the Des Plaines police station after they took Gacy away in the ambulance and went home. I had done everything I could as his lawyer, after all. Now it was up to him to follow my advice and remain silent, keep his damned mouth shut—something John Gacy did not do very well. I would have to wait for the results of the examination from the hospital and, after he was released from care, try to force a bond hearing as soon as it was possible. If Gacy's condition was serious, that might take some time, maybe several days, depending on his condition. Of course, like everything else about this crazy case, that is not what happened.

I hadn't been home more than ten minutes when I got a call from one of Gacy's neighbors. When the surveillance on his home began, Gacy must have bragged that he had hired me to put a stop to it. We were both precinct captains, and people knew that I was a lawyer with some clout, some political friends.

"There are what looks like fifty police vehicles, trucks, lights, absolute chaos over at John's house," the neighbor screamed into the phone. "You better get over there, Sam. They look like they are planning to tear the place apart. You're his lawyer." I remember thinking that I would have to thank John for giving out my home phone number. Why even have an office if strangers were able to call me at home? Then I remembered that I was still listed in the phone book. Perhaps I should remedy that? I made a mental note, but it turned out to be too late.

When I arrived, the street was secured at both ends of the block by squads with flashing lights, and the scene in front of Gacy's house looked like something out of a bad disaster movie. Flashing Mars Lights, spotlights, special floodlights constructed on top of evidence vans, and countless uniformed men scurrying everywhere filled my field of vision. There were squad cars from several different jurisdictions parked haphazardly on the street, on lawns, on sidewalks, basically everywhere. It seems that my very first client, my one client, had caused a bit of a stir.

I made my way past the initial challenges to my presence by asserting my right to be there, louder and more convincingly than the uniformed officers that were positioned at the perimeters.

"I'm his lawyer! That's my client's house! I represent Mr. Gacy!" I shouted to one cop after another as I stormed toward the nucleus of the beehive. I pounded on the locked front door of Gacy's house and peered into the diamond-shaped window at eye level. A face appeared that filled the window. It was a face I knew. Greg Bedoe, the seasoned Cook County investigator whom Terry Sullivan had attached to the unit early during the investigation, looked back at me. I will never forget the look on his face as long as I live. It was a look of sheer horror, the look of a man that had seen something gruesome, grotesque, unimaginable.

"Get the fuck out of here, Amirante!" he screamed at me, pointing.

"Hey, Bedoe, fuck you! I want to see a warrant! What the fuck do you guys think you are doing here? You can't do this! Where is your goddamned warrant?"

"Fuck you, and fuck your warrant, Sam! I said get the fuck outta here! We have a warrant, now get the fuck out of here before I have your ass dragged outta here!"

We were both screaming at the top of our lungs and attracting some attention. I looked around. All I could see were cops . . . everywhere. I made a quick assessment. I was not going to win this argument. My home turf was in court. This was their home turf, no question about it. I backed away from the front door.

Welcome to the private practice of law, Sam, I thought once again. I found myself thinking those words quite a lot lately.

A COUPLE HOURS earlier, sometime shortly after 7:15 p.m., which was the time the warrant was signed by Judge Peters, the first of the members of the investigation team arrived at the home of John Wayne Gacy.

There was the static of pure anticipation in the air. They would have loved to tear into the place and rip it apart, especially the crawl space, but the men knew their jobs. A meticulous process was being followed. An evidence technician named Daniel Genty had the dubious distinction of being the one chosen to go into the crawl space below Gacy's house. While Genty dressed in coveralls and firemen's wader boots, some of the others checked out the house. They removed the trapdoor to the crawl space and peered into it. Evidently, someone had unplugged the sump pump. There were several inches of standing water in most of the crawl, making it impossible to do any real investigation down there. The plug for the sump pump was plugged in, and it kicked on. Immediately, the water was being pumped out. While that was happening, the other officers proceeded to search in various other areas of the house.

Officers Tovar and Kautz had long suspected that they would find items of property belonging to others in Gacy's house. They had been working that angle. During the first search, various officers noticed a small Motorola television on a dresser in Gacy's bedroom. Officer Kautz was with Officer Adams when they visited and questioned Mrs. Szyc, the mother of one of the missing teens, John Szyc. Among the items of paperwork that were given to them, which included the car registration for the 1971 Plymouth, was a registration form and warranty certificate for a small Motorola television that belonged to Szyc.

Tovar and Kautz made a beeline into Gacy's bedroom. They checked the serial number on the TV in Gacy's room. Sure enough, the TV sitting on John Wayne Gacy's dresser once belonged to John Szyc. It had the same serial number. They also found a clock radio that was once the property of young John Szyc. Chills ran up and down the spines of many officers when they thought about what else might be found in the crawl space in light of this new information. What were believed to be sound theories—speculation really, but informed speculation—about the connection to and the whereabouts of the increasing number of missing teens that were once connected to Gacy were becoming more and more plausible.

The time of reckoning had come. After about ten long minutes of pumping, the sump pump had removed enough water from the crawl to allow for a meaningful search. Officer Genty dropped into the crawl space armed with a bright spotlight and a trenching tool. He had to half-crawl to maneuver in the tiny space under the house. The first thing he noticed was the lime spread all around to absorb moisture. Small pools of water still existed in low spots, and it was discolored, brownish. He picked a spot and plunged the blade of the trenching tool into the soft, moist dirt. An odor escaped with only one shovelful of dirt. This was gross—a dirty, horrifying job. The odor was overwhelming. With the next shovelful, Genty stopped. He had hit something solid. He reached into the dirt to see what it was. Although he kind of expected it, what he saw, what he was now holding, stole his breath. Then he turned and yelled over his shoulder, "Charge him!"

Genty had found the first of what would later prove to be hundreds and hundreds of human bones!

THE WORD SPREAD like wildfire, as they say. Radios crackled and squelched. Jurisdictions were notified. The cries went into the atmosphere.

"Charge Gacy with murder."

"Call the medical examiner."

"Get me the mayor."

"Find out about jurisdiction."

"Let the chief know . . . wake him up!"

"See if we can tear this house down."

"Tell my wife I won't be home . . . for a while."

"This is going to be big . . . no, huge . . . no, monstrous!"

"I have never seen anything like this in my life."

"I don't know what we are going to do about Christmas, honey."

The air seemed to echo with the news.

And then . . . the press arrived.

17

AS EVERYBODY KNOWS, the city of Chicago is the third largest city in the United States of America, which, as everybody knows, makes it the third largest media market in the United States. The force and speed at which this story ripped through that media market and was instantly transmitted on to the rest of the world is epic in the annals of print and electronic media lore.

Friday morning, December 22, 1978, every television set and every radio in every home and car and business in the entire city was squawking about one thing: John Wayne Gacy.

The unusual thing about Gacy was that he was no "person in the shadows." This was not an anonymous, work-a-day guy who one day snaps and goes to work and sprays his postal-employee coworkers with a hail of bullets, killing ten or twenty. He was a politician, the guy at the front of the parade, the guy who had the yard parties attended by hundreds. Therefore, this story was a textbook example of exponential growth. Four hundred people tell ten friends that they were at a party at Gacy's house, and suddenly, four thousand people are talking about the guy, and so on, without the help of the press. From the highest reaches of Chicago politics, including the mayor and the governor, to his neighbors and business associates, it seemed that no one in the city had more than one degree of separation from this man. You could not throw a rock in all of Chicagoland—population nine million—without hitting someone that had his or her own personal Gacy story.

And I was his lawyer.

And many of the venerable members of the fourth estate were looking for me, it seems, but I was babysitting Gacy in the bowels of the Des Plaines police station. I had returned to the station after having visited Gacy's house—quite the humbling experience—and I was sitting with him, trying unsuccessfully to remind him of his constitutional right to remain silent. John thought he knew better, though. He thought that he was smarter than people like Washington, Jefferson, Franklin, and Adams. He wasn't.

He asked that I notify his sister Joanne. She immediately came to the station to be with him. He spoke with her and admitted that much of what was being said about him was true. I can't imagine what that must have been like for his sister, but she stoically stayed by her brother's side through the night. By dawn, Gacy had told his story to many of the members of the investigation team. He also said that he would show everyone where he disposed of bodies that were not under the house.

A morbid, sad three-car caravan left Des Plaines, Illinois, as the sun barely showed its first morning light on Friday, December 22. John wanted the first stop to be the Maryhill Cemetery, to pay respects at his father's grave; and he was told that all efforts would be made to grant that privilege by the boys from Des Plaines, provided that he was cooperating with them. Gacy somehow knew that this would be the last chance that he would ever have to stand at his father's grave. His father, the man whose every prediction about his son had finally, ultimately come true—in spades.

The group headed out in three squads to the bridge, where Interstate 55 crosses over the Des Plaines River near Joliet, some fifty miles away. Upon arrival, Gacy recounted the story of the night that he drove Rob Piest's body out to that bridge, ten days previous, and—with Officers Shultz and Robinson grasping his arms to ensure he didn't fling himself over the rail—pointed to the very spot where Rob was released into the muddy water below. He also explained that it was at this spot that he released four other bodies of young men after he had run out of room in his crawl space.

Tears streaked his sister's face, and I think it is fair to say that everyone else on that bridge felt chills. I know I did.

The somber moment didn't last long, however; because almost immediately, the entire troop saw ABC's Chicago affiliate WLS TV newsman Jay Levine running, with camera crew in tow, across the bridge. Gacy was spirited into the back of the squad car and whisked away while Mr. Levine tried futilely to keep up, poking his microphone into the dust from the disappearing Illinois State Police cruiser.

As THIS STORY exploded in the press, there were people that would rather not have become part of it. Me, I'm a bit of a ham. I always knew that my chosen profession might include some press coverage. Cameras don't intimidate me. But suppose that you just happened to live next door to Gacy or down the block from him, or that you once worked for him for a summer three years ago, you just might not want to see reporters camped out on your front lawn or chasing you through the mall when all you are trying to do is buy a bag of dog food.

This was such a huge story, especially in Chicago, that the members of the press were generally tripping over each other to get an angle on the story that had not previously been covered. In the days following his arrest, if you had ever met John Wayne Gacy or had any connection to him whatsoever, chances are that you would have the business end of a microphone shoved in your face, sometimes at the most inopportune times of the day or night or in the most inopportune places. People had to become creative in their efforts to avoid being accosted by eager-beaver reporters on a deadline.

My wife, Mary, was among the folks that were uninterested in having their fifteen minutes of fame happen right then and there. She preferred her privacy. She had enough on her plate. Her husband had been consumed by the whirlwind surrounding Gacy. Her older son was in the hospital and her younger son was an infant who needed constant attention, as infants invariably do. So imagine her surprise when she walked by our front window, dressed in a housecoat and pajamas, curlers in her hair, with Jimmy, our infant son, in her arms, and saw one of those big cumbersome media trucks screeching to a stop in front of our house. Her jaw dropped as she watched John "Bulldog" Drummond, a truly famous face in Chicago and a crime-beat reporter from CBS News, scurrying up our front walk, trying desperately to untangle power cords that connected him to his camera crew, all of whom were also excitedly scurrying behind him.

She had to think fast.

"Ma'am, I'm John Drummond, CBS News, sorry to bother you, ma'am, but is this the home of Sam Amirante, the lawyer, the one that is representing Mr. Gacy? Are you his wife, ma'am? What a cute baby . . . is that Mr. Amirante's son, ma'am? Do you have a moment, ma'am? Can we ask you some questions, ma'am?" A microphone was being waved about precariously close to her face and to the baby, and a four-inch camera lens was staring at poor Mary. She hadn't signed up for this, but my wife was no slouch. She was fast on her feet.

"I'm sorry, who?" she asked innocently. "No, no, no, I'm just the babysitter. No one is home."

The dejected Mr. Drummond dropped the microphone to his side and waved off the camera. The little red light went off, and the camera was suddenly pointed downward.

"Do you know where they are . . . where the Amirantes are, ma'am?"

"At work, I guess. But this is not the Amirante lawyer's house. I think they are a cousin to the lawyer . . . a cousin or something."

The Bulldog turned slowly on his heels, dejected, shaking his head, with his little clipped bulldog tail between his crooked bulldog legs, and trudged back down the walk toward his truck. "Sorry to bother you, ma'am," he said over his shoulder.

Mary had to giggle a little at the sight as she closed the front door, but she was not about to go on TV for the first time ever in a housecoat and curlers. Sorry.

AFTER RETURNING FROM Joliet and the bridge over the Des Plaines River, with Gacy incessantly begging to go to the cemetery, the next stop was Gacy's house. Gacy had admitted that there was at least one body buried on his property that was not in the crawl space, and the prosecution wanted to know exactly where it was. Further, when an accused person points out where the bodies are buried, whether figuratively or actually, it strengthens the State's case. In the event that the defendant later recants and denies his involvement in a crime, the prosecution has evidence that the defendant knew or was aware of information that only the perpetrator could possibly know.

I had advised against all of this, of course, but Gacy was on his "frolic." No one could convince him that he should stop doing the job that the police are paid to do. Frankly, as crazy as this sounds to you and me, Gacy loved the limelight; he loved the attention. It didn't seem to matter that the reason that he had the limelight trained on him was that the prosecution was building a case for murder. He was in his element. How weird was that?

Gacy's entire block had been cordoned off from all except public officials, cops, and those that were unlucky enough to have a house on it. There was a lull in the activity because jurisdictional concerns were being sorted out and new warrants were being obtained to allow a complete and extensive search of the house and excavation of the crawl space. We pulled up, and a brand-new flurry of activity was generated throughout the members of the press and others that were hanging around on the fringes of the crime scene.

Gacy was brought into his garage.

If you've ever wondered what your first concern would be when you are brought back home after being charged with the murder of a missing boy and you are the prime suspect in the murder of many, many others, well . . . apparently, if your name is John Wayne Gacy, your first concern would be the fact that the police that had been conducting a search of your home had left some things—some tools and some other items—out of place in your meticulously kept garage. Gacy immediately started bitching about this mundane issue as if he was going to be back in an hour or so and he was going to have to clean up the mess all by himself. He began picking up items and placing them gingerly into their predesignated spots on walls and in drawers. If not for the solemn gravity of the situation, which was completely lost on this strange little man, it would have been hilariously funny. What was wrong with this guy?

Finally, someone reminded my client that he was not there to clean the garage.

There were moments during this time, this experience, that stand out in my memory. It is all an incredible experience, of course, a tornado of activity. My first case as a private criminal defense attorney was becoming quite an interesting ride. But some moments stand out. What Gacy did next caused one of those moments.

He took a can of black spray paint and drew a box on the concrete floor of his garage. Then he drew an X in the middle of the box.

"Dig here," he said. It was like he was pointing out the spot where a buried water meter could be found. If the foreman of a crew charged with the responsibility of digging a trench for a water main was totally bored with his job, he couldn't have said it more nonchalantly, more offhandedly.

"Do you know who is buried here?" one of the guys asked.

"Yeah . . . Butkovitch."

John Butkovitch had eaten dinner at John Gacy's house. This kid was a particular friend to Gacy's ex-wife Carol. Little John, she called him. There was Big John and Little John. What a kooky pair, always together. John knew this kid's father. John had helped decorate Little John's new apartment. Little John was a regular visitor, a valued employee, a friend.

Now he was under concrete in Gacy's garage.

What was wrong with this guy?

18

AFTER WE RETURNED to the Des Plaines police headquarters, after I had bitched loudly enough, a bond hearing was scheduled.

Gacy was brought to the tiny courtroom that was in the same building as the Des Plaines police headquarters. This courtroom's most common use was for the traffic call for the City of Des Plaines. It was small, and it was not secure. Anyone could walk in, so there were uniformed patrolmen at the door checking credentials.

The hallways outside the courtroom, together with the miniscule gallery where a few rows of churchlike pews existed, were packed with people, mostly reporters; but other government workers and politically connected observers would someday brag that they were in that room. Again, Judge Marvin Peters presided.

I battled my way past cameras and reporters from all over the world. I saw cameras from Greece, England, Germany, France—those were the ones I noticed—together with every network from the United States, as represented by their Chicago affiliates. Microphones were poked and shoved at me, and questions were shouted at the top of lungs.

I had not been home, except for ten minutes for a quick shower that I had taken Thursday morning when I had to return to the office to take my client to his appointment at the Louis A. Weiss Memorial Hospital, or so I thought.

I hadn't changed clothes, shaved, or seen water that hadn't been filtered through ground coffee beans since the wee hours on Thursday. I looked more like a defendant than the defendant.

Gacy was ushered into the courtroom, surrounded by police officers, amid murmurs, yelling, shouted questions, and popping camera bulbs. He was positioned next to me, and the judge slammed his gavel and called for quiet.

The courtroom hushed.

"People of the State of Illinois versus John Wayne Gacy, number 78-3-008080," the clerk called as she passed the file to the judge.

If this scene had occurred during centuries past, the throngs of people that were inside and outside of that courtroom would not have been holding cameras; they would not have been holding pens and paper or tape recorders—they would have been holding pitchforks and torches. They would not have been shouting relatively polite questions from behind invisible lines of demarcation; they would have been attacking, pitchforks and torches raised, and calling for Gacy's head. So to say that my position in that courtroom was unenviable would be a colossal understatement. I was representing the scoundrel, the ne'er-do-well. In the eyes of many, that made me the scoundrel too.

Fortunately, I was unaffected by all of that folderol. In fact, I saw myself as riding the white horse in that situation. As far as I was concerned, I was the person in that courtroom with the moral high ground. It's funny, the people that wrap themselves most snugly in the American flag, the ones that scream the loudest about their freedoms and their constitutional rights are often the very people that lose sight of the meaning of all of that wonderful rhetoric as soon as push comes to shove, as soon as the precepts that we as a people so cherish come to be tested. When the very constitutional concepts that they claim to support are challenged by a hard case, an ugly case such as this one, they run for cover. They run for the comfort of man's basest instincts. It's much easier to hate the bad guy than it is to support the hard reality that if we are to continue to enjoy our freedoms, if our Constitution is to survive, it has to be supported in all circumstances, even when to do so seems hard.

So my job was simple. All I had to do was argue in favor of setting a reasonable bond for Mr. Gacy and see if we couldn't get him released after posting it. No problem.

Plantiff

v.

John W. Gacy Jr.
Defendant

COMPLAINT FOR PRELIMINARY EXAMINATION

No. 783-008080-01

Lt. Joseph Kozenczak
(Complainant's Name Printed or Typed) — complainant, now appears before
The Circuit Court of Cook County and states that
John W. Gacy Jr.
(defendant) — has, on or about

December 11, 1978
(date) — at 8213 W. Summerdale, Cook County, Illinois
(place of offense)

committed the offense of _____ Murder _____ in that he
killed Robert J. Piest without lawful justification by strangling him with a rope
intended to kill said Robert J. Piest.

in violation of Chapter __38__ _____ Section __9__ (A)(1)
ILLINOIS REVISED STATUTES

X Lt. Joseph Kozenczak
(Complainant's Signature)
1420 Miner St., DesPlaines 297-2131
(Complainant's Address) (Telephone No.)

STATE OF ILLINOIS)
COUNTY OF COOK) ss.

Lt. Joseph Kozenczak
(Complainant's Name Printed or Typed)

being first duly sworn, on __his__ oath, deposes and says that he has read the foregoing complaint by him
subscribed and that the same is true.

X Lt. Joseph Kozenczak
(Complainant's Signature)

Subscribed and sworn to before me __December 22__, 19 __78__
Judge or Clerk

I have examined the above complaint and the person presenting the same and have heard evidence thereon, and am satisfied that there is probable cause for filing same. Leave is given to file said complaint.

Summons issued,
or
Warrant Issued,
Bail set at __NO BAIL - BAIL DENIED__
Judge

or
Bail set at _____

It seemed that Judge Peters saw things differently.

I argued that a charge of murder could not stand without a body. There was no evidence that the alleged victim of the murder, one Robert J. Piest, was, in fact, dead. Plus, the State was attempting to proceed on a complaint for preliminary examination. My client had not yet been formally indicted. Under normal circumstances, this would have been a cogent, valid argument and would probably have been sustained by the court. In this case, however, the defendant had pointed out where he had disposed of the body only a couple of hours earlier in front of many police officers and the assistant state's attorney, so the argument was rejected by the court. Go figure.

I was successful in having my client transferred to Cermak Hospital, the hospital that served the Cook County Jail inmate population, rather than into the general population. I strongly believed that Gacy needed psychiatric help, and although Cermak was basically jail hospital and not exactly famous for its compassionate care, it was better than nothing. It was certainly better than the alternative—having Gacy housed in the general population of Cook County Jail, one of our nation's most notorious and dangerous of jails. Frankly, I don't think he would have survived that. He was not only a sickly, blubbery cream puff of a man, he was also suicidal. He hadn't shut up about how he wanted to "do things my way" since the all-night session in my office when he spilled his guts.

The case was continued for further motions and for assignment to December 29, 1978, at 9:30 a.m.

THE DAILY HERALD

Arlington Heights PADDOCK PUBLICATIONS

52nd Year—132 Saturday, December 23, 1978 40 Pages — 15 Cents

Contractor charged with teen's death after bodies discovered

by TONI GINNETTI

A 36-year-old contractor with a criminal record for sex crimes was charged Friday with the murder of a Des Plaines youth hours after police discovered the decomposed remains of two persons in his home.

The contractor, John Wayne Gacy Jr., was ordered held without bond in the murder of 15-year-old Robert Piest, 8213 Craig Dr., who has been missing since Dec. 11. Authorities said Gacy admitted to police late Thursday that he killed the youth.

Piest's body is feared to be among the skeletal remains found early Friday in Gacy's home at 8213 W. Summerdale in unincorporated Norwood Park Township.

THE UNIDENTIFIED remains of

at least two persons, believed to be young men, were found in shallow graves, one in the garage and another in the dirt crawl space of the residence where Gacy also operated his PDM Contracting business.

Robert Piest

Cook County Sheriff's police Friday were dismantling the house looking for more bodies believed to be buried there.

There had been rumors that as many as 24 bodies might be found and Cook County Sheriff Richard J. Elrod said, "It's possible." Three reports and others that there may be as many as 25 bodies could not be verified.

Des Plaines Police Chief Leo Alfano said "several more rounds" that could hold more dead were in the crawl space. He declined to estimate how high the victim total could go.

JOHN WAYNE GACY, 36, was charged Friday with the murder of Robert Piest, whose body could be among the remains found in Gacy's home. Gacy, a contractor, is an accused killer who had been under police surveillance for the past few weeks.

(Continued on Sect. 1 Page 12)

Jet is down in sea

From Daily Herald news services

PALERMO, Sicily — An Alitalia DC-9 jetliner carrying Sicilian emigrants home for the Christmas holidays crashlanded into the stormy Mediterranean early Saturday while making its landing approach to the Palermo airport.

Airline officials said 125 people — 110 passengers and five crewmembers — were aboard the twin-engine plane and at least 21 were rescued by fishing boats and rushed to Palermo hospitals.

The boats also picked up the bodies of at least four people, officials said.

Giuseppe Venturelle, a fishing boat captain who witnessed the crash, told authorities the plane went into the sea a short distance from shore, skimming the stormy sea at such a low altitude before it.

"THE PLANE came down quickly a few hundred meters from us and went into the sea," Venturelle said. "We couldn't see how the people managed to get out but we turned on the search lights and rushed to it.

"Because we were so close we picked up a lot of survivors," he said. "They were all in the water. Evidently the crew didn't have time to put the rubber life rafts."

One of the survivors, Giovanni Macterava, 26, a member of the paramilitary finance police, was seriously injured in the crash.

"As soon as the plane went into the water penetrators broke out," Macterava said. "We didn't understand anything and almost immediately there was a big explosion in the front part of the plane.

"I don't think any of the crew members survived in that place," he added.

THE PLANE, flight AH123 from Rome, was part of a supplementary

'Close to end of road' in SALT talks

GENEVA, Switzerland (AP) — The United States and the Soviet Union tentatively have agreed on a new treaty limiting their nuclear arsenals, U.S. officials said here Friday. But President Carter's confirmation said "several difficult issues" remain unresolved.

White House press secretary Jody Powell, with the president, on a Christmas vacation in Georgia, told reporters that it characterizes progress in the strategic arms limitation talks as "a tentative agreement — that's wrong."

When asked about Powell's statement, the U.S. officials at the strategic arms limitation talks in Geneva stood by their report of a tentative agreement.

THE OFFICIALS said "tentative" meant the Soviets would commit over-night with Moscow about the compromises they had agreed to Friday

and reserved the right to reopen these issues this morning.

Powell told reporters, travelling aboard the Air Force One en route to Carter's home in Plains, Ga., that the president spoke of "moving ahead" on SALT in a telephone conversation with Secretary of State Cyrus R. Vance in Geneva before leaving the White House.

"Based on his conversation with Vance, perhaps reports dealing out of Geneva telling that an agreement had been reached or is a virtual certainty

are not correct," Powell said. "They have made progress, but several difficult issues still are unresolved."

"A tentative agreement — that's wrong," the press secretary declared.

IN GENEVA, the U.S. officials, asking not to be identified, told reporters a tentative agreement was reached after a lengthy negotiating session between Vance and Soviet Foreign Ministers Andrei Gromyko. Speaking privately with reporters,

the officials said Vance and Gromyko would meet again today. They said that session would be followed by an announcement on the talks.

Backing Carter, the Carter administration spokesman at the talks said, "We are close to the end of the road." The spokesman declined any further public comment.

The U.S. officials told the U.S. and Soviet negotiators had reached tentative

(Continued on Page 4)

Darker side of clown

by PAT DOYLE

The sunny side of John Gacy, hidden for years under a clown costume, surfaced for shocked neighbors Friday when police uncovered grisly gravesites at his unincorporated suburban home.

Beneath the respectable image of a Democratic precinct captain and big-hearted jester, the 36-year-old Gacy concealed the record of a violent sex offender with a reputation for dispensing free drugs to young men who befriended him.

It was a record as well concealed that neighbors were stunned and incredulous when they learned that authorities had found him working in Gacy's single-story, brick home at 8213 Summerdale Rd., in unincorporated Norwood Park Township.

"ARE WE TALKING about the same guy, kind of short, who used to dress up as a clown suit?" asked Frank Hedls, 819 Conense, in Norridge. "He seemed like the nicest guy in the world. He made over sure when my people saw doing. My wife saw hysterical and he missed her death."

Just an entirely different picture of Gacy, a genial contractor who offered, emerges from old police records and the experience of a young man who once worked for him.

The picture is one of a man with a boutique for sex with young men and boys, a fondness so strong that he used physical violence and threats to get it.

Gacy was convicted in Waterloo, Iowa, in 1968 for sodomy of a 16-year-old boy he was responsible for as part of the Big Brother program for boys without fathers. After he was indicted for the offense, police say he beat up the boy and plagued him with threats for testifying against him and was charged with assault.

AT THE TIME, Gacy was active with a variety of civilian programs and served as vice president of the Waterloo Jaycees.

Gacy moved to Norwood Park Township after he was paroled from prison in 1971, and seemed to have his troubled past behind him. Soon after his arrival he became Democratic captain of the 51st precinct in Norridge.

(Continued from Sect. 1 Page 12)

A DECOMPOSED BODY dug up from a shallow grave at the home of John Wayne Gacy is carried away Friday. Cook County Medical Examiner Robert J. Stein said an anthropologist and forensic dentist will be used to identify the skeletal remains.

BODIES FOUND HERE

SUMMERDALE

Norridge

FOSTER AVE.

LAWRENCE AVE.

MONTROSE AVE.

19

GACY WAS TRANSFERRED to Cermak Hospital at the Cook County Jail. Naturally, I was disappointed that we did not win the argument at the bond hearing. Nobody likes to lose. However, there was something to be said for being able to actually have a night's sleep. I thought that with Gacy cooling his heels in county, a full night's sleep might possibly be in my future. That's when the death threats to me and, believe it or not, to my family started at all hours. Apparently, death threats have more gravitas at two in the morning than they do in the daytime. Who knew? Those threats, together with endless calls from members of the press, made sleep fleeting. I was young. What did I know?

Welcome to the private practice of law, Sam.

Never would I have believed how crazy people could get. These were people, I might add, who had absolutely no connection to the case at all.

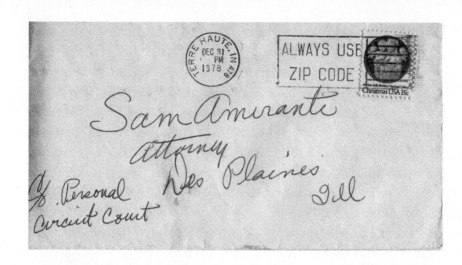

Sam Amirante
Attorney
*Personal
Circuit Court
Des Plaines,
Ill

The citizens in that town
ought to take you out hang
you also run a hat poker in
your rectum torture you like
that S. O. B bastard did all of
these boys you (red mouth)
lawyer) could not make a living
if they did that you are just
as bad as he is then you say
insane ha he is just a rotten
low down no good S. O. B
bastard you (red mouths) crooked
Judges have ruined our country

189

My dad drove a truck for the *Chicago Tribune*. He delivered newspapers to the people that delivered and sold the newspapers to the public in one of the big box trucks with the logo of the paper plastered on the side, one of the trucks you see in movies when the director wants to tell the audience that the story is spreading far and wide.

He worked hard every day, supported his family, saved his money, you know the type—the salt of the earth, never intentionally hurting another living soul. After I graduated from college, my dad saved his money all over again; and slowly, with sacrifice, he finally had enough money saved to go out and buy his dream car: a brand-new Lincoln Continental. It was his pride and joy. He babied that car.

This is hard to believe, but some asshole, some coward felt that the appropriate way to express his anger toward me because I had the audacity to represent one John Wayne Gacy was to vandalize my father's car. The logic escapes me.

On his beautiful car was scratched "Your son must be a fag. No one but a fag would represent a fag like Gacy."

The person or persons that perpetrated the vandalism were not simply misguided idiots with a screwdriver—they were homophobic misguided idiots with a screwdriver. This sad and cowardly act was reported in the paper, in Irv Kupcinet's column, because everything Gacy was reported in the paper.

On Sunday, Christmas Eve 1978, my wife and I had my parents over to the house, as usual, and we were all celebrating the holidays with the kids. Sammy had finally been released from the hospital with a clean bill of health, so this was a special Christmas. I had spent a great deal of time profusely apologizing to my dad for what had happened to his car, as if it was my fault. He knew that I had no power to stop crazy people from acting crazy, but he did use this opportunity to remind me that he had advised me to become a doctor. Parents—ya gotta love 'em.

We were having a traditional Italian Christmas dinner—lots of pasta and fish—and the mood was festive when the telephone rang. It was John Gacy.

"Sam," he said, "I want you to tell your father how sorry I am that his car was vandalized just because you are representing me, because you are my lawyer. I feel kinda responsible, you know? It ain't right."

"John, how did you know about that?" I asked.

"I read about it in the paper. That ain't right, Sam."

"Well, John, I don't have to tell him that you are sorry. I'll let you tell him yourself. He's right here. Hold on."

I tapped my dad on the shoulder. He was playing with one of the kids, not really paying attention to what I was doing. The Christmas tree glowed; the decorations twinkled, presents all over the place.

"Dad," I said, "someone wants to talk to you."

My dad looked at me, a bit surprised. We were at my house, after all. Who would be calling him there? "Who is it?" he asked.

"It's Gacy," I said. "He wants to apologize to you for what happened to your car. He wants to tell you he is sorry."

My dad's eyes became saucers. Then he had on a determined look that I had seen all my life. My dad and I are carbon copies of each other, with twenty-odd years of aging the only difference. His shoulders and back came up, and he scowled.

"No. I don't want to talk to that guy," he growled.

"Come on, Dad." I covered the mouthpiece on the phone. "He wants to tell you how sorry he is." I was loving this, laughing inside. My eyes were twinkling.

"I don't want to talk to him!" My dad's head had sunk between his shoulders. He no longer had a neck. Tiny beads of perspiration popped out on his forehead. He was seething. I was smiling, which, of course, made him even madder.

I shoved the phone at him. "Take the phone!" I said, laughing under my breath. Now my mother and my wife were also goading him.

My dad took the phone. Here's what we all heard . . . in my dad's gruff growl.

"Humm, yeah!"

Silence.

"All right."

Silence.

"OK, OK, yeah . . . yeah. Tanks. Tanks." (Chicago style for *thanks*.)

Silence, as my father's neck fully disappeared and larger beads of sweat popped out.

"OK, OK. Fine, fine. Tanks. That's OK . . . tanks."

He hung up the phone and looked at all of us. "Do you know what that asshole said to me?" he asked, incredulous.

"What?" we all asked, filled with mirth.

"He said, 'I'm sorry, Mr. Amirante, that some jerks vandalized your car just because your son is my lawyer, but . . . ya know, *there are a lotta nuts out there.*'"

We all broke into laughter. John Wayne Gacy—the man that was sitting in Cook County Jail on Christmas Eve, charged with the murder of a young boy, suspected of the murder of many, many more—had been dead serious. He did not even see the irony. He was telling my dad that there were a lot of nuts out there. Perhaps he should have looked in the mirror—if they would let him have one.

What was wrong with that guy?

CHRISTMAS 1978 WAS pretty much a nonevent for me, just another day. I was consumed by this case, and as hard as I tried to take a break from all the mad activity that surrounded it, I just couldn't. I was already planning strategies and seeing scenarios concerning how this was all going to play out.

Gacy had limited his options with reference to his defense by talking to any and all Des Plaines coppers that tapped him on the shoulder and asked him what happened. This had become a bit of a pastime around the station. It actually went beyond what would normally be considered questioning or interviewing of a suspect in a professional manner. That is not to say that the members of the investigation team were unprofessional when they questioned Gacy. They weren't. They would always remind him of his constitutional right to remain silent, and they were all actually trying to develop their case. But they were not bringing Gacy into a room and conducting a formal investigation session either.

Everyone has seen a dramatic depiction of an interview session on TV or in the movies. One would think that the questions would be asked in an interview room, complete with one-way mirrors, tape recorders, and a cadre of high-ranking officers looking on from behind the glass.

While Gacy was in custody in Des Plaines, officers and others would simply stop by his cell to shoot the shit whenever they were bored. On one such occasion, Mike Albrecht and assistant state's attorney Larry Finder were talking with Gacy. He was in his cell, and the others were standing outside. The police officer and the prosecutor were curious to find out just how Gacy accomplished his gruesome deeds. After all, Gacy was pretty much a fat wimp. He had always been a sickly, overweight loser, an outcast from the cool kids, with a heart condition and a fear of confrontation; and he was exactly the same as an adult.

"I used the rope trick," Gacy said, rather nonchalantly, considering the subject matter.

"What's the rope trick?" Larry asked.

"Well, do you guys have a rope?" Gacy inquired, looking at Albrecht as if they were all sitting around at the barbershop or the gas station just jawing.

"I'm not about to give you a rope, John," Albrecht said, looking at Gacy as if he might be out of his mind.

"What? I'm not going to kill you, Mike."

Then Gacy shook his head, disgusted, laughing under his breath. He reached into his pocket and pulled out the rosary that he always carried. He asked for a pen.

"Larry, stick your arm through the bars and make a fist. Pretend that your wrist is a neck and your fist is a head."

Within seconds, Gacy had tied a couple knots into the rosary beads, stuck the pen through some loops, and demonstrated the way the rope trick worked like a tourniquet.

"How would you get the rope over their heads, you know, didn't they put up a fight? Didn't they resist?" The officer and the prosecutor were both intrigued. They couldn't believe what they were hearing.

"Many times they would put it over their heads themselves," Gacy said without skipping a beat. "It was a trick, like a clown trick. They were waiting for the trick."

For me, when I heard this story, I just thought that it was insane on so many levels. Which was crazier, the fact that Gacy always carried a blessed rosary around in his pocket, the holy symbol of the Virgin Mary in the Catholic Church, when he committed his heinous crimes against young boys, or that he used that holy symbol to demonstrate how he killed those young boys? Or was it crazier still to picture a group of grown men sitting around a jail cell—a prosecutor, a cop, and a killer—offhandedly discussing the whole matter as though they were a bunch of asshole buddies in a locker room sharing secrets about a cheerleader?

But that was the dichotomy that was John Wayne Gacy. It was as if Gacy was so happy to be included, to be "just one of the guys," that he would say anything that kept the others listening to him. For once, Gacy was actually the center of attention, and it really didn't matter to him why. If a couple of regular guys, men he respected, guys he thought were cool, were interested enough in his stories to stay and listen to him tell them, he would continue jabbering, without regard to how detrimental the telling would someday prove to be.

Gacy really had only two friends—his employees Mike Rossi and David Cram, two kids barely out of their teens. And they would have had nothing to do with him if he weren't their employer, holding a paycheck every Friday, and a guy that always had drugs and beer and a place to consume them. This was Gacy reaching out, looking for friendship. I'm sorry, but John Wayne Gacy was the epitome of Winston Churchill's famous quote—a riddle, wrapped in a mystery, inside an enigma. Gacy was a psychiatrist's wet dream.

What was wrong with this guy?

I had been asking that question quite a lot lately. It was a fair question too, let's face it. The more you got to know Mr. Gacy, the more confused you became. I think that people like to put individuals like him neatly into a box so as to categorize and understand them. The easy thing to do with a person like Gacy would be simply to put him into the Evil, Crazed Killer box and be done with it. That is what most of society does—and did—with John Gacy. And believe me, John Gacy fit in that box quite well.

The only problem with that, however, is that when we do this, we don't learn anything further about the guy. We don't look any deeper. And when we fail to look deeper, we might miss some of the important reasons, the lessons about how an individual like John Gacy becomes a John Gacy. I'm no shrink, but I would like the people that study this sort of thing to learn as much about a guy like Gacy as possible, only because it might help society to recognize the symptoms or characteristics of a person like him in the future, maybe even before the next Gacy goes on a killing spree like the last one did. I could be wrong, but I think that would be a good thing.

One thing was sure about Gacy. He fit into many more boxes than just one, you know, the Evil, Crazed Killer box. This was a guy that carried a rosary with him at all times, then used it to demonstrate how he killed teenagers; who became a clown so that he could cheer up sick little kids; who had a family that loved him and stood by his side in times of unimaginable strife. When you put a squad of hard-bitten, seasoned, professional cops on his tail, they all became some sort of half-assed, convoluted version of buddies that ate and drank with him, swapping stories like they were bunkmates in the army. One minute this guy is pictured with his arm around the First Lady of the United States of America, Rosalynn Carter, while she was serving as the First Lady; and the next minute he is pictured as the most prolific serial killer of all time. He is standing at your door, grinning ear to ear, asking for your vote as your precinct captain by day; and he is cruising Bughouse Square in his shiny new Olds 98 by night. When he is caught and accused of crimes too numerous and incomprehensible to possibly understand, he sits around and chats about those very crimes like he is telling stories from his days at camp.

Historians chronicle the lives of our greatest leaders; biographies abound about people like Washington, Lincoln, Roosevelt, Kennedy. We even write books about our movie stars, rock stars, and sports stars. Every aspect of the lives of those that excel in life are studied and set to print or celluloid so that we might know how they did it, what made them tick, all in an effort to produce more like them, all in an effort to allow some child to learn, to be inspired, to join the ranks of those we honor and call great.

Shouldn't we do the same thing when it comes to those persons that repel, disgust, and scare us—all in an effort to *avoid* having more like them? Every generation has its famous greats and its infamous worst. Shouldn't we study them both? While we are all learning about what *to* do, shouldn't we spend a little time learning about what *not* to do?

Who the hell knows? Not me. I never smoked pot in college.

20

THE ONLY THING a good lawyer is concerned about at a time like this is that which is in the best interest of the client. That's it. That's the job. We are not social workers or psychologists, policemen or vigilantes. Sometimes we employ such people if it is in our client's interests, but our job is not to moralize or to judge. That is for others to do.

When a profusely bleeding patient is brought to the emergency room of a hospital, it really doesn't matter if that patient is the president of the United States or the crazed assassin that just shot the president of the United States. They get the exact same care. A surgeon's calling is to preserve life, to do no harm, irrespective of the patient's station in life, the patient's criminal record, the mistakes that the patient may or may not have made in life prior to his or her arrival in the ER. That is the oath. That is the job. A good doctor lives by that oath and performs that job.

Sometimes, it seems to me, that it is hard for certain people to grasp this concept. That is why my dad's car needed a new paint job and my wife had to pick up the telephone in the middle of the night and listen to some anonymous cretin spit vile, profanity-laced threats into her ear. These people are controlled by their emotions, not their brains; and believe it or not, I would fight to the death to defend their right to be so controlled and to maintain their skewed, uninformed opinions. That is my job. However, I would rather they didn't profess those opinions over the phone at 2:00 a.m. and involve my wife and my kids, but that's America. You have an inalienable right to be a nut, even an asshole.

Generally, people can be divided into two types: (1) those that would rather see ten guilty people go free to ensure that not one innocent person is ever wrongfully convicted and (2) those that would rather see ten innocent people convicted to ensure that not one guilty person ever goes free. It's really that simple, and both views have validity.

Defense lawyers, by and large, subscribe to the opinion of the first of these two groups. Prosecutors often subscribe to the opinion of the second group. In order for our system to work properly, society needs both. One thing that I have found to be true, however—and you can take this little nugget of wisdom to the bank—is that no one who has ever been wrongfully accused of a crime, or accused of a crime at all for that matter, subscribes to the opinion of the second group, no matter what they thought before they were accused, wrongfully or not. In other words, the day that you get your first DUI, you tend to join the ranks of group one. It is very easy to speak abstractly in a bar or at a cocktail party about how tough one thinks the laws should be, but perhaps one should wait until they have actually been wrongfully accused to fully formulate that opinion.

––––––––––––

THERE WAS A lot to do before December 29, 1978, Gacy's next court date. I had to file endless motions and challenges if I were to do my job properly. At this stage of the case, the work never stops. I was beginning to feel the weight of the sheer magnitude of the undertaking, together with the steady drumbeat of hatred that was being spewed by the many people—a minority actually, but a minority among millions can still be quite a large number—that could not wrap their heads around the concept that in this country everybody and no matter what they are charged with, no matter how heinous the crime, is entitled as a matter of law, and a matter of right, to a vigorous and proper defense. It's required by our Constitution, by our democracy.

I got wind of a planned interview that the medical examiner of Cook County, Dr. Robert J. Stein, was going to give, which was scheduled to air on WMAQ radio, the NBC affiliate. Dr. Stein was prepared to discuss whether or not a person that murders numerous people could be sane, to give his expert opinion on the subject. I had to try to stop that from happening, if I could. There was a great potential for poisoning the jury pool.

I was in my office when I received something unusual—a telegram. Gotta say, it's not every day that I receive a telegram. Think about it, have you ever received a telegram? Probably not, unless you're over eighty years old. So I'm interested. Maybe it's a very creative death threat, who knows? As it turns out, that telegram happened to be a godsend.

The telegram was from an old friend—Bob Motta.

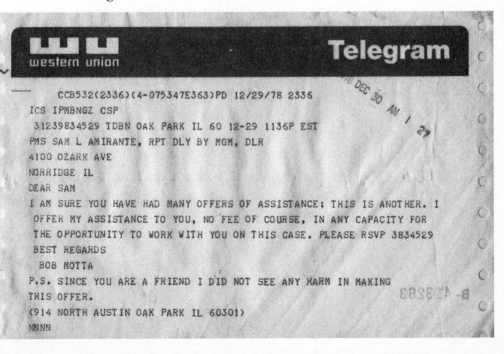

```
CCB532(2336)(4-075347E363)PD 12/29/78 2336
ICS IPMBNGZ CSP
 31239834529 TDBN OAK PARK IL 60 12-29 1136P EST
PMS SAM L AMIRANTE, RPT DLY BY MGM, DLR
4100 OZARK AVE
NORRIDGE IL
DEAR SAM
I AM SURE YOU HAVE HAD MANY OFFERS OF ASSISTANCE; THIS IS ANOTHER. I
OFFER MY ASSISTANCE TO YOU, NO FEE OF COURSE, IN ANY CAPACITY FOR
THE OPPORTUNITY TO WORK WITH YOU ON THIS CASE. PLEASE RSVP 3834529
BEST REGARDS
  BOB MOTTA
P.S. SINCE YOU ARE A FRIEND I DID NOT SEE ANY HARM IN MAKING
THIS OFFER.
(914 NORTH AUSTIN OAK PARK IL 60301)
NNNN
```

Robert M. Motta and I had worked together at the public defender's office; plus, I had worked with Bob's mother years earlier at Resurrection Hospital, so I knew the family. He was an honorable man and a good lawyer.

I had received previous calls and votes of confidence from lots of other lawyers I knew, some offering their help; but Bob was the only one who thought to send a telegram to express this. What a great idea, right?

All I could think about every night when my head hit the pillow were the four assistants that had been assigned to this case by our esteemed state's attorney, Bernard Carey. I thought about the limitless amount of money that would be spent to prosecute such a high-profile case. Then there was the small matter of the endless investigatory resources available to the State of Illinois, every police officer on every police force in every corner of the state would love to have a crack at helping convict the most prolific serial killer of all time.

I was just one guy.

So I decided to call Bob. Maybe he would really like to get involved in the case. I could certainly use the help. Plus, maybe he could help fend off some of the nice people who had promised to hang me from the highest oak tree in Cook County by my genitals and gouge my eyes out with hot pokers. If you think that sounds scary, you should have heard what they were promising to do to my kids, to my wife.

I didn't actually pay much attention to the death threats, as disconcerting as they were; they were being made by misguided cowards with a snoot full of liquid courage who didn't have anything better to do with their time. But I was concerned about the ever-increasing magnitude of work that was beginning to pile up. Someone had to do something about this planned broadcast by Dr. Stein, and it really didn't look like I was going to have the time.

"Hi, Bob, how are you doing?"

"Fine. Who is this?" I don't think Bob was expecting my call.

"It's Sam. Sam Amirante."

"Hi, Sam. Jesus, how are ya?" Motta was pacing now, thinking about a conversation he had had with his young son about this very phone call. It was his son that had said, "Why don't you call him up, Dad?" It was that conversation with his son that had led to the telegram idea.

"Fine . . . tired," I said.

"Yeah, I'll bet you are. Christ, this case is unbelievable. How's it going?" Motta could hear his own heart beating. He didn't know what to expect, but he figured that I had called for a reason. I hadn't called just to chat. He knew a request to help out on the case was probably coming.

"It's going, you know. I got your telegram. Thanks."

"Yeah . . . well, you're welcome."

"Do you know Dr. Stein, the medical examiner?" I think I sounded as tired as I felt.

"I know who he is, seen him on TV. Why? What about him?"

"Well, it seems that Dr. Stein is going to be interviewed on WMAQ radio, and he intends to give an opinion as to whether or not a person who commits these types of alleged crimes, kills this number of kids can be considered sane. This doctor will certainly be used by the State as one of their chief medical witnesses. I'd like to stop the broadcast. I don't want him to poison the jury pool."

"Well, I think you're right. No question, you have to file a motion. But can you abridge the freedom of speech? Wouldn't that constitute prior restraint?" Motta had crystallized the issue.

"I don't know," I said. "But I'd like to try. Hell, I have to try—which, by the way, is why I called, Bob. I was wondering . . . would you like to do it?"

Motta's heart stopped. No matter how you slice it, this was a career decision.

"Well . . . ah . . . when . . . ah . . . I don't know. When?" he stammered.

"Monday," I said. We were speaking on Friday, so yeah, two days of prep.

"Monday? This coming Monday? Well . . . ah . . . can I let you know later? I think I have something else up on Monday. Can I call you later?"

"Well, Bob, I would need to know fast, you know. I need to get the research and pleadings done for the TRO by Monday in order to file and ask for an emergency hearing. The broadcast is scheduled for Tuesday. Get back to me as soon as possible, OK? Check your calendar." I hung up.

Motta stood there, a bit dumbfounded, with a dead telephone in his hand. He slumped into his chair. "Jesus . . . Jesus . . . Jesus," he kept silently repeating, shaking his head. He realized that he had just hesitated to be part of what was being referred to as the trial of the century because of some silly little commitment to a misdemeanor case on Monday, which could easily be continued with a telephone call.

"What the hell am I doing?" he asked himself aloud in his empty office. He began to pace, stared at the phone, picked it up, set it back down in the cradle, paced some more, mumbling. Then he stopped, stared at the telephone once more, grabbed it, and punched in my number.

"Sam, OK . . . of course I'll do it. I'll do anything I can to help. When would you like to meet?" he said.

"Well, that's the thing, Bob. Actually, I'd like you to handle this yourself. I'm tired. I'm swamped. I'm getting overwhelmed with paper over here."

"Alone? Ah . . . OK." Bob was a bit surprised once again. "OK . . . ah . . . how will I . . . how do I get the facts?"

"Do you have a pen and legal pad handy? I'll give them to you right now." As I talked, Motta scribbled. This was a load off my mind, I had to admit. I was beginning to breathe a little easier.

The best word to describe Bob is *irascible*. *Ornery* would be another. That may sound like I'm not being too complimentary; but if you think that, you would be wrong. Those are words that describe a good lawyer, one who cares little about the opinions of others, especially when it comes to their opinions about him. Bob couldn't care less what one person or another thinks about him, his methods, or his ways. He just puts his head down and plows through what he needs to plow through to get the job done. Another word to describe Bob—*tenacious*. You can't stop him once he sinks his teeth into an issue.

For the next thirty hours, Bob was buried in books and research materials, reviewing and learning the fine points of the law as it pertains to the First Amendment of our Constitution and, in particular, as that First Amendment, which guarantees freedom of speech, applies to the press. These are lofty, high-minded issues that lawyers have fought over throughout the history of our republic, important issues that require a delicate balance to preserve free speech without allowing the press to overstep and do harm. Few areas of the law are more voluminous. Bob knew by late Sunday night that he had little chance of prevailing on this motion. It was an uphill battle, at best. It is almost impossible to stop someone, especially a member of the press, or a person being interviewed by a member of the press, from saying something before they say it. This is what is known as prior restraint, and it is frowned upon in a free society. However, a good lawyer does not cower from a fight just because the deck is stacked against him. That is when a good lawyer bares his teeth the brightest, and Bob was a good lawyer.

He drafted and personally typed up a complaint for temporary restraining order; and on Monday, armed with a briefcase full of case law and a bushelful of determination, he set forth to the Daley

Center to file his emergency motion for TRO in the Chancery Division of the Circuit Court of Cook County. The clerk at the counter who accepted the filing and file-stamped the documents had barely lifted the stamp off the paper—the ink was still drying—when the press, including radio station WMAQ, was alerted to the filing of these documents. The call went out to their lawyer.

Don Reuben was probably the most famous attorney in the city of Chicago. Other high-profile attorneys would dispute this, of course, out of jealousy or pride; but Don Reuben represented Fortune 500 corporations, big-name media types, the crème de la crème of the city. If you were in law school or a member of the legal profession, you knew who he was, and most of the population of the city had seen his mug on the news at one time or another even if they didn't remember his name. When Mr. Reuben walked into the courtroom at precisely 3:00 p.m., the scheduled time for the emergency hearing, and announced that he would be representing the National Broadcasting Corporation and their affiliate WMAQ radio, Bob swallowed hard but was immediately surprised to see how slight of a man Mr. Reuben actually was. He was such a little guy—really little.

Unfortunately, size doesn't matter in the arena of the courtroom, especially when precedent and case law are on your side. The judge ruled that he could not see a compelling reason to bind the hands of the press or the doctor to air or state an opinion prior to the stating of it.

Bob didn't have time to be too dejected, however. As soon as he exited the courtroom, he was besieged by a throng of screaming reporters, with microphones and camera lenses recording his every word. Yesterday, Bob was a relatively obscure but happy young lawyer who had recently opened his small office in Oak Park, Illinois. Today, his rugged face, with his trademark bushy mustache, would be plastered across all three local network news broadcasts as each covered the story on the evening news.

Bob stopped by my office the following day to debrief and discuss the case. He had done a great job with the motion and with the press. He had really stepped up to the plate on short notice and without much help from me—without any help from me, let's face it. I told him that I could use help on the case in its entirety. We talked about how it would likely be an unusual ride with an unpredictable ending. I mentioned the steady flow of death threats and criticism that had been leveled at me and would now be leveled also at him. I explained to him that John Gacy was a lot of things and that one of those things was pure crazy. Bob was not intimidated or concerned. I made a formal offer to him to become cocounsel on the case, pending approval by the client, and we shook hands. From that moment on, we were partners on the case titled *People of the State of Illinois v. John Wayne Gacy*, and we never looked back. The handshake was enough for us. Now we just had to hold on tight because the ride was starting.

21

WE **HAD TO** go out to Cermak Hospital to visit Mr. Gacy. Motta had no idea what to expect. He had been up most of the night before agonizing over this first meeting with his new client. It is only natural to wonder a bit about what the country's worst, most prolific serial killer might be like.

Parking your car and strolling into the Cook County Jail is an experience that you will never forget. You travel through several levels of chain-link fence, topped with gleaming rolls of razor-sharp barbed wire, enough barbed wire to slice a fly in half if that fly is foolhardy enough to attempt a buzz through it. The pea gravel crunches under your feet as you approach the first of many gray cast-iron doors that clank behind you, much as you might expect they would if you have ever watched a prison movie. Only a jail door sounds like a jail door. The clank sounds quite final, quite irreversible. The doors are guarded by uniformed men or women that block out the sun with their size. When they ask for your ID, it is not a request, it's a command. They smile sometimes, but you know from their tone that not one thing that they say is in any way negotiable.

Motta and Gacy hit it off just fine, or as fine as anyone gets along with that unusual little man. Gacy smiles and shakes your hand, but that doesn't mean he won't talk shit about you behind your back. That depends on what suits him at the time. What surprised Bob was the level of cream puffery that he met. Gacy strikes you upon first meeting him more as the old Polish plumber who, like an old *Saturday Night Live* skit, exposes his butt crack every time he bends over to fix the toilet. He is not an immediately intimidating person by any stretch of the imagination. Instead, you are more likely to laugh. He is more of a wimp with a thick Chicago accent, who obviously spent a great deal of time caring for his mother. *This is the monster that everybody has been talking and writing in the papers about?* Bob was thinking. What Gacy did more than anything else during their first meeting was whine and bitch like a little old lady in a bad restaurant. He had complaints about nearly everything. Bob and I just looked at each other, incredulous, as if to say, "Yeah, John, it's *jail.*" We refrained from stating the obvious. After some time, our actual mission was finally accomplished in that Gacy approved Bob Motta as my cocounsel.

One problem that loomed ominously in the distant future was a simple concern about how we were going to get paid. Money was not our first concern; but we had to pay the rent, we had to eat, and we had to feed our families. Gacy had paid me a retainer when he had an ongoing business. Now he had jobs lined up that he would never finish. He had accounts receivable that he would never collect. And most of his other semiliquid assets, tools, vehicles, and the like had been confiscated and were being held by the State as evidence. His primary asset, his house, was being systematically destroyed as body after body was excavated from the crawl space. No one was suggesting that the investigation and excavation of the crawl space be interfered with; however, there was talk about getting court approval to raze the structure to make the investigation easier. That we would have to oppose. Otherwise, how would we get paid?

THE CASE HAD been up in court on the twenty-ninth, and the following orders had been entered by the court:

The case was continued by agreement of the parties to January 10, 1979, where the matter would be reassigned by the chief judge. Now the case was being transferred to the Criminal Courts Building at 26th Street and California Avenue, one of the most famous courthouses in the country. Clarence Darrow, among other noted attorneys, argued cases in its hallowed courtrooms.

The night before that court appearance on the twenty-ninth—the night of December 28—was a lesson in humility for me. I was in my office feverishly trying to prepare motions—motion to dismiss, motion to transfer, et cetera, et cetera. These were preliminary motions that I needed to file with the court. And in general, I was attempting to prepare for this big, important case. I was feeling pretty full of myself. My picture had been in the paper, and I was the hotshot criminal defense attorney charged with representing the defendant in this huge case. Hell, it was going to be the trial of the century. Everybody said so. My secretary, Erlene, and I were in the office well into the evening hours. Even she was proud to be working for such a famous guy, and on such a famous case.

Suddenly, panic struck. I looked at the clock on the wall and realized that my suit—my one and only suit—was at the cleaners. I had dropped it off to be cleaned in anticipation of this big day. If I didn't pick up that suit, I would have nothing to wear to court the following morning.

I begged Erlene, "Would you please pick up my suit while I finish making copies and getting everything ready for court?"

"I suppose," she said, teasing me. "But don't get used to it."

"I'll meet you at my house," I called to her as she hurried out the door all bundled up in coat and scarf against the weather.

Erlene had her own problems getting the suit. First, the snow and ice were making driving a chore. Then, when she finally arrived at the cleaners, it was closed. Luckily, she saw a light burning in a back room. She pounded on the door. The owner responded, shaking his head and pointing at the "Closed" sign in the window, pantomiming his regrets.

"Please, sir," she pleaded through the glass. "You have to help me! My boss is Sam Amirante, the attorney representing John Wayne Gacy, the guy in the news, that guy with the bodies under the house. He has to have this suit for court tomorrow. He needs it!"

Erlene was proud. The guy was totally impressed. He immediately opened his doors and made the extra effort to help. She was working for a pretty important guy. How cool?

With perfect timing, Erlene and I arrived at my house at the same moment; we both pulled up to the house together. I thanked her profusely as she ran up to meet me with the suit. We stood there on the walk, surrounded by piles of snow, both of us excited about this important case and all that was happening.

The porch light came on, and my wife, Mary, appeared in the doorway.

"Hi, Erlene," she said politely, smiling at her. Then she turned to me. "Honey," she said, still smiling brightly. "We need toilet paper. Go buy some toilet paper."

Did you ever hear air escaping from a balloon? That is the sound that my ego was making as I dutifully trudged through the snow back to my car as the two women in my life silently giggled. I drove away.

No job is finished until the paperwork is done.

BOB AND I huddled and began to plan strategy and assign ourselves specific areas of concentration. We began to see the path on which we would attempt to walk through the minefield that lay ahead. We immediately became a team of two—partners.

THE CASE WOULD ultimately be assigned to the Honorable Judge Louis B. Garippo, which was a testament to the wisdom of the chief judge, the Honorable Judge Richard Fitzgerald. It was well known that the normal process of computerized assignment of judges was circumvented just this once by the chief due to the particular sensibilities and temperament of Judge Garippo. Nobody questioned this assignment—with good reason—because Judge Garippo was clearly the right man for the job.

The evening before my first appearance before Judge Garippo proved to be an interesting one. The death threats and criticism in the press were increasing as more and more bodies were recovered from the crawl space beneath Gacy's house. I tried hard to ignore the onslaught, but it was wearing on me. I had always tried to keep a reasonable relationship between myself and the venerable members of the press. However, I was fielding questions that didn't sound right to me, not in a free society where a defendant's presumption of innocence is paramount.

Finally, it was time to set the record straight once and for all.

After being asked a particularly snotty question by a particularly snotty, faceless reporter somewhere in the back, I finally went off. I wanted the sad little anonymous commentators out there, the purveyors of the ugly threats to my kids and to my wife, hiding in their homes and fortified with a bottle, to hear me clearly. I looked squarely into the lens of the camera in front of me, pointed at it, and by extension at each and every one of the little cretins hiding on the other side of it, and screamed a tirade at the top of my lungs. I went on and on, paraphrasing the Constitution, railing on about how every person in the country was entitled to a trial in which he or she was able to confront his or her accusers and the witnesses against him or her no matter what the charges may be. I talked about the sanctity of the right to a trial by a jury of our peers. I was worked up. It finally ended as follows:

"I will defend this man, my client, until the last drop of my blood, if necessary! This is America!"

It is my understanding that this interview was widely disseminated. It seems that everyone saw it, and that included Judge Garippo.

Therefore, when I approached the bench the following day on my first day in front of the esteemed judge, the following exchange took place:

"Good morning, Your Honor, Sam Amirante representing the defendant, Mr. Gacy—"

Before I could say anything else, Garippo interrupted.

"Excuse me, excuse me, is someone talking. Stand back a little farther so I can see you."

I backed up.

"Yes, back up some more," said the judge, motioning to me.

Needless to say, this threw me just a little. I took another step backward and eyed the judge. He smiled down from the bench, peering through wire-rimmed glasses with what I thought to be a particularly mischievous look, a smirk, maybe.

"Well, Mr. Amirante, I expected to see some kind of six-foot-four gargantuan kind of guy, based on what I saw on the TV last night. That was you pointing and screaming into the camera, right? Now here you are, and I could hear you talking, but I couldn't see you. You are not six foot four, are you?"

"No, Your Honor, I'm not."

I guess the camera shot on the news the night before was a head-and-shoulders shot, and the judge could not get a perspective on my actual size. We stood there, appraising one another for a long moment. It was a moment that I will always remember. But I had something up my sleeve that I believed would cause him to always remember the moment as well. I handed up a piece of paper, a small card, passed it up to him as he sat perched on the bench.

"Well, Your Honor, allow me to present our first motion."

Here's what I handed to him:

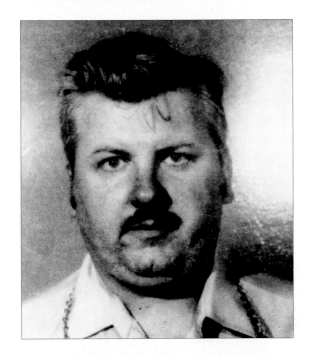

The world saw Gacy as this.

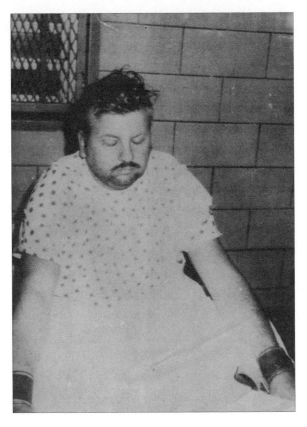

Sam saw Gacy as this.

Crime Scene Photos

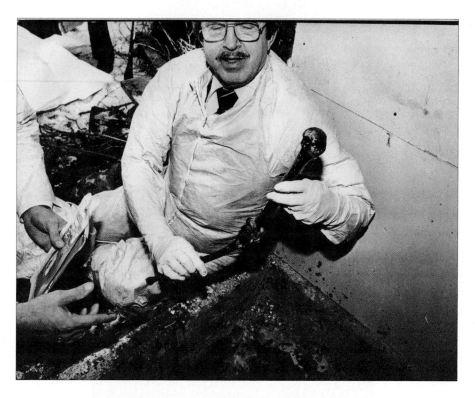

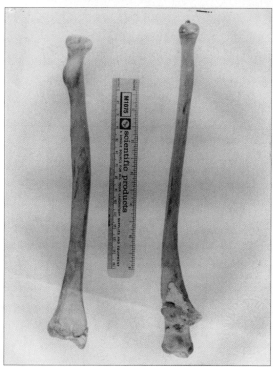

Photo used in Kunkle's closing argument.

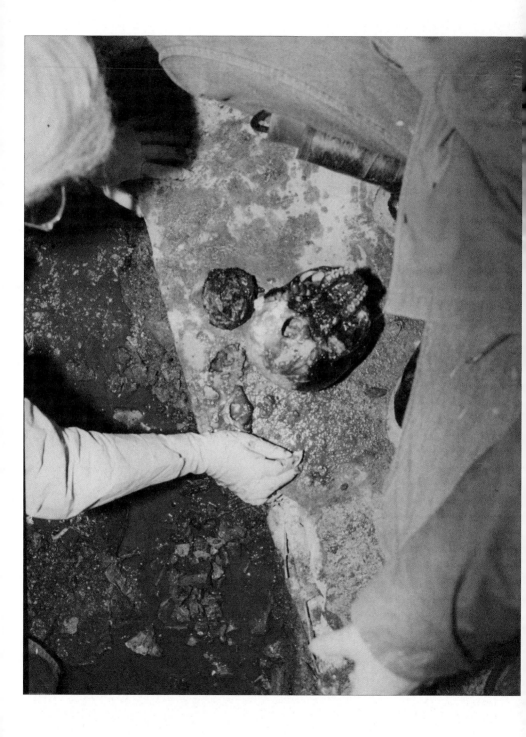

Rope from body 8 ››

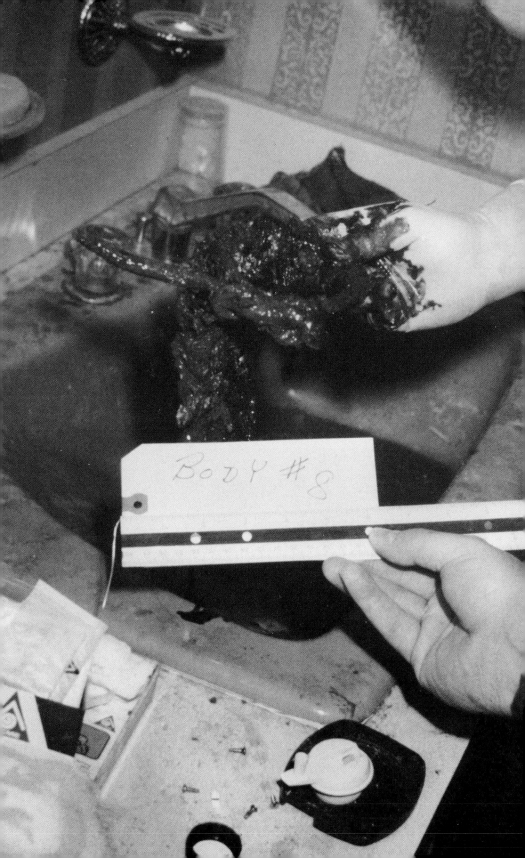

Rope from body 8

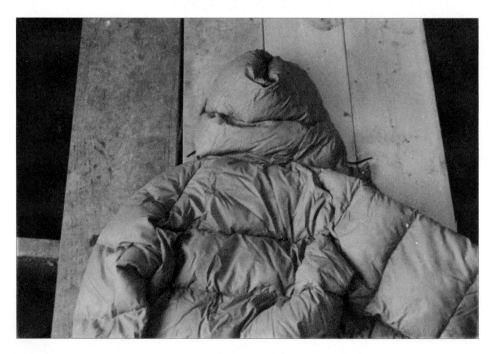

The blue down jacket.

John Sync's car.

John Sync's television.

The receipt found in Gacy's
house that broke the case.

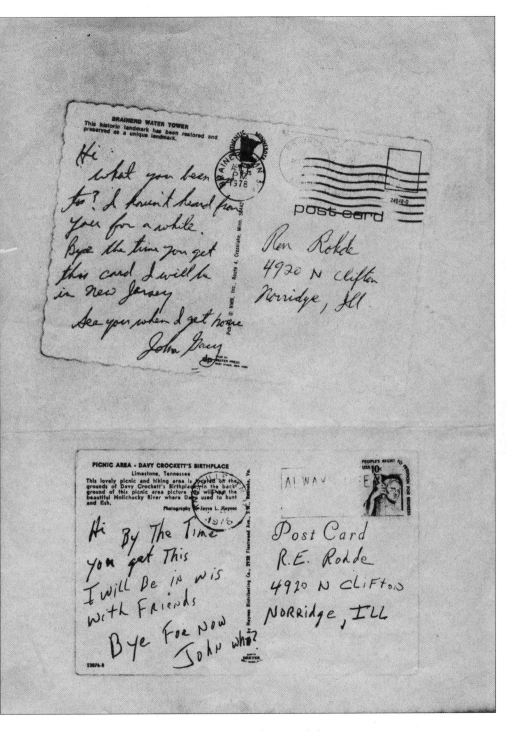

Postcards that Gacy sent his friend while on vacation.

Motta   Amirante

John Wayne Gacy Jr., center, is shown as he arrived with guards late Saturday night at the Winnebago County Public Safety Building. Jury selection for his trial begins today. (Copyright The Chicago Tribune 1980). (AP Laserphoto).

The prosecution team. From the left: Terry Sullivan, William Kunkle,
Cook County State's Atty. Bernard Carey, and Robert Egan.

Spotlight report: The Gacy jury

Trial starts Wednesday

By MARJORIE RUSCHAU
Staff writer

Accused mass murderer John Wayne Gacy Jr. and his traveling media road show have moved on to Chicago for the next phase of his trial.

A five-woman, seven-man Winnebago County jury was selected after four days of in-depth questioning. One man and four women will serve as alternate jurors, replacing any regular jurors who cannot serve for some reason, such as illness.

THE TRIAL begins Wednesday morning in Cook County Criminal Courts. The jurors and alternates will be brought in sometime Tuesday.

There the prosecution is expected to produce the grisly details of the deaths of the 33 Chicago-area young men and boys Gacy is accused of murdering — one by stabbing and 32 by strangulation.

Graphic video tapes showing the discovery of 29 of the partially decomposed bodies beneath the home and garage of the defendant may be shown.

If the Winnebago County jury judges Gacy to be insane, another hearing will be held to determine whether he should be hospitalized.

Jurors will be lodged at a Chicago hotel for the duration of the trial expected to last six to eight weeks. Friends and family may visit on Sundays in Chicago.

Things seemed unnaturally quiet in the Winnebago County Courthouse Friday following the excitement of the past week.

The uproar of the area, Chicago and national media attending the jury selection at times equaled, if not overshadowed, the actual jury selection. The familiar faces of Rockford television newscasters stood out to the local people as much as the NBC and CBS logos on the network cameras.

Journalists gathered early Monday morning in the courthouse lobby, hoping for a chance to talk to some of the prosecution and defense attorneys and eager for a good seat in the courtroom.

THE BRAZEN TV and newspaper cameras, barred from the third floor of the courtroom, struggled to get enough film footage. When the two defense attorneys went to lunch Monday, their every step was photographed as they came out of the elevator, walked through the lobby and walked out the door. The crowd even stopped traffic as it doggedly followed the attorneys across State Street.

In the courtroom, the first row of seats was filled with media artists. Using such mediums as ink, chalk, magic marker, pencil and water colors, they tried to capture the hypnotic presence of Gacy and the tension of prospective jurors.

Reporters filled the next three rows, notepads in hand, leaning forward to catch the answers of the soft-voiced prospective jurors. The situation was so tense any light answer came off as a fantastically-funny joke.

"Have you any relative or friend who is afflicted with mental illness?" one woman was asked.

"Not that I know of," she answered. The entire courtroom, including Gacy, broke up in laughter.

COOK COUNTY Judge Louis B. Garippo excused 246 prospective jurors during the four days of jury selection before the jury and alternates were chosen.

Members of the Cook County contingent had nothing but praise for the way they were treated and the people they found in Rockford.

"(Rockford) was quite different from the popular conception that some news people tried to depict," Garippo said. (Some newspapers had analyzed Rockford residents as poorly-educated, lower middle class factory workers eager to hang Gacy.) "We found a great cross-section of people, well-educated, honest, forthright and willing to answer questions."

"We're happy we came here," said defense attorney Sam Amirante. "Everything went smoothly."

"I REALLY believe IN The AMERICAN SYSTEM
oF JUSTICE EVErybody IS ENTITLED TO
The best deFense Possible."

SAM AMIRANTE

chgo Sun-Times 1-5-79

J. GACY
12-25-79

A sketch Gacy gave Sam.

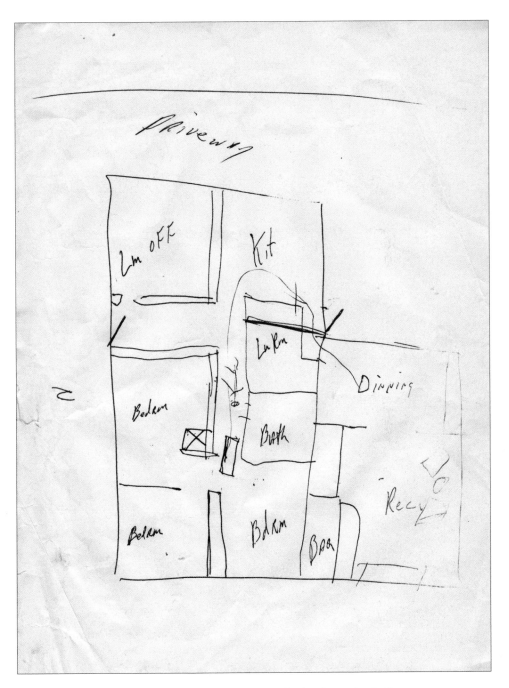

Gacy's sketch of his house. Note the body in the hallway.

11-10-79

your task is to build a better world said God.

And I asked how? this world is oh so large and vast and yet I'm so small what can I do?

And God in all of his wisdom said.

just Build a better you.

John Gacy

Witness - Investigator Julianne Weiss -
Witness - Cf. Fitzgerald

Judge calls off demolition of Gacy home

A judge called off the demolition of John Gacy's home Wednesday as wreckers were maneuvering heavy equipment into position for the razing.

Circuit Court Judge Richard H. Jorzak stayed his previous demolition order for at least a week after lawyers for the accused mass murderer argued that Gacy 'didn't get his day in court" when demolition was being considered.

Specifically, attorneys Sam L. Amirante and Robert M. Motta contended that Gacy didn't get a fair hearing because a third lawyer, LeRoy Stevens Jr., failed to appear for Tuesday's hearing when Jorzak issued the order to allow the demolition.

Amirante and Motta have been representing Gacy in his criminal troubles, while Stevens had been retained independently to represent Gacy in civil matters. Stevens couldn't be reached immediately for comment on why he failed to appear Tuesday.

Gacy lawyer trying 1st private criminal case

By Maurice Possley
and Bob Olmstead

The prosecution of suspected mass murderer John Gacy will pit three of State's Atty. Bernard Carey's veteran trial lawyers against a seasoned ex-public defender tackling his first criminal case as a private attorney.

Gacy's lawyer is Sam L. Amirante, 30, who never thought he would be fighting a murder charge against the man he once knew only as a trustee of the Norwood Park Twp. Lighting District.

Amirante, a gravel-voiced veteran of criminal trials, spent 4½ years in the Cook County Public Defender's office, handling hundreds of felony cases in suburban courts and in the Criminal Court Building at 26th and California. During that time he did occasional legal work for the lighting district and met Gacy.

AMIRANTE'S name appeared in a federal lawsuit filed in Gacy's behalf Dec. 19, charging that Des Plaines police were harassing him. Amirante said attorney LeRoy Stevens is handling that suit.

On Dec. 22, after Gacy was charged with the murder of a Des Plaines youth and investigators began uncovering bodies under Gacy's home, Amirante quit his position as supervisor of the 3d Municipal District for the public defender to devote full time to the suspect's defense. Amirante said he previously had planned to leave the office in February.

He took the case because "I'm an attorney. The man's entitled to the best defense. It's the American way."

Gacy, who allegedly has told investigators he killed 31 or 32 people, was scheduled to appear in the Des Plaines branch of Circuit Court Friday, but the hearing was conducted without him because authorities feared for Gacy's safety. The case was continued to Jan. 10.

AMIRANTE, a graduate of Loyola University Law School, is married and has two young sons. While working as supervisor in the suburban district, he compiled a record of eight acquittals and two convictions in felony jury trials, he said.

Taking on Gacy's defense places the feisty, scrapping Amirante against a familiar foe in Terry Sullivan, 34, a 10-year veteran of Carey's office and supervisor of the 3d Municipal District for the state's attorney.

Sullivan is part of Carey's team, which is headed by William J. Kunkle Jr., 37, and anchored by Robert R. Egan, 30.

Also a Loyola Law School graduate, Sullivan describes Amirante as "energetic, very competent, and a gentleman. Sam is a very good lawyer."

The sandy-haired Sullivan, who is single, and the dark-haired Amirante have gone head-to-head in several previous cases, including the trial and conviction of Everett Bowen on charges that he

killed his three children by setting fire to their Northlake home.

SULLIVAN'S prior experience also includes investigative and supportive trial-work in the trial and conviction of Patricia Columbo and Frank DeLuca, for the murder of Columbo's family.

Kunkle is chief deputy

state's attorney and a former public defender who switched sides to become an assistant state's attorney in 1973. He lost election tries for a Cook County judgeship in 1976 and 1978.

A graduate of Northwestern University Law School, Kunkle served as Carey's chief of the criminal prosecutions bu-

reau and has considerable experience in the prosecution of criminal cases involving a defense plea of insanity.

Kunkle helped pioneer the first use in Illinois of two juries to hear a murder-arson trial against three South Side men accused of killing four members of the same family.

An avid softball player,

Kunkle and his wife, Sally, have a young daughter and live on the North Side.

EGAN, a prosecutor since 1973, is officially the state's attorney's trial specialist in Criminal Court, a position he calls "a sort of trouble-shooter." He assists other assistant state's attorneys in the more difficult cases.

cost of the cars as they are

. Funeral Arrangement

John V. May Funeral Home
4600 N. Milwaukee Ave
Chicago Illinois

Casket: Silver/Gray - White Interior
          From Loyal Casket Co
          28 So. California
          Chicago, Illinois

Clothing: Dk. Blue 3 pcs. Suit
            White shirt
            Red + Blue Tie
            Black Rosary in hand
            Black shoes

Flowers: lot of Flowers

Music:
          Amazing Grace
          How great thou are
          Holy God we Praise Thy Name

Service:
          St Francis Borgia Catholic Church
          7950 W. Addison
          Chicago Illinois
          10 Am. White Mass

          (I became a Catholic here in 1950)

Interment
          Maryhill Cemetery
          Milwaukee Avenue
          Niles Illinois
          Grave side
Plot: At The Head of My Dad grave
        Next to my Uncle Raymond Robertson

I

Dear Mom, Joni, Karen, Sam, + Bob;

By the time you read this I will have already died. I don't want you to be sadden by my passing, but happy that I am at Peace and Rest, and Remember God's word:

"Albowiem tak Bóg umiłowaї świat, że Syna swego Jednorodzonego dał Aby Każdy Kto weñ wierzy nie zginał ale miał żywot wieczny."

For Sam
"Poiche Iddiö ha Tanto Amato il mondo, che ha dato il suo unigenito Figliuolo, affinche chiunque crede in Lui non perisca, ma abbia vita eterna.

Almost all of my life I have been on the go trying to prove that I would Amount to something and be excepted by my Father. Although I have only lived to three/fourth of my Thirty seventh year. I feel that I have lived three life times.

I am tired, so very tired, I have worked all of my life and have shared it with everyone. I have never asked for or gotten anything for nothing. But then,... that also is the way I wanted it. As I was growing up I don't think I could ask for a more understanding Mother, you were always there when I needed someone to comfort me, or to give advise, and even make me feel wanted when I was sick. Of course I let you down when I ran away at Twenty, but somehow I think you know and understood. I never was any good at keeping things from you. I am sorry I let you down when Dad died. I know that I should have been there, and I have never forgotten or forgave myself for it. Just one more reason why dad was right about me.

Joni, you and I were close when we were growing up, and shared alot of things mostly good, but some how a cloud came between us as we became older, maybe it was marriage or just not living close enough. And even then I don't understand why you changed I still loved you just as much. I know now you have your own life to live and a beautiful family to care for.

Karen, you,... I don't know where to start. I can remember our ups and downs, and our good times and bad ones, and I wouldn't trade any of them. You too have a nice family and beautiful children. I guess it was meant to be, you have come out to be the strong one. Of course you had good teachers, you watch + learned from Joni and I and benifitted from our mistakes.

I don't want you to think that my whole life was sad + lonely, because you shared alot in my happiness. Oh I think I have traveled more than the entire family, having traveled over forty states of this great county of ours, and loving every inch of it, making decision for alot of people and making things work. As you know big things have never bother me, always little things have upset me the most. But I guess that normal when your a little man. I have met many many people in my life from presidents to common people like me... And I have found one thing that holds true... That weather your black, white, red, or brown., we're all brothers in God's eyes. All we want from life is to be treated like a human and given a chance.

All my life I have believed that I was self-motivated and that I could accomplish anything that I set my mine to doing. You know God never said life was to be easy, He just gave us the tools and the time to mold it into a labor of love in our own image.

But Karen, there were other things in my life that I did that I am responsible for, and that I am the only one who can understand the feeling I got from them. Like the first time I was in charge of the largest christmas parade in Springfield. Everyone was concerned with how big and how good it was. While in 6° degree weather I was happy when I seen the warm glowing faces of children waiting hours to see Santa Claus, and some for the first time. To know that you in a small way was in part responsible for that happening that was my reward for over two month of work. And then the time I was a clown and went to the hospital to visit the children, and I went into a room by myself where a little boy was, and his mother started to cry, and after I visit with the boy I went out and asked the mother if I had did anything wrong. She said, No... it just that her son who was hit by a car had been in there for six weeks and that was the first time she seen him smile. That feeling you can't put into words, and it something that no one can take from you. Thats what my life has been all about. Making others happy and helping people These are the simple things in my life which I can take with me forever.

It's too bad that I didn't apply the same love, the same feeling to my own family. Maybe I would have never lost Carole. God knows I love her and the girls.

My work was my life, working for others, doing things for others, weather I made money on not. I have never been able to figure out why? Why did I drive myself so hard it was almost like I was punishing me for not being better. Oh well I know that God understands and maybe with all the sickness I had that was His way of making me strong.

And Then There the other side, The side That I Really don't Know where it Fits in, but it there. Why? How? What happen To make it happen in me. It doesn't Fit? It don't belong,.. I hate it, yet it didn't go Away, No matter how hard I worked or how many hours I stay up, To Keep it From happening.

Sam and Bob, I guess I was hard to get along with And hard on you both. But Please Forgive me As I Am Sorry That I couldn't be of more help To you with Your case. The Last seven years have been moving So Fast That I have yet to catch up with Them. It has been Like Living without Any Feeling This Last year has been Longest + worst, in That being Alone And not understanding what happen To everyone you new.

My Last year has been Like being A witness to A very close person ... me, And not Knowing what Really happen. I Find it hard to believe That I can Know so much About so many things And yet Know Nothing About myself. I have had a heavy broken Heart Split in A body with A mind of Two different people Fighting For control, And yet not Knowing who was Responsible For what. I only wish I could have explained it or Remember what Real was going on in my Life I can not help to think That maybe I could have helped to make things better or at Least clear up some of The mystery in me, Have you ever Reached For some thing that no matter how hard you tried, you could not Grip it. But you never Stop wanting it. That's Alot The way my Life was, but the hardest thing to understand is that you don't understand why? In The Last Eleven month I have gone over and over my entire Life. Not only in dreams but even my Fears, And yet I still don't Know The Answers. Maybe it was not God's will For me to Know or maybe I Am Looking For Answers to something that was None of my business to begin with.

You Know I have never Quit at Anything
I set out To do. And yet my Life is Ending
with me being more Confused Than I've ever
been. Oh I Talked of Death And even taking
my own Life, but I don't Think I could do
That. Besides that wasn't GOD's Will For
me, As you see that I Join him Anyway!

I hope to Find Dad Now That I have
Time, maybe we can Talk And go Fishing Providing
I don't get blamed For Everything That goes
WRong.

I have made my peace with The Lord,
my GOD And I hope that he give you All good
Health and happiness. I have to go Now,
Thank you For Everything

God bless
Love always

John Wayne Gacy

5-14-80

Judge Louis B. Garrippo

Dear Judge Garrippo,

I would like for you to order one Julie Weiss to return to your court the following letters, that at the time they were written she was given by me under pretext that she was working for my attorneys. The dates are as followed:

MARCH 21-80   1 Page
MARCH 31-80   1 Page
APRIL 10-80   9 Pages
APRIL 27-80   8 Pages
APRIL 30-80   2 Pages

ALSO ON A APRIL 30, 1980 visit she pick up 4 Letters Addressed To me From Limestone High, 2 From Gary Porter, 2 From Linda Schneider.

There is two Letter in Particular Both dated april 27th. One deal with authorization from me to her to seek out a civil attorney to represent me. I am CANCELING that order.

The second letter with the same date is regards to authorization for her to look for a new criminal attorney. since she stated that my present attorneys were droping me. Which I have now Found out to be False.

That same Letter which runs 5 pages contain statement which in part could lead someone to misunderstand what I am saying. As you know throughout my whole trial and before many people including mostly the news media has taken things out of context. It seem because of greed now everyone wants to destroy the images of my attorneys both Sam Amirante + Robert Motta because they put on such a fight for me. It is bad enough that I was of no help in my own defense because of the lack of understanding of criminal procedures and what really happen Its like working at great odds when it seem that

II

everyone hates the Accused and then I myself
wasn't Able to help Them.

In that letter mrs weiss told me that
she was working for me and that she needed a
fast breakdown of the events of my
case as she investigating something for Sam.
So that letter contains the following:

First when all attorney started working on
my case and how I obtain them. etc etc.

Please feel free to write if
you have any other question

Sincerely John W. Gacy

The translation from Italian to English is loosely this: "Sir, please don't break my balls."

A hidden smile flirted at the corners of the esteemed jurist's mouth and filled his eyes as he looked back at me. He kept his judicial demeanor, however, never wavering.

"Hmm, I see. OK, OK, Mr. Amirante, step back. We will proceed accordingly. Any other motions?"

And with that, the case of *the People of the State of Illinois v. John Wayne Gacy* officially began. We had a judge and a courtroom assigned, a place to do battle. Of course, it would be just over a year before the actual trial would start, but the preliminary struggles would start today.

22

As IT TURNS out, Jack Hanley was a real person—sort of. Plus, he was really a cop. It seems that Gacy and Officer Hanley had met sometime while John was working at Bruno's, a restaurant where he worked for a while as a short-order cook after he was released from the prison in Anamosa. Of course, Officer Hanley's name wasn't actually Jack, but in John Gacy's wandering, lost mind, it was. Officer Hanley was not a homicide detective either. However, if you asked John, he would tell you that he was.

Without explanation, John Gacy would occasionally use this name when cruising Bughouse Square. He always believed that it was much cooler to say he, John Gacy, was a homicide cop named Detective Jack Hanley, a suave badass who solved the unsolvable crimes, rather than the truth—that he was a dumpy, boring small-time contractor who lived with his mother in the suburbs. Now in his defense, John Gacy was not the first guy in the world who has told a little white lie in an attempt to get laid. I have seen a lot of multimillionaires with really bad shoes and worse haircuts in meat markets and watering holes. Most of these stories fade with the morning sunlight as the alcohol is metabolized and eliminated from the body.

For some unexplainable reason, though, John Gacy decided that it would be in his best interest to claim that Jack Hanley was his alter ego, his second personality. Unlike other men who have lied in pursuit of poontang, John seemed to adopt Jack as a second persona. So when John was flitting from cop to cop and prosecutor to prosecutor confessing his awful crimes like a bumblebee goes from flower to flower, he was telling many of them that John Gacy did not commit these grotesque acts—Jack Hanley did.

Now please keep in mind that Gacy did not mention the name Jack Hanley during the endless drunken ramblings that spewed forth during his soul-searching confession at my office with Leroy Stevens. However, he suddenly had a second personality buried deep inside when he told his story to the police. This was simply Gacy being Gacy. John always knew best, you know, or so he thought. These were self-serving statements—a silly, uninformed attempt to set into motion some sort of flimsy departure from reality.

What this accomplished, together with the fact that Mr. Gacy could not simply just keep his mouth shut, was to set in stone the only defense available to him. Motta and I would have no choice in the matter. We would be required to assert the insanity defense at trial. It was John himself that left us no other alternative. Oh yeah, there was one other reason why we were limited to asserting the insanity defense: John Wayne Gacy was certifiably, without a doubt, with all certainty batshit, bonkers, cuckoo, crazy, insane. This fact would become painfully obvious over time.

BOB MOTTA AND I had our work cut out for us. We solidified as a team and began the process of representing America's most hated man.

It has been said that when the prosecution builds a case in court against a defendant, it is like building a wall one brick at a time. Each brick has to support the bricks laid on top of it in order to support the wall. If the defense can chip away at a particular brick, or at several of them, this can cause the whole wall to come tumbling down.

Bob and I sat in the office spitballing, looking over some of the evidence that the State had against our client, tracing the steps that they had taken that brought us all here. It was our job to challenge each and every one of those steps and then to devise some sort of affirmative defense based on our client's inability to understand his actions or to conform his behavior within the confines of the law.

We started at the beginning, the very first search warrant that, among other things, turned up the photograph receipt that first tied Gacy to Rob Piest, the original item of evidence that put Rob Piest inside Gacy's home.

"Look at this." I was waving the very first complaint for search warrant around, which had been drafted by Lieutenant Kozenczak and Terry Sullivan. "There is nothing here about a photograph receipt."

When a complaint for search warrant is presented to a judge in an effort to procure an actual search warrant, it must be quite specific. The items that the officers and the assistant state's attorney wish to recover must be delineated in the complaint. Representatives of the State cannot enter a suspect's home and simply look willy-nilly for just any old thing that they think might help their case. That would fly in the face of the Constitution. If during the course of a legal search the officers conducting the search come across items that are on their face illegal and those items are in plain sight, then those items can be legally confiscated. However, items not delineated on the warrant, which are not per se illegal, are not subject to confiscation.

"There is nothing illegal about a photograph receipt. Why would they have a right to grab that item out of the house?" Bob asked, with full knowledge of my answer.

"They shouldn't be able to," I said. "Even if this photo receipt document was in plain sight, it is not contraband. It is not something they can just grab. This item should be excluded. Where did they find this?"

"They found it in the garbage in the kitchen, in the garbage bag. They cannot go snooping in the guy's garbage, can they?"

"They may be able to, once it is thrown out by the curb. There are cases that say that at that point it is discarded, abandoned. You know all those cases where private detectives go snooping on celebrities, but this garbage was still in his house, under his control. It may not have even been garbage. Maybe it was just a bag of items that he intended to keep. But we don't even have to get to that issue. This item was not delineated in the warrant, and it could never be considered contraband, so they cannot seize it, right? What possible theory could they use?"

"And look at this." Bob was now looking at the second search warrant. "They got a warrant based on a smell? A smell—jeez, the smell of putrefied bodies? How can anyone tell the difference between a decaying human body and the decaying body of any other kind of animal—hell, of an old, moldy half-eaten piece of steak in the garbage, for that matter? Decaying flesh is decaying flesh."

And so it went. We picked through the documents and each item of evidence that we knew about, through every single move that was made in the collection of the evidence. Every day and night we would pour over the minutiae of the case. We were back and forth to Cermak to interview Gacy. Sometimes Bob would go out and talk to Gacy; sometimes I would do it. Often, we would go together.

We told Gacy to write down every thought, every memory, anything and everything that came to his mind that could help us to better understand the case, to better understand him. On one of our visits, he gave us this:

#1 John WAYNE GACY Life HighLights High (H) + Low (L

1942 BORN MARCH 17, 1942. Edgewater Hospital 12:25 A.M.
1943 Nothing
1944 Nothing
1945 Nothing
1946 OLSEN girl Took my clothes OFF. ~~Going~~
      going To SpringField First TRAIN Ride
      getting whipping From DAd. messing up CAR Parts
1947 Starting school
      Being AFRAid of Fire Engine sireN
1948 HAving stitches in Right Hand
      Being scared of The BLACK HAND Kids game
1949 getting beating From Dad For messing with Roberta Richie
      Didn't Like Contractor TAKing me For Rides, messing with Me
1950 changed From Public school to CAtholic
      DAd is operated on BAck INJurxe (L)
      mother scared us kids that she WAS LeAving (L)
* 1951 DR. BARROWs Tells of my Heart condition (L)
1952 moved To 4505 N. MARMORA (H) HAppy Adventure
1953 going to Wisconsin Fishing with DAd Alone (L) Blame For Any thin
1954 Nothing
1955 cutting school Alot (H) Failing
      sickness (L)
1956 changed To Vocational school (H)
      DAd Putting me down (L)
      Started working (H) First Job IGA Store
1957 sickness, 2 operation (L)
      Hit with A swing in the Head (L)
      WorKing + going to school
1958 June grad. #1 in my class of 79 students (H)
      Received American Legion Scholastic AWARd (H)
      Starting High school (H)
      sickness (L)
1959 Hospitalized Alot (L)

#2

1960 Sickness (L)

Accident, Fell From 2nd Fl. of Building, Spine injuries (L)

got my First car with Dads Help (H)

1961 Asked To leave High School because of Health Risk (L)

Sickness (L)

Dad down on me (L)

1962 Fought with Dad, Ran Away From Home in may (L) Depressed

Lonely + Lost Returned After 3 months (L)

older Sister got married (H)

1963 Traveled For Nunn Bush Shoe Co As manager (H)

1964 Jan younger sister got married (H)

Parents 25th wedding Anniversary (H)

moved To Springfield (H)

girl Friend moreen Died (L)

march Engaged To marry (H)   Sept J married marlynn (H)

Ran Largest Xmas Parade in central Illinois (H)

First male sexual Experience (L)

1965 great married Life, marlynn Pregant (H)

Honored As "man of The year" Springfield, Ill. (H)

Chosen outstanding First yr. Jaycee Local, District And 3rd place

in Illinois out of 13,800 member (H)

1966 michael John was born (my son) (H)

moved To waterloo, Iowa   New Job (H)

1967 Honored As "man of The year" waterloo Iowa (H)

unhappy working with Father in Law (L) Hated him

1968 Sodomy conviction (L)

Prison (L)

Divorce (L)

1969 Completed Schooling (H)

Sick Heart Attack (L)

Dad Died Christmas day (L) December 25th

1970 Honored "man of The year" Anamosa, Iowa 1967 (H)

Declined Parole march (L)   Granted Parole may (H)

Return to chgo, start new Life

1971 moved To 8213 Summerdale

#3

1972   got married To Carole (H)
      Self made Family 2 beautiful little girls (H)

1973   Problem with mother-in-law (L)
      Sickness, Hospitalized June (L)

1974   First yard party "Lulu" (H)

1975   Problem marriage (L)
      2nd yard Party "western Bar B Que (H)
      Appointed To county Board (H) Lighting District
      Divorce (L)
      Director of Polish Parade (H)
      Became "Pogo the clown" (H)
      Business good (H)   Confused Not Happy (L)

1976   Divorced Final (L) Depressed (L)
      3rd yard Party "spirit of 76"(H)   Polish Parade Dir (H)
      Business Booming (H)   Not Happy (L)

1977   Business Sky Rocketing (H)   Lonely, Confused, not Happy (L)
      4th yard Party "southern Jubilee" (H) Polish Parade Dir (H)
      Engaged to marry 3rd Time Broken off (L)

1978   Business Pecking (H) Lonely, Depressed (L)
      Carole Pregant (not By me) (L)
      5th yard Party "Italian Festival" (H)
      Polish Parade Dir. Pres. Carter wife visit in charge (H)
      Nov. Carole married (L)
      Arrested Dec. Confused (L)

1979   Lost, Lonely, Confused, no Will To Live
      December 25th Died

As Bob and I reviewed this disjointed document, we were per-plexed. John had included some of the oddest references—refer-ences that no one would expect—together with many of the most obscure moments from his life. He also included his most hated activities, his first sexual acts with men. However, he failed to include any reference whatsoever to one very important aspect of his life—the fact that he had killed, that he had killed over and over again. Mundane, minute details from his life were there on each and every page. Yet according to this document, John Wayne Gacy had never taken a life. Was he still attempting to hide this part of his life even though he had confessed it to me and to others, or was it something deeper?

23

WHILE **B**OB **AND** I were preparing and filing stacks of preliminary motions and investigating the case during its early stages and while these various motions were being set for hearing in the months to come, another true emergency arose that required our immediate attention. This turned out to be an emergency of epic proportions because it involved money—our money, our own money.

The excavation process that was necessary to recover the bodies was ongoing. Day after day the body count rose. The staggering number of bodies, together with their location, was causing significant damage to the structural integrity of Gacy's house. However, at least so far, the process had left the building intact and standing.

In the wind was this nagging assertion about a plan by the sheriff's department to raze the house entirely, thereby making it easier to search for and recover any bodies not yet found. There is absolutely no question that the excavation process was made more complicated by the fact that a house stood over the hideous burial site, and Bob and I could certainly understand why the guys working on the tedious recovery process would love to work without a house overhead, but we could not stand by and let this plan come to fruition without a fight, a serious fight.

There were constitutional issues at stake as well as other issues of great concern—money.

It was true that our client, Mr. Gacy, had been charged with crimes more grotesque than any in recent memory. Some would say that the charges were unparalleled in all of history. There is a tendency, when an alleged crime is particularly horrifying, to forget the rules or to attempt to bypass those rules altogether. The idea that the sheriff's department could simply tear down a man's house in order to make it easier to reach undiscovered bodies was a classic example.

"There is talk that they want to tear down Gacy's house. I got this from a reliable source inside the sheriff's office. They want to tear the whole goddamned thing down and cart it away in trucks!" I said excitedly as I burst into the office, shaking and stamping off wet melting snow. I threw my overcoat on the couch. I was freaking out. "This time I think they are really going to do it."

Bob was alone at the desk we shared with a single lamp burning, buried in books and paper that continued off the desk and onto the floor all around him. He hadn't even noticed that it had gotten dark outside. He was researching issues that had to do with all of those previously filed preliminary motions—motions to dismiss, motions to quash, motions to suppress. He looked over the top of the mounds that covered our one desk with an incredulous look. If it wasn't one thing, it was another thing! We had heard talk of this motion, this rumor, in days past; but now it seemed to be imminent—at least that was the buzz.

"They can't do that." Bob was shaking his head in disgust. "We still have a Constitution in this country, right? They didn't do away with it while I wasn't looking, did they? I think there is something in the Fifth Amendment that has to do with not depriving persons of life, liberty, or *property* without due process of law. I'm sure I read that somewhere, maybe it was in law school." Sarcasm dripped from the walls. "Oh yeah, I think it goes on to say something about no private property being taken for public use without just compensation. So there's that too. Have these people lost their minds?

"I hate to admit this because I am as idealistic about the Constitution as anyone on the planet. You know that. But that's not the worst part—that house is our fee. Our fee is in that house! Nobody is going to pay this guy for work that he has already completed, so his accounts receivable are worthless. He has basically nothing to speak of in his bank account. His cars, trucks, and virtually any other big-ticket items that he owns have been confiscated. That house is Gacy's only asset. It's the only thing that he has left to pay us with."

Hmm . . . this was serious.

The thought of starvation hung in the air. I had two little kids and a wife. Bob had a child, an ex, and child support. Plus, *we* had to eat. That is not being selfish, is it? That's not too much to ask? We needed sustenance in order to have the energy necessary to defend this guy. We would pass out right there in the courtroom if we didn't eat, right? That would never do; that would be a bad thing. We had no savings. Public defenders aren't paid enough money to save any of it. Both of us were fresh from the PD's office. We could barely pay the day-to-day bills, let alone save. Now we were on our own, which was worse. We had no other clients, and Gacy had sucked the air out of any other potential ones. We didn't have time to do anything else but work on this case. Just ask my wife about that one. We barely saw each other anymore, and she was none too happy about that, by the way. Wait until I got home and tried to explain to her that we were destitute. Fireworks were in my future.

So like I said, this was a bit of an emergency.

What we did not know was that the rumor that I had heard was actually much more than a rumor. It seems that a notice of a court appearance had actually been sent to Mr. Gacy and to his civil lawyer, Mr. Leroy Stevens. A pending court action had already been filed and a hearing was scheduled on Tuesday, March 27, in housing court in front of the Honorable Judge Richard H. Jorzak. Bob and I were completely unaware of this pending court date. The petition before the court alleged that the excavation process had rendered the structure unsound, that the whole structure was on the verge of collapse, and that it was a danger to the men working as part of the excavation process and to the residents of the neighborhood.

For some unknown reason, Leroy Stevens failed to appear at that Tuesday-morning hearing. As a result, Judge Jorzak entered an order that the house be razed, having heard no evidence whatsoever opposing such an order. Huge yellow bulldozers, a towering crane, together with several imposing dump trucks and other items of demolition equipment, had positioned themselves in the front yard and in front of the house on Summerdale Street. Our client, Mr. Gacy, was about to become financially insolvent.

Wednesday morning Bob and I appeared before Judge Jorzak on an emergency motion to stop the demolition. We explained that we had not been informed of the hearing that was held the previous day and argued that the demolition of the structure was an unconstitutional taking of property. We insisted that a full hearing be held to determine whether or not the structure was actually unsound. The judge agreed. He would not have entered his original order if someone had only stepped up to represent Gacy's interests.

Armed with an order of court, essentially a flimsy little piece of paper, we careened through traffic at dangerous speeds and slid to a stop in front of Gacy's house amid the hulking trucks and bulldozers. There were always gawkers in front of Gacy's house, curiosity seekers huddled behind yellow police tape. Today, however, the crowd was unusually large and included at least one camera crew. The demolition of the Gacy home was big news. We waded though the pack of onlookers and ducked under the police barricades, waving the court order and hollering a single word. "Stop!"

Hard-hatted construction workers holding clipboards and screaming over the rumble of diesel engines were pointing and planning where to begin the teardown. Bob and I slogged through the mud and slop that was once the meticulously manicured yard and circular drive in front of our client's house, looking for the guy who seemed to be in charge. We presented the order to the foreman on the job, who shrugged, shook his head vigorously, then zipped a flat hand back and forth in front of his throat, signaling the guys in the bulldozers and trucks to cut their engines and stand down.

This disappointed many in the crowd and the boys with the TV cameras. A collective groan could be heard. As the crowd groused and grumbled and then slowly dispersed and the camera crews packed up and went on their way, Bob and I silently basked in our minor victory. You really have to stand in front of a huge wrecking ball hanging from a crane, feel the earth rumbling under your feet from many idling diesel engines, smell the burning fumes, hear the deafening sound of it all, and confront a big, burly man in dirty dungarees and wearing a hard hat, who is totally committed to his mission, with an 8½ × 11 piece of paper before you can fully appreciate the feeling. It was a feeling that says that this country and the people in it still live pursuant to the law, pursuant to a constitution, which was more powerful than all the swinging wrecking balls, all the huge towering cranes, and all the rumbling dump trucks. It had nothing to do with Bob or me. This was much bigger than a couple of young lawyers. This was the best parts of our system of government, of our laws at work. We were proud to represent that system that day.

A victory, yes, but a hollow one as it turned out, because on April 4, just eight short days later, the date on which the matter was set for full hearing, we appeared with our expert witness, Paul Gordon, an independent, private structural engineer. The State's primary witness was William Harris, the Cook County building commissioner. There, a battle of the experts took place in which

Harris testified that the structure posed a hazard to the health and safety of the public in that the house could collapse or flood or both. Gordon testified that the particular clay-laden soil that existed below the house had stiff characteristics and that due to this, the excavation had resulted in no damage to the footings, foundation walls, or the concrete piers that supported a steel I beam, and therefore, the structure was sound, in spite of the extensive damage that had been done to it.

The judge ultimately ruled in favor of the State and ordered the razing of the house. Again, our system of laws had worked. We just were not on the winning side.

This presented a huge problem for Bob and me. We hit the books.

IN THE STATE of Illinois, as in many other states in which the death penalty is available, if a defendant is indigent, the presiding judge may appoint outside or private counsel on behalf of the defendant, and that counsel is paid by the county essentially as a public defender, although the private attorney is not an employee of the County or the State. The hourly rate is set by statute and is far less than that which a private attorney would normally charge. However, a private attorney would pay many of his or her own expenses out of the fee that would be charged to a wealthy or well-off client. Subject to court approval, a private attorney that is appointed by the court may apply for the payment of certain expenses, including the sometimes rather-exorbitant fees charged by expert witnesses.

After a great deal of research, many long hours, gallons of coffee, and several packs of cigarettes, we emerged from the office with another emergency motion to present to Judge Garippo. This was becoming routine of late, nothing new; however, this time it was quite personal.

We must have done our homework because, without much fanfare, we were appointed as counsel for the defendant, Mr. Gacy. We breathed a collective sigh of relief. We would now be able to continue on the case *and* feed our families, which was a good thing. I don't think I would have stayed married very long if I had come home and announced that although I would still be working twenty hours a day, I would not be getting paid for it.

Appointment as counsel had other very positive results. I say positive because it was positive for our interests and the interests of our client. There are those individuals that held the opinion that any funds spent by the State or the County on Gacy's defense was a travesty, a waste, money spent in the devil's defense.

We would now be able to proceed to provide our client with a proper defense. In the long weeks and long months that followed, Bob and I would turn over every rock, every stone to ensure that our client had that proper defense. As those days became weeks, and those weeks became months, an entire year would pass before both sides of the case would be prepared to collide in a battle that would be reported worldwide and cause the very tenets of our democracy to be tested—nearly to its breaking point. Passions would flare at each and every turn. Criticism of our efforts was relentless. Gacy was the most hated man in America, and by proxy, so were we. He was the monstrous clown killer that did not deserve to breathe the same air as normal folks. He certainly didn't deserve to be defended.

24

THE YEAR **1979** passed in the blink of an eye; a whirlwind of day-to-day investigation and preparation blurred together like a pipe dream. The Gacy file—a small cluster of papers, written interviews, a few court documents, and various notes written on a yellow legal pad, all of which once fit into a single-file jacket and could be carried under my arm or in my briefcase—had ballooned into a mass of paper, documents, exhibits, photos, and paraphernalia that filled an entire corner of our small Park Ridge office. Boxes stacked haphazardly on top of other boxes threatened to push the ceiling tiles through the floor of the office above.

Suddenly we had a trial date staring ominously, stubbornly at us from the calendar on the wall. Gacy had consumed our existence for an entire year. We were both totally committed to the defense of this man's life, and now it was time to lay it all on the line. Every waking moment had been dedicated to the investigation and preparation of this case.

Don't get me wrong, Bob and I did not spend all of that time cloistered in a dark office with our noses buried in law books. A large part of the job was spent very much out in public. We were being stalked by the print media and interviewed on TV almost nightly. We had meetings with psychiatrists and psychologists, investigators, jury consultants, and witnesses from every walk of life and from all parts of the country.

Our small, shared office space was a bustle of activity and excitement, which included a few extra members of the team. A young, freshly graduated female paralegal, Julie Weiss, had volunteered as an intern, and the public defender's office had assigned us two investigators, Nick Mestousis and Lindy DiDomenico, to help with the overwhelming workload.

Nick and Lindy had traveled all over the country interviewing witnesses and taking statements from any and all persons that had ever had a connection to John Wayne Gacy. This included all the people who knew him in Springfield, in Iowa, in Las Vegas, any out-of-state job on which he ever worked, anyone anywhere that had met Gacy was sought out, contacted, and statements were taken. We were looking for anything that could lead to a better understanding of our client, to help in his defense. Boxes were filled and stacked with the results. We left no stone unturned.

Our days and nights were chaotic.

Flashing camera bulbs and shouted questions often began in the morning on the way out to our cars in our driveways and didn't end until we locked our doors behind us at night. It was fun . . . for the most part. If you loved the law and the insanity that accompanies a high-profile, internationally reported press case, if you didn't mind giving your life over to the scrutiny of the public eye, if you didn't mind being associated with America's most hated citizen and being personally scorned and hated for it in some circles, it was great fun. We were the center of attention in all of Chicago. Not everybody hated us. After all, we really were becoming local celebrities—hell, national celebrities. We got along with all the press people who followed us around all day and night. Most people had stayed awake in civics class. They knew that everyone is entitled to a defense and a trial. We were just lawyers doing our jobs to the majority of folks, just lawyers being lawyers. There were even

"Gacy groupies," women who were interested in us just because they had seen us on TV. Of course, that didn't matter to me. I was married . . . but Bob wasn't. Bob was quite single, quite available. So if you viewed it from a distance, it probably looked fun. In truth, it had its ups and downs.

Nobody likes to be relentlessly vilified, especially when you know deep in your soul that the job you are doing is absolutely necessary to the administration of justice. Wives and family members were involuntarily swept up in the tornado of activity that came with the territory. They hadn't signed up for this level of crazy. The death threats and late-night telephone calls from the truly stupid and cowardly became part of our lives. Members of the press at times bothered my wife, and even my parents. Our kids were occasionally teased and chided at school. Everybody on the planet seemed to have an opinion on what we were trying to do, and they were none too shy about sharing that opinion, sometimes at the most inconvenient times and in the most inconvenient places. People would stop us in the supermarket or the church parking lot on Sunday morning to let their opinion be known. We actually could not take a piss in a public restroom without hearing the well-reasoned pontifications of some drunken expert on the subject of John Wayne Gacy.

But all in all, considering that both Bob and I had always had dreams of being retained on that really big important case that made a difference, that mattered, the whole experience was exciting, and yes, it was fun.

However, in spite of the mind-numbing roller-coaster ride that we had been on, this was only the beginning, the preparation stage of the case. Now we had to try that case in a court of law. A man's life was at stake, and the true gravity of it all grabs at you when you look at that calendar and see those days ticking off. Had we done everything? Had we turned over every rock and every stone? Did we interview every witness, search our client's past, hire the appropriate experts, categorize each and every piece of evidence, take every available step in the furtherance of our client's cause? Were we ready?

The resounding answer to each and every one of those nagging questions and a hundred more was quite simply *yes*.

Bob and I had done our part.

In spite of what the world thought about John Wayne Gacy, in spite of the efforts and the protestations of the cuckoos and the crazies and the uninformed, Mr. Gacy was going to receive a fair trial in accordance and in keeping with the dictates of our Constitution.

Then it would be a jury of his peers that would decide his fate.

IT WAS A tumultuous year, and it started off with a bang. On Friday, January 12, 1979, it started snowing blizzard-style, and it didn't let up for two full days. On top of approximately 10 inches of already-accumulated snow, there fell another 20.3 inches of freshly fallen white stuff, setting new records in our fair city. By the end of January, there was an approximate accumulation of 47 inches of snow and compacted ice covering all of Chicagoland and making travel next to impossible. Every time you left the house, it was an adventure.

Amid this external chaos, Bob and I were sinking our teeth into the specifics of our task. After researching, preparing, and filing the numerous preliminary motions, we began the search for some of the best psychiatrists and psychologists in the country. Gacy had confessed to his crimes. His crimes were hideous and unprecedented. He had painted himself into a very small and very specific corner, and he was caught holding a very wet paintbrush. His one and only course of action, aside from simply pleading guilty, was to enter a plea of not guilty by reason of insanity.

After having spent a great deal of time with John in recent weeks, I was convinced that this plea was not only his best and only course of action and in his best interest, it was absolutely true. As far as I was concerned, John Wayne Gacy was bonkers. He was clearly insane. I had watched him go to places in his mind I had never seen anyone go. I had represented hundreds upon hundreds of criminals during my years as a PD, and this guy took the cake.

The disjointed and rambling tale of horror that he had disclosed to Stevens and me on that eerie, crazy night in my office the night before he was arrested was evidence enough. On that night, when Gacy spoke, it was as though he was not even present, like he was not even there. I saw his eyes flutter, and it seemed as though he became a body inhabited by another, something unholy. He didn't even remember telling us about his endless, disconnected dissertation of the grotesque events of his life over the past two years.

Of course, I'm no shrink. As far as I was concerned, this determination was a job for professionals. Bob wholeheartedly agreed on both counts. Bob was quite sure that our client was crazy as a bedbug, and he thought a professional head shrinker should confirm his "diagnosis," for the record.

What began as a rather routine, offhanded statement of fact by a couple of young lawyers about their client—"We will have to start looking into who are the best psychologists and psychiatrists in this field and line up some interviews and examinations for him"—turned out to become a major preoccupation of the field of psychology. Every local member of the fine profession of men and women who were involved in the field of the study of the human mind wanted a crack at him. It was not hard to find shrinks to become involved in the case. During that year, our client was subjected to psychological and psychiatric probing and poking on a level beyond the imagination. While incarcerated, he was drunk, drugged, hypnotized, interviewed, and cross-examined. He saw charts, graphs, inkblots, story lines, and forms of all color and description; he drew pictures, looked at pictures, analyzed pictures, and became a picture. They talked to him while he was standing, while sitting, and while lying down, while sleeping, waking, half-asleep and half-awake, while in conscious, semiconscious, and unconscious states—all this in an effort to determine that which Bob and I knew in an instant. Gacy was nuts.

The big question, however, still remained unanswered: Was he nuts enough? Could John Gacy appreciate the criminality of his conduct and conform said conduct to the requirements of the law? That was the question for the jury.

When all was said and done, there were almost as many opinions on that issue as there were psychologists and psychiatrists who were studying it.

One fact unearthed during all of the interviews and interrogations by the various renowned shrinks that hit home for me and which always anchored my belief that my client was insane on a level sufficient to have him found not guilty by reason of insanity was this: When John Wayne Gacy was five or six years old, he developed a fetish for his mother's silk undergarments. He said he liked the feel of them. He would fondle his mother's lacy panties and rub them on his little body. When he was done doing what he did with these items—and this made the hair on the back of my neck stand up straight when I heard it—he would bury them under the house. When John's mother began looking for several pairs of underwear that she thought she had lost, she found a small bag filled with panties partially buried under the porch of the Gacy home.

John was punished by his parents, and his mother's panties stopped disappearing. However, by the time John was a teenager and reaching puberty, he had graduated to stealing these coveted items from neighborhood clotheslines. He now was old enough to use these items during masturbation, which he regularly did; and when he was finished, he would revert to his original behavior and bury those items, often under the house.

This simple revelation, especially when taken in conjunction with everything else I knew about this sad, sad excuse for a human being, which appeared in report after report from doctor after doctor who had interviewed him, basically cinched it for me: John Gacy, my client, was on a psychological choo-choo train that went off the tracks many years before. The destination of that train had been predetermined. The normal synapse that happens in your brain and my brain and the brains of everyone else we know just did not happen in the brain of Mr. Gacy. He had, in fact, been miswired at the factory. He had a broken brain, and that brain had been broken long ago.

That was my opinion then, and it still is, and I sleep very well at night while holding it.

The theory that allows me to comfortably hold this opinion is surprisingly simple and has been stated in many ways throughout time. Here is one.

If a person who has reached the age of majority becomes angry with another person and says, "I'm going to kill you," then that person methodically walks into another room with plenty of time to think about his actions, grabs a loaded shotgun from the closet, walks back into the first room where the other person is standing, and proceeds to blow this person's brains all over the wall behind him, we call that murder.

However, if the same set of circumstances occurs and the perpetrator is a minor—let's say he or she is seven years old—it becomes a terrible, tragic accident, like lightning striking or a collision in traffic. Why? Because we don't blame small children for their actions no matter how sad and terrible, no matter how horrific the results may be. We know that seven-year-old children are not responsible for their actions. This is not a hard concept to grasp. Their little brains have not matured enough. They cannot understand the consequences of their actions. Hell, the Catholic Church takes the position that they cannot even commit a sin.

Everybody understands this.

Where the waters become muddy, where understanding becomes fleeting is when the "child" is six feet tall, weighs two hundred pounds, and has a five o'clock shadow or has long blonde hair and big perky breasts and chain-smokes. That is when the problems arise.

However, the brain of an adult can be so broken, so dysfunctional, that it is of no more use to that adult than the brain of a seven-year-old child. It just does not work properly—it's broken, and it causes the adult to act in ways that are unacceptable without the willing consent of its owner.

25

I**N SPITE OF** the very serious nature of the matter at hand—the trial of
a man accused of the murder of thirty-three young boys—when
you live with something every single day, no matter how serious
the subject matter, one must break free of the solemnity on occasion just to remain sane.

At the outset, in any trial where the mental heath of a defendant might be an issue, a determination as to whether the defendant is mentally competent to stand trial must be made. Counsel
for the defense usually makes a routine motion, and the judge will
then order that basic psychiatric and psychological evaluations
be administered to determine whether the defendant is mentally
capable to assist in his own defense. Bob and I made the motion
early on in this case, and the judge immediately ordered the tests,
all quite routine.

When the results of the tests were completed and were available, Judge Garippo called in the lawyers, both defense and prosecution, because he intended to make a ruling as to the competency
of the defendant—nothing unusual.

What the judge didn't know, but what everyone else in the
room did know, was this: A very special report had been transmitted to the esteemed Judge Garippo.

Another judge and dear friend of Judge Garippo, a person that shall remain unnamed because Judge Garippo still doesn't know who was ultimately behind the ruse, and I refuse to be the one to break the silence, had a phony report prepared and delivered to Garippo in place of the real one. The delivery was made in the normal course of business and in a manner that would lead the judge to suspect nothing. The sealed, official envelope, embossed with the characteristic markings of the Psychiatric Institute, Circuit Court of Cook County, R. A. Reifman, MD, Director, was lying on Judge Garippo's desk in his chambers. It was the normal practice that the report remain sealed until opened in the presence of counsel for both sides of the case.

So there we were, six lawyers—with straight, solemn faces—and the judge, whom everyone in the room respected greatly. He opened the envelope and pulled out letterhead stationery indicating that the letter was from Robert A. Reifman, MD, Director.

It read,

Dear Judge Garippo:

Pursuant to your honor's order, the above named defendant was examined by the undersigned psychiatrist.

Based on the above examination, it is my professional opinion that the above named defendant is COMPETENT to stand trial. Further, it is my professional opinion that the said defendant was legally INSANE at the time of the alleged offenses. He did NOT have the substantial capacity to appreciate the criminality of his conduct or to conform his conduct to the requirements of the law.

However, the above defendant is now legally SANE and in no need of further treatment at this time.

Very truly yours,

The judge stared at the letter in front of him for a very long time. He seemed to be reading it over and over again. He looked up at all of us with a look that none of us will ever forget. "This can't be right. Something is wrong here," he mumbled, shaking his head slowly. He put the letter down on the desk. He looked back at us.

"It says that he is competent to stand trial, insane at the time of the offense . . . and sane now." We watched as he contemplated what that meant. He seemed to be somewhere else as we watched him trying to imagine just what it was going to be like to declare that he had no choice but to find the defendant not guilty by reason of insanity, but that because the defendant was now sane and in need of no further treatment, he was free to leave the courtroom. He was a free man.

"Well, Judge, in that case, I think we will opt for a bench trial," I said, with complete sincerity.

We watched as the judge saw the headline in the *Chicago Tribune* and then the *New York Times* flash before his glassy, bespectacled eyes: GARIPPO FREES GACY!

We all felt the laughter welling up inside. We fought it as long as we could.

Then Garippo said with a slowly creeping smile, "You guys are in on this, aren't you?"

Lawyer jokes—ya gotta love 'em.

I TELL THIS story as a prelude to the truth, which was that Dr. Reifman found just the opposite when it came to Gacy's sanity at the time of the offense. He found him sane. Of course, this was only one man's opinion. However, it did guarantee a jury trial. We also knew at least one of the experts who would be testifying on behalf of the State.

As the weeks and months passed, one by one, the judge ruled in favor of the State on the majority of our pretrial motions. We challenged the indictment, the warrants—we challenged each and every step the police and the state's attorney's office took during the initial investigation, the collection of the evidence, and ultimately the arrest of our client.

During a hearing on one of our motions to quash the warrant and suppress evidence, Judge Garippo threw us a bone when he declared from the bench that many of the warrants had been "inartfully drawn," by which he meant that the warrants were, in some cases, flimsy. However, he allowed the evidence into the case in spite of the weakness of some of the warrants.

While we were having hearing after hearing on our motions, body bag after body bag were being dragged out of Gacy's house, all of this in front of TV cameras, which broadcast their gruesome tale to the world. The brighter the light that shines on a case, the harder it becomes for a judge to exclude evidence that is found, whether that evidence is found legally and in keeping with the Constitution or not. Although I would strenuously argue—and Bob and I did so argue—that this should not be a consideration, sometimes it cannot be helped. Judges are human beings.

However, in my humble opinion, if the constitutionality of a search of the residence of a United States citizen is at issue, the Constitution should always win—always, no matter what. If the Constitution says one thing and our emotions say another, the Constitution should be followed rather than the emotion, every single time. It is that very Constitution that protects those rights that we like to call inalienable.

Too often, when a defense attorney wins a case on constitutional grounds, it is offhandedly described in the press, and sometimes even by our society in general, as a "loophole." This is always done so in the pejorative sense, as in, "That scumbag lawyer got his terrible criminal client off on a goddamned loophole. It's a travesty of justice."

Unfortunately, this statement, this sentiment is completely assbackward. When a defendant is convicted of a crime in spite of his or her constitutional protections, that is the loophole—that is the true travesty.

Otherwise, why have a Constitution? Why don't we just revert to mob rule, mob lynchings? Why is it so often accepted practice in the minds of some in this country that the police can break the law in their efforts to get the bad guy, as long as they get the bad guy? How silly is that, the police can break the law in order to arrest a person that broke the law? What?

Every oath that is administered to our leaders invariably includes the sacred phrase "to preserve, protect and defend the Constitution of the United States." Perhaps we as a people should decide if we really mean that, or not.

So when Bob and I argued that the second warrant, the warrant that unearthed the first body, was insufficient at law because it was based on the claimed presence of an odor—an odor that was indistinguishable from many other odors—and a photo receipt that was not listed in the original inventory from the first warrant and was illegally taken during the execution of that first warrant, and the judge ruled against us, we were disappointed, to say the least.

However, we were very pleased when Judge Garippo, with the Wisdom of Solomon, ruled in favor of our motion for change of venue but kept the trial in Cook County.

A motion for change of venue is filed when it is believed that a defendant cannot receive a fair trial in the jurisdiction where the crime was committed due to a predisposition on the part of the entire community, especially the jury pool, which is usually the result of an oversaturation of press coverage in a given area. When that press coverage is particularly biased or the crime is particularly grotesque, or both, the judge must consider whether or not a fair trial is available to that defendant in that jurisdiction. No case has ever stood as a better example of this concept than the *Gacy* case. Judge Garippo knew this, and he was faced with a difficult problem: How would he protect the rights of the defendant to a fair trial without dropping this monumental case in the lap of some poor unsuspecting judge in some other jurisdiction?

The answer was a stroke of genius and surprisingly simple all at once.

The judge granted our motion for change of venue and ordered that the jury would be picked from another county where less press coverage existed, and then the jury would be transported to Cook County and sequestered to protect them from the ongoing press coverage in this county. You didn't need to transfer the entire case to a different county because the only persons that mattered in the case, the only persons that would actually be judging the case, were the twelve men and women of the jury.

Studies were commissioned by the court to determine a county in the state where press coverage was less pronounced.

Winnebago County was chosen as the county from where we would pick our jury. Rockford, Illinois, its county seat, a bustling city of approximately 150,000 residents, is closer to the Wisconsin border than it is to the city of Chicago. It boasts of its almost-equal proximity to Madison, Wisconsin; Milwaukee, Wisconsin; and Chicago, Illinois. At about ninety miles away, it was close enough yet far enough away from Cook County. Of course, no jurisdiction on the planet existed that had never heard anything about the *Gacy* case. However, Rockford was a city unto itself with its own radio, TV, and newspaper outlets; and all parties agreed that it would serve well the purpose of a change of venue on the Gacy matter.

As the trial date approached, every person involved in the case temporarily moved their entire operation—lock, stock, and barrel—to the fair city of Rockford, Illinois.

The night before jury selection was to begin, everybody met for drinks at a local watering hole not too far from the Winnebago County Courthouse. I don't think that this little get-together was planned; it just happened. Rockford is quite cosmopolitan, but it is small compared to Chicago. Therefore, only so many hotels existed that were conveniently situated near the courthouse and could accommodate the number of lawyers and staff that descended upon that poor unsuspecting town.

The Clock Tower Inn turned out to be the place that everybody involved in the case stayed, so the bar at that fine establishment, with its walls completely covered by vintage clocks of every description, was packed to the rafters with people that were involved in some way with the Gacy matter.

The place was packed, the bar was elbow to elbow and knees to knees, and the tables throughout were full. Everybody was taking a well-deserved and short-lived break from the grind.

It's funny—most people believe that prosecutors and defense attorneys are mortal enemies. That is just not true . . . usually. Many people thought that William Kunkle and I actually hated each other. Nothing could have been farther from the truth.

When you work with someone on a case, an occasionally grudging, mutual respect grows, if it is deserved, of course. As a result, often, just the opposite is true. Prosecutors and the defense counsel can be quite close friends; some are even married to each other. The relationship is much more akin to the members on opposing sports teams. Even as kids, it will sometimes happen that your best friend is on an opposing team.

Of course, from time to time, even the closest of friends or colleagues have the occasional minor disagreement. It can happen to anyone, right, in the heat of the battle and all?

I am not a big drinker, never was. I am that guy who is still drinking the first beer that he ordered four hours after arriving at the bar. Only my closest friends know this about me. I party with the best of them, so it is not obvious. I just never liked to drink much, not even in college. Bob, on the other hand, enjoys his beer. Bob never does anything half-assed. If he walks into a bar to have a few, that is just what he does.

On this particular night, however, I don't know—maybe it was the tension of the moment. Everyone was realizing that we were all actually, finally, after all those many long months, on the verge of one of the biggest trials of our lives. Once the jury was selected, we were all headed back to Chicago to put on this case. The day of reckoning had arrived.

Whatever the reason . . . everyone may have had a few more drinks than usual that night. Even I was not immune. Pitchers of beer, shots of booze, mixed drinks of all colors and concoction were being passed around like candy on Halloween. Prosecutors, defense counsel, their staff members who took the trip, investigators, police officers, and, let us not forget, the venerable members of the press—everyone who was involved with this tough, high-profile, high-pressure monster of a case was blowing off a little steam in a very big way. It was fun.

No one really knows, or remembers, just exactly how the brawl began. It's fuzzy at best, no matter whom you ask. Many of us have tried to reconstruct the events of that night in the days since, but to no avail. All I can say about that particular night is this: As barroom brawls go, this was a doozy!

I have heard errant speculation that my partner and dear friend, Bob Motta, may have had some involvement with the first salvos of the melee; perhaps he and Bob Egan or Jim Varga or one of the others were having words, and maybe that discussion became heated; but no one really has ever confirmed that, at least not in public, or out loud. You see, Bob has always been the type of guy that has never taken a grain of shit from anybody, ever. So it stands to reason that it would be unlikely that anyone would publicly blame him for such a thing, at least not without very clear and convincing evidence, and certainly not to his face.

What does it matter who started it, anyway? By the time it was over, every single person in that bar was involved whether or not they were participants in the case, save two. Glasses flew and smashed against walls, chairs were thrown, tables were tipped over, things of all shapes and sizes were broken or used as weapons. The place looked like a good old-fashioned Irish wedding, or funeral.

By some miracle, no one was seriously injured.

I said everyone was involved, save two. Who were the two that remained above the fray, you ask? Well, by the time the fight broke out, most of the members of the press had either gone back to their rooms or moved on to another dramshop. One lonely reporter remained. I believe that his name was Galloway; I think he was with the *Chicago Sun-Times*, but don't quote me on that. Let's call him Galloway, though, just to give him a name. Let's say his name was Paul Galloway.

Mr. Galloway was passed out, mouth agape, drool glistening on his chin, head hanging askew over the back of a wooden bar chair, snoring, while chairs and bottles flew over his head. He never moved a muscle during the entire conflagration. He slept like a baby throughout. Therefore, the rare and rather embarrassing departure from professionalism was never reported in the newspapers, thank God.

Number two was even more unusual.

While the gates of hell were opening up all around him, while glass missiles zinged past and various items of furniture and the odd human being flew by his person, Bill Kunkle, who never drank anything stronger than a Diet Coke, sat engrossed in a game of solitaire or some sort of game that he had been playing all night long. He sat in his chair, as if in a bubble, with Armageddon occurring all around him, and never looked up, never threw a punch, never took a scratch.

As for the rest of us, we all did our best to obscure our bumps, bruises, and minor cuts and to caffeine away our hangovers as we dutifully appeared to questioned prospective jurors the following morning.

26

THE ROCK RIVER lazily snakes its way through downtown Rockford, Illinois, the county seat of Winnebago County. A block away from its banks stands the Winnebago County Courthouse. Life is noticeably slower there than in the chaos and clamor of the sprawling city of Chicago and its environs; however, don't get me wrong, Rockford is no small town. It is a vital, bustling city with a long proud history and a tough, professional criminal justice presence in an area that is surrounded on three sides by rolling farms and just south of its counterpart city, Beloit, Wisconsin.

The Chrysler Corporation has a huge automotive manufacturing plant in nearby Belvedere, Illinois; and many of Winnebago County's citizens work at the plant or in Rockford as merchants. The rest of the population is dedicated primarily to farming in the surrounding open miles of the northwestern part of the state of Illinois. This cross section of people provided an eclectic and interesting mix to the members of the jury pool.

Jury selection has gone from the gut-based art form once practiced by country-style lawyers like Lincoln or Darrow to a science, where lawyers are often assisted by elaborate, targeted firms dedicated solely to that purpose. These firms test mock jury after mock jury and meticulously and scientifically study human behavior, particularly as it pertains to everyone's "favorite" civic responsibility—jury duty.

We were consulting with a firm from Minnesota. No one from the firm would be there at the defense counsel table with us. However, we would be armed with their reports and recommendations, together with their graphs and charts and professed expertise. Ultimately, it would be up to Bob and me to pick the jury that would sit in judgment of our client, Mr. Gacy. Today was the day, Monday, January 28, 1980.

———————————

I CAME TO from what was for me an uncharacteristic alcohol-induced coma in my room at the Clock Tower Inn and was immediately filled with the memory of the previous night's antics. Ya know, I'm Italian; and I believe that you can be excommunicated from the Italian American population if you openly disagree with anything that Frank Sinatra has ever said. But just this once, and just between you and me, I have to state categorically that I part ways with one of the long-held and widely quoted positions of Old Blue Eyes, the Chairman of the Board. Sinatra always said that he felt sorry for people who didn't drink because if you don't drink "the way you feel when you wake up in the morning is as good as you are going to feel all day." I have to say, I don't agree. I rather like waking up in the morning without a hangover, and I swore that I would never pull anything like that again. Sorry, Frank, just this one time, you were wrong.

It's amazing how healing a long, hot shower and a fresh, crisp suit and tie can be. If that doesn't do it for you, then you should try walking into a totally packed courtroom where it is your job to pick the jury that will sit in judgment during the trial of the century. That will clear up any lingering cobwebs from your brain right quick.

Every available seat was taken in the smallish courtroom in the Winnebago County Courthouse, and when all of the seats were occupied, people stood and crammed the aisles, craning their necks to get a glimpse of the proceedings and at the alleged monster from the big city. Extra uniformed bailiffs had been brought in, and they stood at parade rest at the edges of the crowd to ensure order. To many in that room, it was a silly exercise to have moved the jury selection to their county; it was not as if they hadn't all heard every gory detail that the strange portly little man seated at the defendant's table was supposed to have committed. It was 1980, not 1880. This was Rockford, not the moon. News traveled fast.

I think, however, that in spite of the smattering of criticism, the general consensus among Rockford residents was that they were excited to be in the bright spotlight, to have us all in their town for a while, and to have the jury that would sit in judgment of this monumental case selected from its citizenry.

With the help of a uniformed sheriff, Bob and I pushed our way through the sea of bodies in the gallery and past the soft murmur of voices and the pointing fingers. We seated ourselves at the defense table and smiled knowingly at our opponents.

Gacy was brought out from custody wearing a pale lime green polyester suit, off-white button-down shirt, and a printed burgundy tie. It was the first time that he had put on civilian clothing, worn anything besides prison garb or a hospital gown in over a year. All he needed was a cigar, and he would have looked like the cheap pol that he fancied himself to be. He looked around the courtroom in amazement, like a child.

The names of each prospective juror, together with minimal pertinent information about them, had been placed on three-by-five-inch index cards, which were being shuffled by each member of the prosecution team as if in a riverboat poker game. This time-honored practice assures a random selection of prospective jurors. The cards were passed to us. I picked up the stack, cut them, shuffled the deck twice like an old pro, and handed it off to Bob. He held up the deck dramatically, ran his thumb along the side of the stack, split them, cut them, shuffled them, and set them on the table in front of him. The order of selection had been chosen. A bailiff swooped in and scooped up the deck.

Then those familiar words from the head bailiff rang out and filled the silent courtroom. "All rise!"

Judge Louis B. Garippo entered the courtroom with a flourish and glided up the short steps to his perch atop the bench, black robe flowing behind him. Once seated, he nodded to his bailiff.

Sixteen names were slowly called out by the bailiff. As each name echoed throughout the courtroom, a man or a woman that had been previously seated in the first rows of the gallery stood up and tentatively walked to the jury box and took a seat. When the twelve spots in the jury box were filled, the remaining four took their seats next to the jury box as potential alternates.

Judge Garippo folded his hands in front of him on his desk. His favorite tie peeked out from the top of his robe and splashed the only color against his serious black presence. His prominent gold-rimmed glasses reflected the lights above. He had been a judge for ten long years. He had been here many, many times in the past; and he knew better than most exactly what to do, how to handle the intensity of such a scenario. He smiled a quick, calming smile at the nervous members seated in the jury box. His firm but kindly, somewhat-fatherly manner immediately put the jury members at ease.

"Ladies and gentlemen, good morning. You have been selected as prospective jurors in the case of *People of the State of Illinois versus John Wayne Gacy*. John Gacy has been charged with thirty-three counts of murder in indictment no. 79-69 to 75 and 79-2378 to 79-2403." Garippo looked up, expressionless, at the prospective jurors. He paused for just a beat, and continued. "Because of the nature of the offenses of which Mr. Gacy is accused, he is eligible for the death penalty."

You really have to be in a courtroom where the penalty of death is at issue to feel how the gravity of the moment pounces upon every single person in the room. There is something about hearing those words spoken out loud from the bench that does it. In spite of the fact that everyone in attendance knows full well in advance what is going to happen, there is a lightning bolt, a charge of electricity that fills the air. An imperceptible collective gasp happens out of nowhere and out of no one. This isn't a movie; this is real. Hearts pound, pupils dilate, ears perk, attention focuses.

Judge Garippo reached for a glass of water and took a sip. He adjusted his glasses and went on.

"The State of Illinois has elected to seek the death penalty."

Again, Garippo paused to let this sink in. A couple of the prospective members dared to look at the oaf sitting next to me. Gacy looked like he might have to pee or something. He wasn't there. He wasn't present. His mind was somewhere else. The rest of the panel purposely avoided looking at the defendant and the defense counsel. Many had suddenly found something interesting on their shoes or on the ceiling. I made some notes.

"The matter before the court is a capital offense. If Mr. Gacy is found guilty beyond a reasonable doubt and is legally eligible for the death penalty, the state's attorneys, representing the People of the State of Illinois, will ask you to impose a sentence of death."

Just when you might think it impossible, the electricity in the room intensified by a power of ten. This time many of the panel members, both in the jury box and in the front rows of the gallery, locked their gaze on William J. Kunkle, Terry Sullivan, Robert R. Egan, and James M. Varga. They didn't seem to mind, although they each shifted slightly in their chairs.

Garippo continued, "The indictment in this case is the formal manner of charging Mr. Gacy with the offenses—it is not to be considered as evidence and carries no inference of guilt. Mr. Gacy, under law, is presumed to be innocent."

Again, the seasoned judge gave his audience a moment. This, of course, was important information that everyone already knew;

yet they needed to hear it directly and specifically from him and on the record.

"This presumption remains with him throughout the proceedings and may be overcome only by proof of guilt beyond a reasonable doubt."

Garippo sipped more water. He wanted his words to sink in as if they were being heard by every person in the courtroom for the very first time. It was working too. He had the entire room. He certainly had me. I couldn't hear those words enough. He began again, as he looked at each of the prospective jurors in the jury box and at those seated in the gallery.

"The State has the burden of proof, that is, they must prove beyond a reasonable doubt that Mr. Gacy committed the crimes as charged."

I hoped that everyone in the room felt the lump that I felt in my throat. It appeared every time I sat in that chair at that table. It didn't matter in what courtroom that chair and that table were situated. It didn't matter if my client was charged with a traffic ticket or the worst of all crimes. To me, this was like church, and Garippo was reciting gospel. I believed those words and believed in those words to my very core.

I searched the faces in the jury box for a time and then looked out into the others in the gallery. I knew what I would find. I'd seen it before. There they were, the men and women that would sit in judgment of my client. Most had the look that I needed to see, the look in their eyes that betrayed the same feelings that I felt, that feeling of pride and love of country, that misty-eyed reverence for the best system of criminal justice on the planet. There too were the others. They were the dolts, the pinheads, the adult human beings, U.S. citizens, all that Washington, Jefferson, Adams, and Franklin hadn't counted on. At least two were sound asleep; several were so distracted that you could only imagine the silly cartoons playing in their useless minds. There was the blonde bimbo playing with her hair and cracking her gum. They fidgeted and daydreamed, they stared out into space or down at their fingernails, they wished that they were not missing their daytime soaps and had made specific arrangements with a friend to take notes so they could catch up after this stupid nuisance of having to serve on a goddamned jury was over. There were also the scary assholes, the ones that had already made up their minds. After seeing one or two reports on TV, they couldn't wait to cast their vote to string the bastard, my client, a human being by the way, from the highest tree in the county, evidence be damned, so that they could brag about it to chicks in bars. These were the people, mostly guys, who took some sort of sick pleasure in the revenge death of another human being.

And these fuckin' people have the vote, I thought to myself. I wanted to stand up and go out there and shake them.

I think Garippo saw the same thing that I did. He suddenly stood up and in a loud, resonate voice, he asked, "Are there any among you that because of the nature of the crime cannot be fair and impartial to the defendant?" He continued standing, looking at the entire panel, first at those seated in the jury box and then at the rest seated in the gallery. That snapped them all to life. Something must be happening; the judge was standing. What's up? Even the snoozers were wide-eyed and paying attention, wondering what they had missed. I had to chuckle silently.

"Please raise your hands if your answer is yes." The judge had the attention of everyone in the room once again. He stood there waiting.

Slowly, tentatively the first hand was raised by a woman seated in the gallery. After her, others seemed to have permission to do so. Two more followed in the gallery. Then three more went up in the jury box. The judge waited. Every other person in the courtroom waited. After several minutes, eight hands were raised. When the judge was reasonably sure that he had coaxed every hand up from the panel, he addressed a woman who was seated in the front row of the jury box. He had her name. He had the three-by-five-inch cards with the names of all the jurors in his hand.

"Your name is Mrs. James Labuda, correct, ma'am?" (The names of the jurors have been changed.)

She was clearly very nervous. She began to nod her head in the affirmative before she spoke. Her bottom lip trembled. Then came a very timid "Yes, sir."

The judge sat down. He had achieved his purpose, and now it was time to lower the level of intimidation and tension. Everyone in the courtroom was motionless; nobody made a sound.

"As a juror, your responsibility is to be fair and impartial. Can you meet that responsibility? Can you be fair and impartial to Mr. Gacy and to the State of Illinois?"

You could see the inner conflict raging. It was there in her facial expression, in her demeanor. She sat silent, not wanting to voice her true feelings but unable to deny them. The petite woman simply blinked and shook her head. Her eyes glistened with emotion.

"Please, Mrs. Labuda, you must answer audibly for the court reporter," the judge gently prodded.

"Well, I, I . . . I just think it's too horrible." She paused and took a breath. "I mean, what he did to those boys. I don't think I can be fair," she admitted.

If the judge let this go without further comment, the rest of the panel would become convinced that if they simply said that they couldn't be fair, they would all be able to walk out and go home. He couldn't have that. At the same time, the frail but determined little woman seemed on the verge of a nervous breakdown. A single tear dripped from the corner of her eye as she trembled in her chair.

"Can you agree that a defendant is presumed innocent until proven guilty beyond a reasonable doubt?" The seasoned jurist was pushing her a little further.

Mrs. Labuda fidgeted and shifted uncomfortably in her seat, but she was not about to relent. "Yes, I do, sir, but I just don't think I can be fair to him."

Garippo had been a judge for a long time. He had questioned hundreds of jurors in countless trials. In his opinion, this prospective juror was not malingering. She was sincere. He felt he had to excuse her, and did so. Mrs. Labuda stood and hurriedly walked out of the room. It had been a trying experience for her. As the courtroom door closed behind her, the judge turned to the next panel member who had raised a hand, this time an elderly man with gray tufts of thick hair poking in errant fashion in all directions. The man did not seem to be as affected by the proceedings as the first woman. He voiced his concern, said that he thought the whole matter was quite horrible, but admitted that he could reserve judgment until he heard all the evidence. He remained seated for the next phase, the lawyers' questions.

And so it went, the judge continued his preliminary questioning of the eight persons who had raised their hands. The answers that were elicited had a common theme—the subject matter of the case was horrific, the newspaper and TV stories had been shocking, but they would listen to the evidence before deciding. Garippo's gaze settled on an overweight middle-aged white man with a ruddy farmer's tan, a scowl, and a buzz cut. The man wore a long-sleeved hunting shirt, buttoned to the neck, which strained and stretched to cover his huge rotund beer belly. The judge pointed at him.

"You, sir, in the second row of the gallery, please state your name," he called out.

"My name is Vern Bergquist," the man grudgingly offered.

The judge proceeded, "Can you be fair, Mr. Bergquist, to the defendant and to the State of Illinois?"

"He should be hanged . . ." The answer was mumbled and trailed off. The judge couldn't hear any of it, but I had heard enough. I leaned over to Bob, whispering urgently. I pushed my chair back and began to stand.

"Please speak louder, sir, so that the court reporter can hear you." The judge was now stretching in his seat to better see past the first row of the panel.

"I think they should take him out and hang him! He doesn't deserve—"

The guy was no longer mumbling. I'd call it screaming. He was raising his huge form up out of his chair, pointing at Gacy. I shot to my feet.

"Objection, Judge, may we have a sidebar!" I was trying unsuccessfully to make my voice heard over the rising clamor.

Bergquist bellowed at the top of his lungs. "He doesn't deserve a trial! They should do to him like he did to those kids!"

He pointed at Gacy and shot daggers of pure hatred at him. The courtroom erupted. Garippo pounded his gavel. Uniformed sheriff's bailiffs descended on the man causing the disruption. Bergquist continued in a frenzy, waving his arms and spewing venom. A few others in the gallery stood and began to join in as the rest cringed in disbelief.

This was life imitating art. Hadn't I witnessed this very scene being played out in the movie adaptation of some legal thriller? I was beginning to wonder if Bergquist was about to pull out a secret pouch of animal blood and smear it all over his chest. Tension grew. Bob was on his way to the bench, as were Kunkle and Sullivan. I momentarily put a hand on Gacy's shoulder, looked at him, and then joined the rest, screaming for a sidebar.

For the first time, Garippo raised his voice, and with a final bang of his gavel, he commanded, "Ladies and gentlemen, please, may we have order in the court while I confer with counsel!"

The room immediately quieted. Bergquist stood flushed and glaring at Gacy and at Bob and me, surrounded by wary bailiffs.

It's always the most patriotic asshole in the room that has absolutely no concept of what patriotism actually means. By the look of him, I was willing to bet green money that he had an American flag plastered somewhere on the back of his rickety old pickup.

The mood of room changed from momentary chaos to a buzzing calm. People whispered excitedly to one another without making any noise.

The prosecution team, the defense team, and the court reporter huddled at the side of the bench with the judge, out of earshot of the jury.

Motta was screaming a whisper through his teeth. "Judge, this juror has contaminated the entire venire!" Bob had his hands on the corner of the bench and was leaning forward toward the judge, insisting that a new panel be chosen.

I continued on the theme. "I ask the court to discharge the entire venire."

I believe it was Kunkle who leaned in close to the judge, trying to express his urgency in a whisper that could only be heard by the judge, the lawyers, and the court reporter. A sidebar is an art form in and of itself. You have to learn to yell your argument, while whispering.

"Your Honor, you should simply admonish the prospective jurors to disregard the comments of Mr. Bergquist. It isn't necessary to discharge this venire. Simply excuse Mr. Bergquist, and instruct the jurors." The prosecutor may have had more to say, but he was being upstaged by Motta's feisty presence.

"That won't do," Motta hissed. "The comments were so inflammatory the jury will not forget or disregard them. They are poisoned!" Bob was adamant, as usual. He stepped it up a notch. "And further, I request that all voir dire of jurors concerning the death penalty be conducted individually out of the presence of the other prospective jurors."

These requests by Bob and me were perfectly reasonable from our perspective and had precedent in other cases where the death penalty was at issue. The court must take every precaution to ensure that one juror is not significantly influenced by the words of another and thereby tainted. However, a judge has a great amount of leeway in these matters. He can use admonitions to guard against undue influence of jurors. Plus, Judge Garippo had no intention of requiring the entire cadre of court personnel, the lawyers and their staff, and all others involved in the case to take up residence in beautiful downtown Rockford for a month or more, which were the logistical ramifications of such requests.

"Motion for individual voir dire will be denied," Garippo calmly said. "I will admonish the jury to disregard the comments of Mr. Bergquist and excuse him from duty."

"Objection," I strenuously interjected. "Our client is prejudiced by this prospective juror. The court has just begun voir dire. It would not unduly delay the trial to impanel a new venire. If the court refuses to impanel a new venire, the defense is compelled to request a mistrial at this early juncture."

Garippo was unmoved by my brilliant argument and unimpressed that I was demanding a mistrial. I wasn't exactly surprised, but I had made my record. I had barely gotten the words out of my mouth when he cut in.

"Objection denied. Motion for a mistrial denied."

The players returned to their respective places, and all was returned to normal. The tenor of the trial had been set, however. The barroom brawl of the night before at the Clock Tower Inn, now a distant memory, would seem insignificant and paltry, and pale in comparison to what was to come.

Judge Garippo focused his attention on Mr. Bergquist.

He explained to this nincompoop that we had a constitution in the United States of America, maybe he had heard of it? That it was this very document that guaranteed his right to stand up in a courtroom and make an absolute fool of himself, screaming and yelling his silly opinions about not having a trial. That in many countries, he would be on his way to jail right now, or worse. However, because of the document that he sought to usurp, he was simply going to be excused from jury duty and sent on his way.

The judge didn't say it quite that way. I said it that way. Garippo was much more diplomatic, but his message was the same.

Mr. Bergquist slithered from the courtroom, escorted by an enormous sheriff's bailiff.

Four days later, twelve members and four alternates had been selected as jurors to sit in the matter of *People v. John Wayne Gacy*. The judge explained some of the logistics regarding transportation and lodging during what would prove to be a six-week sequestration. He gave them a couple days to make their arrangements and pack. He scheduled the trial date and told everyone that he would see them all back in Chicago.

After a year of toil sweat, and arduous and meticulous preparation by all parties, the trial of Mr. John Wayne Gacy had, at long last, begun.

27

THE CRIMINAL COURTS Building at 26th Street and California Avenue in the city of Chicago, Illinois, had been a place of legend long before the trial of John Gacy. It has a rich and storied history. Many famous, high-profile attorneys have argued many famous, high-profile cases in its hallowed courtrooms. However, there is no question that the *Gacy* case was the trial of the century of its day.

Judge Garippo's courtroom on the sixth floor of the old building could have been the set of a Hollywood movie, an aesthetic mix of dark hardwoods and smooth marbles, built by proud craftsmen and intended to stand forever. One enters through heavy eight-foot oak doors that open into a cavernous room with twenty-five-foot ceilings trimmed by ornately carved crown moldings high above. Rows of churchlike pews serve as seating and end abruptly at the bar between the gallery and the well of the court, where long tables for the defense and prosecution are clearly marked and positioned before an imposing bench where the judge presides high above all others. Eight-foot windows, cut into the stone on the room's south wall, reveal streams of morning sunlight that streak the room in the early hours. A green desk lamp sits next to a brass nameplate on the bench, which proclaims that the courtroom belongs to and is presided over by just one man. This was Garippo's room, his court.

For several weeks prior to the trial date, workmen had been busy making minor alterations to accommodate a trial of this nature and scope. The jury box was expanded to allow seating for the twelve jurors and the four alternate jurors who would sit and hear all the evidence, in case they were needed. Sections of bulletproof plate glass were erected to separate much of the gallery from the well of the court. Other minor changes were made so as to accommodate press coverage. No cameras would be allowed inside the courtroom, but reporters would be positioned and able to report on the proceedings without disruption or distraction to the court.

Outside the courthouse, areas were set aside for press and cameras, and the streets surrounding the courthouse were dotted with the cumbersome white trucks crammed with the equipment that would immediately beam the news of the trial to the world, each of which had the call letters and logos of their respective television networks emblazoned on the side, advertising their presence.

Electricity filled the air for miles around. If you read the papers or watched TV, you would think that nothing else was happening in Chicago or the world. All that was needed were a few balloons and a few barkers, and we would truly have had us a circus.

The lawyers met with the judge in the days prior to the actual start of the trial to work out preliminary matters and actual logistics for the trial. It was decided that we would all work six days a week with full days on Saturdays. Garippo fully intended to plow through the truckloads of evidence and exhibits and the unending lists of witnesses that may or may not be called, depending on the particular twists and turns of the trial, in a timely manner. He had no intention of dragging out what we all knew would be a protracted trail any longer than was absolutely necessary.

We fought long and hard over whether the State should be allowed to use certain exhibits. They had prepared a huge easel on which the pictures of twenty-two identified victims and eleven question marks appeared and were easily removable from the slots that held them to use during testimony. Bob and I argued that having the easel in plain view of the jury throughout the whole trial would be inflammatory and prejudicial. The judge ruled that it could remain in the courtroom, out of the way, unless the State was referring to a specific victim. The upshot of this resulted in our having to sit with the State's gallery of grief, sometimes with all of these pictures on this huge board, behind us in the courtroom day after day during the entire trial.

There was also an argument over the State's plan to bring into the courtroom a huge chunk of the flooring from Gacy's house, which included the trapdoor that was the access to the crawl space. Essentially, they were bringing the damned crawl space right into the goddamned courtroom. I had to admit to myself that if I were prosecuting this case, I would want to do the exact same thing. Of course, I never said that to anyone, not even to Bob, and we forcefully argued against it. However, the judge ruled that it was simply demonstrative evidence and would be allowed in for that purpose.

After two days of preliminary fighting and informational meetings, we all looked at one another and agreed. We were ready.

On Wednesday, February 6, 1980, opening statements began in the case entitled *People v. John Wayne Gacy.*

The courtroom was packed to capacity, and then some. People sat and stood and crammed into every available space. Judge Garippo swore in the members of the jury, and the entire courtroom fell into utter silence.

Bob Egan, who had been chosen by the team to give the opening statement for the prosecution, stood and walked before the jurors. The long-awaited moment had arrived.

"MAY IT PLEASE the court, ladies and gentlemen of the jury, I want you to picture, if you will: A young boy. He is fifteen years old, he is a sophomore in highschool, he is a gymnast at the high school, and in the evening he works at a pharmacy," Egan began. "He works at a pharmacy because he is fifteen and he wants to buy a car when he is sixteen, so he is saving his money. His name is Robert Piest.

"I want to take you back fourteen months to a place called Nisson Pharmacy. Nisson Pharmacy is in the suburb of Des Plaines, Illinois, a suburb northwest of Chicago. You passed it on your way in as you came in on the toll road."

Egan slowly and methodically told a story about a cold December evening, just over a year previous, when a local contractor kept an appointment to give a quote to the owners of that now-famous pharmacy in Des Plaines, Illinois. He covered every gruesome detail that the State felt they could prove—the chance meeting between Rob Piest and John Gacy, the ride to Gacy's house, the murder of young Rob, the disposal of the body, all of it.

Bob listened as Egan stood in front of the jury and set forth the State's case in a sometimes-dry, sometimes-emotional dialogue, a "We will prove this and we will prove that" kind of dissertation of the facts spun exclusively in the manner in which the prosecution viewed the evidence. That was his job. He did it well. This was an opening statement and not an argument, although most lawyers attempt to stretch the definitional bounds of such a mission. Attorneys rarely miss a chance to argue, even when their antics are subject to objection by their opponents. It has happened that a lawyer will break into crocodile tears, sobbing out his or her version of the facts and evidence, and when the opposing counsel finally stands to rightfully object, it's all apologies and earnest assertions of how greatly affected he or she actually was by this particular case. That assertion is itself, by any definition, an argument; but it gets by many judges, simply because of the waterworks.

Motta was not interested in such theatrics or distractions, and he respected Egan for his lawyerly presentation and professional manner. Egan did, however, refer to Gacy as "the most evil man that ever walked the face of the earth," thus setting up a theme that the prosecution was expected to use, good and evil or, better stated, good versus evil. They would paint Gacy as evil—and, therefore, not insane.

When Egan finished, the judge broke for lunch, and the courtroom emptied. Motta stayed back. He couldn't eat anyway. He sat alone at the defense table with his notes and his thoughts. He flipped through pages without really reading the words; then he stood up and approached the jury box. He had been here many times before; standing solo below the twenty-five-foot ceilings in front of the assembled ladies and gentlemen of the jury, looking at their somber faces, and pleading a case was nothing new to him. However, there was no denying it—this was different; this was, after all, the trial of the century.

Unlike me, Bob was publicly against the death penalty. He had a deep philosophical aversion to the whole concept. I didn't. I was fine with the concept; but he had always thought it barbaric, wrong on so many levels. Although this was a capital case, the death penalty was being sought; he knew he had to stay clear of any such argument. That was not our defense. He had to steer clear of his deep-seated personal feelings and stick to the specifics of the case.

He thought of the hundreds and hundreds of hours that he had spent with the man on trial. A review of that cumulative experience made it simple for him. If he could convey to this jury what he knew about John Wayne Gacy, he believed that a "not guilty by reason of insanity" verdict was a foregone conclusion. Nobody on the planet was surer than Bob was that his client, our nut job of a client, was damaged. He had a damaged, defective mind; he had been miswired. Gacy had killed, yes, but his actions were as a result of an overwhelming compulsion over which he had no control.

In what seemed like seconds, Bob was approaching a full jury box. The throngs had returned from lunch and reassembled, filling the courtroom beyond its true capacity once again. All the jury members and their alternates were seated in their assigned seats with what Bob perceived to be openly skeptical, hostile faces. Many seemed to be unconcerned or uninterested. It was Bob's unenviable task to attempt to begin to pull together what would prove to be weeks of varied and confusing testimony and make it all understandable in a cohesive way that supported our theory of the case.

No place on earth is quieter than the quiet in a courtroom just before a lawyer begins an address to the jury. Whether it is opening statements or closing arguments, everyone in the room seems to be on the edge of their seats. An innocent cough from the gallery sounds like an echoing gunshot. Nobody breathes.

Such was the case when Bob Motta stepped forward to begin his opening statement for our case. This would be the first glimpse into the inner workings of the mind of the man who was accused of being the nation's most prolific serial killer. The waiting masses would finally have the opportunity to hear what kind of defense this monster would put forth.

Bob began by asserting that something had gone sadly wrong during the development of John Gacy's mind. He was controlled by an insidious, rapacious illness. He told John to stand.

"I will show you this man," Motta asserted, pointing at his client. "He is a human being. He was born, held in his mother's arms, nurtured, loved. Now he is the most despised man in the world. 'Every man's death diminishes me,' he said, quoting John Donne, the man who famously said, 'No man is an island.'" Bob felt very much like an island.

He named each of the twenty-two identified victims.

"The lives of those young men," he said, pointing to the State's gallery of grief, "cannot be replaced—the pain of the families cannot be measured or abated." Bob was gripping the railing of the jury box, leaning in, a couple of feet away from the jurors in the front row. "Nothing is more precious than human life," he pleaded, "but hatred and sympathy cannot play a part in the decision you must make. Only clear, rational thought and the strictest objectivity can guide you—a very difficult task."

Bob retreated a bit from the jury box. He began to pace and stalk the area in front of the bench in the well of the courtroom.

"Incomprehensible illness compelled him to the most horrible ends." Motta's voice bounced off the intricate crown molding high above his head in the ornate old courtroom and reverberated throughout its confines. "He understood, he planned, and he routinely killed, again and again and again." These words hung in the room like a dense fog.

"Free will is of what I speak! Something was missing in Gacy, missing from his heart or his mind, some vitally important element that provides the ability to make choices: of right over wrong, morality over immorality, life over death."

All eyes were on Bob. He knew that this concept, which was at the root, at the very core of our case, which he expertly espoused, was all too tough to accept for many people. In some cases, it was simply beyond them. It is so much easier, more comfortable to understand human nature in simple terms, biblical terms, the struggle between good and evil, the devil and the angels. Unfortunately, this sadly uninformed approach leaves out an explanation for so many of life's common conditions: the unfortunate sufferer of cerebral palsy or Tourette's syndrome, the epileptic, the stroke victim. The brain controls our every action. We know that. Even unconscious activities like the pumping of the heart, like breathing, would not occur without the steady support from the computer in our head. When the brain is broken, when the connection between our bodies and our brain fails, we no longer have the choice to do that which we so deeply wish we could.

The stroke victim would love nothing more than to get up and walk—hell, many would be content just to stop drooling, but they can't, because their brain is broken. An epileptic would rather not pitch a fit on the floor of a downtown department store at noon on a Saturday in front of a hundred shoppers. It's embarrassing. But no matter how hard they wish it wasn't so, or try to pray it away or valiantly attempt to fight against it, the inevitable happens, because their brain is broken. These people do not choose to do what they do. They do not choose to have their debilitating malady. They are just plain stuck with it, because their brain is broken.

Motta just hoped that his understanding of the natural order of things, the physiological truths, the psychological facts that exist whether we as a species like it or not could be transmitted to the twelve good men and women sitting, fidgeting, in front of him. He could not have cared less about what another person in that courtroom thought—just those twelve, but that was Bob.

Gacy didn't choose to kill, he told them. "He was unable to choose. There was no choice to be made," Bob said, adding that the choice had been made years ago.

"We have doctors, they will tell you in medical terms that Gacy is crazy and that he is controlled by the darker side of human nature, the basest part of man—that in normal people either never surfaces or is entirely absent. They will tell you of disease that causes the vilest of human behavior, uncontrollable and savage. Men of common decency fear to admit it can exist in the human heart. Men fear such horrors; they have been warned not to look into the abyss where they may themselves . . . become what they see!

"You must not succumb to fear! You will not be condemned for saying the truth—and if you believe Gacy is crazy, then say so. Fear will be a powerful force dictating that this man be excised from humanity, cut out like a cancer."

Motta pointed at our client as he strode closer to the jury box. He approached the railing between him and those twelve, grasped the rail, and leaned in.

"Use all your strength to fight the fear!" he screamed a soft whisper. He looked at the strange little man that we were both representing; he stole a glance at me and then returned his gaze to the jury.

"I ask you to look into the abyss. If Gacy acted out of chronic mental illness, then under our law he is not responsible for his acts. If the disease stripped him of free will and he killed, he must not be destroyed. Is there not one among you that can see past this shroud of death and come to grips with what you must do? You won't like it. The darker side of you will demand revenge despite his illness. You must not allow this to happen."

He closed by saying, "Don't see through anger. See clearly. Use cool, sound judgment, because if you decide that he must be punished rather than treated, that will be far more irrational than any act he has committed or could commit. I thank you."

As Bob Motta took his seat next to me, I realized that he had failed to elaborately thank the jury for their attention, a common courtesy that lawyers usually extend. Instead, just the simple "thank you." Lawyers will usually go on and on about how much they appreciate the jury's service, et cetera, et cetera, as they probably should.

I looked at him. I knew him. I could see that he wasn't convinced that these jury members, our jury members, were capable of seeing past a very powerful emotional desire that is in us all—the desire for revenge. He wasn't concerned about his opening statement. He had covered every base, addressed each and every issue, every point of order. He was concerned about them—that disparate group that had been plucked from their lives in distant Rockford to sit in judgment of our client. What he saw in the faces of that distracted and seemingly disinterested panel worried him. It would be a tragedy if those people had already made up their minds, like much of the rest of the world had.

28

THE MORNING OF February 7 saw the first witness for the prosecution walk to the witness stand, sit, and face the jury. Judge Garippo quite uncharacteristically ended the previous day's proceedings early, immediately after Bob finished his opening statement. This would not happen often.

The circus atmosphere, the crowds, the unprecedented attention given to this case continued unabated both inside and outside of the courtroom. TV trucks and reporters had taken up residence on every sliver of available real estate and on streets surrounding the outside of the courthouse, and cables connected to men and women with microphones filled the halls inside.

Marko Butkovitch, the father of young John Butkovitch, was the first person to testify in the *Gacy* case. He was also the first person in a long parade of life and death witnesses called by the State. A life and death witness is usually the person who last saw the victim alive. One after another—relative after relative, friend after friend, person after person—walked up to the stand to testify about the last time they saw their lost loved one. As you might imagine, there was a significant amount of tears flowing. This is, of course, perfectly understandable. What else would the family members and survivors of a young boy do? The pain that they must have felt is unimaginable.

Bob and I always considered this as one of the toughest aspects of the case. Nobody wants to cross-examine grieving family members about such a tragic event. It is hard enough to do it just once; imagine doing it over and over again.

However, we had a job to do, and do it we would.

We asked a precious few questions of most of the immediate family members; but other persons, friends for example, were considered more or less fair game. After all, we had offered to stipulate to all of the life and death witnesses and the evidence to which they would testify, but the prosecution team would not agree to the stipulation.

Let me state that in another way. Bob and I, as the attorneys for the defendant, offered to forgo any right to challenge any claim made by the life and death witnesses. We agreed to stipulate to their testimony, thereby alleviating the need for any of the family members to testify at all. That would have saved them from that painful experience. After all, our defense did not hinge on that testimony. We were admitting that the victims were dead and that our client killed them.

The prosecution team would not stipulate, however; they would not agree to any stipulation of any kind regarding this phase of the trial. They insisted on the live testimony of the witnesses. Why? Well, the answer to that question is quite simple. They wanted those poor people to cry on the stand in front of the jury. They wanted the sympathy that would be elicited by their testimony.

Don't ever let anybody ever tell you that a murder trial isn't a war, that it isn't pure unabashed hardball. And don't let anyone ever tell you that one side is more sensitive to the feelings of human beings than the other. A trial is an all-out battle, no holds barred. Each side fights to win, and each side has its casualties.

That is why I didn't have a problem with the cross-examination of Donita Gannon.

As a courtroom brawler, I know from experience that if you can bring into question the credibility of any one of the witnesses that your opponent puts forth, it casts a shadow of doubt on the credibility of all the witnesses that your opponent puts forth. It stands to reason that if your opponent is willing to knowingly put one person on the stand that you can expose as an obvious liar, he or she might be willing to put others up on the stand that are willing to lie as well. Makes perfect sense, right? Let's face it, I didn't come up with this theory of trial practice all on my own. It is a time-honored tactic that has been used by trial lawyers for centuries.

So when Donita Gannon sashayed through the huge oak doors at the rear of the courtroom and every head in that courtroom turned to watch this stunningly attractive Asian woman approach the witness stand, I was ready for her.

She was clearly aware of the attention that was being paid to her. You could see it in her walk, in her eyes, in her overall demeanor. Every eye in the room followed her as she strutted her stuff toward the jury box, outfitted in a standard-issue "little black dress" and black patent leather high heels. Her long black hair, with an extra high glossy sheen, bounced behind her. She was a piece of work. She seated herself on the witness stand.

John Gacy nudged me, whispering frantically, "It's a . . . ," he started to hiss. I gave him a stern look and a quick "Shhhoushhh!"

After the witness was sworn in, Bob Egan stepped up to conduct the direct examination on behalf of the State. He began, "Would you state your name and spell your last name for the court reporter, ma'am?"

"Donita Gannon, G-a-n-n-o-n." She smiled demurely.

Egan took her quickly through questions that elicited testimony that she and Timothy O'Rourke, one of the victims, were close friends, that they lived together in an apartment on the North Side of Chicago, and that she had last seen her friend in front of their home on Dover Street and Lawrence Avenue. It was all quite touching. When Bob Egan said, "No further questions," everyone in the courtroom was left with the impression that they had just heard the testimony from a grieving girlfriend about her deceased boyfriend.

Judge Garippo turned the witness over to us for cross-examination.

I approached the witness and asked the following questions and received the following answers:

Q. Miss Gannon, is it Miss or Mrs.?

A. Miss Gannon.

Q. How long has your name been Donita?

A. Since—

Bob Egan was immediately on his feet. "Objection, Your Honor, I don't see how that is relevant."

I shot back, "That is relevant." I was glaring at Bob Egan. He knew where I was heading.

Garippo looked down at both of us with a scowl. Lawyers were supposed to know that they were not to address each other; they should address all arguments to the court. They rarely remembered this rule. "The objection is overruled," the judge said sternly.

I returned to Ms. Gannon.

Q. How long has your name been Donita?

A. Since March . . . 1977.

Q. What was it before that?

A. Don Ganzon.

Q. Don?

A. Yes.

It actually took several seconds for the inhabitants of the courtroom to absorb what they were hearing. Suddenly, it seemed to communally sink in. The beautiful woman that everyone in the room had been openly ogling . . . was a man! A he-she, as Gacy had eloquently called Donita. There was a collective silent gasp.

Q. What was your name when you met Timothy O'Rourke?

A. He started knowing me as Donita.

Q. He knew you as Donita.

A. Yes.

Q. You say Don. Is the long name of that Don or Donald? What name did you have, Don or Donald?

A. Don.

Q. Don?

A. Yes.

Q. When did you meet Timothy O'Rourke?

A. May 1977.

Q. How long have you been a female?

Egan shot to his feet once again. "I don't see the relevancy here, I will object."

Garippo had on a look of total fascination. He waved his hand, as if to sweep Egan aside, without even looking at him, and said, "Overruled." I could tell he wanted to hear the answer. He was riveted on the witness, as was everyone else in the room. I asked the question again.

Q. How long have you been a female?

A. I am in the process of [becoming] a woman.

Q. So when you met Timothy, you were not a female, were you?

A. That is right.

Q. Where did you meet him?

A. I met him at a party.

Q. Where was the party?

A. The party was on Broadway and Surf Street.

I went on to ask questions about their meeting, general background questions. The jury and the gallery were paying attention now, if they weren't before. Everyone in the room had realized that it was true: Black could be white, up could be down, an original perception could be just plain flat wrong. That was my purpose. I wasn't interested in embarrassing this poor little woman, or man, or whatever. For obvious reasons, I needed to show how wrong an original perception could be.

"Where was he the last time you saw him?" I asked.

"He was in front of our house on Dover and Lawrence." Ms. Gannon was angry with me by now. Her eyes shot poison.

"You were living with him?" I continued.

"Yes," she spat.

"Did you plan to marry him?"

"He was just a friend," she stated with emphasis.

"So, you were not in love with him?"

Egan had had enough. He wanted this to stop. He jumped up. "Objection, how is that relevant?"

Garippo agreed. "Sustained," he said, with a look that told me to move on.

"Were you in love with him?" I persisted.

Egan raised his voice. "Objection!"

Garippo glared at me. "Sustained," he said again.

I began walking toward the bench. Egan was right behind me. "May I approach the bench?" I said quickly.

While Egan, the judge, and I were having words, Ms. Gannon answered the question, ending our discussion.

"I was not in love with him," she exclaimed.

I continued to ask questions pertaining to a statement Ms. Gannon had made to some investigators. No new or significant information came to light. I was wrapping up my cross.

"Have you had the sex-change operation yet?" I wanted to ask if she still had a dick under that pretty little black dress, but I thought better of it.

"Objection!" Egan was standing.

"Sustained," ruled the judge.

"No, I haven't," Donita Gannon, or Don Ganzon, again volunteered.

"That means you are still a man?" I shot back.

"Objection, again!" Egan was apoplectic.

"Sustained," Garippo stated. "You don't have to answer."

"Say that again," the witness was saying.

"You don't have to answer the question," Garippo reiterated, with a sharp look in my direction.

I felt that it might be time to change the subject.

"Did you ever hear of a bar called Blinkers?"

Ms. Gannon had calmed down some. "Yes," she answered.

"What kind of bar is Blinkers?" I asked.

Again Egan was on his feet. He was not going to allow me any slack. "Objection to the form of the question," he said.

"She may answer," the judge ruled.

"What kind of bar?" I prompted. I was almost done.

"It is predominantly a gay bar," she responded.

"No further questions." I hoped I had made my point.

"Nothing further." Egan had no redirect. He then said, "Thank you, Ms. Ganzon." He called her Ganzon, her old name, her man's name. I thought that was funny.

"You may step down," the judge said without expression.

As Donita Gannon walked back down the aisle and out through those huge swinging oak doors, she seemed to have lost a bit of the swing in her step. Once again, every eye in the courtroom was glued on her, but I am not so sure it felt as good as it did during her grand entrance. If she was embarrassed, I'm sorry. But like I said before, this was hardball. That woman had stood there at the outset of her testimony with her hand on a Bible and sworn to God that she would tell the truth, when, in fact, she was living a lie. Although it was not her fault—it was probably just a cruel trick of nature, like hurricanes, tornados, pestilence, or the like—her life was one confusing, tragic, incomprehensible lie, just like my client.

I hoped someone on the jury got that.

29

Testimony in the trial continued. One after another crying, devastated witnesses testified on the stand; a couple of them became so emotional that the judge had to momentarily stop the proceedings for fear that they might collapse. Those fears were all at once realized when a woman named Bessie Stapleton, the mother of fourteen-year-old victim Samuel Stapleton, fainted dead away upon being shown a bracelet that had belonged to her son by Mr. Egan. She uttered the words "God, why," exhaled loudly, and slid like a piece of wet spaghetti toward the floor of the witness stand. The woman was helped from the courtroom by the sheriff's deputies, and order was restored, but not before the incredible heartbreak and grief of this aspect of the proceedings had been amply demonstrated.

Many of the witnesses' names were the same as those represented on the State's gallery of grief—fathers and mothers, sisters and brothers of the deceased. Some, however, were close friends. Often, it was a close friend that was the last person to see the deceased. There was a reason for this. The largely unspoken truth that hung in the air like a thick, silent haze was this: Many of the victims had long ago left their homes or, in some cases, were kicked out of their homes due to conflicts with their families over their perceived lifestyle choices. The majority of the victims were homosexual. Not all, but most of them were male prostitutes, and the others clung precariously from the fringes of society. The incredibly enormous and truly tragic elephant in the room were the eleven nagging question marks posted as victims on the gallery of grief. There they sat, below the pictures of the identified victims, from time to time throughout the entire trial—eleven unidentified victims.

One can't help but wonder why. There was not a nook or a crevasse or an isolated burg or tumbleweed-swept town at the very end of a long lonely road in the farthest reaches of this nation that had been immune to the relentless press coverage that was attendant on this case. For month after month, every newspaper, radio, and television outlet across this land and abroad reported the horrendous events that took place in the obscure, unincorporated Chicago suburb. They couldn't help themselves. The story was captivating. Twenty-nine young bodies in a crawl space; a strange, gregarious minor politician, contractor, and part-time clown the suspect; pictures of him and the First Lady; male prostitutes as victims; killings that took place over a span of two years; thirty-three victims in all—how the hell could they possibly resist?

Motta and I were interviewed almost nightly, the prosecution team as well, the police, the mayor, the neighbors, former coworkers, prison mates, fellow Jaycees, girlfriends, wives, friends, foes, you name it—the press considered it an angle on the story. You could not hide from this news story if you actively tried to do so.

On top of all that, forensic pathologists and scientists had actually reconstructed the skeletal remains of the unidentified victims in such a way as to recreate their facial structure, and through computerized technology, they created computer-generated likenesses of these victims. You could see what these kids had looked like. These images were broadcast night after night on national television networks and reprinted in newspapers from sea to shining sea.

So the nagging question remained, unspoken and unexplained. Was there not another set of parents out there that looked up from their morning paper or their evening news broadcast and asked each other, "I wonder if one of those kids is our Johnny?"

That question remained unanswered, and remains unanswered still.

This sad fact led Dr. Robert Stein, the Cook County medical examiner, to state publicly that these unidentified kids "were not runaways . . . they were throwaways."

This whole unspeakable facet of the case served to further muddy up and complicate the issues. We couldn't touch this at trial because we felt it would look as though we were trying to imply that the victims in general did not warrant the attention they were getting, that they were all just society's outcasts. Of course, nothing could have been farther from the truth. We believed that every human life was sacred and had merit, including our client's life. We were fighting for that life with everything we had. That was the truth. Yet we had to sit and watch the prosecution drag in every available tearful face to yank on the heartstrings of every member of that jury, and we really couldn't do very much about it.

However, somewhere toward the end of this heartrending parade of life and death witnesses, the State wheeled in a wheel-chair-bound accident victim straight from the hospital. Her name was Mary Jo Paulus. I always thought that they had gone a little too far with her. She was in agonizing pain, both physically and mentally. She cried on cue during her testimony; but on cross, Motta got her to admit that the State had purposely withheld pain medication with some excuse about how she should not be under the influence of drugs on the stand. Bob also pried information out of her that some other person named Weedle was the last to see the deceased victim, William Kindred. So what was she doing there in the first place? Why did she have to be there at all, considering her condition? Where was Mr. Weedle? Wasn't Mr. Weedle pathetic enough as a witness? I don't think that played well with the jury.

Like I said, this was hardball. Don't ever let anyone tell you different.

After the life and death witnesses, the State began to put on persons that were involved in the case at the very beginning. Phil Torf, Kim Barnes, Linda Mertes, and others told the jury about the earliest moments of the story as it unfolded back at Nisson Pharmacy, Gacy's construction estimate, the forgotten appointment book. Jurors were transported to the night of December 11, 1978, and into that now-infamous drugstore in Des Plaines, Illinois. Linda Mertes spoke about how Rob Piest talked to her regarding his interest in the construction job. Kim Barnes testified about the photo receipt and how she had stuck it into the pocket of the blue down jacket that Rob had let her wear because she was cold at the cash register.

The story progressed as the State began to call to the stand the police officers that had investigated the case, the detectives that had followed John Gacy undaunted for days on end, the men that, through diligent effort and tireless hard work, had brought the defendant down.

Through these witnesses, the jury began to hear the story that they were promised in Egan's opening statement, only this time they were hearing it from the stand and under oath. The crying seemed to be over, and the actual participants were setting the nuts and bolts of the case forth methodically and dispassionately. As the story progressed through the officers' testimonies, you could see in certain jurors' eyes that they were fascinated by tales of how the police had chased Gacy all over the northwest suburbs at high speeds, how Gacy had begun telling the officers in advance when and where he was going, how he would invite them into his home for drinks and food, and, especially, how the police and Mr. Gacy sometimes drank together in bars, with John introducing them as his bodyguards. Mouths dropped when they were told that Lieutenant Kozenczak and Officer Pickell were in Gacy's house while Rob Piest's body rested silently in the attic, and many of the jurors looked upon John with disdain and bewilderment when they heard about his indignant statement to Kozenczak: "Don't you have any respect for the dead?"

A week of trial had passed in the blink of an eye, with more drama promised in the weeks to come.

30

THE JURY CONTINUED to hear the story unfold during week 2 of the trial. Early Monday morning they were treated to the rather gruesome story of the disposal of young Rob Piest's body, together with the events that occurred on Gacy's way back from that bleak, eerie bridge. If they had not decided this already, this morning's testimony may have informed them to keep their future breakfasts light.

Minor sparks flew when the tow truck operator, Robert Kirkpatrick, recounted the entire incident concerning Gacy having run off the road on Interstate 294; but he could not make an in-court identification of John, who was seated in the defendant's chair right next to me, as the man that he had seen in the big black Olds 98 that night.

The State called witness after witness intended to fill in the blanks for the jury regarding how they saw Gacy. Business associates were called to testify that he ran a successful business. Others testified that he was a competent worker. The State was offering their theory that Gacy was a normal guy without an apparent mental defect.

They also put on some evidence regarding our client's drinking habits and his drug use. It was their theory that John did not do drugs or drink to excess, and there was some testimony offered to support that proposition. Various Gacy acquaintances testified that Gacy was not a big drinker, and that, although he smoked pot, took Valium occasionally, and maybe popped a pep pill from time to time, these habits did not interfere with his ability to do his job, pay his bills, or live his life.

The State was building up to the testimony that they intended to offer from both Mike Rossi and David Cram. These two individuals were considered key to the State's case. Both of these men had worked for Mr. Gacy for years. They had each lived with John at one time or another, and they were his trusted friends and confidants.

Prior to that testimony, the State quickly called two young men who said that Gacy had propositioned them in a sexual way. The first, Robert Zimmerman, was an employee at Gacy's favorite Shell gas station. The second was Anthony Antonucci. He testified that Gacy had used handcuffs to restrain him while he made unwanted sexual advances toward him. Antonucci was successful in resisting John's advances, which John then dismissed as just a joke, just horsing around.

The testimonies of Cram and Rossi were revealing. These were the two individuals that had spent the most time with Gacy over the years previous to his arrest.

When Cram was called to the stand, we objected strenuously. Every effort that we had made, either personally or through our investigators, to interview Cram before trial had been unsuccessful. He was dodging us. We argued that the State had not allowed us proper preparation for this witness. Garippo overruled the objection. However, he recessed the court and allowed Motta and me to conduct an impromptu grilling of Cram prior to his testimony in a small adjacent room.

With David Cram on the witness stand, the jury learned how a chance meeting where Gacy picked up the young Mr. Cram while he was hitchhiking down Elston Avenue in the city of Chicago turned into an extended working relationship and friendship that blossomed during the following years. For a period of time, Cram lived with Gacy at the Summerdale address. David was on the stand for hours as Sullivan skillfully directed him through the areas that the prosecution team wanted covered.

During his testimony, Cram described events that had an eerie similarity to other events that the jury had heard about from the stand regarding Rob Piest.

Sullivan asked Cram about his birthday in 1976.

"Calling your attention to your birthday, 1976, were you at Mr. Gacy's house on the evening of your birthday?"

"Yes, I was."

"At that time, had you been drinking at his house?"

"Well . . ."

"Yes or no?"

"Yes."

"During this time that you were drinking, was Mr. Gacy drinking with you?"

"Yes, he had a couple with me."

"Did anything unusual occur that evening?"

"Yes. When I came in, it was my birthday, I believe, and I came into the house, and he had a clown suit on. He said that he was preparing for the next day. He had some kind of benefit charity to do with some kids with the clowning, and he thought it would be rather cute if, you know, seeing it was my birthday, that he leave the uniform on, and he was showing me some of his puppets and so on and so forth. Then he came up with a handcuff trick and—"

"What do you mean a handcuff trick?"

"Well, how you can escape from handcuffs."

"Did he in fact demonstrate how he—"

"He demonstrated them, and he took them off. I was so plowed, I didn't . . . you know, really pay attention to it."

"Did he ask if he could perform the trick on you?"

"Yes, he said to me, maybe sometime I'll need it."

"Were you sitting down at the time?"

"Yes, I was."

"In the family room?"

"Yes."

"Did he, in fact, put the handcuffs on you?"

"Yes, he did."

"Were they in front of you or in back of you?"

"In front of me."

"Were you able to escape from the handcuffs?"

"No, the trick was, you needed the key."

"At the time you were handcuffed, did Mr. Gacy say anything to you or do anything to you?"

"Well, I held the handcuffs up and I told him, you know, get them off, and he grabbed me between, by the chain, and swung me around the room a couple times, you know, I just, you know, said get these off me, you know."

"Did he say anything to you at that time?"

"Yes, he said, 'I'm going to rape you,' and I kind of freaked out, straightened up a little bit."

"Did you do anything at that time?"

"Yes, I ended up kicking him in the head."

"You what?"

"Ended up kicking him in the head."

"Did Mr. Gacy then take the cuffs off?"

"I did."

"How did you get them off?"

"With a key."

"Where did you get the key?"

"Out of his pocket, because they were lying on the counter, or one of the two."

"You needed a key to get out, is that correct?"

"Oh, for sure."

No one in the courtroom could escape the skin-crawling feeling that they had heard a story that was creepily similar to that one before. We could not avoid the sting that was left in the air. Some jurors looked down their noses at Gacy.

They hated him. I had to remind the jury that my client was crazy, that he was insane. I had my opportunity on cross-examination of Mr. Rossi later that day.

Rossi's testimony was limited because he had retained counsel. He was being represented by Edward V. Hanrahan. Mr. Hanrahan had served as the elected state's attorney of Cook County prior to being defeated by the now-sitting state's attorney, Bernard Carey. He was a good lawyer and had already demanded immunity for his client.

The State was just plain stingy with offers of immunity because they had been burned while doing this in the past. When, on cross-examination, a jury finds out that a witness is testifying pursuant to an agreement to grant immunity from prosecution, they tend not to believe the testimony of that witness. They think they are just testifying in exchange for the deal and will say anything. Therefore, the State would not agree to a deal for Mr. Rossi.

As such, Mr. Rossi was more or less uncooperative, and the State did not use his testimony as extensively as they might have, had he been more cooperative. However, I was able to use some of Mr. Rossi's extensive knowledge of Mr. Gacy to show the jury how truly insane my client was.

Rossi had been at John's house when Lieutenant Kozenczak and Officer Pickell went out to confront Mr. Gacy for the very first time.

I had to remind the jury that my client was crazy, that he was insane. This was my chance.

On the night of December 12, Kozenczak and Pickell had been out to interview Gacy regarding the Piest disappearance. After they had gone, Mike Rossi came in screaming about the police. I directed his attention to that night.

"After they left, you went into the house, is that right?"

"I was in the house."

"And, Mr. Gacy went up into the attic?"

"Yes, sir."

"Where were you when he did that?"

"In the hallway."

"In the hallway below the attic?"

"Yes, sir."

"What was Mr. Gacy wearing?"

"I believe he was wearing blue pants and a leisure shirt."

"And when he went up in that attic, he went up there to get Christmas tree ornaments?"

"Yes, sir."

"How did he appear to you?"

"Did he appear to be normal at that time, anything unusual?"

"Well, there had been a death in the family, but outside of that, he was OK."

"He was upset? Who died?"

"An uncle or something."

"He was upset about that?"

"Slightly."

"But, that seemed to be all that bothered him, right? Did he seem bothered when he went up into the attic, or was he his old self bringing the ornaments down?"

"Normal."

I looked at the jury for a long minute or two. I couldn't say it out loud, that would be testifying, but I wanted to psychically transmit to them the memory of the other testimony that they had heard about that night. If John Wayne Gacy was retrieving Christmas ornaments from the attic in his house on the night of December 12, he had to reach over the naked, dead body of Rob Piest to do it. Michael

Rossi was standing at the bottom of the ladder while Gacy noncha-lantly got the ornaments, probably humming Christmas carols as he reached for the box. No one except a person that was filled with madness, that was clinically and permanently insane, could perform such a task and arrive back at the bottom of that ladder looking . . . normal.

DAY AFTER DAY, Saturdays included, the story of John Wayne Gacy unfolded. Slowly, carefully the State filled in the details. Officer David Hachmeister and assistant state's attorney Lawrence Finder both testified to the continued impromptu confessions by Mr. Gacy, including the hair-raising tale about his demonstration of the rope trick on Larry's arm.

The jury heard from Dan Gentry, the evidence technician that unearthed the very first bone of the very first body and uttered the now-somewhat-famous declaration, "Charge him!"

In a trial, you cannot simply point to a picture and say, "That's victim number 1, Butkovitch. He was strangled by the defendant." A painstaking and elaborate process is necessary to establish the iden-tification of bodies and the cause and manner of death. Forensic dentists and forensic doctors must be called to the stand to offer grotesque and mind-numbing testimony as to each and every little aspect of the process. When doctors testify, the room usually goes to sleep quickly, not always figuratively.

Dr. Robert Stein, the Cook County medical examiner, was one of the doctors called to testify regarding cause and manner of death. We had been concerned about his testimony from the very begin-ning because he had been the doctor that was interviewed on NBC, when Bob first became involved with the case. He gave the hypo-thetical opinion that a man who killed thirty-three kids could be sane. We had to ensure that he stayed far away from any kind of testimony like that on the stand. Although he was a doctor, he really wasn't qualified to make that assertion. But because he was a doctor, if he made such an assertion, the jury might believe it.

The lawyers and the judge wrangled over this in chambers and outside the purview of the jury.

Stein primarily testified that the victims were strangled. Many were found with ropes still around their necks when they were removed from the crawl space. Many had some kind of cloth stuffed into their throats. The testimony was gruesome and graphic. However, he stayed away from giving his opinion as to the sanity of Mr. Gacy.

The State filled in whatever holes they believed were left to fill with their remaining witnesses.

The issue of sanity was for us to raise in our case. Once raised as an issue, the burden of proof shifted to the State to prove beyond a reasonable doubt that the defendant was sane at the time of the offense, or in this case, offenses. Therefore, the prosecution would not call any doctors to testify as to Mr. Gacy's sanity until their rebuttal case. Everybody in all of Chicagoland and the world knew that there would be doctors called to argue over John Wayne Gacy's sanity, but that is just the procedure, that is how it is done. So with no further witnesses to testify regarding this phase of the case, after three and a half weeks of testimony designed to prove that John Wayne Gacy was a murderer, the State of Illinois rested its case.

The lawyers retired to their corners to lick their wounds and prepare for round 2 of the battle.

31

On Thursday, February 21, 1980, Bob and I presented our first witness on behalf of the defense of our client, John Wayne Gacy.

I never knew what to believe regarding most of Jeffrey Rignall's tale of woe regarding the night that he and Gacy met. The story from my client and the story from Mr. Rignall diverged on many points. However, that is often the case when a lawyer puts a witness on the stand to testify. We, as lawyers, were not there at the time of the occurrence. We only know what we are told by our witnesses. Many times, memories fade, and agendas fill in the blanks. We have to trust that when a witness is sworn before God to tell the truth, he or she takes it seriously.

In Jeffrey Rignall's case, he had already published a book regarding his expected testimony and appeared on several talk shows and radio broadcasts to tell his sad story. John Wayne Gacy had made him famous.

Bob and I both felt that to call on one of Gacy's most vociferous accusers was a risk, but we felt it would show that we were not afraid of the horror that this story would unfold. There was no question that our client was seen as a monster by most of the country and the world. We had to show that in spite of the horrific nature of the crimes committed, our client was unable to control his actions.

Jeffrey Rignall dutifully related his now-famous nightmare, exactly as he had described in his book, with all the gory details about chloroform and a bleeding rectum. Either he was a very good actor, or he was still quite shaken by the experience that he had endured nearly two years earlier, because he broke into tears at one point and suddenly vomited.

The judge recessed court.

When all was returned to normal, after the cleaning crew had gone, Jeffrey returned to the stand. The following very important testimony was elicited:

"Sir, you are Mr. Jeffrey Rignall?"

"Correct."

"You are the same Mr. Rignall who testified earlier in this trial, right?"

"Correct."

"And you realize you are still under oath, correct?"

"Yes."

"OK, now, Mr. Rignall, I want to once again ask you if you recall the early morning hours of March 22, 1978."

"Yes."

"And that is the morning to which you testified earlier, is that correct?"

"Correct."

"OK, based on your own personal observations, all the surrounding circumstances involving those personal observations, do you have an opinion as to whether John Gacy, at that time, during those attacks, could conform his conduct to the requirements of the law?"

Kunkle: "Objection."

Court: "Overruled."

"Do you have an opinion?" I asked, disregarding Kunkle and his objection.

"Yes."

"What is that opinion?"

Kunkle: "Objection!"

Court: "Overruled."

Mr. Kunkle did not want Jeffrey to say the words that he knew were coming. I raised my voice over his.

"What is that opinion?" I persisted. "Could he conform his conduct to the requirements of the law?"

"No."

"How did you reach that opinion?"

"By the beastly and animalistic ways he attacked me."

I continued with my voice at high decibels.

"Do you have an opinion as to whether he appreciated, could appreciate the criminality of his acts at the time?"

Kunkle: "Objection."

Court: "Overruled."

"Yes," Rignall answered over the din of lawyers and judges sparring.

"And what is that opinion?"

Kunkle: "Objection."

Court: "Overruled."

"No," Rignall said, shaking his head vigorously. He was telling the court that our client could not appreciate the criminality of his acts at the time, answering my underlying question.

"And how did you reach that opinion?"

"By the way he attacked me . . . in the beastly manner that he did it, what he did to me."

I was praying that this kid was not going to puke again. He was shaking and quite upset.

Kunkle had lost that little volley. I calmed down and asked a few more questions about Mr. Rignall's ongoing medical treatment and his ongoing therapy. Then I said, "I have no further questions."

Mr. Rignall was excused from the witness stand, and he tentatively and carefully escaped the courtroom, shaking frailly as he walked.

Bob and I gave each other a knowing look. Our first witness had given his personal opinion from the stand, based on his personal experience, his encounter with the defendant. And his opinion was that John Wayne Gacy could not conform his conduct to the requirements of the law, nor could he understand the criminality of his actions. In his humble opinion, Gacy was nuts.

We wanted to show the erratic, changing nature of our client. Gacy would act pleasant and charming one minute, and then without warning, he would be somebody else the next. So we called Lillian Grexa, Gacy's longtime neighbor.

She told the jury that John was warm and generous, always smiling, that he had wonderful block parties. He was a good daddy and good neighbor, but he kept his bushes too high. He didn't trim them. Other than that, he was a great guy.

This woman looked like the lady that lives in every neighborhood, on every block, in every city, a nice-little-old-ethnic-lady-that-smiles-and-bakes-cookies kind of woman. The jury knew her. The jury believed her. And so the dichotomy appeared—apparently, Mr. Gacy was not just the monster they had all heard about; he was something else too. Now these fine men and women of the jury would actually have to think, to listen to the evidence.

We put on a couple of other witnesses that testified regarding the good side of John Gacy. Then we ended the day with testimony from Michel Ried. Mr. Ried had lived with John years earlier and had actually considered John a dear friend.

"Sir, could you please state your name and spell it for the court reporter?"

"Mickel Ried. M-i-c-k-e-l R-i-e-d."

"Where do you currently reside?"

"1349 W. Touhy."

"Are you married?"

"Yes."

"Do you have any children?"

"One."

"What is your business or occupation?"

"Welder."

"Are you currently employed?"

"Yes."

I continued asking perfunctory questions before I got down to the point.

"Mr. Ried, do you know the defendant, John Wayne Gacy, in this matter?"

"Yes, I do."

"Is he here in court?"

"Yes."

"Point him out please."

"Green suit." Mr. Ried pointed at John.

"Could you please tell the ladies and gentlemen of the jury where, when, and under what circumstances you met Mr. Gacy?"

"I met John . . . 1971."

"Would it have been around November 1970?"

"Could have been. I am not sure about the date."

Mr. Ried testified that he and Gacy had become friends, that he moved into Gacy's house, that he got to know him as a good person, a good father, and a good family man.

"Now, while you were still living with him, do you remember when you moved out of the house?"

"I think it was September."

"September of . . ."

"Like fall, '71 I believe?"

"Nineteen seventy-one?"

"Uh-huh."

"And why did you suddenly move out—did you suddenly move out, or did you plan to move out, had another place to stay?"

"Well, I just suddenly moved."

"Now calling your attention to, I believe, the day before you moved out, could you please tell the ladies and gentlemen of the jury if you observed anything unusual about John Gacy?"

"Well, we came into the garage one night. It was dark, we went to unload some of the equipment, and we got out of the car and the lights went out in the garage, and John told me to get some fuses under the workbench. So as I was doing that, on my hands and knees, I got hit on the head with something. I later—"

"Did you later learn what that was you got hit on the head with?"

"Yeah, hammer."

"What, if anything, happened to you when you got hit with the hammer?"

"I stayed down for a couple of seconds, and I kind of stood up and saw that John was looking like he was going to hit me again."

"Now when you say—backtrack just a little bit—did anything happen physically when you got hit with the hammer?"

"Well, I hurt my head."

"Did you bleed at all?"

"Yes."

"You say you did get up then?"

"I did."

"When you got up, what was John Gacy doing?"

"He had his arm back with a hammer in it, looked as though he was going to hit me again."

"What kind of look did he have in his eyes?"

"Well, kind of strange."

"Had you ever seen that look before?"

"No."

"Had he ever done anything to you like that before?"

"No."

"Before that, did you threaten him or try to hurt him, or did you try to strike him or anything?"

"No."

"Did you threaten him with anything at all?"

"No, I didn't."

"Any kind of extortion?"

"No."

"You say you got up and looked at him and he had a strange look in his eye? What, if anything, did you do?"

"I put my hand to stop his hand from coming back down, and at the same time, I asked him what he was doing or why he wanted to hit me."

"It was calm? Like that in an instant, or did it take a long period of time?"

"He hit me. I stood up and grabbed his arm and asked him what he was doing or what he thought he was doing."

"What, if anything, did he say to you?"

"He just looked at me and then put the hammer down."

"Did his expression change at all?"

"Yes, it did."

"How did it change?"

"He seemed like he was sorry he hit me."

"He put the hammer down?"

"Yes."

"What, if anything, did he do to you at that point?"

He told me that he didn't know what came over him, but he felt like he wanted to kill me."

"Now, after he said that, and he put the hammer down, what, if anything, did he do?"

"Well, I guess he patched up my head."

"Patched up your head?"

"Yes."

"Where? Right in the garage, or in the house?"

"No, we went into the house."

"And what was he doing or saying?"

"He was sorry that he did it."

"And then you moved out the next day?"

"The next day."

"Now, as you look back at that, Mr. Ried, have you formed or do you have an opinion as to that particular time with the hammer in the garage? Do you have an opinion as to whether John Gacy knew or could conform his conduct to the law? Do you have an opinion?"

"Yes."

"What is that opinion?"

"I don't think he knew what he was doing."

"Do you have an opinion as to whether or not he could appreciate the criminality of that act at that time?"

"No."

"You don't have an opinion?"

"I do. I don't think he knew what he was doing."

"Was that behavior different from the John Gacy you had known for those six months?"

"Yes."

"Other than that behavior, what kind of guy was he?"

"Well, he was like a brother to me."

"He treated you good?"

"Yes."

"No further questions. Thank you, Mr. Ried." I looked at the prosecution table. "Your witness."

As we closed in on the end of week number 4, we believed that we had successfully upset any plans by members of the jury to politely listen to what was said from the witness stand and then quickly vote to convict this bastard. They were going to have to really give the case their serious consideration. At least, that's what we thought.

On Friday morning we put on several more character witnesses to testify to the various sides of Mr. Gacy.

Finally, it was time to break out the shrinks, the testimony of the men and women on which the entire case would hinge, would turn, would be ultimately decided—the doctors that would make it simple for the jurors to understand the case and the defendant, John Gacy. Right.

32

BEFORE **D**R. **T**IMOTHY Leary was known as the LSD guru and he coined the phrase "tune in, turn on, and drop out," he was a very well-respected man in the field of psychological sciences. He was a member of the team at Harvard University's Department of Social Relations and a frequent speaker and writer regarding psychiatric and psychological research and study. He was credentialed. He was a big-time, hotshot shrink.

I read something that he said, which was quoted in the popular book *I'm OK, You're OK* many years ago, that has stuck with me ever since. Here's the quote:

> I would like to share with you some of the histor-ical background of my immobilization as a psychological scientist. As I look back I can see that there were three stages of my own ignorance. The first, which is by far the most happy, you could call the stage of innocent igno-rance when I was possessed with the notion that there were some secrets of human nature, there were some laws and regularities, some cause and effect relationships, and that through study, through experiences, through reading, some day I would share these secrets and be able to apply

my knowledge of these regularities of human behavior to help other people.

In the second stage, which might be called the period of illusion of non-ignorance, came the disturbing discovery that, although on the one hand I didn't know what the secret was, suddenly I discovered that on the other hand people were looking to me as though they thought I might know the secret or be closer to the secret than they . . . None of the research that I did worked nor did any of my activities provide any secret, but again I could always say, "Well, we didn't have enough cases," or "We must improve the methodology," and there were many other statements which I'm sure you are familiar with. One can postpone the painful moment of discovery but eventually the unhappy truth finally becomes apparent—that although many people may be looking to you and listening to you—you have patients and students and you're going to PTA meetings and they are looking to you for the secret—still eventually you begin to think maybe, maybe you don't know what you're talking about.

By no means am I trying to imply that psychiatrists or psychologists or others in their field do not know what they are talking about. I would never say that, and I do not think that—heaven forbid, perish the very thought.

What I can say is this: Of the seven major psychiatric and psychological experts that testified either on behalf of the State or on behalf of the defense, doctors and PhDs all, no two of them diagnosed the defendant in the same way. They all said that he was crazy. On that there was a consensus. But nobody seemed to know why or to what degree.

They did, however, have plenty to say about the subject of John Wayne Gacy. The standard-issue testimony of an expert witness in any field begins with an hour or so of credentials—every school, every degree, every treatise, every book, every speaking engagement, every teaching position, all of it must be painstakingly and carefully testified to from the stand. Otherwise, what the heck are they doing up there, right? They are experts, after all.

After they are through with the accolades, and everyone in the courtroom has gone somewhere else in their minds, they begin to expound. That's when the fun really begins.

Let's just say that for days and days the jury learned more about the field of psychiatry and psychology than they ever planned to know. This knowledge came to them from the stand in a foray of fifty-dollar words and ten-cent examples. They did, however, hear some incredibly interesting nuggets about our client interspersed between the mumbo jumbo. Let's give credit where credit is due.

And truth be known, the testimony was absolutely essential to the defense. Bob and I would not have been able to make our case without them.

Let me try to encapsulate days of testimony into sound bites that set forth their primary message.

Dr. Helen Morrison, probably our best expert witness, shocked the jury with the information that Mr. Gacy, as a child and adolescent, would steal silk women's underwear, use them for private sex, and bury them under the house. That information will kinda take your breath away when you first hear it. It does lend itself to the possible interpretation that maybe the defendant went off the proverbial rails long before he had a fighting chance to change directions.

That story was repeated by other shrinks as well.

The fine doctor used many big words to explain to the jury that John Wayne Gacy was insane. The big question remained, however: Was he insane enough? Was he insane at the time of the crimes?

Her testimony was clear.

"Now, Doctor, based on all that you have reviewed, your clinical evaluation, your expertise in the field of psychiatry, do you have an opinion based on a reasonable degree of medical certainty as to whether John Gacy, as a result of the mental disease you have described, lacked substantial capacity to conform his conduct with the requirements of the law at this time of each of the alleged acts?"

"Yes."

"What is that opinion?"

"That because of the continuous mental disease, he was unable to conform his conduct at the time prior to and during each of those acts."

"Doctor, did you further have an opinion based on a reasonable degree of medical certainty as to whether or not Mr. John Gacy, because of the mental disease that you have described, lacked substantial capacity to appreciate the criminality of his conduct?"

"Yes."

"What is your opinion?"

Her opinion was the same as her original report. According to this highly respected woman, whose field of study was specific to serial killers, whom she considered a special breed of individuals, persons that did not fit the standardized molds of human behavior or the ways in which these persons are categorized. It was this:

"Although superficial evaluation could not permit the development of other than an almost simplistic view of the mental disease of the defendant, a continuing evaluation shows a complexity of profound psychopathology not limited to one diagnostic category. Indeed, there is an incomplete recognition in the psychiatric diagnostic literature of the complexity and exact nature of the psychopathology. At least he may be said to be suffering from a psychosis with paranoid, intermittent delusional thought processes that is layered by a borderline syndrome of extremely low-level functioning. As such, the above results in a profound impairment that severely affected his ability to appreciate the criminality of his conduct and to conform his conduct to the requirements of the law."

Dr. Richard Rappaport had a different diagnosis, a different take entirely, from Dr. Morrison's. However, he seemed to arrive at the same place. Gacy was crazy. This after hours of testimony containing information like this:

"An electroencephalogram is a brain wave test which enables one to get a rough idea or approximation of whether or not there's any gross pathology in the brain—brain tumors or space-occupying lesions in particular."

And an hour later, he was saying this:

"The first characteristic under sensorium is orientation. Is the person oriented as to time, place, and person, and he was. He knew where he was, what time it was, who I was, and who he was. An individual with organic brain illness or psychosis might not be able to differentiate himself from another person."

Finally, thank heaven, he said the following to Bob Motta on direct examination:

Q. "Now, Doctor, based on your examination, everything that you have reviewed in this case, your diagnosis, your expertise in the field of psychiatry, do you have an opinion based on a reasonable degree of medical certainty as to whether John Gacy suffered from a mental disease continuously and interruptedly prior to and including the date of January 1, 1972, through the present?"

A. "Yes."

Q. "What is that mental disease?"

A. "Borderline personality organization."

Q. "Now, based on a reasonable degree of medical certainty, was he suffering from that disease at the time of the alleged acts?"

A. "Yes."

Q. "Do you further have an opinion based on a reasonable degree of medical certainty as to whether John Gacy, as a result of that mental disease, lacked substantial capacity to conform his conduct to the requirements of the law at the time of each of the alleged acts?"

Kunkle. "Objection."

Court. "Overruled."

A. "Yes."

Q. "And what is that opinion?"

Kunkle. "Objection."

Court. "Overruled."

A. "He did lack substantial capacity to control his behavior at the time of each of those crimes."

Q. "And conform his conduct to the requirements of law?"

A. "And to conform his conduct to the requirements of law."

Q. "All right. Now, Doctor, I want to ask you a few further questions. Would it change your opinion in any way if John Gacy had, prior to his arrest, told the police that he had no knowledge of the missing Piest boy?"

A. "No"

Q. "Why not?"

A. "Well, it is consistent with his ambivalent way of expressing his feelings. Sometimes he has knowledge, sometimes he has no knowledge, sometimes he denies, sometimes he acknowledges. His wavering and inconsistency is a great part of his disease."

And so it went. So thank you, Doctors. Thanks to everyone. I guess that pretty much cinches it. All questions about our client have been answered. He's nuts, just like we have been telling you. I guess we can all pack it up and go home, huh? I mean, if a doctor testifies that a guy has a broken leg, he has a broken leg, right? So if a doctor—hell, two doctors—testifies that our client has a broken brain, I guess that does it. Game, set, match. Let's go. Don't you people miss your wives and kids?

Apparently, I was jumping the gun a bit. It seems that all shrinks, although they are all doctors studying the exact same thing, don't always agree. Plus, Kunkle wasn't done with Dr. Rappaport. He cross-examined that man for over an hour. He actually tried to bring the fine doctor's opinion into question. It wasn't pretty.

He especially liked it when Dr. Rappaport described Gacy's personality as being like an onion—many, many layers, which had to be peeled back—and Gacy's alter ego as swiss cheese, with many, many holes, therefore he had no conscience. Kunkle had a bit of a field day with that on cross.

All in all, however, the fine doctor held his own against Kunkle.

———————————

THE STATE HAD their doctors as well, of course. Sparks flew during the direct examination of one of the State's experts, Dr. James Lewis Cavanaugh Jr.

Again, Bill Kunkle was asking the questions.

"During opening statements in this case, Mr. Motta referred to his desire that the defendant would be put in some mental institution or hospital for the rest of his life. Is that possible in Illinois, Doctor?"

I stood up. "Objection," I said.

The judge asked, "Is what possible?" He was looking at Kunkle.

I continued my objection. "As to what is possible?"

Kunkle continued without a ruling. "Is it possible to guarantee a person found not guilty by reason of insanity, and then committed to a mental hospital, Department of Mental Health in Illinois, will remain there for the rest of his life?"

Cavanaugh answered with the following words:

"Absolutely impossible, a guarantee. The whole thrust of legal impact changes on the ability to keep individuals many times—in my opinion, who need to be in hospitals—has been so extensive that we find it very difficult to keep people in hospitals who in fact need to be there because of concern, which I can understand that to hospitalize is a deprivation of civil rights, and we live in a—"

He had gotten these words out. Then a small version of hell broke out.

What the fine doctor was saying was that there was no guarantee that if Gacy was found not guilty by reason of insanity, he would stay in an institution. He was implying that Gacy might walk out of court a free man.

Obviously, this was a terrible problem for us—actually, for everybody. This could be grounds for a mistrial. We all might have to start this whole thing over!

If the jury thought John was going to walk out of court, they would never vote for a "not guilty by reason of insanity" verdict—hell, would you? The only other problem with the testimony, aside from it being told to the jury, was this: It was not true!

This was the voice of an airhead academic spouting puffy, fluffy academic theory and speculating about his civil rights, not an area of his expertise. And even the puffy, fluffy academic theory was wrong.

Motta jumped to his feet. "Objection, Judge. Can we have a sidebar please?"

"Mistrial!" I said, as all the lawyers headed for the bench.

As we surrounded the judge and frantically whispered, tempers flared a bit.

"I am objecting to the materiality," I began in hushed but heated tones. I went on. "He's talking in terms of possibilities, talking in terms of civil rights, and none of it is material to the case. It creates an inference for the jury that may or may not be true. A guy like Gacy, I think, should spend the rest of his life in a mental institution."

Garippo said, "Well, I don't know." The judge didn't get to say anything else just then.

"Nobody knows!" I hissed. "How can he testify to that? If you are going to let him testify [to that], then I'll call back every one of our doctors."

The judge ruled that for now the testimony would stand.

Kunkle said, "All right." He was just trying to calm things down.

"Mistrial," I said, but this argument would have to be shelved for later. We had a jury staring at us.

We returned to our corners. Kunkle continued questioning the witness, staying clear of the speculation that had been said.

When Mr. Kunkle was through with his witness, Bob stood up to cross-examine him.

Q. "Dr. Rappaport—oh, this is Dr. Cavanaugh, I see. Is that a Freudian slip? Dr. Cavanaugh, do you think that Mr. John Gacy needs to be in a mental hospital?"

A. "I don't believe he would benefit from treatment . . ."

Q. "Do you think he needs to be in a mental hospital?"

A. "No, I don't."

Q. "You don't? Could you describe the procedure regarding commitment after a finding of not guilty by reason of insanity?"

Kunkle. "Objection, the judge has already instructed the jury as to that."

Judge. "Well, he may repeat it."

Q. "He asked the question, Judge!" Bob was pointing at Mr. Kunkle.

Judge. "He may repeat it."

Q. "We'll find out."

A. "The procedure is identical to that of any other patient when the issue of potential and involuntary commitment is raised. In order to involuntarily commit, the individual must demonstrate imminent danger to himself or others or has to be in such a state as to be adjudged essentially unable to care for himself or herself."

Q. "Do you think that John Gacy presents an imminent danger to himself or others?"

A. "Imminent danger?"

Q. "Right."

A. "No."

Q. "All right, if he was found not guilty by reason of insanity, do you think he would pose an imminent danger to others?"

A. "I believe if he was found not guilty by reason of insanity, he would not meet the State's involuntary commitment standards."

Q. "Would you say that Mr. Gacy would be released?"

A. "If the law were followed, I believe he would have to be released."

Q. "You would testify he was not a danger to the other people, Dr. Cavanaugh?"

A. "I would testify that he were not imminently—"

Q. "Do you call killing one person after another a danger to people or society?"

A. "It is certainly a danger to society. The standard—"

Q. "If he were released—"

Kunkle. "Objection."

Q. "Would there be an imminent danger?"

Judge. "Should we go off to the side?"

33

WE WERE BOTH concerned about the lingering sting left over from the battle over Dr. Cavanaugh's testimony. It was devastating to think about how that information was going to affect the jury's collective thinking. It was an easy issue to obsess about. It could have put us off our stride. However, we had forgotten one thing: We were the attorneys for Mr. John Wayne Gacy and where Mr. Gacy was concerned, there was little time to obsess. There was always something new on the horizon.

On Friday morning of week 5, Gacy decided to be Gacy and add to the theatrics. Unbeknownst to Motta and me, Gacy had written a letter to the judge from jail two weeks prior. The judge gave it to us, and we read it and pretty much dismissed it. We had better things to worry about. Evidently, Gacy had not forgotten about the letter, and he had sent word to the judge that he wanted to discuss it.

Judge Garippo came out of chambers first thing Friday and explained that he had some matters to attend to before the jury was called. You can't make this stuff up.

"Over two weeks ago, the record should show that Mr. Gacy wrote me a letter with a few complaints. I gave that letter to his attorneys and was assured that there was no problem. Today I have received another letter from Mr. Gacy. Mr. Gacy, if you will step forward . . ." Gacy tentatively stepped up to the bench. "Is there anything you wish to say before this court?"

"No," Gacy answered.

Garippo couldn't believe his ears. "Pardon?" was all he could say. After all, it was Mr. Gacy who had contacted him.

Gacy stood there, arms at his side, shoulders slumped. "No," he repeated.

The judge simply stared at him. "With respect to the letter?" he prodded.

Gacy was a study of befuddlement. He looked like a twelve-year-old boy that didn't want to admit that he broke the window. "Well," he said, "it's written to you. The letter is between you and me."

Garippo actually smiled ever so slightly and shook his head. "Well, under the law, there can be nothing between you and me. It has to be on the record."

Gacy was downcast and slouched. I expected him to kick the toe of his right shoe into the heel of his left, the classic "Aw shucks" move. "You could do what you want with the letter," he mumbled.

"Do what I want with the letter?" Garippo's eyes twinkled.

"Yes."

"All right, here's what I will do with the letter. First, the letter will be made part of the record." The judge raised the letter to eye level and peered through his gold-rimmed glasses. "It reads:

"Over two weeks ago, I asked that my trial be stopped, and I haven't heard from you.

"When I asked my attorneys as to why we are not putting on more witnesses, I am told that we don't have money to bring in an expert. I also asked for a mistrial. As never before has this court allowed a professional witness plants a seed in the jury head like it was done yesterday.

"I think that you can give them instructions until you're blue in the face, and you won't take that out of their heads. When Cava-

naugh said John Gacy would not qualify for commitment to a mental institution and would have to be set free if he were found not guilty by reason of insanity, as you know, other than so-called statements made by me and given in a self-serving manner by officers for the prosecution, there is only evidence that I own the house that was used for [bodies] their safekeeping.

"Until something is done to correct this injustice, I will no longer have anything to do with my attorneys, and I am taking back my word in regards to not saying anything in the courtroom.

"The prosecution continued to tries to make me mad while the trial is going on with the taking of my PDM contractor labels and putting them all over the place. That's receiving of stolen properties, as I have never given my permission, and when yesterday, Greg Bedoe came up to me in open court and told me that I should stop smiling, and swore at me. I don't have to take that; I don't think anyone should come forward to the prosecution tables until I am out of the courtroom.

"I await to hear from you, and I will abide by your word."

Judge Garippo declared, "Well, first, with regard to the mistrial, I have made my ruling on the question of a mistrial. As far as your bringing in experts, at no time have you been denied the opportunity to bring in experts—any expert that was requested. The court has allowed any expert requested to come in and make examinations and testify. As far as reimbursement, I have indicated that each expert will be paid a reasonable amount. So that that is clear in your mind, at no time have you been prevented from obtaining any witness because of expense."

Then the judge leaned forward on the bench. His eyes bore a hole in Gacy.

"You said you would no longer have anything to do with any of your attorneys, is that your position?"

"That's correct," Gacy answered.

Garippo seemed exasperated. He wanted this to be over.

"I will continue for now the balance of the trial," he said, "and we will take that up—why won't you have anything to do with your attorneys?"

"Because I'm not running the trial."

"Are there any tactics that the defense is using . . . that your attorneys are using that you don't agree with?"

"I was against the insanity defense from the beginning."

"You were against the insanity defense from the beginning?"

"That's correct. While I may not be capable of defending myself, I was against the insanity defense. I'm sure Mr. Amirante, Mr. Motta will both tell you that."

"Have a seat," Garippo said. Gacy moped off and sat down at the defense table. Garippo looked at me.

"Do you have any statements to make, Counsel?"

I could barely talk. The only statement I could make was, "Mr. Motta and I have been indicating to Your Honor since prior to the inception of this trial on the record, I think we have just had an example of the problem with the degree of a defendant's mental illness addressed in our laws right now. Mr. Gacy should have been committed prior to trial. He should be committed now and because of the degree of his mental illness, we wind up with problems like this."

"Explain yourself," Garippo said.

I went on to explain that it had been my position from the beginning of trial that, although Mr. Gacy complied technically within the competency statute, the statute itself was unconstitutional as it applied to Mr. Gacy.

"Obviously, Judge, based on what you just saw and heard, he's actually not fit for trial."

The judge allowed us to make our record, during which Gacy blurted out from his seat at the defense table, "I did not commit the crimes!"

However, the judge was not about to end the trial and rule that Gacy was unfit. After an impromptu hearing ensued outside of the presence of the jury, in which Bob and I argued the merits of our contention that the competency statute was unconstitutional as it applied to our client, the judge began to nudge the trial back onto the tracks from which it had derailed.

"All right," he declared. "I make a further finding that based on my observations of the defendant in the courtroom, his demeanor, and all of the evidence in the trial, I would enter a finding right now. In a hearing as to fitness under Section 1005-2-1, I would enter a finding that the defendant is, in fact, fit to stand trial.

"Now, with respect to the question of dispute with his attorneys, is there anything you wish to say, Mr. Amirante or Mr. Motta, with respect to that?"

Bob said, "No."

I said, "Nothing," both of us looking behind us at our client.

"Mr. Gacy, if you will step forward again," the judge said.

Gacy trudged up to the bench like a surly teen.

"Do you stand by your statements relative to your disagreement with your attorneys?"

At that point, Bernard Carey, the elected state's attorney of Cook County, Illinois, a very high-profile and powerful figure in Illinois State politics, had wandered into the courtroom to check on the progress of his trusted assistants and to check on the progress of the biggest and most widely publicized trial his office had ever prosecuted. He had heard about the commotion that Mr. Gacy was causing with his letters and his craziness.

When John Wayne Gacy saw Bernard Carey, he went off.

"What the hell is he doing in here?" Gacy screamed, pointing and turning toward Carey.

Immediately, the sheriff's deputies came off the walls and out of seats, their designated positions, and moved closer to Gacy.

"You have no business in here! Leave this trial to the guys that know how to handle it, who know what they're doing! You aren't qualified to be in here. You have three of the best attorneys in your office working on this case—real attorneys, not political hacks like you!"

Bernard Carey was a Republican. To see an actual Republican in a Chicago courtroom was a rarity. John Gacy was a lifelong Democrat, a democratic precinct captain for his voting district. I guess John didn't like Mr. Carey.

By now, the sheriff's deputies were closing in on Gacy. The judge put an end to the disturbance right quick. He waved off the uniformed deputies. The whole exchange had lasted only a few seconds. Gacy had turned back to face the bench.

"John," he said, "you will be the democratic precinct captain till the end."

The judge was waiting for an answer to his previously posed question.

Finally, Gacy complied. "I don't know," he said sheepishly.

"You don't know?" The judge just shook his head, bewildered. "All right, have a seat."

Gacy shuffled off back to the defense table. As he walked, the judge went on. "While we are on the subject right now, between now and the time . . ." Gacy stopped. Garippo pointed at the defendant's chair. "You may sit right there. I will address you, Mr. Gacy. Between now and the time your attorneys rest your case, you have to decide whether or not you wish to testify before this jury. Do you understand that?"

Gacy had sat down. "Yes," he said from his chair.

"OK," said Garippo, always the protector of the record. "Call the jury."

After the jury was seated, and for a very short time, the courtroom was treated to more mind-numbing testimony from a doctor. This time, Dr. Tobias Brocher was called to sing everyone a lullaby. I shouldn't say that. He was our witness, but doctors bore me.

Thankfully, it was almost lunchtime.

OVER THE LUNCH break, the entire courthouse was abuzz with the rumor that Gacy had fired Bob and me. It has always been amazing to me how a story like that can be felt in the air. It's like static electricity. People look at you differently. Some avert their eyes. Others come up and pat you on the back and say things like, "Tough break," or "You're better off," and walk away, leaving you wondering what the hell they meant.

Outside the courthouse the talking heads could hardly contain themselves; they barely even took a breath while reporting the breaking news. Everyone wanted to scoop everyone else. They broke into soap operas and afternoon game shows with bulletins. It was hilarious to Bob and me. Funny that we were not informed.

When Gacy heard about the news in prisoner holding, he was flabbergasted. He had already forgotten all about his earlier miff over his own lawyers in favor of his shining moment with Bernie Carey. He wanted to hear the judge's compliment about him being a democratic precinct captain to the end on the air. Where was that story?

After lunch, Gacy called us back into prisoner holding and told us he wanted to make a statement concerning the morning's brouhaha.

We informed the court.

Upon reconvening, the entire courtroom was treated to a little piece of insanity, compliments of John Wayne Gacy.

"All right, before the jury comes out, do we have a statement to make?" Garippo was sitting tall on the bench with that familiar twinkle in his eye. He went on. "Mr. Gacy wants to make a statement. You wish to make a statement, Mr. Gacy?"

Gacy simply said, "Yes." I believe the words "Your Honor" stuck in his throat. He could never seem to get them out. Then a miracle occurred.

The judge said, "All right."

And Gacy said, "Your Honor," and then he was off. His statement was priceless.

"It seems to me like, as with everything else in this whole case, everything I seem to say has been misconstrued in the press. And I would like to set the record straight that I did not fire my attorneys.

"I did not ask for their leave from this case. It's just that I stated and will state again that I do not understand everything that is going on, and I am against the insanity defense because I lack the understanding or the appreciation of it because I don't truly understand it myself.

"I stated earlier that I do not feel I committed the crime, and anything I say is considered self-serving. All the statements, in retrospect, that I have given are confusing enough to me, that at the time that I made the statement, I believe I would have confessed to the Saint Valentine's Day massacre if it was put to me.

"I believe in this courtroom you have probably five of the finest attorneys that there are in the country. And I listen to them work as if it's a pretzel factory twisting every which way other than the truth. The papers, the newspapers especially, have taken everything out of context and have actually run everything one way or the other without ever bringing out the whole truth and nothing but the truth. And I thought that's what you are after.

"I can see with the seed planting done yesterday before the jury that no matter what you do or how you instruct the jury, you will never reverse what you have told the jury. I had stated before we started the trial to my attorneys that I would like to know myself if I committed the crime.

"I had talked to Dr. Friedman for a long time. As you know, I have seen doctors for over three hundred hours, and in so doing, I have been still left in the same confused state that I am right now.

"While I am not denying the commission of the crime, I don't understand it. I don't understand why—why it happened. And that is why I don't understand the proceedings.

"I have been called every name under the sun in this courtroom, and half the time I leave the courtroom here not even knowing who I am—from an onion to a piece of swiss cheese to somebody that is sane and somebody that is crazy. And quite frankly, I am completely confused as to what has been going on.

"The state puts on a witness who claims to be my best friend, and in all actuality, it's just a person that I felt sorry for because of his illiteracy. Mr. Rohde took the stand and claims he was my best friend. He was just a business acquaintance of mine. You put on different officers from the different varying police departments, and they all do self-serving statements. I am at a point where I don't know what is right and what is wrong and what is truth and what is not the truth because of the mass confusion that has been going on since the thing started.

"I believe I have been tried and convicted and sentenced in the news media already. However, I understand that they are not the ones trying me, but I also feel that nowhere in this land can I get a fair trial—before this started and even now.

"I think it's more prejudicial now than it was before, and again, I don't blame, like I say, the counsel, because I think—as well as for my own defense and for the prosecution—I think you have got some of the finest lawyers here in the country. I can see why Bernard Carey is not here, because he is not qualified, but the thing of it is, is that be that as it may, everybody is going to twist everything to their own liking, and to me, its just like they're playing a chess game. One move, and then another one moves, and I am totally confused as to what is going on. That's why I told you I would abide by your decision and go on with the case."

Garippo, very seriously but still with a twinkle in the eye, responded, "Well," he said, "apparently from your statements, your attorneys are doing an excellent job of presenting, I think, the feelings that you have expressed here in open court."

"The biggest problem," Gacy continued, "I have had with my attorneys is that I have not been able to help them because I cannot remember. It's not that I am denying anything—I have never denied any of it—it's just that I don't know if when it happened, was I aware of what I was doing?"

Garippo had seen enough of the Gacy show.

"All right, now, all right, you may be seated," he said, dismissing Mr. Gacy. "All right, call the jury."

The rest of the trial went pretty much without incident.

The State called Dr. Jan Fawcett, the last of their shrinks. He thought Gacy was crazy, but not crazy enough. Dr. Fawcett testified that John Wayne Gacy was able to understand the nature of the crimes committed and that he could have conformed himself to the law. Gacy, according to Dr. Fawcett, was quite sane.

This testimony was given with the sound of Gacy's letter and statement still ringing in the jury's ears.

All parties rested their case. It was time for closing arguments.

Bob and I had returned to feeling that our case was strong. The State had to prove beyond a reasonable doubt that the man sitting next to me was sane. Was that possible?

34

TERRY SULLIVAN HAD shepherded this case through each phase of the investigation from the very beginning to the present. Ever since Terry moved himself and his personal coffeepot into the makeshift command office in the Des Plaines Police Department, he had been the representative from the Cook County State's Attorney's Office and the supervisor that kept the investigation on the straight and narrow. His closing argument in the *Gacy* case was the culmination of long hours, dedication, and hard work, on which he had spent just over a year of his life. This was his baby; and his passion was apparent as he spoke.

He approached the lectern in front of the jury box, grabbed it, leaned forward, and began.

"Judge Garippo, Mr. Kunkle, Mr. Egan, Mr. Varga, counsel for the defense, ladies and gentlemen of the jury: Today is March 11, 1980. On Thursday, March 13, two days from now, John Mowery would have been twenty-three years old, if he had been allowed to live. Instead, his body was uncovered from John Gacy's crawl space.

"On Sunday, March 16, Robert Piest would have celebrated his seventeenth birthday. Instead, his body was recovered from the Des Plaines River, the very river that he had volunteered to clean to become an Eagle Scout.

"On Monday, March 17, John Gacy will celebrate his thirty-eighth birthday. Before that, you will have the opportunity to decide whether or not John Gacy is allowed to be sitting somewhere in an easy chair, with his legs propped up, in his casual clothes, puffing on one of his big cigars, and making another one of his famous phone calls. Before that, you will decide whether or not he is allowed to tell a friend, such as Ron Rohde, on the telephone, on Sunday or Monday, 'Ron, didn't I tell you, didn't I tell you I'd be out. I beat the system again.' Or, you will be the ones to tell John Gacy, in a loud and clear tone, a message that says, 'John Gacy, your cruising days are over. Young boys need fear you no more!'"

You didn't have to study the jury to determine if they were paying attention. One quick look, one passing glance, and anyone could see that Terry had captured the rapt attention of each and every jury member. He was painting a picture. He began to pace and move about the well of the court.

"You will have the opportunity to tell him, 'John Gacy, you will not manipulate us.' You will be able to send him a message: 'You are guilty.'

"You people have served a long trial and in a very unselfish manner. On behalf of my partners, on behalf of the People of the State of Illinois, whom we represent, I wish to thank you."

Terry was settling in, finding his stride. After having lived with this case every day of his life for such a long period of time, he knew what he wanted to tell this jury. He had been preparing for this moment for over a year.

Terry began by reminding the jury of the initial questions asked of them back in Rockford, when they were being selected as jurors, bringing them back to the beginning, reminding them how it felt to be told that they were going to be sitting on a jury where a man who was charged with thirty-three counts of murders would be judged.

He reminded them that this case was "not a single incident, not just one single massacre like a berserk person who maybe would take a machine gun and fire into a grade school for an hour. That is not what we saw here for the past month and a half. This wasn't a single incident, this went on for years. I believe that the evidence has shown you that these killings were carefully planned, that they were calculated, and then, that they were carefully covered up. That evidence should have shown you people that John Gacy could make conscious, responsible choices.

"I'd like you to recall through your lifetimes that there have been other mass murderers, but seldom, if ever, has anyone been so cold, so cunning, so calculated over such a long period of time as John Gacy has."

Terry was about to slice very thinly the primary issue in the case. He knew he had to do it. He also knew it was a risky move. He took a breath, and continued.

"Now, I am not going to stand here for one minute and tell you that he is normal. No, I couldn't do it, and I wouldn't expect you to believe it. I'm going to tell you, right up front, that we consider him to be abnormal, not normal. You folks probably consider yourselves normal—you have never killed anyone before, let alone thirty-three people. He is abnormal. The very dictionary says that abnormal is a nonconformist, someone who is peculiar, bizarre, one who infringes the law, one who doesn't conform to what society dictates, someone who puts himself above. Yes, that is abnormal, that is John Gacy. But because he is abnormal doesn't mean that he doesn't know the difference between right and wrong. If he does, he is legally responsible. There is quite a difference between being abnormal and legally insane. Nobody who murders is quite normal."

So there it was—the crux of this case, the basic question, that searing question that had landed in the lap of this jury. It seems that everyone could now officially agree that John Gacy was crazy, that he was nuts, that he was abnormal. But was he nuts enough?

Here was Terry Sullivan, arguing that our defense was right, agreeing with our basic premise that John Wayne Gacy was insane.

He just didn't think he was insane enough. It would have been nice if he took a seat at that point. You know, thanked the jury and left it at that. Of course, he didn't. He had plenty more to say.

"We must stress to you people the concept of responsibility, the concept upon which our laws are created, that concept of criminal responsibility that a person must be held responsible for his acts. Just because a person has a personality defect doesn't mean that he is insane, and just because he has a complex personality doesn't mean that he has a mental disease. Criminals don't make our laws, ladies and gentlemen. He is abnormal, but he is rational and he is sane.

"Now, you were instructed, and His Honor will instruct you again, that we had a burden to prove the defendant guilty beyond a reasonable doubt. We had that burden on two issues: number one, we had to prove the defendant guilty beyond a reasonable doubt of thirty-three murders; and [two] we also had to prove that he was legally responsible beyond a reasonable doubt.

"I feel there is no doubt but that we have proven both of those. As to the former, the fact that he has murdered thirty-three people: twenty-seven of those individuals, those young boys, were found under John Gacy's house, one was found under the driveway, one under the back of the garage—twenty-nine on his property. Four were found in the river—Robert Piest, Tim O'Rourke, Frank Landingin, James Mazzara. You may recall that he said there were five that went in the river. We even may be missing someone still—that is by his own statement.

"In addition, Robert Piest's jacket was found in his home; in addition, Frank Landingin's bond slip was found in the defendant's house; and in addition, he talks about the Mazzara boy as Joe from Elmwood Park. He has admitted to at least thirty murders. He said thirty or more.

"Subsequent to the recovery of the identifications, identifications were made. You heard Dr. Pavlik, the dentist, advise you on how he made identifications from teeth. You also heard Dr. Fitzpatrick, the radiologist, testify about certain X-rays in which he said he based his identification. I am not going to bore you with all of that testimony, nor am I going through all of that again. We have proven that he has killed thirty-three people.

"I think we have also proven that the defendant has also taken other advantages, with which he is charged, with Robert Piest.

"As to the second point, the defendant being legally responsible, His Honor has told you before, and I will advise you of this again right now, that the only definition for being legally responsible is the one that has come from the court in Rockford, and the one that will come to you again. And that is simply [this] . . ."

Terry paused for effect. He eyed each and every member of the jury.

"A person is not criminally responsible for his conduct if at the time of such conduct, as a result of mental disease or defect, he lacked the substantial capacity either to appreciate the fact that his conduct is criminal, or to conform that conduct to what is required by law.

"Those are the words that you are going to get again later from Judge Garippo. That is the only basis upon which you should make a decision.

"I suggest that the evidence here just does not show that the defendant was not criminally responsible. In fact, when you look at all of the evidence, it shows that he did have the capacity to appreciate what he was doing and to conform his conduct to what the law requires. It shows further that the defendant was for years, and is, sane and calculating, and premeditating, and cunning, and manipulating, and evil, and rational. His acts and words, ladies and gentlemen, show that. The evidence shows that.

"I think it further shows that the defense of insanity, as used by John Gacy, is a fraud, plain and simple.

"Now, as we talk about the evidence, what I would like for you to do, if you can, is to keep in mind certain of the categories that have been gone over and over again, but maybe during the evidence they haven't been all drawn together into neat little niches. Some of those categories that the psychologists and psychiatrists base some of their decisions on, things that they were looking for, things that you should have been looking for, using your common sense as to what makes a sane or an insane individual. Some of those things that I would ask you to consider again would be intelligence, his memory, his ability to manipulate or con people, his credibility or lack thereof, his self-control, the emotions that he may or may not have had, his use or misuse of alcohol or drugs, his work and sleep pattern, his physical acts or strengths, and finally, a category that I call consciousness of choice, that is, during his life, could he make conscious decisions?

"Now, back when this case first started, Mr. Motta, Mr. Gacy's attorney, made certain statements to you. In his opening argument, Mr. Motta said certain things that I would just like to reflect upon for a minute.

"He said that the evidence will show that John Gacy is insane under any standards. Whether it be that standard of your own good conscience or your common sense, the evidence will show, undeniably, that he could not control his conduct. Well, now, I'm not sure which courtroom Mr. Motta was in during this court case, but I don't think that the evidence has shown that at all. He said that our psychiatrists—that is, their psychiatrists—will testify that Mr. Gacy is incapable of forming an intent because his intelligence and thought processes were helpless, incapable of forming an intent. Well, I think the evidence shows quite the contrary. It does show conscious choices."

Terry went on to give an extensive restatement of how the State interpreted the evidence. He went through the witnesses he thought important and tried to emphasize testimony that he thought pertinent or helpful to his case. He talked for hours. Sometimes he had the jury's attention, and sometimes he did not. But he covered the evidence and related that to the story that was John Wayne Gacy. He did his job. He rarely looked at notes except when he wanted to offer a direct quote. He was leading the jury to a place where he wanted them to be. Then he began to sum up. His passion for this case was unleashed.

"Finally, ladies and gentlemen, thank you for bearing with me. I know you're probably very hungry. Finally, I ask you only, what was the evidence that we have seen? What picture do we now have after all of this evidence? We have a man who has led a life with no regard for the law or people in general. A man who has shown a consistent pattern of antisocial conduct from as far back as Iowa in 1965. He's intelligent. He's cunning. He decided that he enjoyed having sexual relationships with males, and in particular, with boys. And he went about setting up, like a hunter, ways in which to lure and trap his prey, and then ways in which to disarm them. Then, to use them for his own gratification. He got caught once, but there were too many other boys in the future. Only henceforth, he was to be more careful. Shows how he thought those who would later cause him trouble he would kill. Keep them out of his way.

"So like tumbleweed that just keeps rolling along, John Gacy rolled through Iowa, being stopped only for a short time by prison walls, and then he rambled to Illinois and rolled and rolled and rolled through some of our younger citizens, making sure along the way that nothing got in his way and being ever so careful to think before he acted, and then, to cover up when he was done. And he left a path of destruction in his way. Thirty-three boys were dead; and the lives of parents, brothers, sisters, fiancées, grandmothers, friends were left shattered."

Motta couldn't take it anymore. He half-rose from his seat. "Objection," he said. The judge didn't respond. He let it pass. Sullivan continued.

"Even though technically he left some of the surviving victims, they were little more than void shells—you saw them—and perhaps described best as living dead. John Gacy has accounted for more human devastation than many earthly catastrophes, but one must tremble. I tremble when thinking just how close he came to getting away with it all. Further, [the] evidence shows that his intention was to concrete that entire crawl space in the very near future, a move that certainly would have kept him from detection.

"John Gacy's freedom would no doubt have meant for others, somewhere, more shattered lives, and it surely would have meant that Rob Piest would have died in vain. John Gacy had caused misery and suffering enough to last a century. Thank God, he's been stopped. John Gacy is either evil or crazy, said Mr. Motta in his opening statement. I submit that beyond a reasonable doubt, he is evil. He is vile. He is base. He is mean, he is diabolical, and he is a murderer who must be held responsible for his conscious acts. He used all of his victims, both the dead and the living victims, for his own selfish, egocentrically physical pleasures."

Terry pointed at Gacy. He walked toward him.

"John Gacy, you are the worst of all murderers, for your victims were the young, the unassuming, the naive."

Gacy, true to form, totally unable to act appropriately, laughed nervously at Sullivan.

"You truly are a predator," Sullivan went on. "John Gacy, you have pilfered the most precious thing that parents can give: that of human life. John Gacy, you have stolen the most important thing that any person has: his very life. John Gacy, you have nipped in the bud thirty-three young lives, and you have deprived them of everything that this country, based on laws and justice, stands for and guaranteed to those people: their lives, their liberty, and their right to pursue their own happiness. Finally, John Gacy, you have snuffed out those lives like they were just candles. You have snuffed out the very existence of those thirty-three young boys forever. Those candles can't be lit again for all eternity."

Terry turned back to the jury. He walked to the jury box and placed his hands on the wooden dividing railing. He peered at each juror.

"Ladies and gentlemen, the decision of guilt or innocence is now yours. You have the opportunity to prevent the future slaughter of other young men and boys by that sadistic animal. You saw him laugh at me. You are the only ones who can tell him loud and clear, 'We refuse to be used or manipulated by you, John Gacy.' The snows of winter are fleeing, and the miracle of spring will soon arrive here, folks, but you can tell him that 'you, John Gacy, will not partake in that annual miracle, not this time, because we find you guilty.'"

Terry paused. He walked to the prosecution table. He picked up the stack of 8½" × 11" pictures that the State had compiled for their gallery of grief, which they had been using throughout the trial. He had a plan for those pictures. He walked over to the empty easel, which stood in plain sight of the jury.

"You have, on the other hand, the choice of finding John Gacy not guilty," he said quietly.

He paused again.

"If you find him not guilty, that is your choice. If you find him not guilty, then do so. Do so remembering that eleven unidentified male bodies are still in the Cook County morgue."

As he said this, Terry placed eleven pictures that were mere question marks with only the known vital statistics of those victims into slots that secured them to the board. These were the unidentified victims. He then turned back to the jury. He went on.

"If you do so, do so in spite of body no. 2 medical examiner no. 1065 found with a clothlike material on his throat. Male, white, five nine, 150 pounds. Last seen July 29, 1975, Chicago, Illinois. Identified December 29, 1978, as John Butkovitch."

Terry placed John Butkovitch's picture into the slots that secured it to the board.

"If you find him not guilty, do so in spite of body no. 29, medical examiner no. 494, clothlike material on throat. Male, white, five foot five, 140 pounds. Last seen April 6, 1976, at Chicago, Illinois. Identified November 18, 1979, as Darrell Sampson, age eighteen."

Terry placed Darrell Sampson's picture into the slots that secured it to the board.

"If you find him not guilty, do so in spite of body no. 6, medical examiner no. 1274. Male, white, five foot six, 145 pounds. Last seen alive May 14, 1976, Chicago, Illinois. Identified November 14, 1979. Sam Stapleton, fourteen."

Again, Terry placed the picture in the slot.

"If you find him not guilty, do so in spite of Sheriff's body no. 7, medical examiner no. 1277, clothlike material in throat. Male, white, five foot nine, 145 pounds. Last seen alive May 14, 1976, in Chicago. Identified in the spring of 1979 as Randall Reffett, age fifteen. Student."

Again, the picture went up.

"If you find him not guilty, do so in spite of body no. 18, medical examiner no. 1379, ligature around the neck. Male, white, five foot seven, 150 pounds. Last seen alive June 3, 1976, in Chicago. Identified, January 6, 1979, as Michael Bonnin, seventeen."

The picture went up.

"If you find John Gacy not guilty, do so in spite of Sheriff's body no. 23, medical examiner no. 1452. Male, white, five foot six inches tall, 130 pounds. Last seen alive August 6, 1976, Chicago, Illinois. Identified December 29, 1978, as Rick Johnston, seventeen. Student."

Picture added.

"If you find John Gacy not guilty, do so in spite of body no. 22, medical examiner no. 1439, clothlike material on throat. Male, white, five foot eight inches tall, 160 pounds. Last seen alive June 13, 1976, in Chicago. Identified March 17, 1979. That's William Carroll, sixteen, a student."

William's picture went up.

"If you find him not guilty, do so in spite of body no. 4, medical examiner no. 1122. Male, white, five foot nine, 140 pounds. Last seen alive August 6, 1976, in Chicago. Identified December 29, 1979, as Gregory Godzik, seventeen, student."

One by one each picture went up on the gallery of grief.

Terry continued, naming and describing each victim in the same manner, giving each the full respect they deserved. When finished, their picture was reverently placed with the others.

John Szyc.

Jon Prestidge.

Matthew Bowman.

Robert Gilroy.

John Mowery.

Russell Nalson, Robert Winch.

"Tommy Boling. Twenty years old, married, wife, Jolie, and son, Timmy."

David Talsma. William Kindred. Timothy O'Rourke. Frank Landingin and James Mazzara."

Finally, Terry was holding one last picture.

"And, ladies and gentlemen, if you find him not guilty, do so over the body No. 30, Medical Examiner No. April 231, paper-like material in the throat. Male white, five foot eight inches tall, a hundred forty pounds. Last seen alive December 11, 1978, in Des Plaines, Illinois. Identified April 9, 1979, as Robert Piest. Student. Birthday is Sunday."

Terry put Robert's picture up on the board. He addressed the jury from in front of the gallery of grief. He spoke softly at first. Then his voice rose in volume.

"Ladies and gentlemen of the jury, we have proven John Gacy to be criminally responsible. We have proven that he has committed the crimes charged, and we have proven this beyond a reasonable doubt.

"Justice is the very reason we're here. They—they deserve justice." He pleaded, pointing at the board, "That gallery of grief deserves justice! Society deserves justice! John Gacy deserves justice!"

Sullivan approached the easel. He pointed to each picture as he spoke. Each point was a poke that landed with a quiet thud on the board. He bellowed.

"This was murder! This was murder! This was murder! This was murder! Murder! Murder! Murder! Murder! Murder! This was murder! So was this! Murder! This was murder! This was murder! This was murder! Murder! Murder! Murder! Murder! Murder! Murder! And this was murder!"

Sullivan faced the jury, and in a controlled but shaking voice he said, "Justice implores you to find John Gacy guilty of murder—murder in the worst degree! Thank you."

Terry Sullivan took his seat.

The air had been sucked from the room. It was like a vacuum—not a sound, not a peep, no movement. People felt exhausted.

Even the judge could only muster a quick statement: "Ladies and gentlemen, we will now recess and resume at three o'clock."

35

AFTER TERRY SULLIVAN'S closing argument, Motta and I let the court-room empty out before we stood and headed toward the doors. As we walked, I looked at Bob. He knew me. He immediately said that he was going to go get a sandwich, which was his way of saying that he was going to leave me alone to get ready. He knew that was exactly what I needed just then. I was going to have to walk back into that courtroom in an hour and a half and give my closing argument. No problem.

Welcome to the private practice of law, Sam.

I pushed past screaming reporters poking microphones and scribbling furiously on notepads, back to the little office that they had provided us during the trial and shut the door. I was surrounded by boxes and files and pictures and exhibits, by chalkboards and dry-erase boards and corkboards. On those boards were notes and strategies, lines and arrows, pictures and plans that had accumulated over the protracted weeks of trial. It was all a bit of a blur.

I thought about the buffoonery that my client had displayed time and again during the long days and nights of the cockeyed, erratic course of this crazy trial. I thought about the insanity that I had witnessed over the past year, beginning with that night just before Christmas in my office. What a heart-stopping memory. I was preoccupied by the illness of my son, distracted by the Christmas season, pissed off about the fact that I had to waste time talking to this weirdo. But he was my client, my very first client, and I felt I had to do it. There I was, waiting patiently for this nut job, making small talk with Leroy Stevens. Then he walked into the office with all of his apologies and his bullshit. I just wanted this silly, unnecessary little meeting to be over so I could go home to my wife and kids. Then he opened his mouth.

I got the chills just thinking about that night. Never in my life had I seen, or would I even have believed that there could exist, such a deranged individual. There have been few like him in all of human history. He was in a very small club, the members of which make our skin crawl.

I saw the whole scene replayed in my mind, the insanity of it all. This human being, this man, my client right in front of me, right before my eyes, pacing, grunting, sweating, spewing pure horror. I was in a small room with pure evil. I was looking at it. I had met the true-life incarnation of Mr. Hyde. I knew at that moment that my life had changed forever. The Christmas season disappeared. My petty worries dissolved. I suddenly had a purpose that few men could claim.

I chuckled to myself, thinking about the two sworn officers of the law, Albrecht and Hachmeister, thirty feet away behind a plate of glass, one trying to catch a quick nap on the floor of my reception area. Who would believe it? What a ride this had all been.

I looked at the clock. It was almost time. I had given this closing argument to the walls of my bedroom, to the showerhead in my bath, and to the windshield of my car at least a hundred times. Now, it was time to give it for the jury.

I walked into the courtroom and was immediately struck by the fact that the lunch break had not cured the quiet that followed Terry's closing argument. There was a perceptible hush in the over-packed gallery.

I felt the eyes of everyone in the room on my back. I walked up to my partner, who looked me in the eye and simply said, "You good?"

I smiled a quick, serious smile at him, sat down next to our client, leaned back in my chair, and crossed my legs.

"All rise," the bailiff called.

Judge Garippo swept into the room and up the steps to the bench.

"Court is in session," he said as soon as he was seated. "All right, you may call the jury."

The jury filed in. It was as quiet as an empty church.

The judge looked at me. "You may proceed, Mr. Amirante."

I stood up and approached the jury box.

I had lived with this case every single day and night for thirteen long months. It was in me. I had no notes in my hands. I didn't need any. What needed to be said was etched in my psyche. As I approached the lectern, I began.

"May it please the court, distinguished gentlemen of the prosecution, Mr. Motta, Mr. Gacy, ladies and gentlemen of the jury."

I pulled the lectern backward from where Terry Sullivan had left it.

"Excuse me while I move this back. People tell me I look too short here if I stand right up in front there."

The muffled sound of its base dragging across the carpet cut through the stillness. It was the only sound in the overpacked, standing-room-only courtroom. Then when I stopped, incredible silence. The expression "You could hear a pin drop" was created for that moment in time. I smiled a grim, serious, but still pleasant smile at the jury, taking in the faces of each and every member.

"The first thing I would like to do is thank you. Thank you for, first of all, all the time, the listening, the patience you have had with us, especially during, as Judge Garippo said, 4:30 lawyer talk and

4:30 arguments. I want to thank you for listening to that, and I want to thank you for listening to all the evidence.

"I also want to commend and congratulate Mr. Sullivan for giving you—for giving all the people in this courtroom—a fantastic and brilliant, persuasive closing argument; but I must remind you, ladies and gentlemen of the jury, that that's what that was, a closing argument. It is not evidence. That is the way Mr. Sullivan—that is the way the prosecution sees the evidence in this case."

I cleared my throat a little. I felt myself settling in. I was beginning to catch my stride. I continued.

"He made a number of inferences. He speculated a lot. As a matter of fact, he very rarely talked about the evidence. Think about it. Think about his argument.

"He told you how manipulative Mr. Gacy was. He told you how Mr. Gacy planned the insanity defense. He told you how he fakes heart attacks. Did he plan the insanity defense all the way back in Iowa when he attacked Lynch back then? Did he plan to call himself Jack Hanley for this purpose in 1980? When he told Mike Ried that his portrait on the wall was his twin brother Jack, was he planning that far ahead?

"But I can tell by the way you look, I could feel the tension in the courtroom in the last part of Mr. Sullivan's argument. He pointed to all the pictures. He slowly went through them: murder, murder, murder, murder. All that is to arouse your sympathy, and what did Mr. Motta ask you way back in the beginning of this case? Please, ladies and gentlemen, you must not, you should not, you must not consider sympathy in making your verdict.

"He attempted to arouse your emotions. That is manipulation. He didn't talk about the evidence. He just . . . he tried to get your emotions aroused, your basic emotions, your sympathy, and your anger.

"I felt anger and tension in this whole courtroom, this whole courtroom."

I swept my arm across the room, casting my gaze around. My assertion was verified in the eyes of many. There was anger in that room. I walked away from the lectern and never returned to it. I had been told that because of my size, when I stand behind a lectern, it looks like just a head is talking, no body attached. I began to pace, to prowl. I was in my element.

"He tried to get you to really hate my client. He tried to make him into an evil, vile, premeditating, rational, evil man."

I thought I saw at least one of the jurors nod ever so slightly, as if to tell me she agreed with Terry.

"Mr. Gacy is not an evil man. He has done some evil things. He has done some incredibly horrible things, but he tries so hard, so hard from when he was a little kid. He tried so hard to be good. He tried to please his father, and he kept doing it throughout the course of his life. He kept trying and trying and trying.

"He became a clown, he became precinct captain, he became a good husband and a good daddy.

"He wanted . . . [tried] so hard to be good, but he could not be good. There was a bad side to him, an uncontrollable side. He was caged in his own flesh. He was eaten up by this raving, or raging, disease in his mind. He just could not control that. He just could not control that!

"He," I said, pointing at Terry Sullivan, "talks about temporary insanity. He talks about temporary or episodic psychotic states. That's not the case here. You didn't hear the psychiatrists talk about temporary. They came up here and told you he was a sick man—he's psychotic all the time. Dr. Reifman himself told you, about the only good in this he said was that a psychotic person can plan, a psychotic person remembers his acting out, remembers his overt psychotic episodes like a normal person remembers a dream.

"Mr. Sullivan talked about Mr. Gacy's memory, how good his memory was. How many cases did he talk about? He kept going over the same three or four cases all the time.

"He did have a good memory." I pointed at Gacy. "The man does have a good memory, his wife told you that. He is intelligent. The psychiatrists told you that. So when he can't remember the kind of details that the police were looking [for], when he can't remember the kind of details that would help out, there's something wrong somewhere. He's remembering it like a dream. Think about the statements he gave to the police.

"He told them things as if they were coming out of a dream. Some things of the cases he remembered vividly, just like if you have a dream. Sometimes you remember it vividly; sometimes you have a dream and you only remember parts of it. Other times you have a dream, and you don't remember it at all. That's exactly the way Mr. Gacy related the story to the police, to the psychiatrists, to everybody.

"Mr. Sullivan didn't talk about these things. All he talked about is sympathy, anger, hate Mr. Gacy, hate him, hate him, hate him, put him to death."

I had to take these good people to a different place. They could still hear Terry Sullivan's "murder, murder, murder" tirade ringing in their ears. I had a plan, though. I would take them to a place where injustice reigned as the result of groupthink, as a result of fiery speeches, as a result of hateful rhetoric.

"Well, you know, back in 1692 in Salem, Massachusetts, it was July of 1692 that a lady named Sarah Good went to trial. She went to trial accused of being a witch, and when she went to trial, after the evidence was heard—and the judge's name was Nathaniel Corwin. Now, Magistrate Corwin, or Judge Corwin, sat over the evidence. Sarah Good sat at her trial, and the evidence went in; and after the jury deliberated on that evidence, they came back with a finding of not guilty.

"When Judge Corwin heard that, he became enraged. This was the first of the Salem witch trials. He became enraged; the courtroom became enraged. People were shouting. 'Put her to death, put her to death.' The jurors became frightened. Judge Corwin had no other choice but to send the jury back into the deliberation room, send them back in there. He said, 'Please reconsider your verdict, ladies and gentlemen of the jury.'

"They went back in there. They reconsidered based on all of that anger, based on all of that witch hysteria. Then came back out. They did not decide that case on the evidence; they decided it on emotion, and they found that lady, Sarah Good, guilty, and they hung her three weeks later, and everybody was pleased."

I noticed that this analogy was getting through to a couple of jury members. I could see them thinking, contemplating. This was a witch hunt, after all, wasn't it? This was an emotional exercise. When all was said and done, who in that courtroom was actually listening to the evidence unaffected by the overall horrific nature of the case, the gruesome pictures of all those boys? I had to try to get the members of the jury to focus on the testimony, the evidence. I wondered, was that possible?

"Well, we have come a long way in this country since 1692. It is now 1980, and we don't have judges or magistrates of the caliber of Jonathan Corwin. We have fine judges like Judge Louis Garippo. We have judges like Judge Garippo who can control and guide the attorneys through the mass of evidence that you ladies and gentlemen have to picture when you go into the deliberation room; and we also have what we call now, we would hope, impartial juries, and we selected you way back in the beginning of this case.

"We asked each and every one of you if you could put aside the emotion, if you could put aside your bias, your prejudice, if you could listen to all the evidence and give both the State and my client, Mr. Gacy, a fair trial. That's all we ask, and when you say that, and when you are selected as jurors, you then take an oath, and that oath swears you to the duty of being a fair and impartial juror.

"Now, that concept of duty and impartial jury did not develop overnight, because less than a century or a little more than a century after that travesty in Salem, Massachusetts, the United States government passed the Constitution of the United States, and that was in 1787; and just four years later, the government added to that Constitution the first fourteen amendments, and those amendments are commonly referred to as the Bill of Rights.

"Among the first fourteen amendments, we find the Fifth and Sixth Amendments. The Fifth Amendment guarantees my client, and every man in this country, whoever stands accused of a criminal act of any sort, guarantees him a fair trial, guarantees him not to have to take the stand and testify against himself."

Terry Sullivan had given a very powerful closing argument. It is common during trials that after one lawyer has completed a strong, persuasive close, the jury is predisposed to his or her point of view. It is the job of the opposing attorney to remind the jurors that there are two sides to every story. I could feel that happening. I could see it in the eyes of many of the jurors seated in front of me—not all of them, but many of them—an almost-imperceptible subtle shift. At least a few of these fine men and women had decided to listen to another point of view.

I walked toward where John Gacy was sitting at our defense table, pointing at him.

"The Sixth Amendment guarantees him the right to a fair and impartial jury, and it also guarantees him the right to be represented by counsel. Now, those two amendments have been in our laws now for [over] two hundred years, and they have not stood up easily. It's been tough; it's been tough to keep the ideals, the American ideals going.

"Now, in how many countries in the world can a man charged with thirty-three murders stand before a jury and get a fair trial? Not many. I'd go so far as to say this might be the only country where he can. In Iran, he probably would have been beheaded already. In many countries he would have been strung up as soon as it happened, but here he has an opportunity to tell his side of the story.

"One of your fellow citizens way back in the beginning of jury selection told His Honor, Judge Garippo, 'I have a philosophy that will straighten you out. Don't judge a man unless you have walked a mile in his moccasins.' And that's really what we're doing here. You have to sit back and listen to all the evidence and reach a fair and impartial decision based on the evidence.

"With regard to that concept of duty, I said it hasn't been easy. There have been wars, wars with England, a Spanish War, the Civil War, the great world wars, Korea, Vietnam—an unpopular war, but the men and the boys, the women who were over in Vetnam, did those people who died, did the people who became maimed, did they worry that it was an unpopular cause when they were there? They might have thought about it, but they did it, and they did it out of a sense of duty. They were there—they were there fighting for the ideals. No matter how unpopular the war itself was, they were fighting for the ideals in the body of the Constitution and in the amendments to that Constitution; and I'll tell you, I never really felt that sense of duty until about ten years ago.

"Ten years ago I stood on these yellow footprints over in a place called MCRD, and you stand there shivering and shaking and scared to death, and you are standing there scared, and the drill instructors are yelling in your ear, and you see a sign above you. There's a big red sign with yellow letters on it, and that sign says, 'Duty to My God, Duty to My Country, Duty to My Corps,' and I'll tell you, as scared as you are, you get that sense, and you feel—you feel the sense of duty that men and boys and women have felt for two hundred years now.

"Again, it is something that has not come easy, and the duty that you have in the courtroom right now, as jurors, is no less serious, no less serious than the duty that every marine or every sailor or every person that ever served in the armed forces of this country ever had. It's no less serious, because you are keeping the ideals of the country going, and you have to keep that sense of duty in mind all the time. That's why you have to wipe passion, wipe hatred, wipe emotion as best you can out of your minds, because the men and the boys and the women who have died over the last two hundred years, as Mr. Sullivan has said, 'these boys shall not have died in vain.' Well, all those thousands of people shall not have died in vain either, and we're here to see that they should not; and referring to these boys, they should not have died in vain, and if you do what Mr. Sullivan wants you to do, if you use your anger, if you use your vengeance, if you take it out on John Gacy, if you bury your head in the sand, if you blind yourself to the facts, if you don't want to find out what makes this man tick, if you don't want to study him, if you don't want to prevent something like this from happening again in the future, then you will do what Mr. Sullivan asks. You will find him guilty.

"You either trundle him off to the side and forget about him, or you will later have him put to death and forget about him, and you never, ever, will find out what makes a mind like that work, what makes it tick. Then, if you trundle him off to the side, then these boys shall have died in vain, because the next Robert Piest, or the next Gregory Godzik, or the next boy or girl, or anybody who falls prey to a mass murderer—whether they be my children, your children, your grandchildren, if we don't do something about it now, God help us. We can hang our heads in shame."

I was pacing now, pointing at my client when appropriate, walking over to him, and then pointing at Sullivan and the prosecution team when necessary. Occasionally, I would walk right up to the jury box and lean in to make a point. I wanted these selected, dedicated people in front of me to feel the passion that I felt. Killing this man was not the answer. He had to be studied, probed by the greatest minds in psychiatry and psychology in an effort to learn how to recognize a damaged mind such as his in the future. Perhaps, armed with the knowledge that could be gained from such study, a tragedy like this one could be avoided in the future.

"We have an opportunity here in this court. We have an opportunity to learn what this man is all about, to find out why, to find out how."

I walked over to the prosecution's gallery of grief. Standing to the side of that tragic depiction of faces, I pointed to each person to whom I referred.

"Believe me, if vengeance, if passion, if sympathy would bring back any of these boys, if it would bring back John Butkovitch or Darrell Sampson or Randall Reffett or Sam Stapleton or Michael Bonnin or William Carroll or Rick Johnston or Gregory Godzik or John Szyc or Jon Prestidge or Matt Bowman or Robert Winch, Tommy Boling, David Talsma, William Kindred, Timothy O'Rourke, Frank Landingin, James Mazzara, and Robert Piest—you see them up there—if revenge, if sympathy would bring back one of those boys . . ."

I walked the full length of the courtroom, past the faces of the jurors, past the overpacked, crammed gallery and stopped in front of the doors in the rear of the courtroom. I grabbed the brass handle on that huge oak door.

"If one of them could come and walk through the back door of this courtroom right now, this minute, or if they could ever come back to life, Mr. Motta and I would join hands with you. We would join hands with you in putting Mr. Gacy to death or trundling him off to the side—if we could exchange it, but we're not here to exchange."

I returned to the well of the court.

"As Mr. Motta told you in his opening statement, unfortunately for all of us, the fact of death is a final one. No man is an island, and we all feel it; but again we are here to decide the case based on the evidence, based on the facts as presented to you through the testimony from that witness stand."

I reminded the jury again that all of the arguments that they were hearing were just that, arguments. The lawyers were arguing, trying to persuade, but the evidence had already been heard. The arguments did not constitute evidence.

"Now what about the evidence? How do you take apart a case like this? In five weeks you have heard a lot of testimony. You have seen some witnesses for the prosecution that very well could have been witnesses for the defense. You have seen witnesses for the defense that very well could have been witnesses for the prosecution. You have seen a lot of doctors; you have seen psychologists, psychiatrists, all kinds of people. How do you take the evidence apart? Well, the way I have done it is, I have divided the case in seven parts."

I began to take the jury through the evidence in an organized, systematic way; step-by-step we would begin to look at the case together. We would review the testimony regarding the following: death witnesses, police investigation, confessions, medical examiners, family and friends, modus operandi, and the psychologists and psychiatrists.

Life and death witnesses are called to elicit evidence that a victim lived and then died. The testimony is normally limited to dry statements in support of that premise. However, over our repeated objections, the prosecution used this opportunity to tug relentlessly at the heartstrings of the jurors. These witnesses were primarily the relatives and friends of the various deceased boys, a very tough part of the case. These were mothers, fathers, brothers and sisters, friends, and relatives in the throes of indefinable grief. There is nothing harder than listening to the grieving relatives of the departed in any situation, but it is excruciating beyond description when the departed are the young victims of indefensible foul play.

"Now, the first part, the life and death witnesses. Well, you know that State started this case the same way they ended it— sympathy, sympathy, passion, prejudice, hate Mr. Gacy. There are twenty-two identified victims, twenty-two. They put more than twenty-two life and death witnesses on that stand. A life and death witness is put on the stand for the purpose of telling you, of putting into evidence that somebody lived and somebody died. That's the purpose. Do you think that was their purpose? No. Their purpose was to make you cry. Their purpose was to arouse your sympathy. That's what their purpose was.

"You think it's easy to sit here and watch mothers cry up there? It's just as hard for us as it is for you. Nobody likes to see it. Do you think it's easy to see friends and family crying up there? It's not easy, but it's not evidence. An example is—"

At that moment, Judge Garippo stopped me. "If I can interrupt one minute, we'll take a brief recess."

I wish I could tell you that the interruption was for something profound. However, the judge just wanted to give everyone a pee break, including himself, I'm guessing. I suppose he had come to know me over the last six weeks, and he figured that I'd be up there for a while.

"May I proceed?" I asked after we had reconvened.

"Yes," said the judge.

"OK, I believe I left off where I was talking about the beginning of the State's case, the life and death witnesses.

"They put more than twenty-two on there, and I was going to give you an example of the way in which the State attempts to arouse your sympathy without going into the facts.

"First, let's look at Mary Jo Paulus. Remember her, the little girl with the brace on her neck? This girl was straight from the hospital. No pain medication. Mr. Motta asked her about it. She said, 'No, I didn't take any medication.' In pain, she sat up there—in pain.

"Mr. Motta also asked her, 'Were you the last one to see William Kindred alive?' She says, 'No, a guy named Weedle saw him last.' Where was Weedle? How come Weedle didn't come in here and testify? Did he get in an automobile accident too, or was it better to see this poor girl suffering, in pain, so your hearts could go out to her?

"What about Donita Gannon? Remember Donita Gannon? That's the little [Asian] registered nurse. Now, you think the State came out and told you that Ms. Gannon was really Mr. Ganzon? Oh no. No. They left that up to the defense. Let the defense lawyer be the bad guys. 'We'll put this poor little girl up there, say she's a registered nurse, talk about how much she misses Timothy O'Rourke, but don't say anything else.'

"So then, we have to get up and expose this poor person to the whole world. Why do we have to do that? Why did we have to look like the bad guys? Because we are concerned with the facts—the facts, the evidence.

"Talking about Ms. Gannon—now here's a person who actually is having a sex-change operation. She shouldn't have any fear, any worry, or anxiety about people thinking anything about her. Maybe she was intended to be that way; she was intended to be a female. So she's having a sex-change operation. If that's what she wants to do, fine, but she should not have to be afraid of it. She should not have to not want to say it on the stand there.

"Another person, Roger Sahs, I asked him, where did you meet the person you dropped off at Bughouse Square? Did you meet him in a gay bar? Wouldn't admit that, wouldn't admit he met him in a gay bar. These are examples of the way people feel about homosexuals.

"Now, this girl, Ms. Gannon, I guess you can say, is a blatant homosexual, or whatever—transvestite, whatever you want to call it.

"Objection, Judge." It was Kunkle. The judge never bothered to respond or rule. I elicited the exact reaction out of Kunkle that I wanted, the visceral reaction that still existed at the time in opposition to the very mention of gay or transsexual persons. I let that reaction hang in the air for a beat. Then I continued.

"Well, whatever it is, you could imagine—you could imagine the torment, the torture that goes on in the mind of a man like John Gacy, a man whose father was a real man, his mother said. A man whose father was a good provider, a tough man. John Gacy wanted to be like his dad.

"John Gacy slowly found himself going more and more and more the other way. He did not want to. He hated the whole idea of homosexuality. He hated himself for being a homosexual, and he still does. He still does.

"As Dr. Reifman said, he is a homosexual, but he won't admit that to himself. Why? Because he does not want to—the torture, the pain.

"In the voir dire, a few of you indicated that you were repulsed by the idea of homosexual conduct. Picture yourself, use your common sense, what if you suddenly found yourself going the other way, becoming a homosexual, becoming a homosexual, becoming something that repulses you, something that you do not want? Think about the confusion of identity, think about the inner conflict you have. That's what the doctors were talking about up there, and I want you to keep that in mind. Keep in mind the evidence.

"Think in your mind the kind of person John Gacy was—a construction worker, a guy who wanted to make his marriage succeed, a good daddy. Yet he caught himself going farther and farther the other way. Mr. Sullivan said it's by choice.

"In May of 1975, he cut off his wife. He said, no more. Then— why was it later on he buried his head in her lap when he could not have sexual relations with her? He cried, he cried, and he said, 'I'm afraid I have gone the other way completely.' He did not want that. It was a horrible, horrible thing for him."

The conflict that raged internally in this sad specimen of a human being, our client, had to be brought home to this jury. Gacy was the poster boy for the argument that homosexuality is not a choice. He was raised by a rough, tough, hard-to-deal-with tool-and-die man—a man's man, a guy who hated homosexuals, the classic homophobic. Gacy was raised to do the same, to be the same.

When John Gacy acted in any other way, if he cried or played with the dolls, or girls, his father called him a sissy, a fruit picker. He was teased relentlessly, often shunned entirely, this by the one man from whom Gacy most wanted acceptance and love. Gacy fought desperately against this predisposition toward homosexuality with every fiber of his being, and lost that battle. This conflict was basic to his psychosis, to his derangement. I hoped the jury understood this essential fact. I wasn't getting a lot of confirmation in the faces that I saw in front of me. I plodded on.

"Anyway, beyond those types of witnesses, there [were] some other interesting facts brought out by the life and death witnesses about John Gacy.

"Mr. Marko Butkovitch said, 'Well, when I met John Gacy, when I talked to him, he seemed like a good man, a good man.' He didn't say he was evil. He didn't say he was vile. He seemed like a good man.

"Mr. Butkovitch also begged and pleaded with the police to investigate John Gacy. 'My son worked for him. Find out, please find out for me,' [he pleaded.] Did the police do anything for him? No. No. Had they done something, we would not be here today, but they did not want to investigate John Gacy.

"Gregory Godzik's sister said that John Gacy used to 'make my brother laugh.' Her brother enjoyed working for John Gacy, and then Gregory Godzik's girlfriend said, 'John Gacy said he was in the syndicate.' This is way back when. Was John Gacy planning the insanity defense? Was John Gacy planning and having these ideas and feelings of grandeur—or, as the doctors called it, grandiosity? Was he in the syndicate?"

Of course, John Gacy was not in the syndicate. I wondered if these fine men and women could see how crazy that was, how telling. Gacy was a pudgy, sickly cream puff that desperately needed acceptance. Did they see that? I took in their faces one at a time. I searched. I wished that for just one second I could read minds.

"After the life and death witnesses, we go into the police investigation. And the police investigation starts off with Officer Pickell, I believe, and Lieutenant Kozenczak; and there was a man named Kirkpatrick from Kirk's Towing in LaGrange, and another officer named Loconsole, and it started with Pickell and Kozenczak going over—after we see in the reports on the missing boy, Robert Piest, they went over to John Gacy's house, after hearing that he had been at Nisson Pharmacy."

I described in some detail the events that occurred the night Kozenczak and Pickell visited Gacy's house the very first time, while young Rob Piest's body was hidden in the attic. It was impossible, in my view, to interpret this any other way. Our client was insane. Think about it. His house was a ghoulish, gruesome, illegal morgue; and he was inviting the cops in for a chat.

"Then as Lieutenant Kozenczak and Officer Pickell are walking out the door, he gets a dislike for Kozenczak, and the reason he got a dislike for Kozenczak, which he carried on all the way through his statements, he did not like Kozenczak, and that was because he said Kozenczak did not show any respect for his uncle who died. He's sitting there with twenty-nine bodies, thirty bodies in that house with no emotion, but yet he's worried that Kozenczak did not show any respect for his uncle.

"Is that the act of a sane man, of a normal man? Does a rational man let the police into his house with all those bodies? He may have appeared rational on the outside to his neighbors. A rational man would not do that; an intelligent, rational man would not do that.

"Then he got stuck—well, apparently he said that he took the body of the Piest boy out to the Des Plaines River, and again, by the way, that was supposed to be the fifth body he threw in that river, all in the same place. Patterned—obsessive, compulsive pattern. 'The crawl space is full. I have to find another space.' Pattern, that's not plan. Pattern is not plan. Pattern is sick, and pattern was sick, and it was based on an obsession. Why at the same point? Why did he drop them off at that same point?

"He rode out there, and on the way back this alert, awake man goes off the road. He gets stuck in a ditch. What did he look like at that time? Kirkpatrick couldn't even recognize him in the courtroom. He's looking around, looking around; he looked at me for a little while, and finally he said, 'I'm sorry, I cannot positively identify him.' Why not? Well, he looked different that night. He looked different. 'When I went up to the car, he was slumped over at the wheel. He was groggy. He looked like he had been under the influence of something.'

"Time and time again people had seen and then later testified to the transformation that took place in John Gacy. One minute, John was congenial, with an ear-to-ear smile that would light a room. The next minute, he would turn dark hearted, evil, scary. Rob Piest had seen this transformation just before he died. Stevens and I saw it that night in my office when John confessed his dastardly deeds—the flutter in the eyes, the apparent switch from Jekyll to Hyde that made John Gacy unrecognizable, that turned him into a different person.

"When asked on redirect examination, well, was he under the influence, was he drinking, he said, 'I didn't smell anything.' Why did he look so groggy? Why did he look like he was under the influence? Beats me. I don't think the State has the answer, but he certainly did look different, and that's when he disposed of that body of Robert Piest.

"Now, he was supposed to have gone on to the police station at eleven o'clock. He disposes of the body of Robert Piest, and on the way back he gets stuck, and as soon as he gets pulled out, he remembers. I had an appointment with Lieutenant Kozenczak. I better get to the Des Plaines police station. Rational? Walking into the Des Plaines police station at three o'clock in the morning, covered with mud, when you are under the investigation of a missing boy? You are under suspicion for kidnapping and possibly murder. Do you do that? Do you walk in a police station at three o'clock in the morning and say, 'I'm here, I'm going to talk to you?'

"That is not the act of a rational man, as Mr. Sullivan would have you believe. If anything, it's that act of a man who wants to get caught, a man who was reaching out, saying, 'Stop me before I kill again.' It's a man who wanted to be stopped, but could not control himself to stop himself.

"He was reaching out at that point. Sure, he was caught in a web. Mr. Sullivan said he was in a web. He wasn't in any police web; he was in his own web. He was tangled in that web of his mind, encased in his flesh for so many years, and the killing had to stop. It became more and more frequent all the time.

"The reason it had to stop was because, by his own statement, John Gacy said Robert Piest was different. He did not fit the mold. He did not fit the pattern. He wasn't picked up in Bughouse Square. He wasn't picked up on Clark Street somewhere. He was snatched out of a drugstore where he worked. He's a boy who John Gacy never saw before. You tell me that's planned? You tell me that's premeditation, that he went there purposely to get Robert Piest, he didn't even know his name.

"That is the drive of a madman, a driven man, driven by perverted obsessions and compulsions, but perverted obsessions and compulsions that he could not control. Why Robert Piest?

"So it went on. He was sent home from the police station at three o'clock in the morning. He then returned at 11:40 the next day. Again now, this is a man under suspicion of kidnapping. He voluntarily goes into the police station and says, 'I'll give you the statement now.' He talks to Officer Pickell again, gives him a statement, exactly the way Officer Pickell wanted him to do it. He not only gave the statement, but—I'll show you the exhibit. I don't know which one it is. He signed his name in the wrong place."

I found the exhibit and showed it to the jury.

"In the statement he gave, the first statement, he said he could account for just about every minute of his time. Maybe he was lying. Maybe he was lying at that time. He signed his name in the wrong place, and he also signed PDM Contractors. You tell me why, for what purpose the man would sign his name and put PDM Contractors? When you sign your name to something, do you put the name of your job or your company below your name? It makes no sense.

"In addition to doing that, Officer Pickell said, 'Well, Mr. Gacy, write in here that you used to hire young people for summer help.' Mr. Gacy said, fine, 'I used to hire young people for summer help,' and signs his name again. Again, this is a man under suspicion for kidnapping. He's in there cooperating. He stays in there.

"While he's in there, Lieutenant Kozenczak has a warrant to issue. When a warrant is issued, they say, 'John, we're going to go over to your house. Could we have your keys?' 'Fine, take my keys, go to the house.'

"He stays at the station. He's not under arrest. Maybe he was being detained, but he did not have to give them the keys, but he did voluntarily give them the keys to his house, that house where those bodies were. Is that the act of a rational man? Is that the act of a professional or intelligent criminal? 'Go look in my house, see what you find.'

"He was calm and cooperative. He wasn't at all nervous, and he bragged. He bragged about his connections. He bragged about his running the National Polish Day Parade in Washington. He bragged he was a precinct captain—he bragged about this and he bragged about that. Why brag? What does that show?

"Anyway, after that initial search, certain things were found in his house. Lieutenant Kozenczak ordered surveillance. He put Officer Hachmeister, and he put Lieutenant, or Detective, Schultz on the surveillance. Now, the man is being tailed. He's being tailed; they are watching him constantly. Does he run? Does this evil man run? No.

He enjoys the tail. He plays games with them. He plays hide-and-seek, but does he try to leave the jurisdiction? Oh, no. 'Here, guys, I might lose you because I'm a fast driver, so here's where I'm going. I'm going to tell you where I am going. Meet me there.'

"He became friendly with them. And he invited them in his house. He cooked for them; he gave them a tour of his house. He showed them photo albums. One of the officers' car was broken down, and when the car broke down, you think he kept going? Do you think he ran? No way. He stopped his car; he went back and gave the officer a ride. He gave him a ride and put him in his car and said, 'Come on, I'll take you along with me.'

"He offered to take a polygraph. As a matter of fact, there was testimony that when they were on the elevated train, on the el, going downtown, his lawyer at that time, Leroy Stevens, told him, 'Leave the country.' Did he do that? No.

"When they went to look for him at the airport, was he at the airport? No. He was at a Christmas tree lot two blocks away from his house. Is that the act of a man who is running scared? Is that the act of a man who was tied up in a web, in a police web? No. Those are the acts of an irrational man, or a man who wants to get caught.

"He was speeding . . . sixty, seventy miles an hour down side streets, erratic driving. They had to tell him to slow down. Did he want to get taken into custody?

"He introduced them as his bodyguards. He told them he had a bodyguard with a .357 Magnum that would not hesitate to waste them. They never saw a bodyguard. They never saw anybody with a .357 Magnum.

"He told them that other people were following him. He said they must have others working with them, because he thought he saw somebody following him. The detective said, 'Nobody else was following him; only we were following him.' He felt the cars were bugged. He told them that he worked hand in hand with Mayor Daley running the city of Chicago.

"He joked, he laughed. They said he didn't have a harsh word to them. He just went right along with their surveillance. Did he want to stop the killing? Did he want to get arrested? He drove fast and erratic. He told them he [couldn't] look at clowns as people, guys, because clowns could get away with murder. Now, this is a man under suspicion of murder. He's under suspicion of kidnapping, and that's what he told them.

"He passed—the morning he got arrested, he pulled into the gas station and passed marijuana cigarettes into some kid's pocket in the gas station right in front of the policemen. Then he tried to—they said he tried to take off. He left the gas station. Did he keep going? No way. He came right back. He came right back into the station and says, 'Come on, Dave, let's get going.' He wanted to get arrested, and they gave no indication even up to that time, with the marijuana, with the speeding, and with everything—they never gave any indication of arresting him.

"Now, when he did get arrested, he finally—he went on that morning and finally got arrested. They took him to the station, and he was there all day, and Mr. Sullivan says he got one of his famous heart attacks, implying he got a fake heart attack. This man had a whole history of fainting, of heart attacks. No medical basis, no physical basis, but that was the history. He had this throughout his whole life, when he was a child.

"Mr. Sullivan calls it a fake heart attack. On the way back from the hospital, after he had his seizure or collapse, whatever it was, he then confesses. Now he has lawyers. His lawyers aren't there at that time. He went to the hospital and voluntarily says, 'I want to clear the air. I want to clear the air. I want to talk to you.' Finally, he was there. He finally talked. He got arrested; the killing could finally stop.

"And how did he talk? He gave a very rambling, disjointed statement. They only asked him one or two questions. This was at three thirty. The first thing he told them was—the first thing he told Officer Albrecht—that he was not a homosexual, and he had a strong fear of being a homosexual. He said, 'A man is a man, and he should stay that way. There's something wrong with a man if he's gay.'

"Then he said 'Jack does not like homosexuality.' Well, the State says he planned this multiple personality thing. Jack, whatever Jack is, we know it's not a multiple personality, but it's something for him to get rid of that guilt. How could a man live in a house with all those bodies, all those years, with all that on his mind if he does not have some mechanism, some relief mechanism? So he blames another part of himself. He blames a guy named Jack. They tried to make you think James Hanley up there was Jack Hanley. His name was James Hanley.

"He talked about Jack [first] to Michel Ried in 1970, before he ever met or before James Hanley ever saw him or [John] ever saw James Hanley, if he ever did. He told them at that time that he never forced sex upon anybody. It was always consensual, and he had a heart condition.

"He told them at that time that he slept with the Piest boy after he was dead. He told them that he did not even know Piest's name, and he told them they were all strangled, and I want you to keep that in mind. When I talk about the medical examiner later, he said they were all strangled. He said he put a rope around Piest's neck, and while he did that, he went and answered the phone. No feeling, no emotion. That's what the doctors are talking about—lack of affect.

"Did you see what he did when Mr. Sullivan was calling him a murderer, murderer, murderer? He was laughing. Laughing. Put yourself in that chair over there. Somebody calling you a murderer, somebody asking the jury to find you guilty of this crime, are you going to laugh? That is what they talk about when they say lack of appropriate affect or lack of appropriate feeling.

"He said they killed themselves, and he wasn't blaming Jack— he was blaming the victims. He said they killed themselves because they sold their bodies for $20. He said he used a rope on every single one of them. Again, remember when I go into the medical examiner. He said all of the killings were related to homosexuality.

"He said he lost count of the bodies, that the crawl space was full. He said he did not like Kozenczak because he did not have any respect that his uncle had died, and then again at three thirty, as I indicated, he went into another rambling—a long, disjointed statement with only one or two questions.

"He did not like homos; he was afraid he was becoming one. He denied any encounter with Jeffrey Rignall. He said Rignall—then he went on to tell them that when he went to court on the Jeffrey Rignall matter, Rignall was the guy who did not show up in court. Actually, Rignall testified John Gacy was the one that did not show up in court. Twisting things backwards, talking in opposites. His statement is a good example of tangential speech. He went from here to there, changing the subject back to something else again.

"Officer Bedoe described it as 'Mr. Gacy skipped a lot back and forth.' He freely gave his statement. There was a definite pattern involved—now, not planned, but pattern. He could remember who many of the victims were. He rambled, skipped, went back in years, then back to the present again; and then he told them that Piest might have been dead when he was in the attic. He said he wasn't even sure if he was dead.

"At the house later in the morning, when he was taking them to show where the bodies were—a man who was arrested, now the man who was trapped, as Mr. Sullivan would have you believe, in his own web, takes the police to show them where Butkovitch is, where he is buried.

"On the way there, he goes in the garage, wants to know why his garage is so messed up. He starts closing cabinets, straightening out drawers, picking things up. He wants to know how come there's mud on his floor.

"Officer Pickell had to remind him three times why he was there. The compulsiveness of his behavior . . . he gave statements compulsively. He's compulsively cleaning, compulsively taking care of things all the time—nitpicking, little things. He's doing it right when he's arrested, right when he's showing where the body is.

"Later on that day, he called Larry Finder into his cell. He said he wanted to talk to Larry. You have never done anything to hurt me, and he read the Miranda rights again. This is a man who has just been arrested for murder. He told him that he felt relieved, but he was unhappy, but he did feel relieved. He said he accidentally left his book at Nisson Pharmacy, and had he not left his book, he never would have killed Piest. Is that . . . a rational, premeditated, planned act? Is that the act of a man who is planning something?

"He left the book somewhere. He goes back to get it, and he kills somebody. That is not premeditated, that is not planned.

"A week later at Cermak, he gave the other statements. Again Mr. Sullivan talked about memory. He remembered that. What did he remember? In all of those statements, what did he remember? He remembered Robert Piest. He remembered something about Szyc, how he spelled his name. He remembered something about Gregory Godzik. He remembered something about—he remembered the first name of Rick Johnston. That was about it—that he was from Bensenville, and he remembered one other thing about somebody.

"Now, Mr. Sullivan went over and over and over the rope trick and the Piest thing, over and over again. There's thirty-three of them. How many did he go into? He only went into a few. Again as I told you in the beginning, a psychotic state, either somebody remembers everything or nothing at all. That's how he told what happened, just like he was dreaming about it.

"OK. Then we had the part of the case, the part of the police investigation that involved the excavating of the property. Now the State would have you believe that the excavation or that the burial was planned, was organized. He had holes dug down there, and they bring out these maps, and they show you—look at how nice and neat everything is. All right, down here, it looks nice and neat. It's not the way those bodies were buried. That's the way they were taken out.

"They were buried, the first one being buried under the cement, then out to the garage, then into the dining room, going like this: garage, dining room, and then the third one in the dining room, and the fourth and fifth over here. The sixth was way down over here, and the seventh was way back over in this corner, and so on and so forth.

"As Dr. Morrison said, John Gacy has [somewhat normal] intellectual capability, but he probably has the emotions of a baby. Somewhere, something stopped. Now why? How? Somewhere something went wrong. Look at his medical history; his medical history that Mr. Sullivan said was average, [this] medical history that was totally discarded by Dr. Leonard Hesston in Anamosa twelve years ago, his medical history that was totally discarded by Dr. Cavanaugh and Dr. Reifman as being average.

"You know it is lengthy. You know a lot of things happened to him with no physical bases. Some of the things, as indicated by Dr. Morrison, were, in 1958 he fainted, he had shortness of breath, there was a request for psychiatric consultation.

"In 1959, in the hospital, he was found on the floor. He was complaining of a headache. He appeared to be disoriented and confused about what happened and why he did it. He was laughing to himself, and he would not answer questions relating to any accident in the hospital. He was discharged against medical advice.

"Again in 1959, he had fainting and dizziness, difficulty breathing, and a sensation of being choked.

"He had hysterical blackouts. In the nurses' notes in 1959, they said, 'He had an acute convulsive episode last night with loss of consciousness and violent thrashing about, but later he was talking normally. He was acting normal and suddenly he developed extreme restlessness after complaining of chest pains, and then he became impossible to handle, and he went berserk again yesterday and he had to be restrained.'

"In 1963, he had a seizure. He shouted and struggled. He gave strong resistance to ambulance personnel. He had no memory of events until after his admission in the hospital, and on and on and on and on.

"That is an insignificant, average medical history? It goes on like that.

"What did his friends and business associates say about him? You saw Rich Dolke, who said, from even when he was a kid he was friendly. You saw Ken Dunkle: friendly, easygoing, happy-go-lucky person, a sincere and warm person as he grew up. The only time they ever saw him get violent was when he had these fits or seizures, whatever they were. Otherwise, he was fine. He was non-violent. They used to have to protect him. They thought he was a sickly boy.

"It was Rich Dolke who said he used to protect John, because he thought he was sickly. Nothing was wrong with him physically.

"His cell mate, the person he knew at Anamosa, said Gacy was a cream puff, but he was a leader; and he always thought Gacy always gave the impression that anytime anyone wanted a fight with him, what he would do is, he'd have one of his, as Mr. Sullivan calls them, famous heart attacks. They weren't faked. He would get ashen gray. He would pass out. He'd have shortness of breath. He wasn't faking it. It was something that was happening with his mind, even back then and throughout his life.

"It's like Dr. Morrison used the example of your palm sweating, or the heart palpitating. You don't tell your palms to sweat; you know they are doing it. You don't tell your heart to palpitate, but you know it is happening. These are things that are caused by some kind of emotional stress.

"The other day I was sitting here, and I had a little red blotch on my cheek, and it was there, and I knew it was there, and I kept trying to hide it like this, or sitting over by the table. It was like a blotch with a white spot, a hive. I kept trying to hide it. My instinct was, I knew it was there. I knew I had no control over it, and my instinct was to hide it."

I continued, pointing out the crazy person that was my client, painting a picture, asking the questions, reminding the members of the jury that this guy was crazy long before he ever killed anyone. He had left the rails as a little boy, developed fetishes, developed defense mechanisms, passed out for unexplained reasons, was in and out of hospitals—the life of a one-day serial killer. Why not study a guy like this? We study everything from insects to elephants. Why don't we study these guys? Maybe they are savable. Maybe their victims are savable. We study microscopic organisms that can kill us. Why don't we study people that can kill us?

"Instead, we continue to act like we did when we were carrying spears or when we were carrying pitchforks and torches. We haven't changed a bit. Kill the bad guy. Don't try to figure out why he is a bad guy, just kill him. Emotion is a powerful thing, isn't it? Funny, though, if you ask anyone, anywhere, they will tell you the same thing: 'No one acts rationally when they act upon their emotions.'"

I spoke for hours. I tried to cover everything. I was fighting for a man's life.

Finally, I said, "Now, bear with me. I will be done in just a few minutes. Go back to 1886, right around the time of that thing they were talking about, dementia praecox, paranoid schizophrenia. Well, in 1886, an author by the name of Robert Louis Stevenson wrote a novel—you can still read it today. I am going to read you some excerpts from that novel. While I am doing that, I am also going to quote some of the testimony in this case. I'd like you to see the similarities. I am sure that you will recognize the novel when I start reading it."

I walked over to our defense table and picked up Stevenson's timeless novel. I had previously marked certain passages. I moved away from the table slightly but stayed close by. I had other items that I needed on the table. I was farther away from the jury, so I raised my voice a bit. I read directly from the book in my hands.

"'All at once, I saw two figures: One a little man who was stumping along eastward at a good walk, and the other a girl of maybe eight or ten who was running as hard as she was able down a cross street. Well, sir, the two ran into one another naturally enough at the corner; and then came the horrible part of the thing; for the man trampled calmly over the child's body and left her screaming on the ground. It sounds nothing to hear, but it was hellish to see. It wasn't like a man; it was like some dammed juggernaut . . . . It was a man of the name of Hyde.'

"'What sort of man is he to see?'

"'He is not easy to describe, there is something wrong with his appearance; something displeasing, something downright detestable. I never saw a man I so disliked, and yet I scarce know why. He must be deformed somewhere; he gives a strong feeling of deformity, although I couldn't specify the point. He's an extraordinary looking man, and yet I really can name nothing out of the way. No, sir; I can make no hand of it; I can't describe him. And it's not want of memory; for I declare I can see him this moment.'"

I looked up from the book and let the passage linger in the air. I looked at each member of the jury while I did this. I set the book down on the table and picked up a transcript of testimony previously given in our case.

"And then you remember the testimony of Jeffrey Rignall," I continued.

"'Nothing ever showed on that guy's face. He just went around torturing me like it was something that happened every day. My assailant was an oddity, a person so evil, so vile, so malicious and cruel that he was almost inhuman.'

"Now, the novel goes on:

"'There is something more, if I could find a name for it. God bless me, the man seems hardly human.'

"Back to Rignall: 'It was another case of somebody wanting control of another person who loathed himself for having those desires, his sexual desires must have been so disgusting he had to punish that stranger, the other person involved in the act, he himself detested, a way of purging the demons from one's soul, punishing someone for the crime you yourself were committing. He was incapable of registering the same kind of emotion as other people.'

"Back to Hyde:

"'This Master Hyde, if he were studied, must have secrets of his own, black secrets, by the look of him; secrets compared to which poor Jekyll's worst would be like sunshine.'

"In describing his Jekyll, the other part of Hyde:

"'A large, well-made, smooth-faced man of fifty, with something of a stylish cast perhaps, but every mark of capacity and kindness, you could see by his looks that he cherished for Mr. Utterson a sincere and warm affection.'

"'He became once more their familiar guest and entertainer; and whilst he had always been known for charities, he was now no less distinguished for religion. He was busy, he was much in the open air, he did good; his face seemed to open and brighten, as if with an inward consciousness of service; and for more than two months, Dr. Jekyll as at peace.'

"He writes of himself: 'If I am the chief of sinners, I am the chief of sufferers also. Both sides of me were in dead earnest.'

"'I have been doomed to such a dreadful shipwreck; that man is not truly one, but truly two. I say two, because the state of my own knowledge does not pass beyond that point.'

"'I saw that, of the two natures that contended in the field of my consciousness, even if I could rightly be said to be either, it was only because I was radically both.'

"'Hence, although I had now two characters as well as two appearances, one was wholly evil, and the other was still the old Henry Jekyll, that incongruous compound of whose reformation and improvement I have already learned to despair. The movement was thus wholly toward the worse.'

"'Henry Jekyll stood at times aghast before the acts of Howard Hyde.'

"It goes on and on and on. I am sure you know the story, the Jekyll and Hyde story, the words that were used so often in John Gacy's house as a child.

"You heard how Jeffrey Rignall described him. You heard how Lynch described him. You heard how Cram described him when he was attacking Cram. You heard how Donnelly described him. You heard what Michel Ried said about the hammer, the strange look in his eyes, the bizarre behavior.

"The man who lived with bodies underneath him—here is what his friends and neighbors, his family said: 'John Gacy was a very nice person . . . he was jovial, kind, genuinely happy . . . he enjoyed people . . . he was always busy . . . he was a good daddy . . . he seemed to show deep and sincere affection . . . he was generous . . . he was not selfish . . . when he would smile, his smile would light up his whole face . . . he was not a vile, evil person . . . his house was open to people all the time, he engaged in charitable activities, he was warm and considerate, he was a good man, a nice man, a friend . . . 'I can't fathom that the John Gacy I knew would have done what he is accused of.' But his hours were irregular . . . and his wife, his ex-wife said, 'And now I feel sorry for him.' And Rignall said of him, again, at another time, 'His voice was demanding and demeaning. It was not like a common person talking back and forth, but his voice was like a giggly-type thing, gentleman, and then he became totally violent.' And again, when Jeff Rignall was asked, what is your opinion? [He said,] 'My opinion is that at that time John Gacy could not conform his conduct to the requirements of the law, because he was so beastly and animalistic.'

"That is the same John Gacy, supposedly, that his neighbors and family and friends talked about.

"'My opinion is that John Gacy could not appreciate the criminality of his acts because of the way he attacked me, the beastly manner that he did it.'

"Michel Ried said that when he hit him over the head with that hammer, he had a strange look in his eye. He could feel the tension. 'He changed, he was out of character, and he did not know what he was doing.'

"John Gacy is truly a Jekyll and Hyde, despite what psychiatric terms you put on it, despite what labels you put on it, he is the personification of this novel which was written in 1886. He was so good, and he was so bad, and the bad side of him is the personification of evil.

"I'd agree with the State that he is evil. Now, whether it is premeditated, planned, and so forth, I don't know. Killing thirty-three people is bad, it is evil. The man is insanely evil. He did not want to do it . . . he could not control himself.

"What do you do? Do you hold him responsible for that, or do you take the first step of having him studied to prevent, to at least try to prevent something like this from happening again in the future? My god, take that first step, ladies and gentlemen of the jury. Do it.

"Mr. Motta and I have tried to present you with an open, straightforward case. We put Rignall on, we put Ried on, we put his family on, we tried to tell you what John Gacy was all about. We also put his friends on, we put four independently retained psychiatrists and psychologists on the stand. We wanted to show you the different sides of John Gacy. We wanted to show you that he was acting under constant, raging, mental illness. We wanted to show you that this man should be studied. The most frightening, the most horrible kind of mental illness, the kind of thing you would not recognize—the fact that John Gacy, two years ago, could have been your neighbor, he could have been your friend, he could have been on this jury, he could have been the foreman of this jury. It isn't that—that alone, isn't that, if you use your common sense, enough indication, enough motive to have this man studied?

"Bob Egan ended his opening statement with the words, 'God help all of us if another man like John Gacy walks among us.' Well, if you don't want to find out, if you don't want to have him studied, if you don't want to learn why, God help all of us, because there probably is going to be more John Gacys walking among us.

"Putting him away won't prevent anything. Punishment won't deter a madman. The next mass murderer out there, do you think that John Gacy, setting an example with John Gacy, would help?

"It wouldn't deter him. It didn't deter John Gacy.

"He couldn't control his conduct. He couldn't control his evil conduct, just like Jekyll could not control Hyde; and eventually, Hyde took over, Jekyll lost it more and more and more, and then eventually the evil side of Jekyll's personality took over beyond the control of the good side. Beyond the control of the good side."

I stole a glance at the clock. It was time to finish up. I took a quick second or two as I silently reviewed what I had said. Had I left anything out? One final item came to mind.

"By the way, Mr. Sullivan mentioned that our doctor testified that John Gacy was unconscious. They never said he was unconscious. We said he was reacting to unconscious stimuli. He was awake, he was walking around—he wasn't unconscious.

"His drive was in his unconscious. He is a danger to himself; he definitely is a danger to others. Remember, he began serving that ten-year sentence December 11, 1968; and he ended it on December 11, 1978.

"Do the right thing, ladies and gentlemen of the jury. Don't decide this case with hate, with revenge, with passion and fear.

Commit yourselves to our laws, perform your duty well as jurors, look at all of the evidence; and when you look at the whole picture, you will find that the State has not met their burden of proving Mr. Gacy sane beyond a reasonable doubt.

"We expect you to return a verdict of not guilty by reason of insanity.

"On behalf of Mr. Motta and Mr. Gacy and myself, I would like to thank you again for being such an attentive jury. I would indicate that our work is now on the verge of being over, and your work is just beginning.

"Thank you, ladies and gentlemen."

I turned and walked quietly to our table. The only sound in the room was the muffled sound of my footsteps on the carpeting. I realized that we were done—no more evidence, no more arguments. The case was coming to a close. Memories of the previous fifteen long months cascaded and crashed into one another like in a dream. The courtroom was a blur; faces were unidentifiable. Adrenaline still coursed through me. My heart thumped. For me, it was over.

As I sat down, Judge Garippo's voice resonated and reverberated throughout the room, snapping me back from my rushing memories, back to reality.

"Ladies and gentlemen, this concludes the arguments that you will hear tonight. The schedule of the events would be that tomorrow the State will have the opportunity to give a rebuttal argument. After the rebuttal argument, I will instruct you as to the law, and then you will begin your deliberations.

"Again, as each day goes by, it becomes easier, and the temptation is deeper to begin making judgments in your own mind about the believability of witnesses and as to what your verdict will be. It would not be fair to either side to do this at this time. Because you have not at this time heard all of the arguments, and you haven't formally been instructed as to the law.

"Further, I just want to correct one thing—a mistake that I made during the course of Mr. Amirante's argument. I sustained an objection relative to testimony of Dr. Cavanaugh relating to suicide. I sustained the objection of the State, and I erroneously sustained that objection. There was testimony relative to that subject. You have heard the evidence, and you are the judges of the evidence.

"We will resume tomorrow at ten o'clock. Please do not discuss this case in any way. Thank you."

36

BILL KUNKLE STOOD well over six feet tall, and his bathroom scale bumped up against 250 pounds when he stood on it, maybe even a little more. In summer, when it was warm enough, he arrived to work on a big ol' Harley Davidson, with chrome gleaming and the deafening blast from hot pipes reverberating against the Chicago skyline. It's a hog on which any denim-jacketed Hell's Angel would ride his colors proud.

He considered himself his own man, and the deep, stern creases etched by time into his bulbous, ruddy face dared anyone on the planet to say otherwise. A serious man—one only needed to be in his presence for a very short time to learn his personal views on a myriad of subjects, strongly held opinions that he would share without much provocation. He was an imposing figure, not a man who fit the cookie-cutter image of what a prosecutor looks like; nonetheless, it was Kunkle that had been chosen by the other members of the prosecution team to present the final word on behalf of the State of Illinois regarding the matter of *People v. John Wayne Gacy.*

At 10:00 a.m. on Wednesday, March 12, 1980, as the players reconvened and the onlookers assembled themselves into the limited seating and the standing-room-only spots, filling every square inch of available space, the cramped courtroom looked noticeably more cluttered than it usually did because of the addition of the huge, irregular chunk of hardwood flooring, which included the gaping trapdoor that once peered down into the crawl space at John Wayne Gacy's house. It had been dragged to a point of prominence before the bench and in full view of the jury box, as had the infamous gallery of grief. It too had been hauled to a place where all jurors could clearly see each and every identified victim's picture.

Kunkle ambled up to the podium like the original John Wayne, the Duke; quietly cleared his throat; and began.

"Judge Garippo, gentlemen," he said with a nearly imperceptible nod to Bob and me. "Ladies and gentlemen of the jury. I'll be the last one to speak to you before you get your instructions on the law from the judge and retire to the jury room to deliberate this case. I'll make you only two promises about my remarks: The first is I won't speak as long as Mr. Sullivan—perhaps not as well either. Hopefully, I won't be as loud as Mr. Amirante.

"Mr. Amirante asked you not to consider sympathy. You should not consider sympathy. Don't consider sympathy for this defendant either. Some of the psychiatrists talked about having computers instead of jurors. They talked about being dispassionate. They left out something called common sense. A lot of us talked about it at the beginning of trial in the jury selection. You can't replace people with computers. You can't do psychiatric diagnosis by computers. We can't take a Minnesota Multiphasic Personality Inventory and get a numerical score and say that a man who has killed thirty-three people isn't responsible for his actions. People aren't that simple. Justice isn't that easy.

"Mr. Amirante told you that John Gacy had an uncontrollable side, that he was 'encaged in his own flesh.' So are we all, ladies and gentlemen. Each of us has good, each of us has evil."

Kunkle eyed each juror to bring home his point.

"And that which separates a social person and a human being with respect for life, with respect for the rights and properties of others, from the animal, from the animals, is the ability to separate those parts yourselves.

"John Gacy separated those parts probably better than anyone I have ever heard of. The defense asked you to excuse John Gacy for the murder of thirty-three citizens of this state because he is so normal. What they are really saying to you is, 'Here is a normal, everyday guy, and, gee, why, we admit he killed thirty-three people, therefore he has got to be crazy. So they put on witnesses to tell you what a great guy he is, to tell you how normal he is, just as we were putting on witnesses to tell you that—when they observed this man at important times, important dates, days of some of the crimes, even the day before some of the crimes, the day after some of the crimes. Those dates that I asked Mike Rossi about, and other people about—those were specific dates. We wanted to show what John was doing on those days. How did he appear to people? They told you he was normal. They told you he was the same as he always was."

As I listened to my opponent speak, as I watched him begin to pace and stalk the limited space just in front of the twelve jury members who would soon decide my client's fate, who would decide ultimately whether he would live or die, I stole a glance at the man sitting next to me—my client, the defendant. It is impossible to describe what I saw. It was as if John Gacy was watching the proceedings as a spectator, like he wasn't a party to the proceedings, like he was watching a baseball game or a Broadway play. He just didn't seem to grasp the fact that Kunkle was talking about him. He was fascinated by the drama without knowing that a very slow-moving bullet was heading directly toward his forehead. He didn't seem to get that this whole scenario was really quite permanent, quite irreversible. Half the time he had the most ridiculous shit-eating grin on his face, like you see on a country kid on his first visit to the big city; the rest of the time he was mugging for the sad and the curious in the gallery.

Finally, at long last, he was truly the center of attention.

"There have been villains throughout history," Kunkle continued, "dictators of totalitarian countries, and mass murderers—all kinds of evil villains put on this earth. I think they probably all loved their children. I think they probably all formed genuine relationships with their wives.

"During the course of the investigation of this case, many of us that have been associated with it have felt, have experienced very strong emotions. There has been a necessity through the presentation of the evidence in this case, for you to experience some of that emotion. As human beings, you will, I know you will, do the best you can to leave that emotion—leave sympathy and pity out of your consideration of the issues of this case.

"But don't for a minute feel there is something wrong with you or you are not doing your job as a juror because you have felt these emotions, because we have all felt them. The time it came home to me in this case was very early on in the first week of the excavation on Summerdale. You have already seen this photograph, People's Exhibit 174 for identification."

Bill Kunkle held up one of the hundreds of photographs that had been marked as exhibits. He showed it to each member of his captive. audience.

"It's a photograph of grave no. 8. Above the numeral in the dirt is a blue tennis shoe. On a plastic body bag to the left of the grave on the dirt is the other blue tennis shoe with a leg bone sticking out of that tennis shoe. I was at the house that day, and I saw it when that picture was taken. The thought that came to my mind at that time was of tying my daughter's shoes that morning before I left. And I thought, *How in God's name did this man, with this tennis shoe, with those legs, with that boy, in that hole, in his basement tie [his] children's tennis shoes?*

"Psychoanalysts can't give you an answer to that question. Medical psychiatrists can't give you an answer to that question. The closest they can come is when Dr. Reifman told you John Gacy has no remorse because John Gacy . . . has no remorse.

"If you think that you can excuse this man from these crimes because he was normal, then every hit man, every dictator, every organized criminals, every person that has learned to kill and learned to accept killing ought to be excused with him, because they are no different. They are no different. John Gacy learned to kill. And he kept on killing. And he knew he was killing. I don't doubt that he was able to show genuine love and care for both of his wives; for his original, natural children; or for his stepdaughters later.

"All the doctors explained to you is that a sociopath or a psychopath has certain areas of certain relationships where his affect is shallow; where he doesn't form a true, loving relationship; where he doesn't really let himself be relied on by other people—in the true sense of the word, doesn't really form a lot of true friendships. But he can still, within his own sphere, within those people that are important to his personality, his ego makeup, the way he looks at life—he can form those genuine relationships. And he did. He did. And that doesn't mean he can't tell and know that he is killing, and know that what he is doing is wrong. And those are the issues that you are here to decide.

"You are not here to decide why John Gacy killed. You are not here to analyze John Gacy, or write a book on psychotherapy, or plan a treatment plan for John Gacy. You are only here to decide the question of whether or not he was legally responsible for his actions at the time of these crimes—and nothing else.

"If you want to restructure our society based on the psycho-analytical theories of Dr. Morrison, Dr. Brocher, and Dr. Friedman and Dr. Rappaport—you know, the psychoanalysts, number one, very seldom cure anyone. Number two, their statistical percentage of predicting human behavior is less than a random guess. And yet they come here on this witness stand and, based on their own high-blown theories, ask you to excuse this man for murder.

"What would they have us do if we are to run our society the way they ask you to? Are we to seek out and find all the three- to five-year-olds that hide silk panties under the front porch and incarcerate them somewhere?

"Because if we don't, certainly they are going to become murderers.

"I'm guessing here, but I don't think there really are a great number of kids that would fit into that group. Maybe it wouldn't be too much trouble to keep a watchful eye on a kid that masturbates into his mother's underwear and then buries them under the house. Just sayin'."

Kunkle continued in a discourse attacking the credibility of the defense's doctors. To listen to him, there were no insane people—only good people and evil ones. There were no gray areas; no nuances; no broken, damaged, or tragic individuals that were incapable of controlling themselves. Certainly, there were no doctors that were able to determine such a malady.

"The bottom-line problem with psychodynamic or psychoanalytic theories as it relates to the criminal justice system goes right to the core of their theories, and that is the predetermination. Because when you turn that around, what it really means is that no one is responsible for their actions. That is really what they are saying to you. We can't run society that way. The laws don't say that. Common sense doesn't say that. We must be responsible for our actions.

"We talk about some of them individually: Dr. Eliseo. First, let me say that in no way am I blaming Dr. Eliseo, or inferring anything improper on his part, in terms of the way that he chose to base his testimony solely on psychological testing, not knowing any of the facts of the case. Now he testified based on what was given to him. On one day of testing, January 13, 1980, after the court has ordered that the jury for this trial will be selected in Rockford, Illinois, suddenly, out of the blue, never having appeared before on any discovery materials or any reports tendered or anything else, we suddenly get a report from a Rockford psychologist. But based on his one day of psychological testing, he tells you that he is able to look back in history, in his crystal ball, and tell you that John Gacy was a paranoid schizophrenia continually for at least an eight-year period of time from 1972 through 1980. I suggest to you that that opinion is patently ridiculous."

It is a wonder why anyone would spend all those years, all that effort and time studying the human mind, pursuing a PhD, when, according to Mr. Kunkle, it was a worthless exercise, it was "patently ridiculous."

One of the hardest things to do in a courtroom is to sit and keep your mouth shut while the other side attempts to take your case apart. At least in a bar, a tavern, or at the dining room table, you can interrupt the son of a bitch that you are arguing with. You can wave your arms around, show your dismay with poignant, well-placed sighs and grunts. A huge roll of the eyes and a disgusted shake of the head always come in handy. In court, however, these antics are frowned upon. They are a good way to wind up being held in contempt. Who writes these rules, anyway? Certainly not an Italian?

Mr. Kunkle went on. He was nowhere near done.

He continued to rail against the defense's expert witnesses and their theories with reference to Mr. Gacy. He was fully convinced that this case was a classic struggle between good and evil. He seemed blinded to the possibility that there are damaged and broken brains in people, which cause them to act in ways contrary to their will. I always believed that this was actually helpful to our case. I believed, and still do, that it is easier for people to accept that an individual is either all bad or all good. The kid that pulls the wings off of butterflies for fun is never the kid that helps little old ladies across the street, and vice versa. However, when someone is capable of great good but still commits unspeakable wrongs, there must be a reason. Something must be broken. Something deep inside that person is not working properly. It was my contention that further study was an absolute imperative if we as a people were ever to understand this dilemma. Evidently, Kunkle disagreed.

"What makes the defendant tick? Let's study him, let's find out. Psychiatrists have been at it for ninety years now, since Freud. And man has been at it since the beginning of recorded history. And there have always been murderers. And unfortunately, there will probably always be murderers. Now, I would like to know just how much time Dr. Friedman, in between testimonials, and Dr. Rappaport, from Highland Park, spend down in Stateville interviewing Richard Speck. Or how much time they spend going around the country talking to Charles Manson, or whoever. What kind of nonsense is this? Decide your verdict so we can study the defendant? That's not an issue in this case. That's not an issue. It's a red herring. It's a phony."

As he continued, Bill shifted his focus from the psychiatrists and the physiologists and on to some of my specific arguments.

"Counsel talked about the Des Plaines police investigation. How can the defendant eat in the dining room with a body under the floor? Well, how do the guys at the morgue have lunch every day? One of the psychiatrists told you, how do the medical students chew on a sandwich that came out of the refrigerator with a cadaver? They get used to it. John Gacy got used to bodies. He was used to killing. He was comfortable with both.

"Why would he invite the cops in without a warrant? He knew they didn't have a warrant. He knew they weren't going to go down into the basement and start digging, or go up in the attic and start chopping. The same bravado, the same con man that he was always. 'Come on in the kitchen, let's talk.' That's not out of character for John Gacy in the least. The concern for the uncle . . . his program wasn't working. He was being his charming self, and they were still hanging around, they weren't leaving. 'Let's get them out of here, get this over with. I have played enough, now let's go on to something else.' That is not inconsistent with his character. Remember that sociopath, that narcissist that is worried about his own hurts. He was worried about his own hurts, like in the comic record *The 2000 Year Old Man*, he was asked—a two-thousand-year-old man was asked to define tragedy and comedy. He said, 'Tragedy is when I cut my finger, and comedy is when you fall in a manhole and die.'

"Well, that's the way a narcissist thinks. That's the way John Gacy thought. When it is his relative that is dead, when it is his wife that is involved in sexual problems, then it matters."

Kunkle continued to attempt to refute specific aspects of my closing argument. He was standing directly in front of the jury, making his claims, selling his side of the story. It was when he moved toward the easel with the pictures, the gallery of grief, that the courtroom and everybody in it found out what his plan was with reference to that little piece of demonstrative evidence.

Bill began to speak specifically about individual victims. He proceeded to give his theory of the case with reference to how he and the rest of the prosecution viewed the evidence, specifically as it pertained to how each victim died and in what order. He used a map of Gacy's property to show where and when bodies were found by police investigators.

"The defendant," Kunkle asserted, "tells us that on January 3, 1972, he picked up a young man in a Greyhound bus station and took him home. And through guile and cunning and talking about sexual acts and 'Let's have a good time and let's party.'

"And he remembers all of these conversations with details. He takes the young man back to his house on Summerdale, and they perform different homosexual acts. His recollection is that in the morning the young man comes at him with a knife as he is waking up. He takes the knife away from him and stabs him to death. Now, body no. 9, stab wounds of the ribs, verified by the radiologist. That's the first victim. He tells us he buried him under the house. Remember the testimony of his wife Carol? Carol said when she moved in, there was an odor in the house. It came from the sub part of the house, this area."

Bill Kunkle was pointing his finger and speaking his words with great emphasis. His passion was welling up.

"She complained about it. She kept complaining about it. There was some lime mentioned. And then she said, 'I want you to take care of it. I want something to be done!'

"And while she was away—I believe she was in Minneapolis—the defendant poured some concrete in the crawl space. He puts the concrete over body no. 9 to get rid of the smell, the only body in the crawl space with concrete over it. That confirms or corroborates his statement that the killing was on or about January 3, 1972, before Carol moved into the house."

He began to become more and more animated. He was speaking faster, moving back and forth between the map and the easel, that easel baring all those pictures. As he finished speaking about a particular victim, he would remove their picture from the easel.

"Later, at her request, he pours the concrete, and for a while the smell gets better. In his statements, he talked about a second victim before John Butkovitch, the next known victim. He said that he had that victim standing up on his head in the closet, and the blood drained out and got on his carpet. And he didn't make that mistake again. And that's when he started stuffing rags in their throats because he didn't want to mess up his carpets. At one time, in one of his statements, he referred to one of the small maps that the police officers had and said he thought the second one was no. 8.

"I think he was wrong in that statement. I think the second one was no. 28. And I will tell you why. Twenty-eight is under the asphalt out in the garage, put in about 1976; 28 also under a couple of layers of concrete; 28 also out in the back, out by John's private domain, the garage. If no. 28 was killed anytime between the time that Carol moved into the house and the time that she moved out, well before Butkovitch was killed, wouldn't it be logical for the defendant—at three o'clock in the morning, protected from view by his ten-foot hedges and the neighbors' garage and so on—to come out here in the back in his private area and bury that body in the yard that he knew was going to be asphalted over? You see, there are only three bodies with concrete over them. As John was learning and as John was practicing, John got rid of the smell here on no. 9 with some concrete, put Butkovitch under concrete. I think it's likely to assume that the one in between, also under concrete, also in back in his private domain, was no. 28.

"Third, John Butkovitch, July 31, 1975. Keep in mind the defendant has supposedly killed unknown body no. 9, and possibly at that time unknown body no. 28 as a result of this snowballing compulsion, this building terror, this conflict within himself over his homosexuality. Well, that's back in 1972, before 1975. And then on July 31, 1975, he kills John Butkovitch. And what does he say about killing John Butkovitch? He wanted to quit. 'He came over to my house and said I should give him his check. He wanted me to give him the money for the work he did for me. He threatened me, and I threatened to call the police. And he left. Later on, I went cruising. I found Butkovitch and took him back to the house. I managed to get the handcuffs on him. He threatens to kill me if he ever got loose. So I killed him by strangulation. I tied a rope around his neck with two knots, placed a stick as a tourniquet behind his neck; and as he struggled or hyperventilated, he strangled himself.'

"Now, that's what he said about killing John Butkovitch on July 31, 1975. Does that sound like a brief psychotic episode to you? Does that sound like an uncontrollable rage attack? He needed a piece of rope in the house. His tools and his other stuff were out in the garage. But he had a two- or three-foot length of rope ready in the house. Butkovitch wanted to quit him. He wanted money. He wasn't about to give it to him. He went out and found him—remember the testimony of Mr. Butkovitch? When John Butkovitch first went to Gacy's house to tell him he was quitting and asked for his paycheck, he went with two friends—witnesses, witnesses. He told him at that time he wanted his money, he wanted to quit. Well, Gacy must have had the compulsion. This is what triggered the rage attack, the brief psychotic episode. He must have killed him right there in front of the witnesses. He didn't do that? No, he went out in the dead of night at two or three in the morning, midnight, whatever, found him, took him back to the house alone.

"'I got him into the handcuffs.' He didn't say he wrestled him down to the ground and put the handcuffs on him. He did it the same way he always did it, the way the living victims on the stand told you he did it, the way that Eddie Lynch told you he did it with the chain all the way back in Iowa in 1967—with talk, with con, with guile, with cunning. Put the cuffs on him. And Butkovitch said, 'If you let me out of these cuffs, you are a dead man.' And John Gacy killed him. It's not a rage attack. It's not a rage attack. It's not a brief psychotic episode. It's not a product of a mental disease or defect. It's murder. Buried him, no. 2, under concrete out by the shed."

Kunkle snatched the picture of John Butkovitch off the easel and added it to the others he was holding. He was beginning a pattern, very deliberate. As he finished speaking about a victim, the picture came off.

"Next, April 1976, Sampson, no. 29. Look on the map for 29, under the dining room."

The skilled prosecutor was leading the jury through the house, "discovering" each and every single body, one at a time. And with each discovery, another picture was added to the stack in his hand.

"After the time Carol was out of the house, the children were out of the house, John was in the house alone. Remember that that dining room and the den, the family room addition, was on the house when John bought it. You remember the testimony of the investigators about recovering that body? Do you realize the work that was required to bury that body under that dining room which was already there? Through the carpet or whatever the top floor surface was, through the flooring, the subfloor, digging in between two floor joists to dig out that grave, put the body into it, cover it up. They told you there was some ceramic tile over the top of the earth when they got to it and it gave way. Well, which one of John's remodeling projects was that? Was the tile from the kitchen, tile from the bathroom remodeling? Working on the dining room? Do you rip up all those materials and replace them in such a way that no one ever notices anything wrong with the dining room floor? Do you do that while you are having a rage attack? Do you do that while you are having a brief psychotic episode? Do you do that when your underlying paranoid schizophrenia erupts?

"May 14, 1976, Samuel Stapleton, no. 6." Again, Kunkle was pointing, telling a gruesome story, telling his version of the story.

Mr. Kunkle was slowly getting louder and more emphatic. He was on the verge of breaking his promise to the jury that he would not be as loud as I was.

"Almost in the same grave, bones intermingled with each other. Randall Reffett, May 14, 1976; June 3, 1976, Michael Bonnin, no. 18. Right here . . . June 8, 1976, Michael Johnston—I mean, Rick Johnston, no. 23. Then bear in mind, 23, 24, 26, 22, 21—all in the same trench!"

He ripped picture after picture from the easel. The number of pictures of dead teens and young men was growing in his left hand. He clutched them, waved them around. He moved between exhibits, the members of the jury gawking.

"Bear in mind that the numbering system used by the sheriff indicates the order of recovery, so that a higher-numbered in relation to a lower-numbered body means the higher number was underneath. OK? So, we have Johnston, no. 23. We have 26, 22, 21, and 24. Twenty-two is William Carroll, June 13, 1976 . . . 24, 26, and no. 21, all in the same grave."

Picture after picture came down as he spoke their name or, in some cases, their number. Soon he was holding them all in his left hand, waving them as he continued. Now the easel was empty and the victims were all together.

"At the beginning of my remarks, as some of the other attorneys have said before, we are not asking you to show sympathy. You cannot—no matter what you do, you can't bring back these lives!"

Kunkle raised the stack of victims' pictures high over his head as he shook them for emphasis. The passion in his voice was apparent. He held them there for a beat . . . then he held them out and showed them as a group one last time to the transfixed members of his jury.

"Don't show sympathy," he bellowed, raising the pictures again. "Don't show sympathy. Show justice. Show justice!" Bill's voice was reaching a crescendo. "Show the same sympathy and pity that this man," he spat this out his words while pointing at John Gacy, "showed when he took these lives . . . and put them there!"

While speaking, Kunkle swept his arm and his accusatory finger away from Gacy and across the courtroom. He was pointing directly at the horrific gaping trapdoor to the crawl space with a shaking fat index finger, the pictures of the dead victims raised high over his head. He took two short steps toward the crawl space and unleashed the entire stack of pictures into that dreadful, horrifying, ominous, cavernous black hole.

I gulped. I heard various muted gasps from behind me . . . then silence. I think I lied before. That expression "You could hear a pin drop" was actually created for this moment in time.

No one talked, or budged.

Kunkle silently repositioned himself back in front of the jury. His voice returned to conversational tones.

"Mr. Egan told you at the close of his remarks, 'If there walks on this earth a man as evil as John Wayne Gacy, then God help us all.'

"Well, you don't have the power to change the past . . . the villains and the fiends that have walked this earth before him. And there is no doubt that there will be some that will walk after. But you can—you can control the future for this fellow. You can affect the present. You can do justice for all the people of the state of Illinois. You are their conscience. You are the People of Illinois now, and you must fulfill the oath that you gave as jurors! You must not allow John Gacy to use you! If you allow this evil man to walk this earth . . . this man . . . then indeed—God help us all!"

The silence in the courtroom was fading. People started shifting and whispering. Not a man to stand on ceremony, and in an effort to move things along, Judge Garippo broke the silence and launched into the next order of business.

He explained to the jury that he was about to instruct them as to the law. Without a lunch or a break, Garippo began reading the jury instructions. He figured that they would all have a nice long lunch while they began their deliberations.

The jury instruction phase of the case was tedious but necessary. The judge read from printed sheets, with one instruction per sheet. It took what seemed like forever, and then as quickly as it began, it was over.

Then the judge simply excused the jury to go deliberate.

37

THERE IS A secret that has been passed down from lawyer to young lawyer for over a half of a century. The secret is kept from even the young lawyer until he or she is deemed ready, deemed worthy. It is the secret of Jean's.

Only after a young lawyer has been bloodied in battle is the secret revealed. Then, and only then, will the young upstart truly appreciate the secret that has been shared by criminal defense lawyers that practice in the hallowed halls of the Criminal Courts Building at 26th and California and, now, has been passed down to him or to her. It is a time-honored tradition, a rite of passage; and when the secret is passed on, it signifies the official acceptance into the small club of courtroom brawlers that prowl the dark wooden churches where criminal justice lives and breathes.

Jean's is a bar, a dark tavern where battle-scarred warriors wait for their juries to return. They wait with glasses full for the thumbs-up, or the thumbs-down. They sit in relative quiet, licking wounds and second-guessing their opponents and themselves, under a picture of Clarence Darrow and others who have honored the tradition before them.

Why is Jean's such a well-kept secret? Well, it is a twenty-foot-wide-by-thirty-five-foot-long dark wood-paneled room without a front door. Its only entrance, its only access is off an alley a block away from the towering courthouse. It is the antithesis of the courthouse—a place to relax, a clubhouse where ties are loosened and wounded opponents sit together, drink together, and wait together. When you enter Jean's for the very first time, you know that you are a lawyer.

On the way to Jean's, we were all laughing and trading Gacy stories. The prosecution team and the defense team, both prepared to wait, both prepared to console the other when the other received the bad news. Only one side could win the trial of the century.

I bought a round as soon as we walked in the door. Kunkle promised that the next round was his. He never got to buy it. The jury was back.

One hour and fifty minutes after they had been charged, they were ready.

This was not good . . .

JUDGE LOUIS B. Garippo addressed the court:

"All right, before bringing the jury out, I have to announce that this jury, depending on the verdict, may not be finished with its duty. Therefore, it is possible, depending on their verdict, that they may be called upon to deliberate again on this case.

Therefore, any visible reaction from the audience could impair and could prevent an orderly hearing, if this jury is called upon to deliberate at any future time."

His eyes peered across the entire length and breadth of his personal domain with a look that said, *Everybody got that?*

"Then call the jury."

The jury filed in. Nobody looked at the defendant.

"Mr. Foreman, has the jury signed thirty-five verdicts?"

"Yes, we have."

"Would you pass them to the bailiff who will pass them to the clerk."

"Each verdict is in order."

"Will you read them please?"

"We, the jury, find the defendant, John Wayne Gacy, guilty of the murder of Robert Piest."

I was thunderstruck. The room was thunderstruck. Emotions poured silently out and turned into electric energy. The collective gasp was respectfully silent, but as heavy as a sledgehammer. Some of the relatives held hands, and tears began to flow. Over the loud silence, the clerk continued.

"We, the jury, find the defendant, John Wayne Gacy, guilty of indecent liberties with a child upon Robert Piest.

"We, the jury, find the defendant, John Wayne Gacy, guilty of the murder of John Butkovitch."

"We, the jury, find the defendant, John Wayne Gacy, guilty of deviant sexual assault upon Robert Piest."

"We, the jury, find the defendant, John Wayne Gacy, guilty of the murder of Darrell Sampson."

"We, the jury, find the defendant, John Wayne Gacy, guilty of the murder of Samuel Stapleton."

And so it went on—each of thirty-five verdicts were read in full, with furtive shrieks and silent sobs accompanying the drone of the clerk.

When the clerk finished, the judge went on, "The attorneys will be seated, please." We all sat. Gacy remained standing. The judge continued.

"Ronald Geaver, did you hear all the verdicts as read by the clerk?"

"Yes."

"Were they your verdicts?"

"Yes."

"Are they now your verdicts?"

"Yes."

"Mabel Loundenback, did you hear the verdicts as read by the clerk?"

"Yes."

"Were they your verdicts?"

"Yes."

"Are they now your verdicts?"

"Yes."

"Dean—what is the last name?"

"Johnson."

"Dean Johnson, did you hear the verdicts as read by the clerk?"

"Yes."

"Were they your verdicts?"

"Yes."

"Are they now your verdicts?"

"Yes."

Again the drone of the voice of the judge continued like that of the clerk's before him, and the continuing recitation of name after name only served to heighten the drama and the sheer emotion.

Then the judge abruptly stopped the repetition. He said, "All right, ladies and gentlemen, this concludes this portion of the trial. You will be returned to your quarters. You will be returned to this courtroom at one thirty tomorrow afternoon. You are not free to answer any inquiries at this time from anyone making any inquiries relative to your deliberations. You understand that? See you tomorrow at one thirty. This case is adjourned until 10:00 a.m. tomorrow. The lawyers are expected to be in court at ten tomorrow for the purpose of preparing for the subsequent hearings."

I blinked my eyes, and I was back, standing next to my client. I really cannot tell you what happened during that blink. It all runs together as a continuous memory.

The judge was talking again . . .

"Call the jury."

"Mr. Foreman, has the jury reached and signed a verdict?"

"Yes, Your Honor, we have."

"If you will pass it to the bailiff to pass it to the clerk. The clerk will read the verdict if it's in order."

"We, the jury, unanimously conclude that the defendant, John Wayne Gacy, attained the age of eighteen years at the time of the murders and has been convicted of intentionally murdering the following individuals: Matthew H. Bowman, Robert Gilroy, John Mowery, Russell O. Nelson, Robert Winch, Tommy Boling, David Paul Talsma, William Kindred, Timothy O'Rourke, Frank Landingin, James Mazarra, and Robert Piest. That these murders occurred after June 21, 1977.

"We, the jury, unanimously conclude that the court shall sentence the defendant, John Wayne Gacy, to death."

The judge looked solemn. This was not his favorite part of the job. He began to poll the jury.

"Ronald Geaver?"

"Yes."

"Did you hear the verdicts?"

"Yes."

"Were these your verdicts?"

"Yes."

"Are they now your verdicts?"

"Yes."

"David Osborne?"

"Yes."

"Did you hear the verdicts?"

"Yes."

"Were these your verdicts?"

"Yes."

"Are they now your verdicts?"

"Yes."

"Ross Putman?"

"Yes."

And so it went.

Tears flowed from every eye in that courtroom—tears of sadness, tears of defeat, tears of triumph, tears of joy, tears of satisfaction. Mothers and fathers, sisters and brothers looked up at the high ceiling, then through it toward the sky. Tears of relief cascaded down their faces.

But most of all, there were tears of pride. Every person in that room had witnessed our system of justice at its finest. Everyone knew that they had witnessed a fair and just trial. Justice had spoken. Justice had won. The Constitution had won; just as its writers, our founding fathers, had envisioned it.

I looked at Bob. We both had tears streaking down our faces.

The flood of emotion was incredible. Every person in the room had shared the experience. It was not an easy moment. It was an overwhelming moment. People looked at the defendant. There he stood, right there, twenty feet away.

We had condemned him, everyone in the room. We all had acquiesced. Did we have that right?

The judge spoke. "Ladies and gentlemen," he said, "this concludes your jury duty. I spoke with the alternates before you. I spoke to them privately because I could not speak to them in open court. But on behalf of the Circuit Court of Cook County, I wish to first commend you for what you have contributed by your service."

The judge had removed his trademark gold-rimmed glasses. He was wiping his eyes.

Only one person in the room was dry-eyed, only one. John Wayne Gacy stood at the defense table, bewildered and lost.

The amount of emotion that flowed forth was like a flood that washed over one and all, even the strong; the ones that thought they would enjoy this could not escape it.

The judge continued, his voice cracking, clearly moved, "A couple of months ago," he said, removing his glasses once again, "a group of prosecutors from another country came and couldn't understand how in the United States you could try a person who was arrested of this type of situation. A lot has been said about how much this case has cost, and I don't know what it cost. I don't know if anyone could put together the cost, but whatever the cost was, it's a small price. My voice is cracking because I really truly feel it's a small price that we paid for our freedom. What we do for the John Gacys, we'll do for everyone. I thank you. You are now excused."

The judge wiped his eyes one last time. His job was not over. He had a task yet to perform, the hardest task of all.

He looked at Gacy.

"Step forward," he said.

"Under the laws, as I interpret the law, this jury verdict, I have interpreted it as not binding on the court. The statute is written in such a way as to indicate that it is binding on the court, but I find it is not binding on the court. Does anyone have anything to say before I impose sentence?"

Bob was first to speak.

"Judge, at this point, I'd asked for—make a motion, just perfunctorily, for judgment notwithstanding the verdict by the jury, based on what I consider to be mitigating circumstances that exist in the record."

I was next. "Just all over the record, Your Honor, there is no question. If anybody ever fit the extreme emotional or mental disturbance in this statute, it's John Gacy. We'd implore Your Honor to give a judgment notwithstanding the verdict of this jury."

Judge Garippo looked at us. He was resolved. He had no choice.

He looked at John Wayne Gacy, who stood before him.

"On the twelve indictments, 79-2382, I sentence the defendant to death; 79-2399, I sentence the defendant to death; 79-2393, I sentence the defendant to death; 2391, I sentence the defendant to death. On all other indictments, I impose a sentence of natural life. I set an execution date of July 1, 1980."

There was a quick discussion about the date. A statute required the date to be in excess of ninety days.

"Oh yes, I have the wrong date. I have the wrong month. June 2. I set the execution date on June 2, 1980. Execution is stayed automatically. Mittimus to issue. Are there any other motions?"

Bill Kunkle moved to dismiss three lingering misdemeanor cases that had been filed against the defendant. It seemed silly.

Garippo said, "Allowed."

And that, as they say, was that. Gacy was taken from the room.

38

JOHN WAYNE GACY died on May 10, 1994, as a result of a lethal injection administered on behalf of the People of the State of Illinois at Stateville Correctional Center, Crest Hill, Illinois. It has been reported that his last words were, "Kiss my ass." Sounds like him, doesn't it? I don't know if those were his last words. I wasn't there.

By the time he died, Gacy had repudiated everything that Bob and I did on his behalf and in his defense. He used ineffective assistance of counsel as one of his many issues on appeal. By the time he shuffled loose this mortal coil, he was not only claiming that he never killed anybody, but I am pretty sure he believed that claim. Crazy people firmly believe their delusions.

There are certain individuals that have lived throughout history that elicit an immediately negative and profoundly visceral response in everyone who hears their names spoken. Just the mention of the name will often launch an argument. John Wayne Gacy has most certainly joined the ranks of these individuals. For a time, Gacy was the most hated man in America. He has since been replaced many times over. America has plenty of "most hateds" to go around. Thousands of people attended parties celebrating his death all across the nation on the night that he died. You've heard of the Macy's Day Parade? Well, on that day in May, there were Gacy's Day Parades all over America.

For me, I didn't celebrate, as you might imagine. Neither was I sad, exactly. It is a hard emotion to describe, actually. I certainly wasn't losing a friend. I never considered John a friend, although I did spend more time with him during the year 1979 than I spent with my wife and kids. I never really even liked him much. He was too much of a braggart and too goddamned weird for me. But John Wayne Gacy did grow on people over time, in spite of his foibles and peccadilloes. Just ask the guys that followed him around the city of Chicago for weeks. If you focused on what he did, of course, he was the worst human being on the planet, no question. But if you actually knew him, it was somehow different. It was oddly possible to look past the monster that the world saw and see the sad excuse for a human being inside—the damaged, broken individual that spent most of his waking hours on earth confused, ashamed, bewildered, totally lost, and still trying to please a father that was both long gone and not able to be pleased in the first place, because he too was a waste of human space. John's aura, if he had one, was not evil—it was pathetic and sad.

Most of all, and in spite of everything else, John Wayne Gacy was my client. When someone hires you to be his lawyer, he or she puts total faith in you. It is a very special and complicated relationship, somewhere between a doctor and a priest, certainly not one to be taken lightly. It is a privilege to have a person seek counsel from you, to put unconditional trust in you. That is no simple thing. You owe that person a duty that is higher than most, and yes, a bond is formed. So I guess I had a bond with John—a singular and convoluted bond, but a bond, nonetheless. I fought for that man's life for over a year, like a medic on the battlefield, knowing full well that the effort would not likely be rewarded. And like that medic on that battlefield, I didn't stop to judge him. I just fought with everything that I had in me.

Did John Wayne Gacy deserve my efforts? Yeah, he did. Every human being deserves counsel in a free society, no matter what the charge, no matter what the cost, no matter what. That was his right, and he had acquired that right from a place far above my pay grade, and yours.

Only one other person on this planet could share the once-in-a-lifetime emotion that was haunting that day: Bob Motta. Like me, he fought tooth and nail for the life of a hated man. Like me, today he too had finally lost that battle.

So, no, I wasn't celebrating, not today.

I called Bob. I hadn't seen him very much during the ensuing fourteen years since the jury's verdict. Oh, I'd bump into him from time to time, of course. We were both lawyers, and there are always functions and chance meetings in courthouses. But we had both moved on, him with his practice and me with mine. I had partnered with Jim Etchingham and had a thriving practice for a time, still in Park Ridge, 200 S. Prospect, right next door to my first office in the 222 building, where Gacy had first confessed his nightmare. Then in 1985, I was appointed to the bench as an associate judge of the Circuit Court of Cook County. I was now dispensing justice instead of fighting for it.

It was good to hear his voice. We made plans to meet at a local bar, a bar where many of my old marine buddies sometimes hung out. The bar, the Northwood, was tucked into the corner of a tiny strip mall where Summerdale Street meets Cumberland Avenue, just a block and a half from where Gacy's house once stood.

I walked into the bar around seven o'clock and looked around. This was a place where men drank draught beer or shots of whiskey and watched sports. A tavern. There were no disco balls or bright lights. The primary color scheme was brown.

There they were, many of my closest friends.

They were all smiling, but not really—Etchingham, Hussey, Joey Etch, Kinahan, what a motley crew. If you knew me, you knew this was no celebration. Of course, it was no wake either. Bob Motta was sitting at the bar eating a beef sandwich. I walked over to him. "I gotta go pick up Sammy in a little while. How are you doing?"

"I think you know," he said.

We talked for a while. I talked to everybody there.

When I left to pick up my son from a school function, I really intended to come back to the bar. Somehow, that idea left me once I got home with my family.

My wife was surprised. I was usually the center of attention. I usually liked crowds.

We all just went for a hot dog. I didn't feel like doing much else.

When I walked into the Plush Pup, a local hot dog stand, the guy behind the counter was smiling at me. "How are you going to celebrate the Gacy execution?" he asked, slapping onions on the dogs.

I chuckled a little. "I am probably one of the only people in this town that is not celebrating," I said, thinking of Bob. "I was the guy who defended him in court. I was his lawyer."

The guy's swarthy, ethnic face went blank. He almost dropped his onion spoon.

"You're kidding!"

"No . . . no, I'm not."

When I got home, my wife and I turned on the TV. There was Bill Kunkle arguing with Walter Jacobson, Chicago's answer to Walter Cronkite.

They were in the throes of an earnest discussion about whether Gacy had been given drugs to ease the tension before he was taken to the gurney.

Jacobson was sure he had taken some kind of drug because he had seen a flutter in Gacy's eye.

A flutter in his eye! A flutter in his eye! I had seen that flutter before. If they only knew, I thought. Gacy wasn't even there. He wasn't even present. He had already gone to that dark place he had been so many times before.

Gacy didn't need drugs. His brain was broken.

I thought about the guy at the hot dog stand. "I was his lawyer," I had said.

I thought about a telephone call that I received fifteen years ago.

"Sam, could you do me a favor?"

Epilogue

THIRTEEN PSYCHOLOGISTS AND psychiatrists testified during the trial of John Wayne Gacy. Each was a noted expert. Most were published authors and professors at this country's most prestigious institutions of higher learning. Yet, after hours of interviews, study and contemplation, none of these learned men and women diagnosed Mr. Gacy in exactly the same manner.

Gacy was an enigma.

After reading the Gacy story, it doesn't take a psychologist or a psychiatrist to see the tormented soul that haunted Gacy's sickly frame. Once he confessed his crimes on that eerie night in Sam's office, he began admitting his horrific deeds to almost anyone who asked. But, there was one thing that he would never admit. This one perceived transgression he took with him to his grave. He would admit to the most heinous string of brutal murders the world had ever seen; but he would never admit that which he considered his most horrendous and well-guarded secret . . . he was homosexual.

Gacy grew up with a father who berated him daily for not living up to preconceived notions of what a "man" should be, school kids and neighbors who bullied and tormented him, and a society that struggled with acceptance of a lifestyle it did not understand. As a result, no one hated John Gacy more than John Gacy.

During the trial, we had a discussion in Judge Garippo's chamber. The issue was whether or not a witness would be allowed to take the Fifth Amendment if he were asked if he had engaged in homosexual acts with John Gacy. The judge never had to rule on the issue. The question was never posed. But, the fact that the issue had been debated at all, even for a minute, says something about the attitude of the time. Homosexuality is not a crime. The Fifth Amendment to the Constitution protects against self-*incrimination* . . . not self-embarrassment. Therefore, the issue should never have come up. Nonetheless, it was the subject of some debate and consideration.

Thankfully, times have changed somewhat. A lawyer concerned with such a question would get laughed out of most judges' chambers.

This country has taken great strides to eradicate the scourge of the many misplaced prejudices from which we have suffered as a nation over the years. The sad results of some of our history's mistakes—slavery, racism, sexism, McCarthyism—are slowly becoming memories of troubled days gone by. Isn't it finally time to assign our most glaring leftover active prejudice, homophobia, to the pages of a history book?

———————————

ARE YOU GOOD with dates? There is one date in this book that kind of jumps off the page: December 11, 1978. Do you remember what happened on that date? John Wayne Gacy brutally murdered Rob Piest, his *last* victim, on that date.

What was supposed to happen on that very same date in that very same year?

John Wayne Gacy was supposed to be released from the Iowa Men's Reformatory in Anamosa. John Wayne Gacy was sentenced to ten years in prison by the State of Iowa pursuant to an order signed by Judge Peter Van Metre on December 11, 1968. If he had served his full term, if he had stayed in that prison for his full sentence, Mr. Gacy's release date would have been December 11, 1978.

Maybe we should stop putting pot smokers, prostitutes, and petty thieves in prison and leave some room for the John Wayne Gacys of the world.

Enough said?

IT IS HARD to imagine that this story could ever have anything akin to a silver lining. However, you know what they say, whenever a door is closed, a window opens.

Sam L. Amirante, my coauthor and friend, may have done the one thing that could possibly qualify as a right to this terrible wrong, as something good coming from this horrible tragedy. In 1984, inspired by his involvement in the *Gacy* case, he personally authored procedures adopted by the Illinois General Assembly as the Missing Child Recovery Act of 1984 (I-SEARCH), which eliminated the seventy-two-hour waiting period to initiate a search for lost children, and he is credited with helping to locate countless thousands of missing children in our state and reuniting them with their parents.

For the first time in Illinois history, the report of a missing child immediately triggered a statewide search, incorporating the resources of local and municipal police forces all across the state in cooperation with the Illinois State Police.

As other states adopted similar laws and similar sensibilities with reference to missing children, it became possible to create the national network, now known as a Child Abduction Emergency, or CAE, commonly referred to as an Amber Alert.

Therefore, these boys . . .

and eleven more, did not die in vain.

ACKNOWLEDGMENTS

WE PUT OFF writing this part of the book until the last possible second because it is the scariest part. That's saying something when you consider that we are writing a book about John Wayne Gacy but believe us; it's true. We were both petrified that we would forget to mention someone, thereby hurting the feelings of a person for whom one of us, or both of us, cares deeply.

However, pretending that we wrote this book without help just because our names are on the cover would be a crime greater than the ones portrayed in its pages. So . . . here goes.

Bob Motta joined with me on a journey that only a very few lawyers would have had the courage to undertake. When Bob sent that fateful telegram and stepped up to offer his help, he was clearly jumping off of a cliff with me and he knew it. Yet, he fearlessly did so without looking back. I could not have done it without you, Bob. Fate brought us together and I am the one who benefited. I couldn't have asked for a better partner, cocounsel, and friend.

We both have to thank Attorney Pam Curran. Pam has been Sam's loyal and dedicated associate and our friend. She puts up with Sam, a daunting task; and she somehow puts up with Danny, who never shuts up. Her encouragement and countless hours of listening, transcribing, reviewing, and critiquing helped to make this book possible. To Lissy Peace, our agent and friend, whose dedication to this project made it a reality after thirty long years, thank you, Lissy. The personnel at Skyhorse Publishing, who welcomed us and made us feel comfortable and confident, especially our editor, Jennifer McCartney, whose knowledge, experience, and incredible attention to detail made this a better book. She also put up with Danny, who never shuts up. Author and friend Georgia Durante shared her expertise and offered her guidance before and during the pendency of the project. Deanna Amirante, Sam's loving wife, offered her input, inspiration, and encouragement. She also opened her beautiful home at all hours to late-night, chain-smoking bull sessions when everyone, including her husband, should have been in bed sleeping. Holly Hueser, paralegal at the Sullivan Firm, Ltd., dragged her boss's files up from storage and facilitated access to those files and provided an office where Danny could work. Terry Sullivan, the "Sullivan" of the Sullivan Firm Ltd., allowed complete access to his files and supported our efforts in the telling of this story. Terry also helped sell the idea of the book to everyone that would listen to him and Sam in Key West, Florida, in spite of the fact that we are now competing with his best-selling book, *Killer Clown: The John Wayne Gacy Murders.* Judge Al Swanson gave us insights and contributed vital information from his days as a reporter covering the *Gacy* case. Steve Veenstra, of Fountain Valley, California, reviewed our first drafts and offered editing advice and constructive criticism beginning with the earliest days of the project. And, thanks to Tim Kiefer for his help and expertise in the making of our videos.

Sam would also like to thank his mentors who taught him how to be a lawyer with passion for our Constitution and the criminal justice system, including Nunzio Tisci, Judge John Madden, Judge James Geocaris, James Doherty, John G. Phillips, Joseph Fasano, Judge Louis Garippo, Judge Robert Sklodowski, and Robert Martwick. I would also like to thank my friends who have encouraged me through the years and never gave up on the idea of this publication, including Gino Peronti, Jeanne Raines, Judge Anthony Iosco,

Judge Les Bonaguro, Judge Annie O'Donnell, Judge Nick Zagone, Judge Howard Fink, Bob Motta, Jim Hussey, Ernie Blomquist, and Judge James Etchingham, the greatest law partner a lawyer could ever have.

I would also like to thank those people who labored with me and took up most of the load during the *Gacy* case in my law office, including Larry Gabriele, Dennis Nudo, Dick Nelson, Lee Poteracki, and their great and dedicated staff who spent countless hours typing, transcribing, copying, and running errands. Thank you, Erlene, Lee, Rita, and Joanne. I must thank Linda Kennedy, Bob Motta's girlfriend, for transcribing the tapes of hours upon hours of interviews with Gacy. She typed her fingers raw. I would also like to thank the numerous investigators assigned to the case, especially Lindy DiDomenico, Nick Mestousis, and Tony Christopher, who not only spent endless hours interviewing hundreds of people all over the country, but also served as our bodyguards throughout the trial. I would also like to express my deepest appreciation to the members of the press, including Jay Levine, Irv Kupcinat, Michael Sneed, Carol Marine, Maurice Possley, Tony Gianetti, Walter Jacobson, Bill Curtis, Dick Kay, John Drummond, Paul Galoway, Tom Fitzpatrick, John Drury, Ron Majors, and all of the others who always treated two young lawyers with dignity, respect, and fairness. In addition, thank you, Marcia Danitz, Verna Sadok, and Andy Austin, the courtroom artists who always made us look better than we really do. I would also like to thank Sheriff Don Gasparini and all of the other court personnel of the Winnebago County courthouse in Rockford, Illinois, for making us feel safe and comfortable during jury selection. A special thank-you to all of the court personnel of the Circuit Court of Cook County assigned to the case for their professionalism. I would also like to thank my fellow marines and all of the members of the other armed forces for giving the ultimate sacrifice so that our constitutional rights may always be protected. In that light, I would like to thank my fellow members of the judiciary and fellow lawyers who ensure everyday in our criminal court system that even the John Gacys of the world receive a fair trial. I would be remiss if I were to not thank two people who, throughout the *Gacy* case, in spite of the great odds against us, and the whole world hating us, put their entire faith, trust, hope, and confidence in Bob's and my abilities to see to it that their brother received a fair trial, John Gacy's sisters, Karen and Joanne.

When Danny left the practice of law, struggling with life, and then suddenly decided, quite out of the blue, to write a book, numerous people supported and encouraged him. It was often just the right word at the right time, especially early on in this unlikely quest. Occasionally, it was what they didn't do. Some were family members and some were friends, some were almost strangers, but each and every one of the following individuals had a hand in helping him find a new path, whether they knew it or not. Vern Bergquist, Jim Labuda, Bob Broderick, John Baumgartner, John Butcher, John Schwaab, Vanessa Trobec, John and Teresa Namy, Gary and Diane Hanson, Dennis and Sue Van Ewyk, Mark and Greg and Katie Van Ewyk, Tim Kiefer, Mike Kiefer, Larry and Nancy Rozzano, Terri and Bridget Rozzano, Michael Broderick, Jimmy Broderick, Steve and Geri Ryan, Bob and Patty Lewis, Mike and Peggy Calebrese, Tom and Mary Gazdik, Dave and Margaret Lombardi, Mark Roth, Katie O'Connor Buckingham, the one that got away. Willie Norris, Mary Griffin Houlihan, Sue Fruzyna Farris, Kelly Torres Tom Eggert, J. Craig Williams, Evonne Kyriazes, Monica Wicklund, June Norris, Ellen Pitt, Hershel "Harry" Heater, Kelly Sutton, Monica Awani, the angel known as Roberta Williams and her husband Dave.

Finally, but most importantly, we would like to thank our families. Sam first. I want to thank my mom, Liz, and my dad, Sam, for being the greatest parents in the world; my cousins, who are more like brothers and sisters to me and stuck by me and supported me when the rest of the world hated me; and Mary Amirante, who struggled and sacrificed to help me through law school to reach my dream to become a lawyer and who, once again, sacrificed so much during the hardships and threats throughout the *Gacy* case; and my sons, who I would live and die for, Sammy and Jimmy, who lost fifteen months of time during their young lives, time they should have been able to spend with their dad, and who inspired me by their presence to author the ISEARCH law (the Missing Child Recovery Act of 1984); and my wife, Deanna Amirante, whose love and encouragement motivated me toward this project; and especially Sofiabella, my princess, the love of my life, who every day with her smile makes me forget about the sometimes unpleasantness of the world we live in and makes me realize what a wonderful life it really is.

Now Danny. I want to thank my mom, Jackie, and my dad, Bill. I wish you were both here to see this. My parents are saints who raised eleven children and who gave tirelessly of themselves every single day until the day they died. They helped me through my darkest days, and I've had a few of those, and also shared my greatest triumphs. My two boys, Jack and Patrick, are my reason for living and the light of my life. Patrick, who lives with me and puts up with me (apparently, I never shut up), has been there every day with encouragement and inspiration. He is a source of great pride in everything that he does. Jack, who lives with his mom, June, inspires me, tests me, and fills me with love and pride as I watch him entering adulthood. My brothers and sisters are amazing. Only those that have grown up in a big family can know the benefits of having so much unconditional love from so many wonderful people. You had to be there in our neighborhood growing up to really appreciate the Broderick call to dinner as it reverberated off the houses and through the trees. Danny, Diane, Susan, Nancy, Michael, Jimmy, Geri, Tommy, Bobby, Patty, Peggy . . . come on and eat! Now all those kids have kids, most have spouses, and some of their kids have kids. So, I'd like to thank my immediate family for their undying support and love: Diane, Gary, Tim, Beckie, Meghan,

Molly, Mike, Eric, Andrea, Susan, Dennis, Mark, Greg, Katie, Nancy, Larry, Terri, Tom, Bridget, Bradley, Michael, Michael, Kayla, Jimmy, Bernie, Geri, Steve, Joey, Katie, Taylor, Brodie, Kelly, Kirk, Katie, Mike, Tommy, Roxanne, Donavon, Little D, Alyssa, Meagan Wren, Jeremy, Darion, Madyson, Natalie, Little Johnney, Bobby, Patti, Bob, Marc, Heather, Peggy, Mike, Joey, and Nick. If we sell just one copy of the book to every member of this loving, caring, eclectic, and wonderful family, best-seller status is pretty much assured.

Although I have mentioned their names before, I would like to take this opportunity to give special thanks to my brother, Tom Broderick, and his wife, Roxanne. Aside from being two of the kindest, most loving people on the planet, Tom and Rox, with their support, have made it possible for me to follow this harebrained idea of mine that I could write a book. Thank you, Tom, and thank you, Rox.

It has been said before, but life really is a roller coaster. You wait for your turn. It goes way too fast. It has its thrilling highs and its scary lows. It ends too soon. And when it's over, you find that you wouldn't have changed a thing, especially the scary parts, and you want to ride it again.

If we forgot anybody, we are truly sorry. Chalk it up to old age.

AUTHOR'S NOTE

ONE OF THE cornerstones of an attorney-client relationship is the privilege of confidential communication between an attorney and his or her client. That privilege is time-honored and sacred and should not be broken, even after death. However, it was John Gacy's desire to have the true story known even after his death. I have labored over the issue of privilege in this matter for many years. Although John Gacy was perceived as a monster, he was, in fact, a human being, who, like any other, deserves to have the historical record set straight. He always wanted his story told and the truth known, as evidenced by a general release and waiver of the privilege given to Bob Motta and me long before Gacy's death. There have been numerous rumors and much speculation, which have embellished the true facts of this case. For instance, there were rumors of cannibalism, mutilation, freezing of body parts, other murders, and bodies being hidden in other parts of the country, all of which are untrue. We write this book to set the historical record straight. Furthermore, all of Gacy's statements contained in this book were also made by him in numerous other and disjointed ways over the years and all have been a matter of public record prior to the writing of this book.

The defense of John Gacy had little or nothing to do with privileged communications. From the beginning, and against my advice, he fully confessed to the police, in his words "to give his victims a proper burial." The basis of our defense was to save his life and allow him to stay in a structured environment where he could be studied and hopefully prevent a repeat of such horrific crimes. This book continues that fight for knowledge, preventive intervention, and human dignity.

—Sam L. Amirante